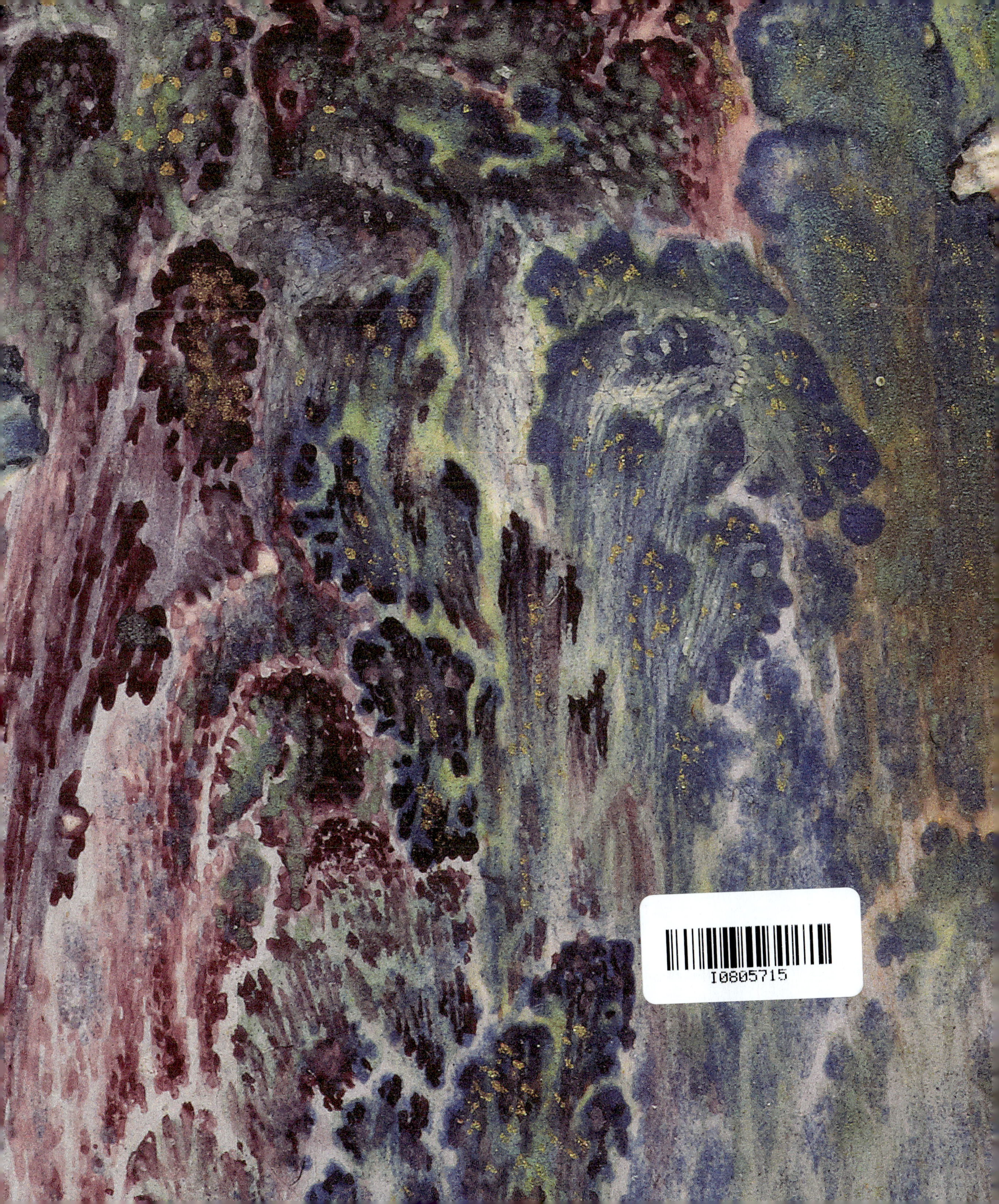

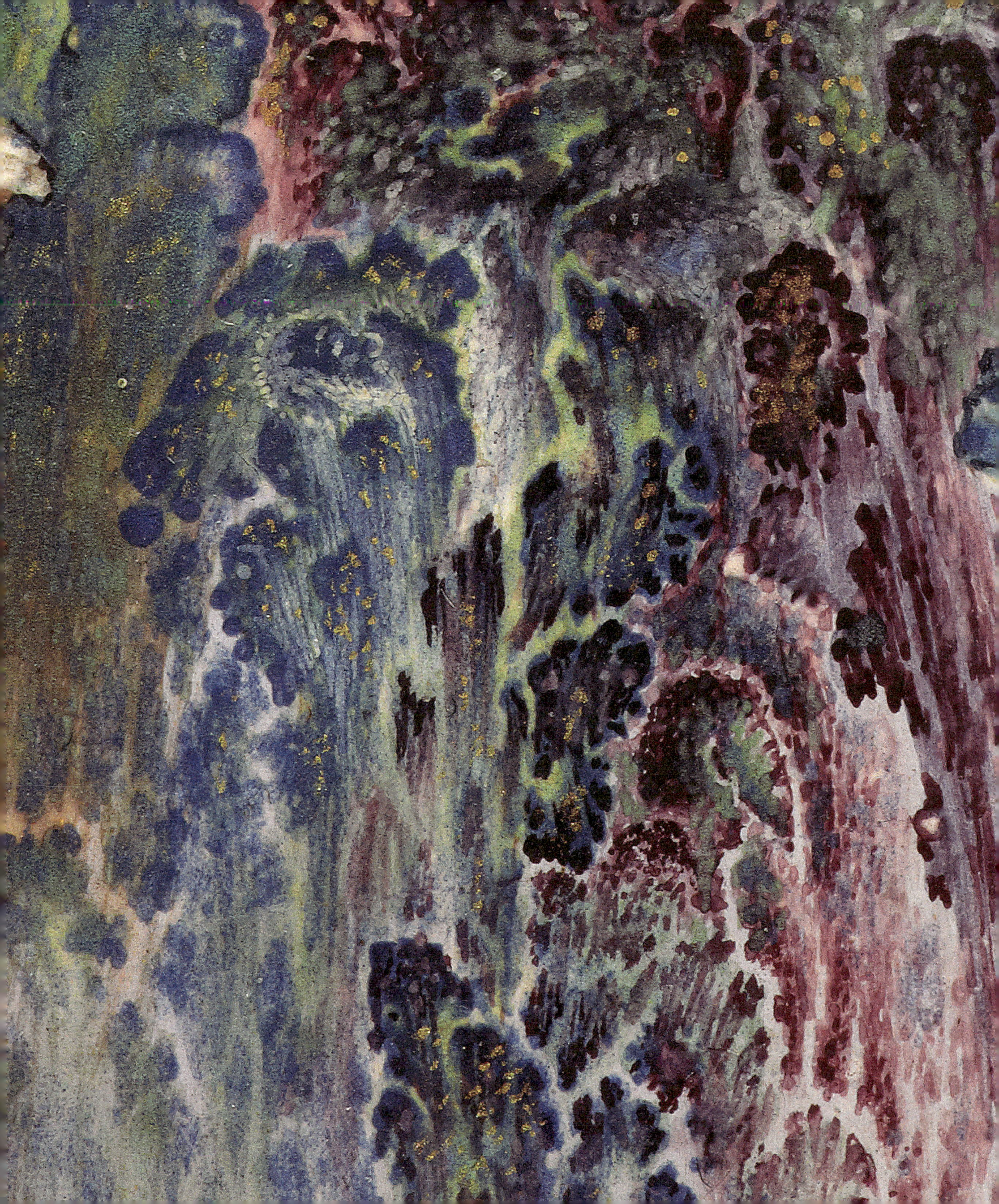

PATTERN AND LIGHT

AGA KHAN MUSEUM

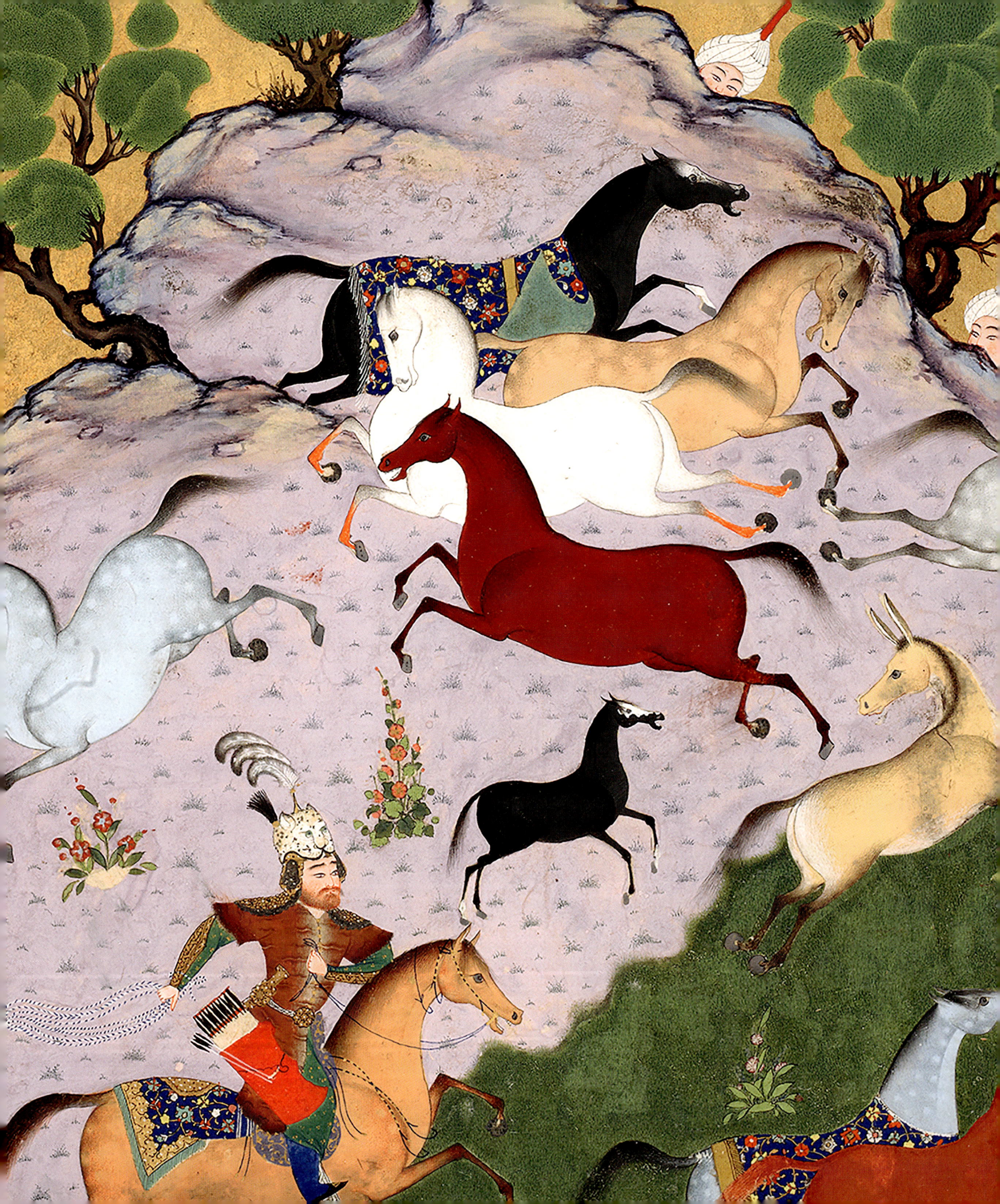

PATTERN AND LIGHT

AGA KHAN MUSEUM

AGA KHAN MUSEUM Skira Rizzoli NEW YORK

Pattern and light : Aga Khan Museum / Henry S. Kim [and five others].
Includes index.
Issued also in French under title : Forme et lumière.
ISBN 978-1-926473-00-0 (bound)
1. Aga Khan Museum (Toronto, Ont.). 2. Islamic art. 3. Art--Ontario--Toronto. 4. Art museums--Ontario--Toronto. I. Kim, Henry S., author II. Aga Khan Museum (Toronto, Ont.), issuing body
N6264.C3T67 2014
709.17'67074713541 C2014-905517-X

ISBN: 978-0-8478-4429-6 (Skira Rizzoli English hardcover)
ISBN: 978-1-926473-00-0 (Aga Khan Museum English hardcover)
ISBN: 978-1-926473-02-4 (Aga Khan Museum English softcover)
ISBN: 978-1-926473-01-7 (Aga Khan Museum French hardcover)

First published in the United States of America in 2014 by
Skira Rizzoli Publications, Inc.
300 Park Avenue South
New York, NY 10010
www.rizzoliusa.com

In association with
Aga Khan Museum
77 Wynford Drive
Toronto, Ontario
M3C 1K1
www.agakhanmuseum.org

FOR AGA KHAN MUSEUM:
Feasibility Studies: Sasaki Associates, Boston, Massachusetts, United States
Design Architects: Fumihiko Maki and Maki and Associates, Tokyo, Japan
Architect of Record: Moriyama & Teshima Architects, Toronto, Ontario, Canada
Landscape Architects: Vladimir Djurovic Landscape Architecture (VDLA), Beirut, Lebanon
Museography and Exhibition Design: Studio Adrien Gardère, Paris, France

Education and Scholarly Programs Department, Aga Khan Museum:
Ruba Kana'an, Head of Education and Scholarly Programs
Michael Carroll, Editor and Publications Manager

FOR SKIRA RIZZOLI PUBLICATIONS, INC.:
Margaret Rennolds Chace, Associate Publisher
Susan Homer, Editor

Design: Gina Rossi

On endpapers: Detail of *The Court of Keyomars*, folio 20v from a *Shah-Nameh* (Book of Kings) produced for Shah Tahmasp I, painting by Soltan Mohammad, Tabriz, Iran, ca. 1522, opaque watercolour, ink, gold, and silver on paper, 47 × 32 cm (18 ½ × 12 ⅝ in.), AKM165 (see also pages 50–53 and 120–21).

On page 2: Detail of *Rostam Pursues Akvan the Onager-Div*, folio 294r from a *Shah-Nameh* (Book of Kings) produced for Shah Tahmasp I, attributed to Mozaffar 'Ali, Tabriz, Iran, 1530–35, opaque watercolour, ink, and gold on paper, 45 × 30 cm (17¾ × 11¾ in.), AKM162.

On page 4: Incense Burner, eastern Iran, 11th century, copper inlaid bronze, 28 × 28 cm (11 × 11 in.), AKM602 (see also page 104).

On pages 14–15: Detail of Tile, Iznik, Turkey, 17th century, fritware, underglaze-painted, 52 × 32 cm (20 ½ × 12 ⅝ in.), AKM587 (see also page 168).

On pages 38–39: Detail of *Découpé* Calligraphic Example from a dispersed *Divan* of Sultan Hosayn Bayqara (d. 1506), Herat, Afghanistan (Historic Iran), ca. 1475, opaque watercolour, ink, and gold on paper, 23.7 × 15.2 cm (9 ⅜ × 6 in.), AKM227 (see also page 144).

On pages 56–57: Detail of *A Resting Lion*, single-page drawing, attributed to Mo'in Mosavvir, Isfahan, Iran, 1672, ink, opaque watercolour, and gold on paper, 14.1 × 22.5 cm (5 ½ × 8 ⅞ in.), AKM111 (see also page 128).

2014 2015 2016 2017 / 10 9 8 7 6 5 4 3 2 1

Printed in the United States of America

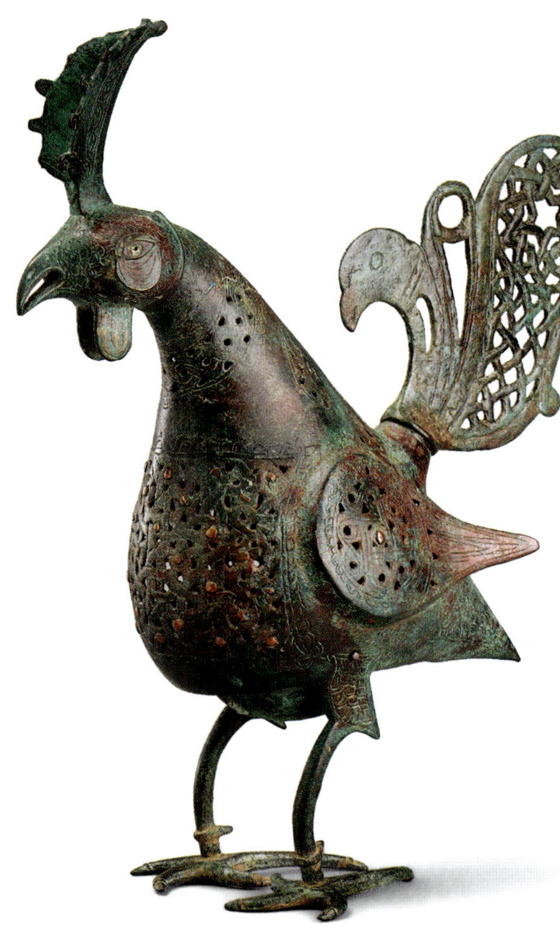

CONTENTS

Foreword

HIS HIGHNESS THE AGA KHAN

The Aga Khan Museum in Toronto reflects my family's and my ongoing commitment to pluralism and to the promotion of understanding between civilizations, religions, and races.

Our plans in Toronto originally called for the construction of a new Ismaili Centre, a space of prayer, contemplation, study, and community interaction. As time went on, however, and added space became available, enlarging our original site, our plans grew to involve three separate yet interrelated developments: the Ismaili Centre Toronto, the sixth such representational building in the world; the Aga Khan Museum; and what we believe is a beautiful, welcoming park, open to the public, that links these two new buildings.

I think one can say that, together, these three projects symbolize the harmonious integration of the spiritual, the artistic, and the natural worlds — in keeping with the holistic ideal and approach that is such an intimate part of Islamic tradition. At the same time they also express our profound commitment to intercultural engagement and to international co-operation. The creative process behind this development has itself been a remarkable international story — it brings together designs of architects from Japan, India, and Lebanon, working with the Toronto firm of Moriyama & Teshima, and adapting age-old architectural traditions in a contemporary Canadian idiom.

The story of this site is connected to Canada's historic welcome to displaced Ismailis in the 1970s and later, and to their successful integration into Canadian life and society. Certainly,

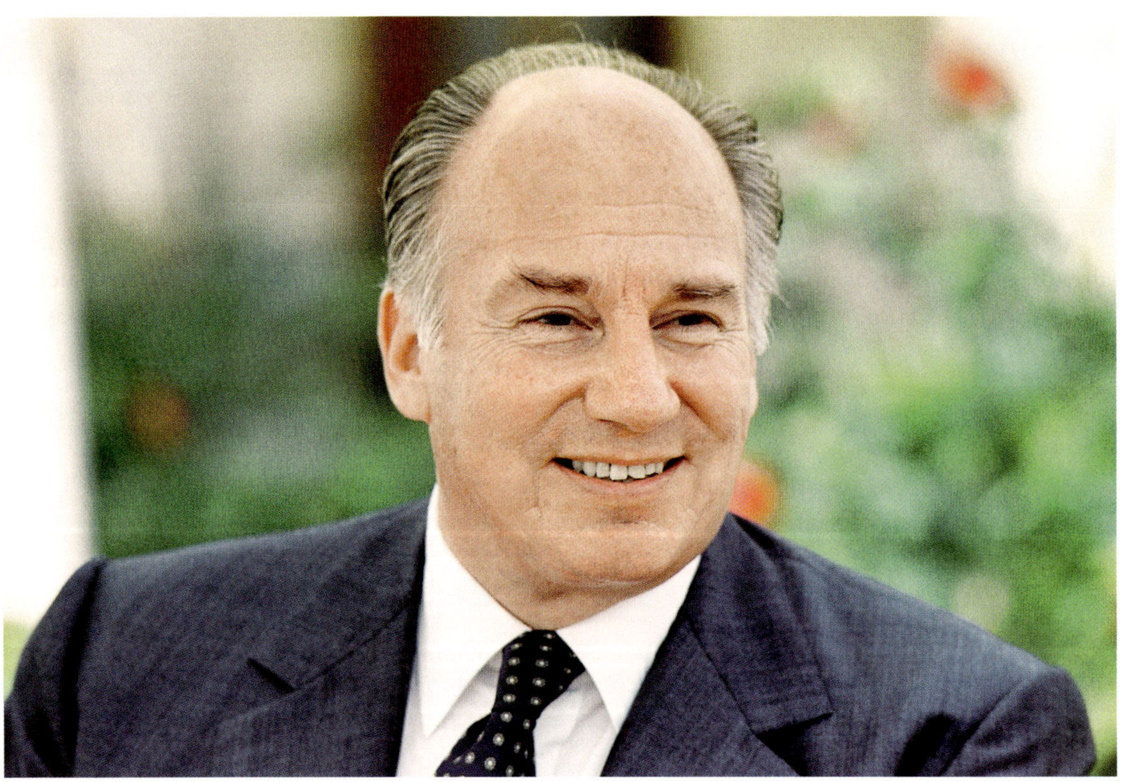

this process and the contributions Ismailis have made in so many walks of life reflect the encouragement they received here to rebuild their traditional institutions and social structures in this country. In looking back over these recent decades, I remember, with deep gratitude, the close collaboration the Aga Khan Development Network has enjoyed with institutions such as the Canadian International Development Agency, which has been and today, as part of Foreign Affairs, Trade and Development Canada, continues to be a key partner in addressing the needs of the developing world. So, too, we appreciate the strong relationships our educational institutions have enjoyed these many years with great Canadian centres of learning such as McMaster and McGill Universities, the University of Toronto, and the University of Alberta. And we are proud of our partnering with the Canadian government in the development of the Global Centre for Pluralism, based in Ottawa, which expresses our shared conviction that the progress of civilization depends on our ability to understand, embrace, and energize the power of human diversity. It is from this strong base of co-operative endeavour covering many years that these projects on Wynford Drive have emerged. They have been inspired, too, by Toronto's own success as a vibrant cultural centre.

The Museum's focus on the arts of Islam makes it something of a unique institution in North America, which will contribute, we hope, to a better understanding of Muslim civilizations — and especially of both the plurality within Islam itself and Islam's relationship to other traditions. It is a place for sharing a story, through art and artifacts, of highly diverse achievements going back more than fourteen hundred years, honouring the central place within Muslim civilizations of the search for knowledge and beauty. And it illuminates both the inspiration that Muslim artists have drawn from their faith, as from the wide and varied array of epics, of stories that recount or reflect the human condition with the universal themes of love and loss, of joy and despair, common to all civilizations at all times. In a world in which some speak of a growing clash of civilizations, we hope and believe that the Museum will help to address what is not so much a clash of civilizations as it is a clash of ignorance. The new Museum has a strong educational vocation: it is a place for active inquiry, for discussion and research, for lectures and seminars, and for an array of collaborative programs with educational institutions, scholars, thinkers, and other museums.

My own family has been intimately involved in Islamic cultural history, notably during the Fatimid Caliphate, which a thousand years ago founded one of the world's first great universities in Cairo. The core collection of the new Museum in Toronto includes elements that have been gathered by my family through many generations, including the miniatures collected by my uncle, the late Prince Sadruddin Aga Khan, displayed in a replica of the Bellerive Room from his home in Geneva. We are deeply grateful to Princess Catherine, his widow, for this generous gift.

The Museum belongs to the institutional framework of the Aga Khan Trust for Culture, already the sponsor of projects for restoring and preserving cultural heritage in places such as Syria, India, Pakistan, Mali, and parts of Central Asia, including Afghanistan, and which has created or promoted museums in Egypt, Zanzibar, and Chantilly in France. The Aga Khan Trust for Culture is active, too, in educational programs, for instance, with Harvard University and the Massachusetts Institute of Technology, and is well-known for its Aga Khan Award for Architecture, an important honour in that discipline.

All in all, the Wynford Drive complex represents a rich tapestry woven from varied strands. And the fact that we have come so far in pursuit of this dream owes everything to those who have believed in it so deeply. We are grateful for the support of so many public officials, successive Canadian prime ministers, regional and city leaders, and local ward councillors. We also salute the contractors, as well as our museum partners from around the world, the members of the Bata family whose support has been so helpful, and the staff and volunteers who have given so much of themselves to this effort. We owe a great deal to all who have made gifts of time and treasure and of endeavour to this project, including, most especially, the Ismaili community in Canada and around the world who have contributed to the development of Ismaili Centres and Jamatkhanas, and to the fund that was set up to commemorate my Golden Jubilee. This project has been designated as a Golden Jubilee project and is a beneficiary of those generous gifts.

I should also say that we hope that the Museum building itself will be recognized as an important work of art, of architecture, designed by the renowned Japanese architect Fumihiko Maki. His beautiful building in Ottawa has already been the home for the Delegation of the Ismaili Imamat since 2008. That building was inspired by the evanescent mysteries of rock crystal. This new Museum here in Toronto takes as its theme the concept of light — suffusing the building from a central courtyard with patterned glass walls and from high lantern windows in the roof. From the outside, this building glows by day and by night, lit by the sun and the moon. The Divine Light of the Creator is reflected in the glow of individual human inspiration. As the thirteenth-century poet Rumi has written, "The light that lights the eye is also the light of the heart ... but the light that lights the heart is the Light of God."

Wisdom Begins with Wonder: The Aga Khan Museum in Context

LUIS MONREAL

> Museums have a strong educational impact: they present evidence of material cultures, without intermediaries, in a direct way that appeals to people both on emotional and intellectual levels.[1]
>
> — His Highness the Aga Khan, Preface to *The Aga Khan Museum, Toronto*

Museums are unique institutions. They display the tangible and intangible heritage of humankind and its environment for education, study purposes, and enjoyment.[2] The confrontation with original works of art that are witnesses to different cultures and epochs strikes an emotional chord. Socrates says: "Wisdom begins with wonder." No other institution has this ability to generate a sense of awakening by placing the visitor directly in front of human artistic creations, from the earliest beginnings to the present time.

Museums induce a sense of wonder and encourage tolerance often lacking in a world filled with instant and frequently biased information. Museums have proven their capacity as catalysts of social change through the educational impact of the art they exhibit.

The Western concept of museums, developed since the Renaissance on the basis of collections amassed by rulers and the aristocracy, has evolved in parallel with a non-Eurocentric vision of world cultures. Today, museums thrive in many different social contexts. They have broadened their acquisitions policies far beyond Western art and acknowledge the creativity of other cultures in a pluralistic world. They have also enlarged their institutional scope by offering artifacts and documents to the public that refer not only to art in a narrow sense but also to history, scientific development, and social traditions, thus providing new opportunities for research and understanding.

The Aga Khan Museum (AKM), an institution founded by His Highness the Aga Khan, is dedicated to the art of Islamic civilizations and to the cultures of the Muslim societies in their historic and geographic diversity. Its institutional mission is to foster knowledge and understanding within Muslim communities and between those societies and other cultures. The Aga Khan Museum will be a gateway between the rich history and tolerant traditions of nearly one-fifth of our world — the Muslim societies — and all those who are open to discovery. Thus, the AKM is by no means solely intended as an art museum. It explores the different dimensions of human culture, from art to science, from literature to music. Furthermore, it is an institution that not only aims to exhibit past cultural and artistic achievements but also to present and make known contemporary creations of artists from the Muslim world and its diaspora.

The selection of Toronto as the location of the Aga Khan Museum was inspired both by the pluralism of the city's social fabric and by its strategic position near the border separating the two great North American nations. It offers an opportunity to reach millions as its potential audience.

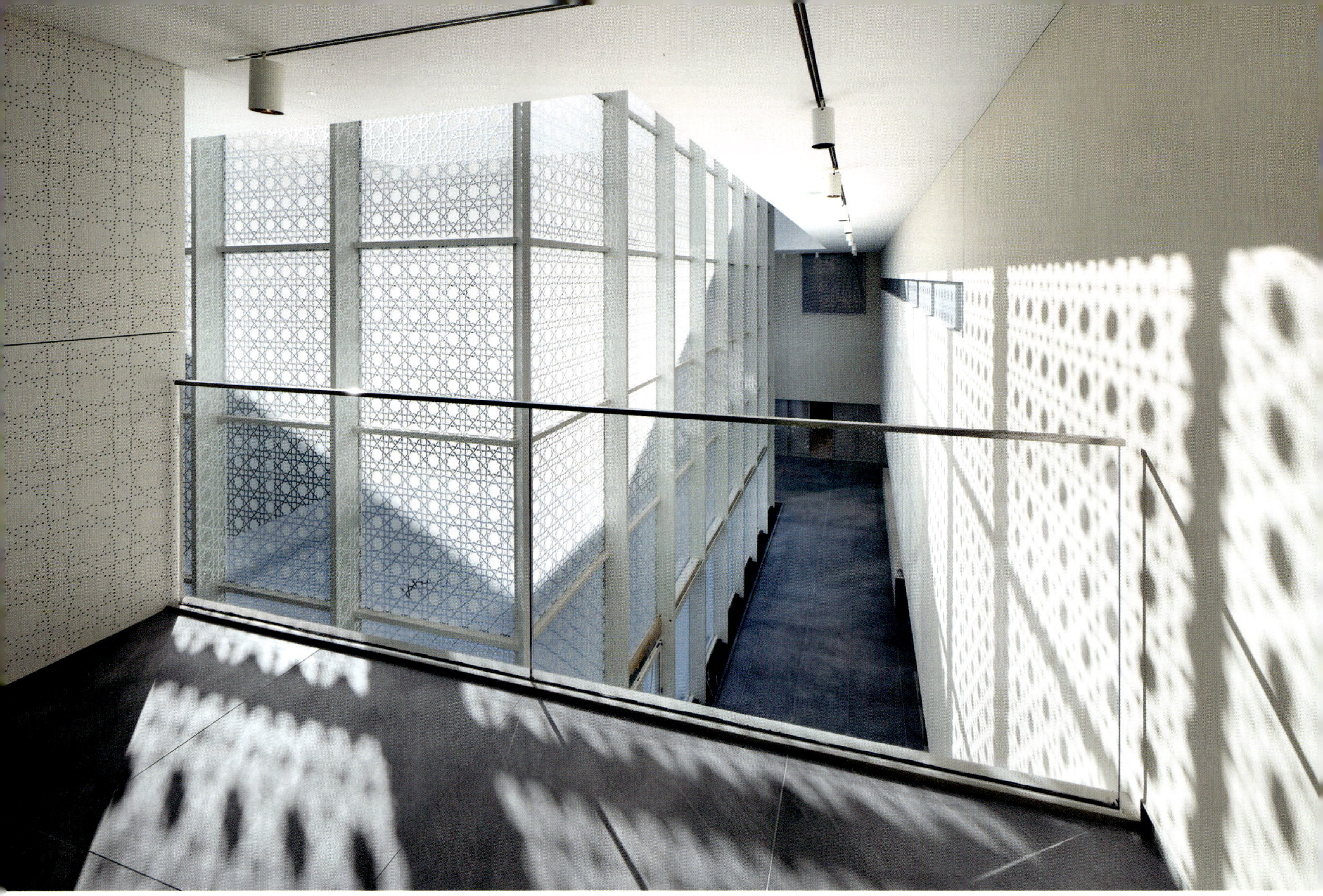

A QUEST FOR PLURALISM

His Highness the Aga Khan conceived the AKM over the past decades, building up its core collection not with the eye of a private collector but with the intention of illustrating the development of the various Muslim civilizations and the pluralism of the world of Islam. The collection of paintings on paper formed by the late Prince Sadruddin Aga Khan — surely the greatest assemblage of such works in private hands — has found its place in the Museum. Aiming to attract visitors from diverse backgrounds, the Museum is developing an active program of temporary exhibitions that will incite visitors to discover cultures and art forms that may be perceived by some as "exotic" when looked at from their personal background.

The architect of the Aga Khan Museum, Fumihiko Maki, who also designed the Delegation of the Ismaili Imamat (Ottawa, 2006–08), worked in close collaboration with His Highness the Aga Khan and found his inspiration in the theme of "light." The correspondence between the Aga Khan and the architect refers in the course of the design process to the Qur'anic "Chapter of Light" (Surat al-Nur) and shows that the AKM wishes to emphasize a common denominator between the Muslim world and nations with other faiths. Light is a metaphorical concept shared by multiple faiths, from Islam to Christianity, from Zoroastrianism to Buddhism. The light that flows through Maki's building, or that radiates from so many of the objects exhibited, is a metaphor of the understanding and tolerance the Museum aims to encourage.

The light that flows through Fumihiko Maki's building, whose interior courtyard is shown here, is a metaphor for the understanding and tolerance the Aga Khan Museum aims to encourage.

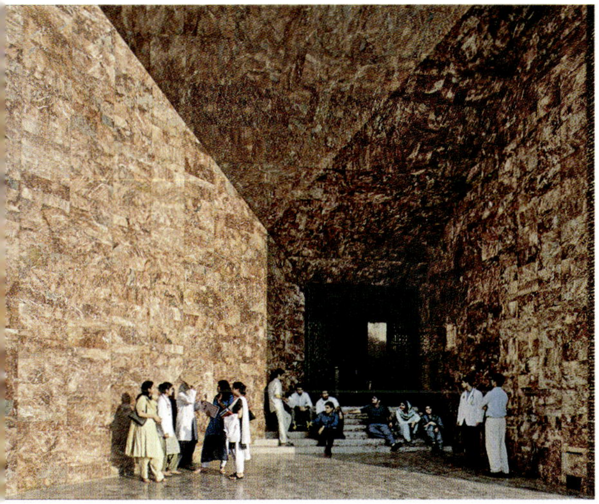

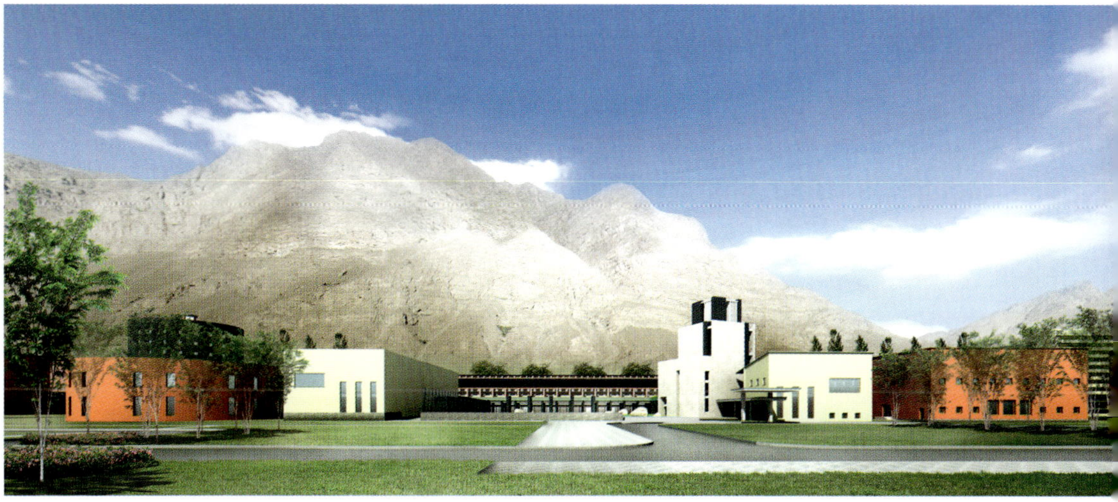

ABOVE LEFT: Students congregate at the Aga Khan University in Karachi, Pakistan.

ABOVE RIGHT: An artist's rendering of the University of Central Asia's campus in Khorog, Tajikistan.

A FAMILY OF ORGANIZATIONS

The Aga Khan Museum is part of a much broader and unique group of organizations: the Aga Khan Development Network (AKDN). A number of agencies, with mandates that include the environment, health, education, architecture, culture, microfinance, rural development, disaster relief and risk reduction, the promotion of private-sector enterprise, and the revitalization of historic cities, form the AKDN. All of its agencies have a common goal: to promote the development of civil society, with the notion of pluralism as an asset in this endeavour coupled with the values of mutual respect and tolerance. This ambition underlies the work of the Aga Khan Museum. Culture in all of its aspects is at the heart of the AKDN's mission, as the education and performing arts programs of the AKM clearly show.

Constituted as an independent institution, the Aga Khan Museum operates in close collaboration with other AKDN organizations, in particular the Institute for the Study of Muslim Civilisations, established in 2002 by the Aga Khan University (AKU), and the Institute of Ismaili Studies. The goal of these institutes is to strengthen research and teaching about the heritage of Muslim societies. They seek to create opportunities for interaction among academics, scholars, and other professionals in order to further the understanding of pressing issues in public life that affect Muslim societies. The Aga Khan University, founded by His Highness the Aga Khan and chartered in Pakistan in 1983 as a private international university, is another of the nine entities of the AKDN that can act as an intellectual partner of the AKM. As a result of treaties signed with the presidents of Tajikistan, the Kyrgyz Republic, and Kazakhstan, the University of Central Asia (UCA) was founded in 2000, also at the initiative of His Highness. This secular and private university offers an internationally recognized standard of higher education in these regions. The AKU and the UCA will develop programs of common academic and research interests with the Aga Khan Museum.

The AKM will also be closely involved with the other educational initiatives of His Highness. Among these are the Aga Khan Academies, founded in 2000 to allow access to education of an international standard of excellence by young men and women from pre-primary through higher secondary education. The academies have been set up in key locations such as Mombasa (2003), Hyderabad (2011), and Maputo (2013).

The Aga Khan Museum operates in close collaboration with the Aga Khan Trust for Culture (AKTC), an agency that comprises a number of programs. These include the Aga Khan Award for Architecture, which has been acknowledging for more than thirty-five years the most significant architectural and urban realizations in Muslim societies and its diaspora. Also under the umbrella of the AKTC, the Historic Cities Programme (HCP) promotes the revitalization of cultural assets

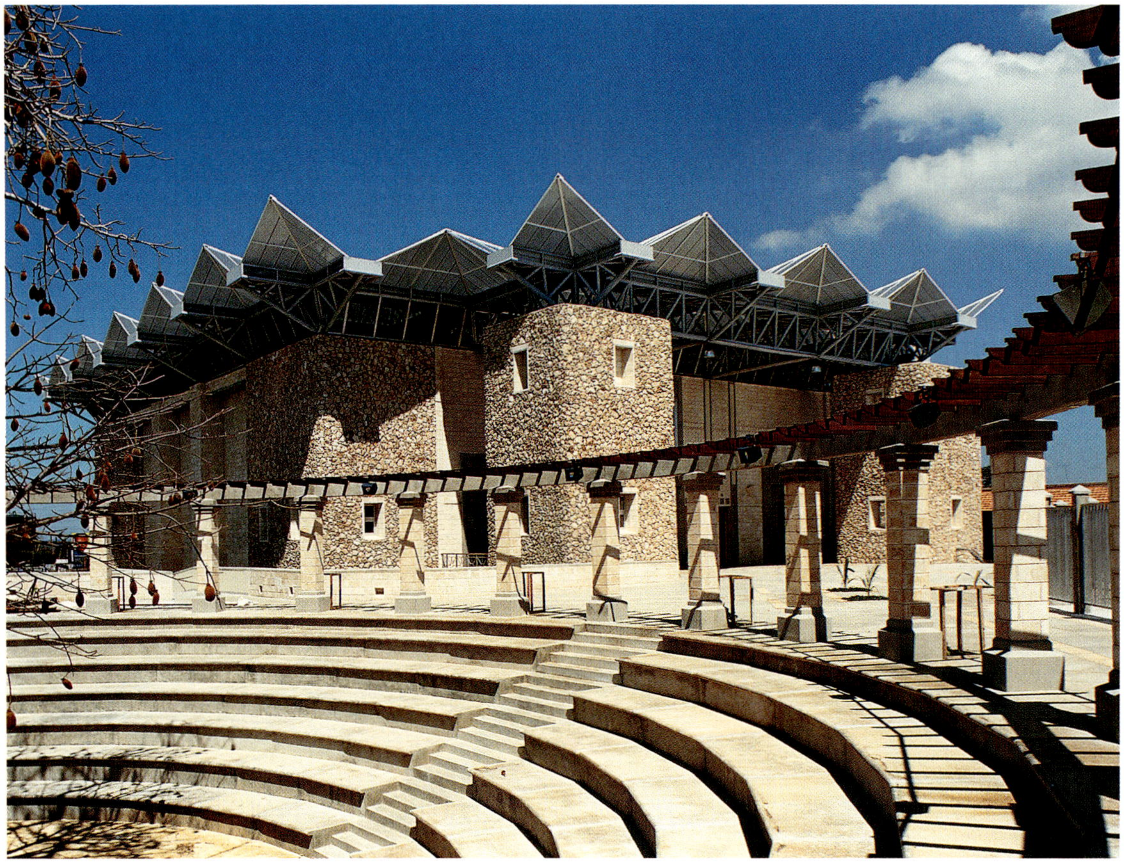

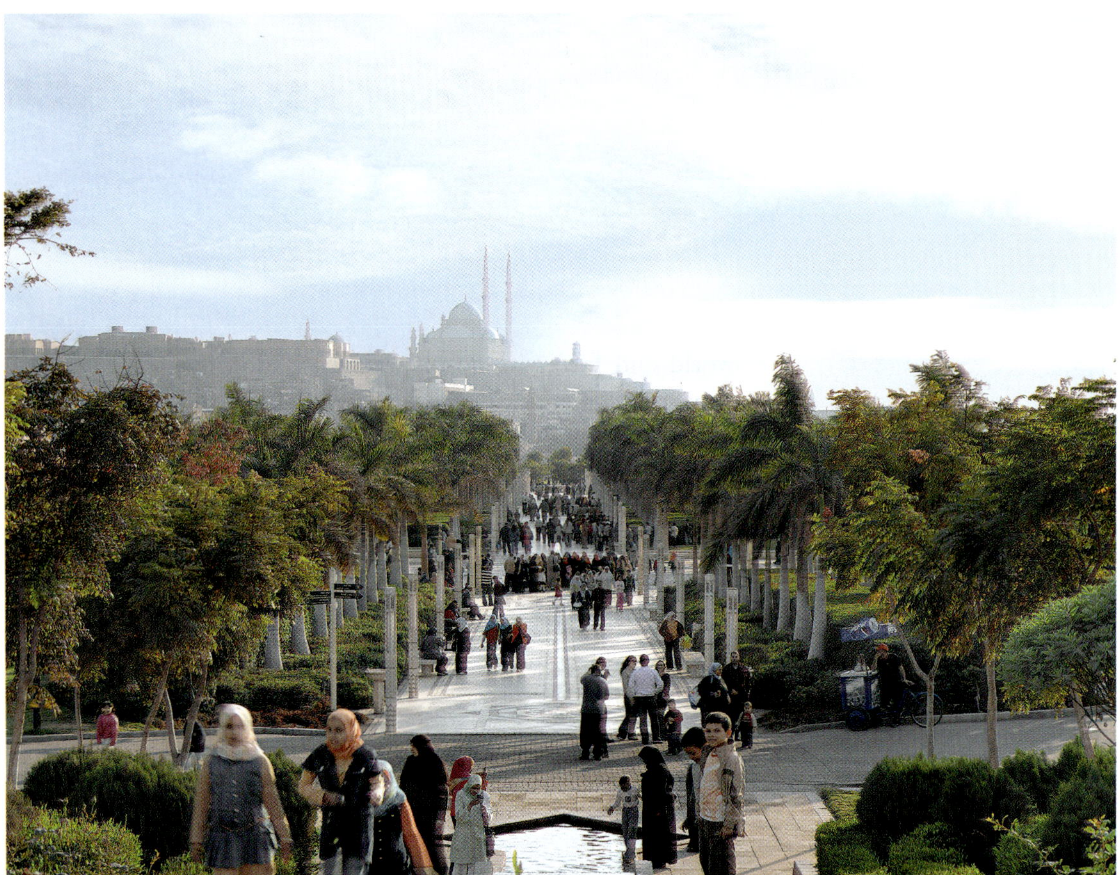

TOP: The Aga Khan Academy in Mombasa, Kenya, follows the widely recognized International Baccalaureate Program.

BOTTOM: The site of al-Azhar Park in Cairo was a debris dump for more than five hundred years until it was transformed by the Aga Khan Trust for Culture's Historic Cities Programme into a vital part of the city.

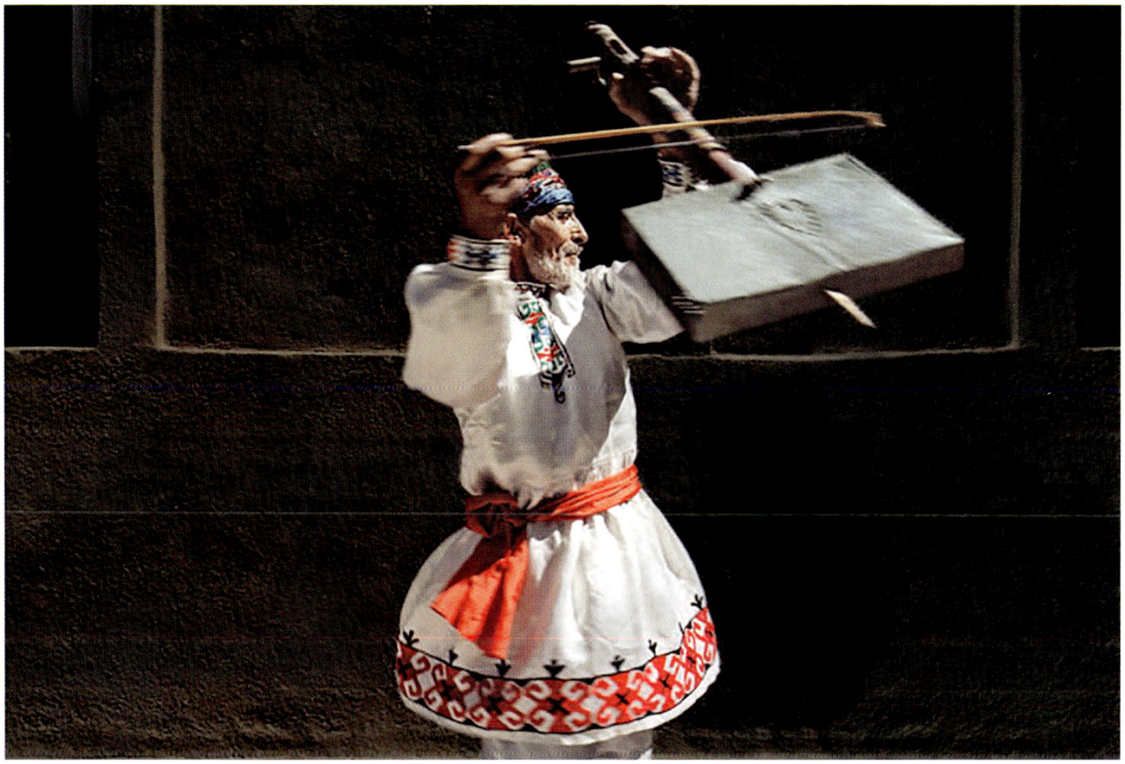

Jonboz Dushanbiev, one of the musicians in the Badakhshan Ensemble, plays a *ghijak* (spike fiddle). Dushanbiev's group, which often performs under the auspices of the Aga Khan Music Initiative, specializes in folk songs and dance music from Badakhshan, a mountainous region straddling Tajikistan and Afghanistan.

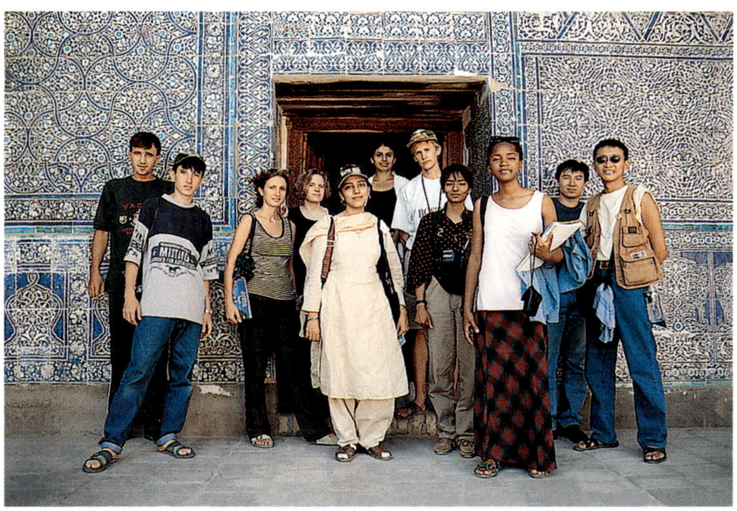

Aga Khan Program for Islamic Architecture students in Khiva, Uzbekistan, in 1996.

in urban areas. It demonstrates through urban regeneration projects in African and Asian cities that such a strategy can significantly contribute to the community's social and economic development. HCP programs and projects go beyond technical conservation and restoration issues, offering opportunities for joint ventures with the AKM.

Another AKTC program that may be coordinated with the AKM is the Aga Khan Music Initiative (AKMI), created in 2000 to support the efforts of musicians and communities in Central Asia to sustain and transmit the wealth of their musical traditions. This program has been expanded to support the transmission of musical heritage in other regions of the Muslim world and foster its development through connections with contemporary musical creation in the West.

In the area of scholarly research and presentations, the AKTC works closely with the Aga Khan Program for Islamic Architecture (AKPIA). AKPIA was established in 1977. It has since become an endowed centre of excellence in the history, theory, and practice of Islamic architecture at Harvard University and the Massachusetts Institute of Technology. AKPIA's mandate is to educate architects, planners, teachers, and researchers who can respond to the building and design needs of Muslim communities today. The program's teaching and scholarly research also serve to increase cross-cultural interest in the arts and culture of the Islamic world. To date, more than 198 professionals, many from Muslim nations, have graduated from the program. Endowments established by His Highness also support the collection and documentation of unique and important textual and material collections bearing on the history of art and architecture in Islamic lands. These together, along with the archives of the AKTC, are available online through *Archnet.org*, a globally accessible intellectual resource focused on architecture, urbanism, environmental, and landscape design. In 2002 the AKTC further increased the resources available to AKPIA by establishing an endowed chair for the Aga Khan Professorship of Landscape Architecture and Urbanism in Islamic Societies at Harvard University's Graduate School of Design.

These and other programs related to the Aga Khan Development Network provide the Aga Khan Museum with a constellation of sister organizations involved in various programs. While anchored in Toronto, the AKM benefits from the worldwide resources of the AKDN. The potential symbiotic relationship between the AKM and the AKDN's agencies opens up the opportunity to expand the outreach of the Museum's programs far beyond its walls and to achieve a truly international cultural project.

A CONTRIBUTION TO A BROADER CAUSE

While museums often work in the somewhat ethereal world of art for art's sake, the Aga Khan Museum finds itself rooted in the real world. His Highness the Aga Khan points out that a close connection has always existed in Muslim societies between faith and the reality of daily existence: "In the Islamic world we always look at the fundamental unity of *din* and *dunya*, of spirit and life, and we cannot tolerate that one functions without the other. The notion of *din* and *dunya* and the integrity of human life is a very important issue."[3]

The purpose of the Aga Khan Museum is by no means to proselytize. It is to create a sense of curiosity and wonder that incites visitors to want to know more. It is there to assist in the acquisition of knowledge.

At the ninth ceremony of the Aga Khan Award for Architecture in New Delhi in 2004, His Highness the Aga Khan declared: "Perhaps these lessons will one day be seen as an important contribution from the Muslim world: A contribution to the broader cause of maintaining and enhancing a multi-cultural, pluralist world and a responsive, appropriate human habitat."[4] These words might well apply to the Aga Khan Museum.

NOTES

1. His Highness the Aga Khan, Preface to Philip Jodidio, *The Aga Khan Museum, Toronto* (Munich: Prestel, 2008), 6.
2. International Council of Museums Statutes, article 3, paragraph 1.
3. His Highness the Aga Khan in conversation with Philip Jodidio, London, United Kingdom, March 6, 2007.
4. His Highness the Aga Khan, Speech at the Ninth Award Cycle of the Aga Khan Award for Architecture, New Delhi, India, November 27, 2004. Accessed at *www.akdn.org/Content/236/Ninth-Award-Cycle-of-the-Aga-Khan-Award-for-Architecture-New-Delhi*.

THE MUSEUM

A Journey Across Cultures and Time: The Aga Khan Museum's Vision

HENRY S. KIM

For visitors who come to the Aga Khan Museum, the objects they encounter can be seen as points in a journey that connect cultures across time. The history of Islamic civilizations is one that can be characterized by continuous encounters with neighbouring peoples over fourteen hundred years. Spread across a vast region that stretched from Spain in the west to China in the east, the opportunities for interactions abounded, fuelled by trading contacts made over the land-based Silk Road and the maritime routes of the spice trade, and through cohabitation in regions such as Spain, Sicily, Africa, the Balkans, Central Asia, China, India, and Southeast Asia.

These encounters left their indelible mark on the arts from the region, something that the Aga Khan Museum is keen to demonstrate in its displays, exhibitions, and performing arts. Included in this essay are some of the more important examples that can be seen in the art from the Museum's collection. Some show remarkable similarities to techniques of decoration and manufacture from the Chinese world. Others reflect styles, forms, and knowledge from the ancient world of Greece and Rome, while certain ones are borrowed directly from Western traditions and some are made by artists from outside the Muslim world. In all cases they show the importance of external influences in the development of the art of Islamic civilizations and reflect the vibrant culture of encounters that took place historically.

A remarkable instance of cross-cultural fertilization over time and regions can be seen in

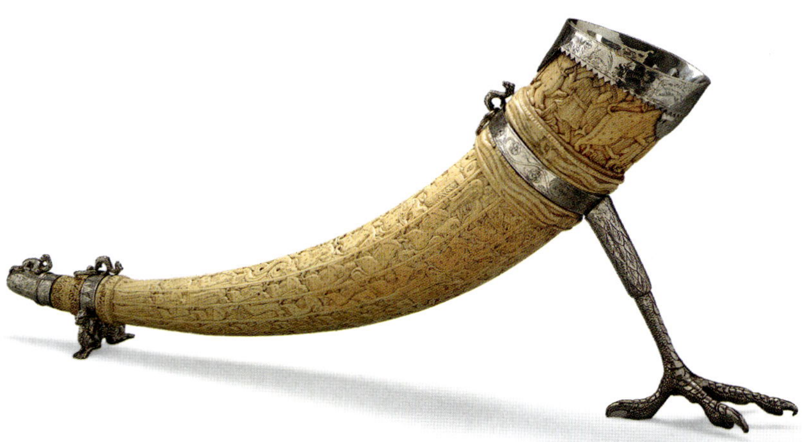

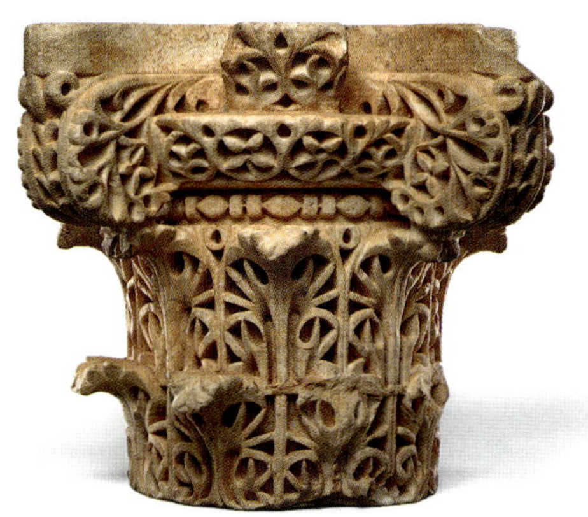

ABOVE LEFT: Ivory Horn (Oliphant,) southern Italy, 11th–12th centuries (mount: Great Britain, early 17th century), carved ivory with silver mount, length 64 cm (25¼ in.), height 34 cm (13⅜ in.), AKM809.

ABOVE RIGHT: Capital, Spain (Historic al-Andalus), 10th century, carved marble, height 28 cm (11 in.), AKM663.

the ivory oliphant or hunting horn in the Museum's collection (AKM809, see also pages 49 and 132–33). The first recorded use of the word *oliphant* occurs in the twelfth-century French epic poem *La Chanson de Roland* where the titular hero, before he dies, sounds an oliphant to warn Charlemagne's army against a Muslim attack during the late eighth-century Battle of Roncesvalles.

Oliphants were likely known in Egypt during the Fatimid dynasty (909–1171), though none have been preserved and they are not found in depictions of hunters in Iranian art. Scholars believe numerous examples were produced in Sicily and southern Italy by Muslim craftsmen after the Normans took complete control of Sicily from the Arab Kahbid dynasty, vassals of the Fatimids, at the end of the eleventh century. The Museum's hunting horn, like other oliphants with iconography such as repetitive real and imaginary animals derived from Islamic traditions, were highly prized by Christian European nobility and often found their way into monasteries and churches.

Silver mounts were added to the Museum's oliphant in Britain in the early seventeenth century, possibly indicating some new ceremonial function and demonstrating further how a device that had already derived much from a confluence of Islamic and European cultures could be repurposed yet again.

In a similar fashion, a tenth-century capital in the Museum's collection (AKM663, see also page 48) from Spain reminds one of the Corinthian capitals found in Roman and Visigothic ruins all over the Iberian Peninsula. The basic structure of Corinthian capitals is maintained here, but the two rows of deeply carved acanthus leaves are rendered sprightlier and with more verve. This capital possibly topped a column in one of the many palaces erected in the Spain of the Umayyads (756–1031) only to be reused by Christians elsewhere later.

The *Qanun [fi'l-tibb]* or Canon [of Medicine] by the Iranian scholar Ibn Sina (known as Avicenna in the West) was written within fifteen years of the polymath's death in 1037. The *Qanun*'s five volumes are a compendium of Greco-Roman medical learning featuring the wisdom of Aristotle and Galen wedded with the Chinese knowledge of Ibn Sina's time. The folio illustrated here is from the *Qanun*'s fifth volume (AKM510, see also page 90), one of two volumes in the Museum's collection (the other is the fourth) and possibly one of the earliest if not the earliest extant manuscript of this work.

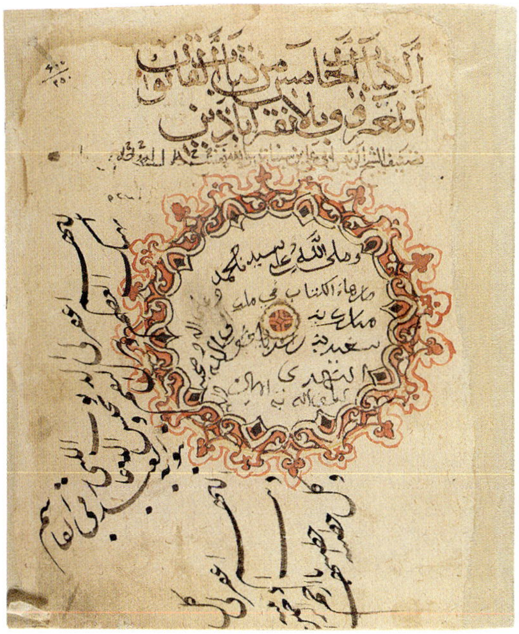

ABOVE: *Qanun [fi'l-tibb]* (Canon [of Medicine]), volume 5, Ibn Sina (d. 1037), Iran or Iraq, 1052, opaque watercolour and ink on paper, folio: 21.2 × 16.4 cm (8⅜ × 6½ in.), AKM510.

Volume five tells of compound drugs and pharmacopoeia, while the other volumes cover topics such as anatomy, the humours, general and specific pathology, diseases, fractures, and surgery. The *Qanun* serves as a tangible bridge between the Classical world, Islam, and Europe, especially since Ibn Sina's great work was translated into Latin in the thirteenth century and eventually into other European languages and became an essential medical text in Western medical colleges well into the eighteenth century. Even today it has an important place in Indian Unani, an alternative form of medical practice related to Ayurvedic medicine.

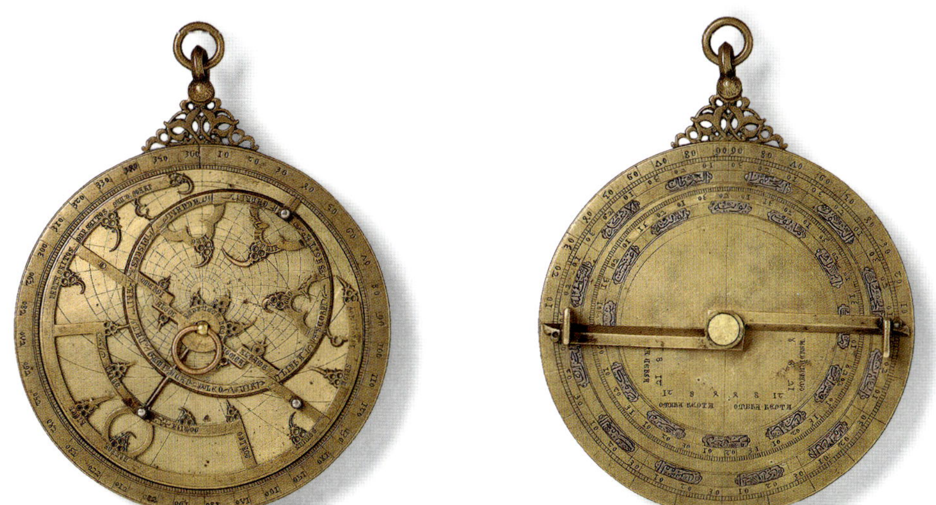

RIGHT: Planispheric Astrolabe, Spain (Historic al-Andalus), 14th century, bronze inlaid with silver, diameter 13.5 cm (5¼ in.), AKM611.

A scientific instrument that is extraordinary not only visually and technically but also for what it can tell us about the time when it was made is the Museum's Spanish astrolabe (AKM611, see also pages 94–95). It is a magnificent object of craftsmanship and science that transforms practical information into an object of beauty. As an object, it represents the advancement of science in the Muslim world and how this knowledge was passed on to other cultures that encountered it.

An astrolabe is a navigational and timekeeping instrument whose name comes from the Greek for "star-taker." The practice of using stars to navigate and keep time can be traced to the ancient world where Greek astronomers developed an advanced knowledge of the stars and their progression across the sky through a year. Instruments that helped astronomers predict the location of stars relative to the ground are believed to have existed as early as the second century BCE and were used into Byzantine times.

What makes the Museum's fourteenth-century astrolabe exceptional are the inscriptions found on it. Most astrolabes have inscriptions in one language, but the Museum's piece has three—Latin, Arabic, and Hebrew. The inscriptions help place where the object was made. It comes from Spain where the cultures of Christianity, Islam, and Judaism met and where Islam had a firm European foothold. The Latin and Arabic inscriptions were written at the time when the astrolabe was originally manufactured, supporting the idea that it was made for communities where Arabic and Latin were both used. Hebrew seems to be a later addition, appearing as light scratches on one of the "maps," suggesting reuse by a Jewish astronomer or navigator.

For millennia the trading of goods has been the engine of cross-cultural exchange. Two fifteenth-century Syrian pharmacy jars or *albarelli* in the Museum's collection (AKM567 and AKM568, see also page 83) are prime examples of how this dynamic worked. *Albarelli* were traded during the

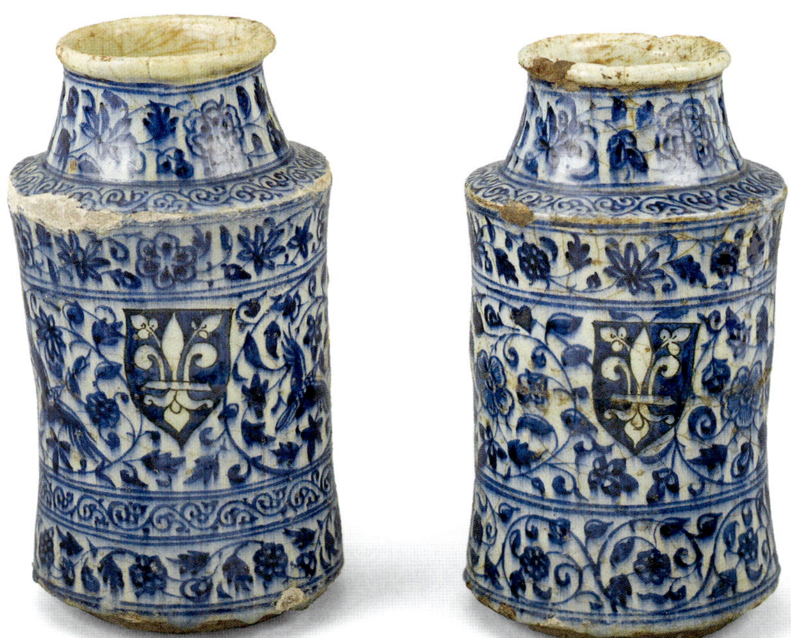

Pharmacy Jars (*Albarelli*), Syria, 15th century, fritware, underglaze-painted. AKM567: diameter 49.4 cm (19½ in.), height 32 cm (12⅝ in.). AKM568: diameter 49.4 cm (19½ in.), height 30.7 cm (12⅛ in.).

Mamluk era (1250–1517) between the Middle East and Italian city-states for their artistic value or as containers of precious pharmaceutical substances. Many French, Spanish, and Italian inventories from the fourteenth and fifteenth centuries record ceramic objects "from Damascus," and more specifically the Medici archives list the presence of *albaregli damaschini* in Florence.

The central, wider band of each of these *albarelli* features a fleur-de-lys heraldic shield that could be the crest of Florentine merchants who commissioned the goods once contained in the jars or it may signify the city the important trade was based in. Italian merchants were often found in Cairo, Damascus, and Beirut in the fifteenth century and it is possible one of them ordered these jars for a Florentine apothecary or perhaps even for medical use in his own home. However, the fleur-de-lys was also used by several Mamluk sultans and emirs until the fifteenth century and has been noted on certain monuments in Syria.

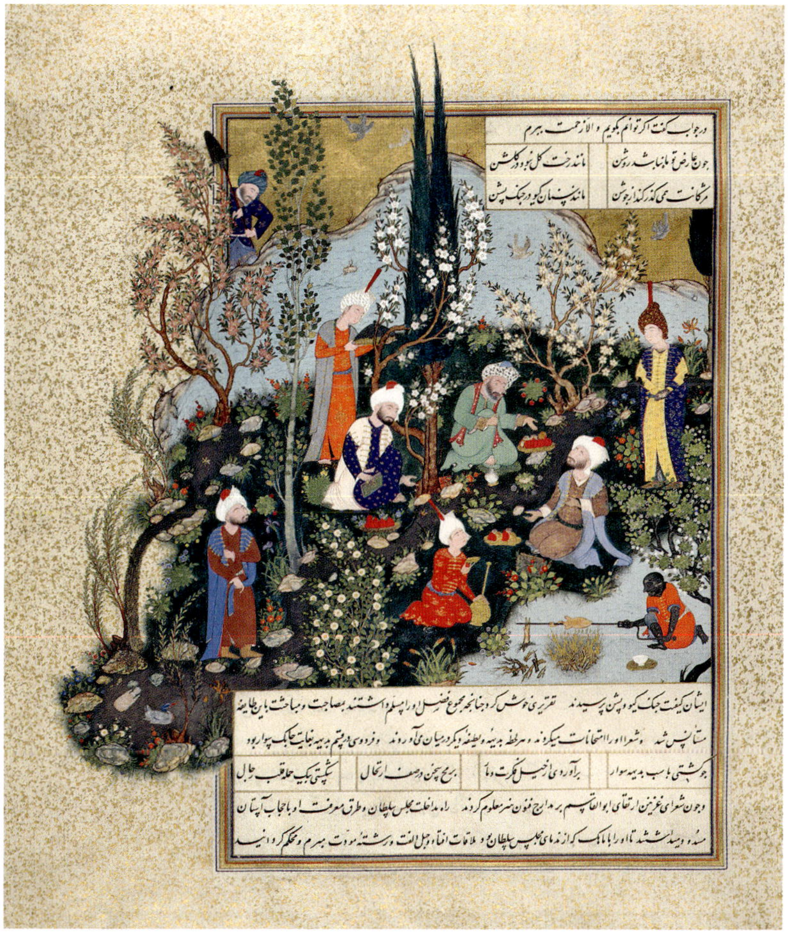

More than a dozen painters, at least two calligraphers, several miniaturists, bookbinders, polishers, gold stipplers, and margin creators, along with a sizable platoon of assistants from various Iranian and Central Asian regions pooled their talents at the behest of the Safavid Shah Tahmasp I (1524–76) to create a *Shah-Nameh* (see also pages 42–45, 50–52, and 114–29) that became arguably the most remarkable Iranian manuscript ever produced. The *Shah-Nameh*, Iran's national epic poem, was written by Ferdowsi in the late tenth and early eleventh centuries and recounts the mythical and historical past of Iran from the creation of the world until the Muslim conquest of Persia.

Ten folios from this extraordinary manuscript are part of the Aga Khan Museum's collection. The folio illustrated here (AKM156) is entitled *Ferdowsi Encounters the Court Poets of Ghazni* and was likely completed circa 1532. Ferdowsi (at the extreme left of the illustration) departed from his native Tus in northeast Iran and journeyed to Ghazni in present-day Afghanistan to seek the patronage of Sultan Mahmud. Before he could meet with the sultan, though, he was confronted by three court poets (the central grouping in the illustration) who challenged his abilities as a poet but eventually recognized his superior talent.

Combining lore and history, the *Shah-Nameh* provides models of conduct that inspired numerous generations of rulers. The poem, in fact, can be considered a "mirror for princes," a popular genre in the medieval and early modern Islamic world that sought to show how rulers should behave. Various neighbouring peoples such as Georgians, Armenians, Kurds, and Pashtuns mined the *Shah-Nameh* for their own storytelling, and Western writers in later periods such as the German author Goethe also found much to admire in Ferdowsi's remarkable achievement and Persian literature in general. Goethe even penned a book of poems — *West-Eastern Divan* — that was inspired by the Iranian poet Hafez.

Ferdowsi Encounters the Court Poets of Ghazni, folio from a *Shah-Nameh* (Book of Kings) produced for Shah Tahmasp I, Tabriz, Iran, ca. 1532, opaque watercolour, ink, and gold on paper, 45 × 30 cm (17¾ × 11¾ in.), AKM156.

Tiles, Iznik, Turkey, ca. 1560, frit-ware, underglaze-painted, each 25 × 24.5 cm (9⅞ × 9⅝ in.), AKM583 and AKM584.

Iznik is the name the Ottomans (1299–1923) gave to the Byzantine city of Nicaea after they conquered it in 1331. The manufacturing of ceramics had been a focus for Iznik even in later Byzantine times, but it was in the fifteenth century that the city truly came into its own as

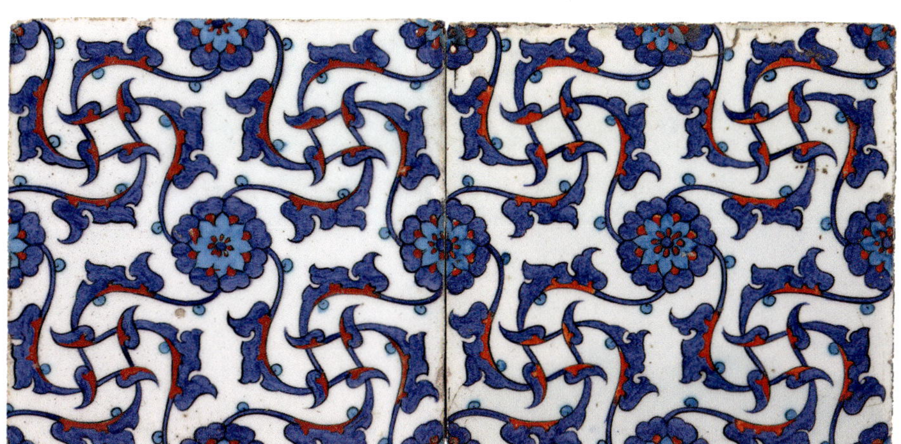

a celebrated centre of ceramic production. These two tiles in the Aga Khan Museum's collection (AKM583 and AKM584, see also page 166) possibly once adorned an Ottoman mosque or palace.

The Ottoman sultans greatly admired Chinese blue-and-white porcelain. Their own potters were unable to reproduce porcelain because of the lack of kaolin as raw material, but they were able to create fritware, ceramics composed largely of silica and glass. Seeming imitation of Chinese originals soon gave way to inventive adaptation so that by the mid-sixteenth century, Iznik had developed its own repertoire of tightly organized floral and abstract motifs as seen in the Museum's tiles. However, as the century progressed, various colours such as red (already seen on AKM583 and AKM584) and green became more common and patterns got more elaborate and even quirky.

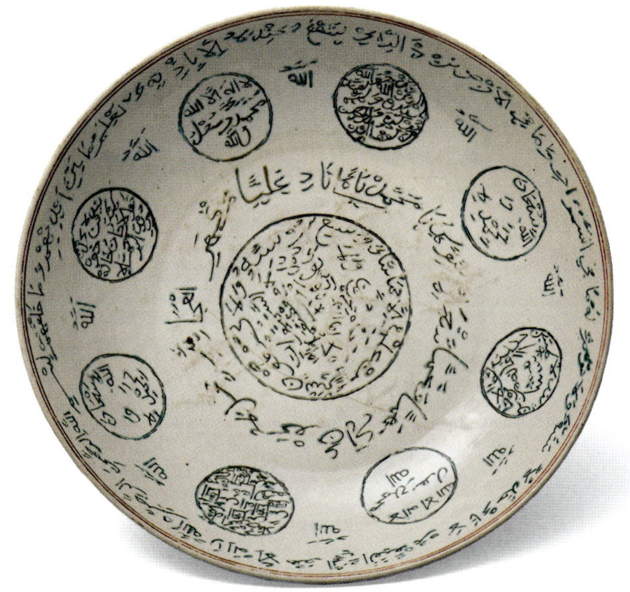

Dish, Zhangzhou, China, 17th century, porcelain, underglaze-painted, diameter 35.1 cm ($13\frac{7}{8}$ in.), AKM591.

A sort of reverse dynamic is represented by a porcelain dish (AKM591) manufactured in seventeenth-century Zhangzhou, China. The Museum's dish is an example of a ware called Swatow, a Dutch mistranslation of Shantou, the port from which such ceramics were supposedly shipped during the Qing dynasty (1644–1912). These dishes were exported to Europe, Japan, and Southeast Asia between the mid-sixteenth and mid-seventeenth centuries, and similar ones appeared in Indonesia and are thought to have been commissioned by the powerful seventeenth-century Shia sultans of Aceh in northwest Sumatra.

The inscriptions on AKM591 feature verses from the Qur'an, including Surat al-Baqara ("The Cow"), Surat al-Ikhlas ("Fidelity"), and Surat al-Nas ("The People"), as well as invocations to Allah. Such inscriptions were meant as protection and assistance for the owner.

One of the foremost Iranian artists was Mo'in Mosavvir (died 1697), who frequently signed his own works and dated them. The main subject and the treatment of clouds in *A Resting Lion* (AKM111, see also page 128), attributed to Mosavvir, exhibit Chinese influence, but the artist

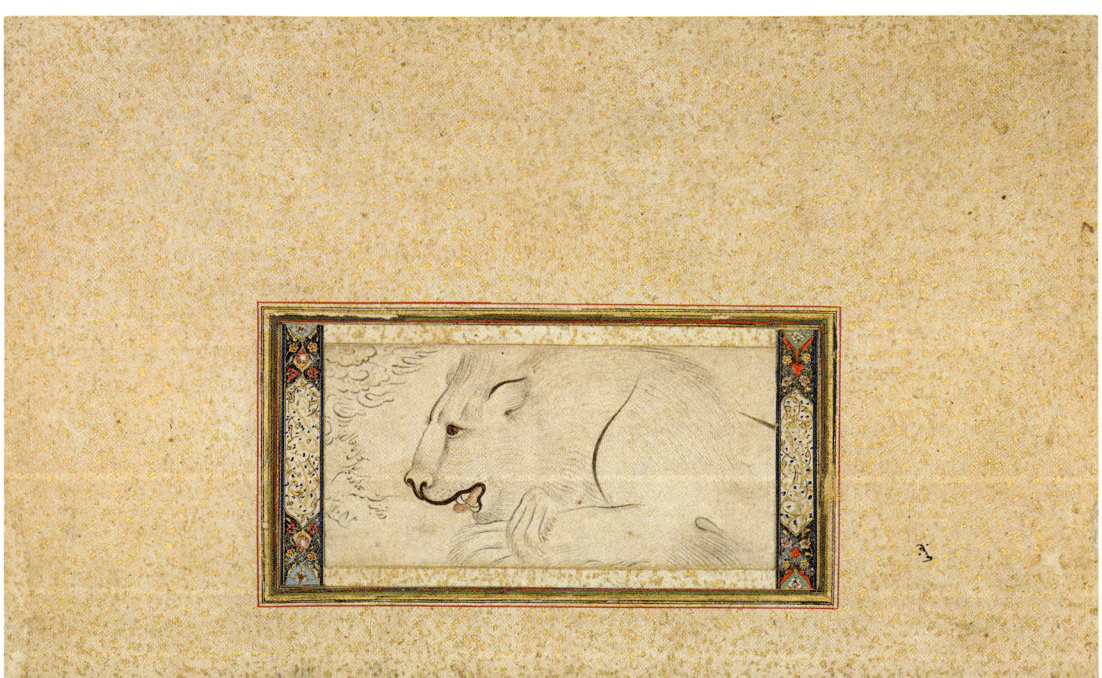

A Resting Lion, single-page drawing attributed to Mo'in Mosavvir, Isfahan, Iran, 1672, ink, opaque watercolour, and gold on paper, 14.1 × 22.5 cm ($5\frac{1}{2}$ × $8\frac{7}{8}$ in.), AKM111.

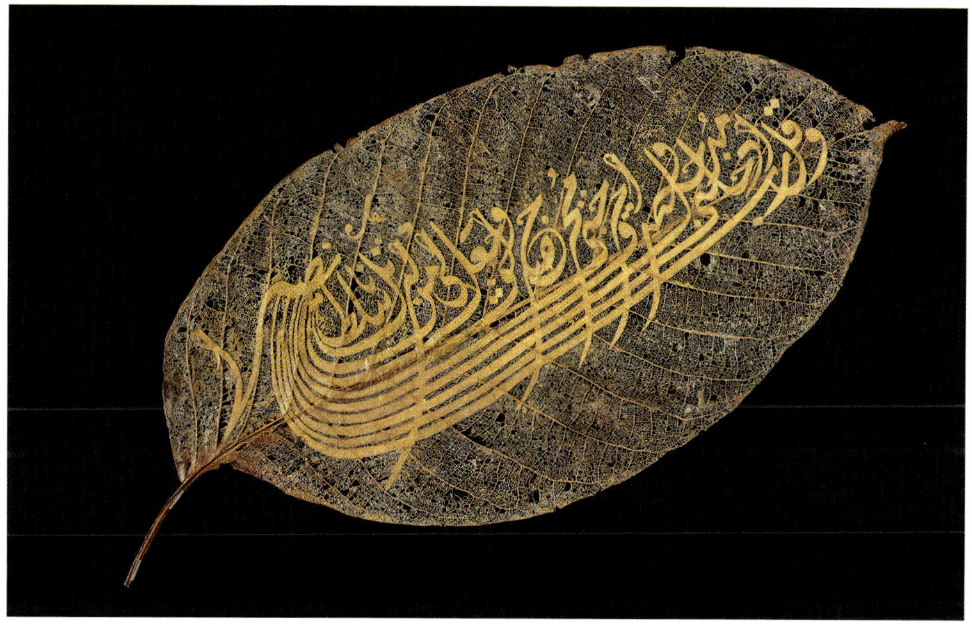

Leaf with Calligraphic Composition, Turkey, 19th century, gold on chestnut leaf, 13.5 × 28 cm (5¼ × 11 in.), AKM538.

has made the drawing his own through his self-assured brushstrokes and playful portrayal of the king of beasts. Although the lion may be "at rest" with his right paw crossed over his left, his open mouth displays a red tongue and deadly fangs.

Mosavvir would have been all too familiar with the danger of wild animals since he showed a tiger mauling a boy in another drawing now in the Museum of Fine Arts, Boston. Apparently, the artist heard about the attack and made the drawing a week later. Resting indeed!

Qur'anic inscriptions are found on all manner of objects, including a mother-of-pearl shell (AKM665, see page 137) and wooden beams (AKM701 and AKM628, see pages 156–59), but one of the most extraordinary media boasting a passage from the Qur'an is without doubt a gilded sweet chestnut leaf (AKM538, see also page 139). The leaf features a verse from Surat al-Isra ("The Night Journey"): "And say, 'Lord, grant me a good entrance and a goodly exit, and sustain me with your power.'" Masterfully, using the characters of the verse, the calligrapher creates a boat filled with people, oars dipping into "water" and perhaps conjuring the journey we all take, a connection all cultures and their peoples should find relevant.

Ten objects, ten illustrations of the cross-cultural nature of the arts of Islamic civilizations. For the Aga Khan Museum, these objects are as important for their inherent beauty as for the wealth of knowledge that comes from viewing and understanding them. The Museum through its public programs will place special emphasis on the culture of encounters that occurred historically to shape the arts of the region. Its goal is to present the arts of Islamic civilizations not in isolation but as an integral part of an artistic and cultural ecosystem that connects East to West from the seventh century to the present day.

A Conversation with Fumihiko Maki, Architect of the Aga Khan Museum

PHILIP JODIDIO

When His Highness the Aga Khan decided that the noted Japanese architect Fumihiko Maki would design a new museum in Toronto,[1] he wrote him a long letter. In that letter he stated: "For the Aga Khan Museum, I thought that 'light' might be a concept around which you could design an outstanding museum. The notion of light has transversed nearly all of human history, and has been an inspiration for numerous faiths, going as far back of course to the Zoroastrians and their reverence for the Sun, to the *Sura* in the Holy Qur'an titled *al-Nur*.[2] Decades of Western history are referred to as the 'enlightenment' for good reason."[3] In a sense, the entire effort of His Highness the Aga Khan, beginning with his ongoing dedication to the Ismaili community and continuing with such initiatives as the Aga Khan Award for Architecture or the Aga Khan Program for Islamic Architecture at Harvard University and the Massachusetts Institute of Technology, has led to this: a museum dedicated not only to the display of exceptional objects of Islamic art but also to music, to education—and to a sense of pluralism and openness that he found in Canada but that he first and foremost finds in Islam.

AN OUTSTANDING ARCHITECT

Born in Tokyo in 1928, Fumihiko Maki received his bachelor's degree in architecture from the University of Tokyo (1952) and went on to obtain master's degrees from both the Cranbrook Academy of Art (1953) and the Harvard Graduate School of Design (1954). He worked for Skidmore, Owings & Merrill in New York (1954–55) and Sert, Jackson and Associates in Cambridge, Massachusetts (1955–58), before creating his own firm, Maki and Associates, in Tokyo in 1965. Maki's study and early work in the United States undoubtedly influenced his extensive list of completed projects. His recent buildings include the Shimane Museum of Ancient Izumo (Izumo, Japan, 2006), a structure similar in size to the Aga Khan Museum that uses a combination of glass and Corten steel, and World Trade Center Tower 4 (New York City), a sleek sixty-one-storey skyscraper completed in 2013. He is also the author of the Delegation of the Ismaili Imamat in Ottawa, Canada (2006–08).

Maki's status in the world of architecture is underlined by the fact that he has been granted three of the most prestigious awards of his profession: the Pritzker Prize (1993), the Praemium Imperiale (1999), and the AIA Gold Medal (2011). The Pritzker Prize Jury Citation offers an explanation of qualities that His Highness the Aga Khan has identified in Maki's work. It reads in part: "He uses light in a masterful way making it as tangible a part of every design as are the walls and roof. In each building, he searches for a way to make transparency, translucency and opacity exist in total harmony."[4]

As Maki explains, his good working relations with His Highness the Aga Khan have developed over time and have been related to the interests of the Aga Khan in modern architecture. "In 1986," recalls Maki, "I was asked to be a member of the Master Jury of the Aga Khan Award for Architecture. At that time the Aga Khan was living near Geneva where we spent a few days selecting candidates for the award. I was invited again in 1992 to participate in the jury, a rare honour! I did not have much contact with His Highness again until the late 1990s when I got a call from a man who asked me if I would be interested in designing a new Ismaili Centre in Canada [Delegation of the Ismaili Imamat, Ottawa]. Of course, I said yes. I met quite a few times with His Highness at Aiglemont near Chantilly [in France] during the design process. Sometimes,

A summer view of the Aga Khan Museum building through trees in the Aga Khan Park.

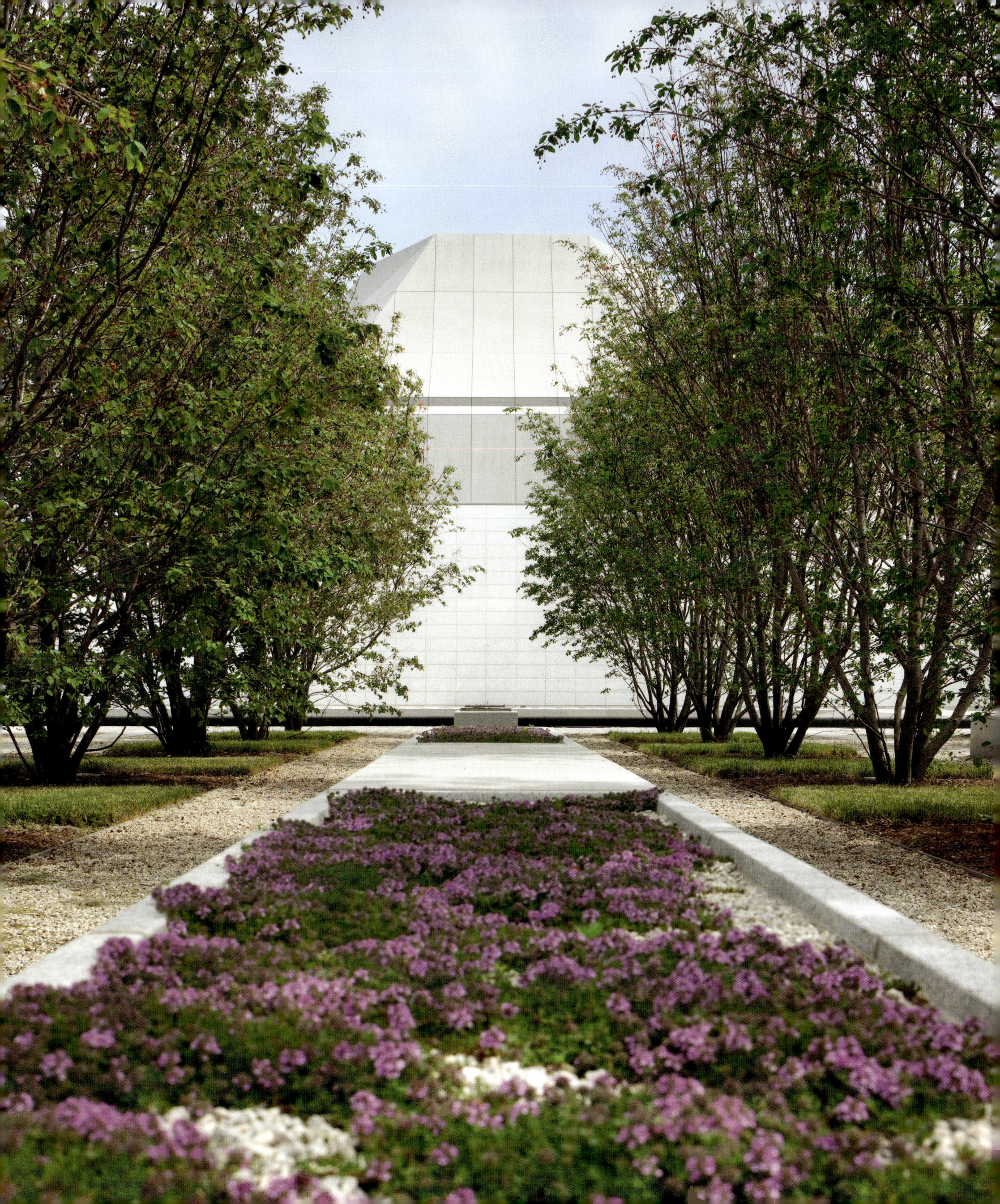

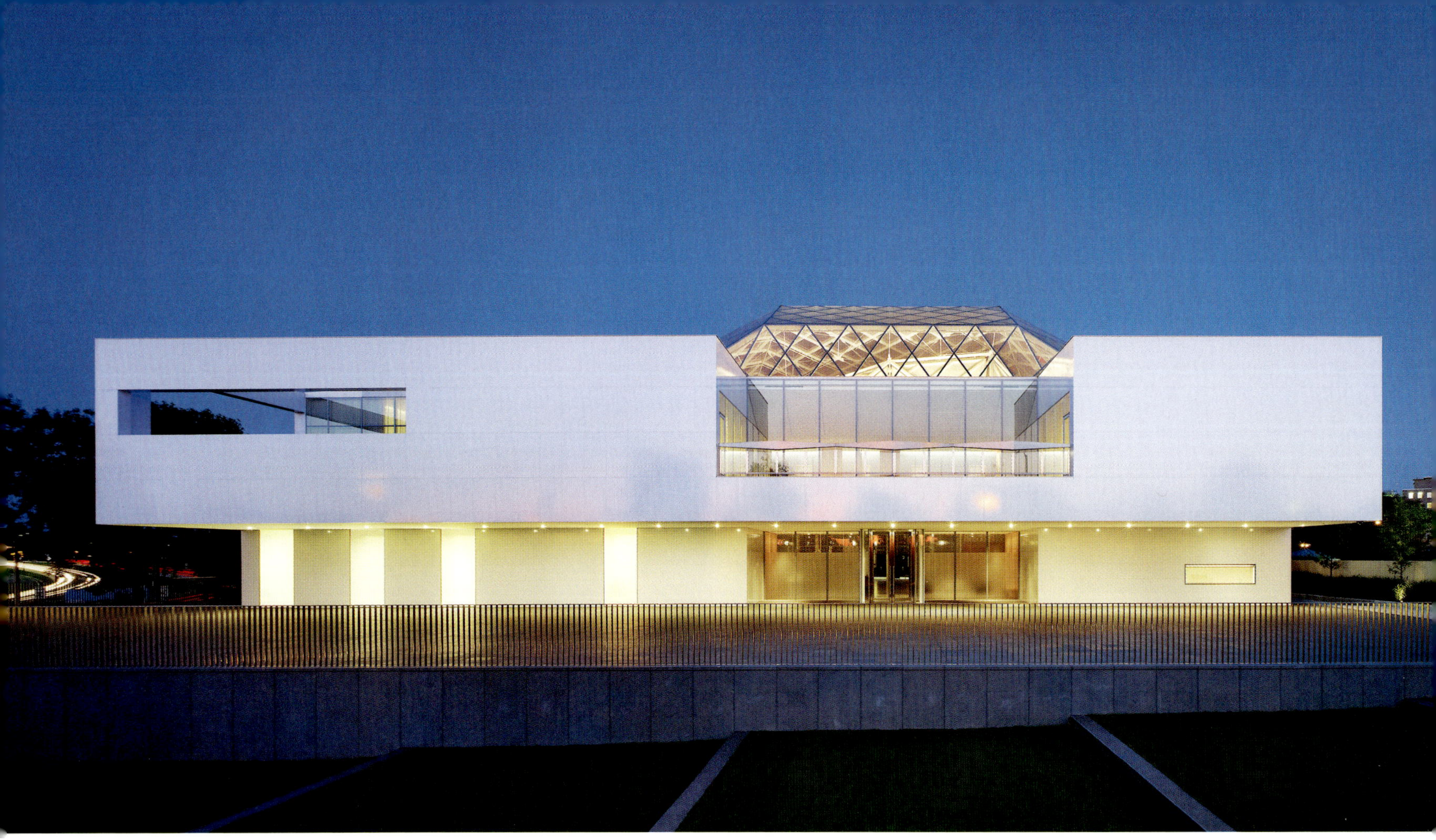

after the construction started, he asked us to be on-site for the selection of exterior stones. The Delegation of the Ismaili Imamat was well received. It was awarded a 2012 Governor General's Medal in Architecture as an example of the architecture of 'peace and plurality.'"[5]

Fumihiko Maki's Delegation of the Ismaili Imamat in Ottawa, Canada's capital, was awarded a 2012 Governor General's Medal in Architecture as an example of the architecture of "peace and plurality."

HOW THE MUSEUM WAS CONCEIVED

Maki explains that the process for the design of the Aga Khan Museum was similar to that of the Delegation of the Ismaili Imamat. He was contacted about work on a new site in Toronto in 2004 before the completion of the Delegation building in Ottawa and was told the construction schedule would be rapid. As Maki says, "There was a meeting with the people from Geneva and Toronto and in particular Luis Monreal, the General Manager of the Aga Khan Trust for Culture. We also visited the site and were given the program, which was quite precise in terms of size and functions. On the way back to Tokyo, I laid out my first thoughts and sketches, which are not far from my final project. This was in August 2004. We made some basic models shortly thereafter in Tokyo. Having prepared a basic concept, we presented it to His Highness at Aiglemont. He approved the scheme subsequent to our meeting."

The architect emphasizes the fact that the completed building is very similar to his initial scheme. "The courtyard has changed in size since then," he says, "but the basic building is much as I originally imagined. I designed the facades to be receptive to natural light according to the time of day and the season. What is interesting about the placement is that north for this project is a diagonal, so every facade has some natural light depending on the time and the season. The same is true of the central court. We made presentations on several occasions during the design process. His Highness was interested in questions such as the textures, the colour of the stone, and also the way the light would fall. We were very fortunate that we encountered no major disapproval from His Highness."

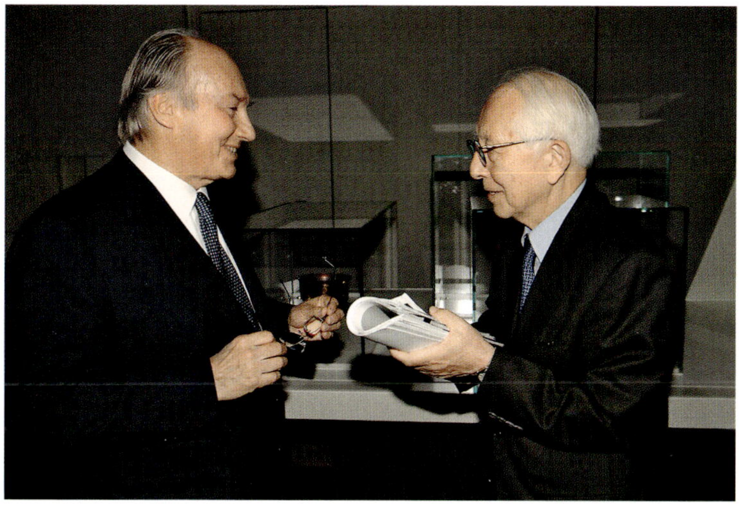

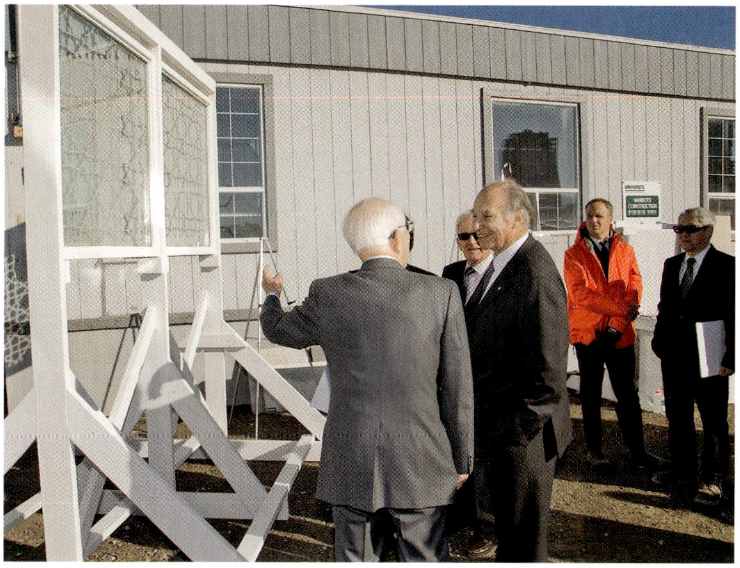

TOP: His Highness the Aga Khan (left) converses with Maki at the Aga Khan Museum exhibition at the Louvre in Paris in 2007.

BOTTOM: In 2009 Maki and His Highness the Aga Khan discuss the glass finish options for the courtyard of the Aga Khan Museum.

As Maki describes the building, "Contained within a simple rectilinear footprint, the primary functions of the Museum revolve around a central courtyard, which acts as the heart of the building and integrates the different uses into a cohesive whole while allowing each space to maintain its independence, privacy, and character."[6] Eighty-one metres (266 feet) long by fifty-four metres (177 feet) wide, the building, as Maki says, is "compact," a fact related as much to the site and its future development as it is to the need to create a cohesive whole.

"We were asked to create a museum of a certain size," explains Maki, "but we decided to make it fairly compact because the possibility of future expansion was part of the program we were given, though no precise size was determined. The placement of Charles Correa's Ismaili Centre and the need to create green barriers around the site to protect it from traffic noise made the precise orientation and location of the Museum fairly evident. Aside from the exhibition of art, His Highness wished to hold events such as concerts in the Museum, and there is also sizable space for educating children about Islamic art. A shop and restaurant that can be used even by those not entering the Museum are provided for. This is not just a museum. It is actually more a cultural centre. We felt that a compact form would allow for the required functions and good communication between them."[7]

EACH DESIGN IS UNIQUE

The completed Aga Khan Museum in Toronto presents relatively closed facades as seen from some exterior angles. "A museum," Maki says, "usually looks closed from the outside because you need wall space to hang and exhibit objects. Except for the entrance and public areas, most of the museum must be relatively closed. Of course, if you have extra passageways outside the exhibition space, you can do that, but that would increase the size. In the Aga Khan Museum the courtyard does bring in a good deal of natural light."

Asked if any specific work of his own or perhaps of other architects influenced his design in Toronto, the architect responds: "Each design is unique in terms of program, site, climate, and the client. I have designed many museums, but each one is very different. I have not been very much influenced by the museums designed by other architects, either. I appreciate many buildings like the Kimbell Museum in Fort Worth (Louis Kahn, 1972), but each architect is different." As for his reaction to the climate of Toronto, the architect states: "I have already designed other buildings in cold regions, so that aspect was not new for me. We had to be careful about frost and snow accumulation. For instance, in the interior courtyard we can't allow snow to pile up, so we have installed a heating system there. But Toronto is not like Maine or Quebec. It is relatively mild there compared to more extreme climates. Noise from the nearby highway is also a factor that required control. This is another reason that the building might appear to be relatively closed. Inside it is very quiet."[8]

The Aga Khan Museum is located on a 6.8-hectare (seventeen-acre) site on Wynford Drive in the northwest quadrant of the Don Valley Parkway and Eglinton Avenue in Toronto. Aside from

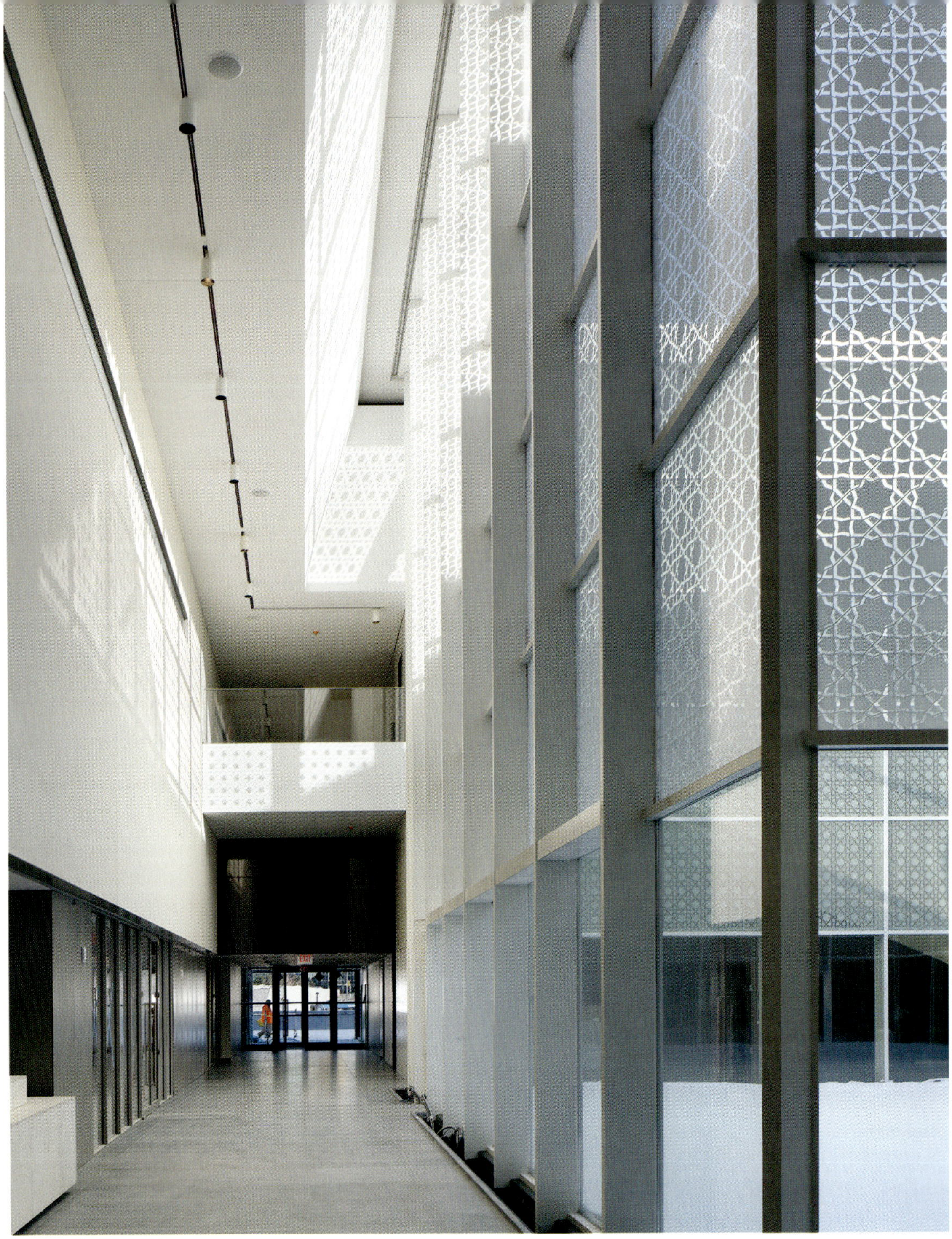

the Museum building by Maki, there is also the Ismaili Centre designed by the Indian architect Charles Correa and a park laid out by the Beirut-based landscape architect Vladimir Djurovic.

Maki explains: "Charles Correa won the competition for the Ismaili Centre in 1998. I was invited to participate as well, but I did not respond at that time. When we did come to be involved in the Museum, Charles Correa's design had already progressed considerably. It was thus a given element for our project. Vladimir Djurovic was invited to participate at the same time as I was. I would not say that my design reacts to that of Correa, but we tried to be very careful about issues such as height. In the Ismaili Centre there is a prayer hall that faces the direction of Mecca. We were asked to make the protrusion of the auditorium of the Museum lower than the dome of the Ismaili Centre, of course. The dome is also on the axis of the entrance to the Museum. I had more discussions with Djurovic than with Correa, since his design evolved at the same time as mine."[9]

The Aga Khan Museum's courtyard (on the right) serves, as Maki says, "as the heart of the building and integrates the different uses into a cohesive whole while allowing each space to maintain its independence, privacy, and character."

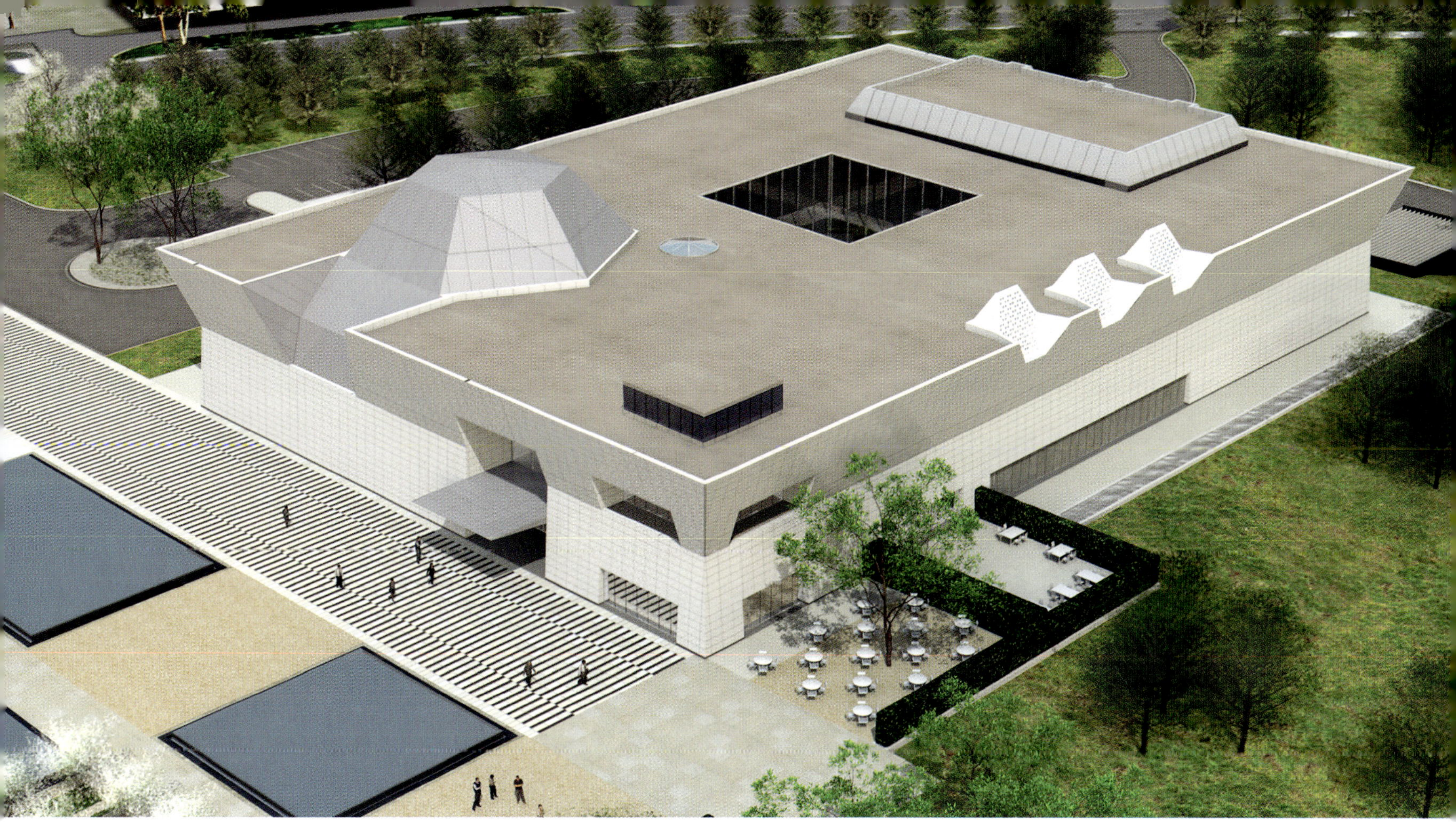

An artist's rendering of the Aga Khan Museum set within the Aga Khan Park.

LIGHT IN ALL ITS FORMS

The Aga Khan's letter sent to Maki at the outset of the Museum project, expressed with reference to the ephemeral but essential qualities of light, sets the tone for the architecture.[10] Quite obviously, Maki has taken these references to heart both in purely symbolic terms and in practical ones. The architect has been careful to create ideal conditions for the viewing of Islamic art, providing very low luminosity where delicate works might be shown, for example. Skylight screens with geometric patterns "inspired by the windows in mosques" and translucent walls are features of the exhibition spaces. The design is centred on a courtyard, intended as "a symbolic space, protected from the outside world," with an "inherent link to traditional Islamic architecture." The exterior of the Museum is "inspired by the forms and shapes of precious stones" and has walls inclined at two distinct angles to accentuate the play of light on the surfaces. White Brazilian granite was chosen as the main cladding material because of its good resistance to the climate. As for the relationship with Correa's Ismaili Centre, Maki states: "The metallic roof of the auditorium space further accentuates the shape and materiality of a precious stone and is intended to establish a formal dialogue with the crystal roof of Correa's Ismaili Centre. The primary entrance and axis of the Museum is aligned with the Ismaili Centre, which provides a subtle relationship between the two buildings, emphasizing the unity of the complex."[11]

Although he wishes for such references to remain discreet, Maki does reveal some of the sources of his thought where light is concerned. "The angular facade is able to refract natural light in quite an interesting way. The cladding of the building, in white granite, assumes different colours according to light conditions." More specifically, Maki says: "At sunset the Taj Mahal glows red or pink, while it appears to be white at noon." The architect goes on to refer to the interior of the Museum, stating: "There is some natural light, but we tried to design the openings very carefully, since much of the material exhibited is sensitive to light. I feel that

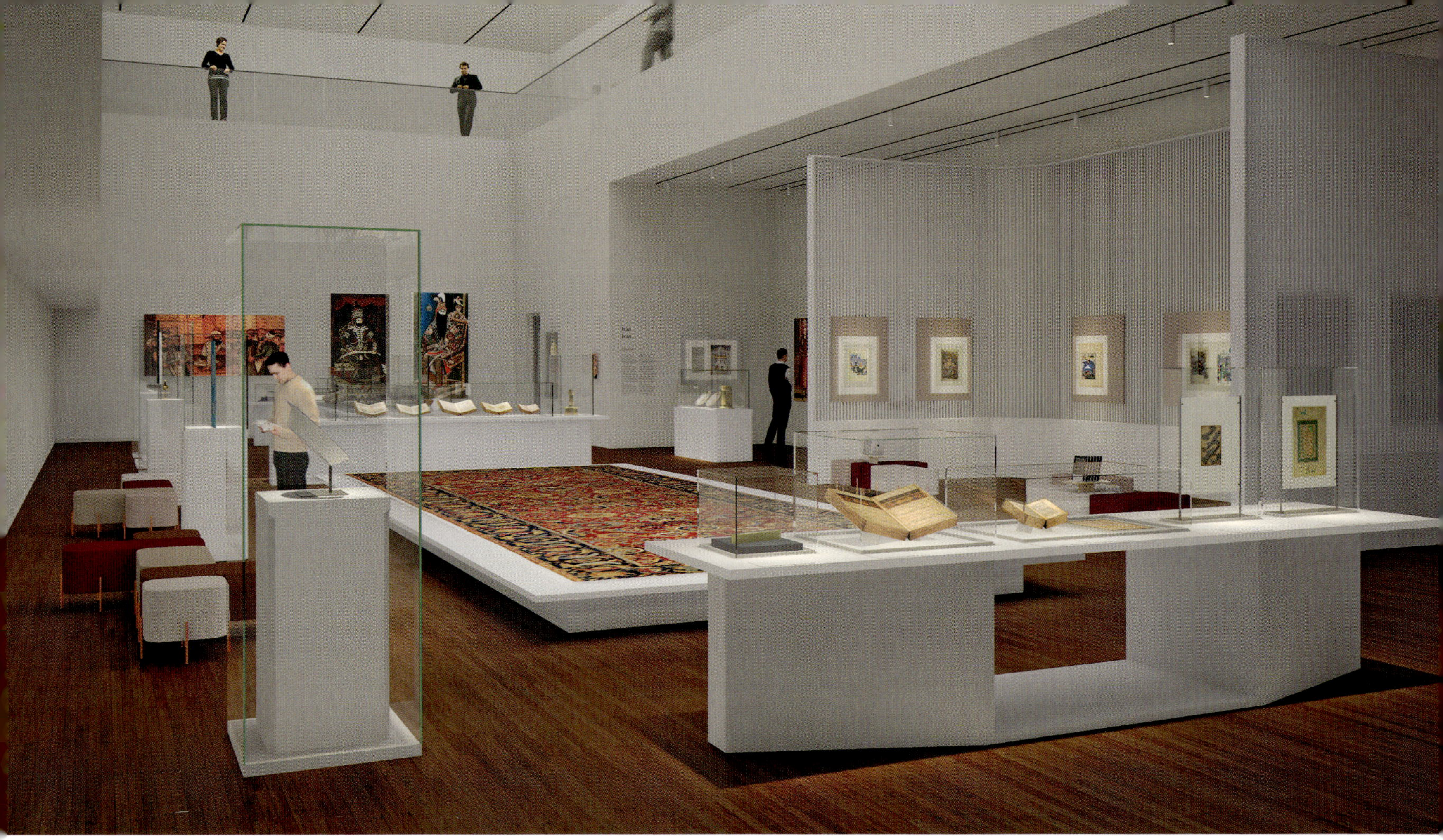

An artist's rendering by Studio Adrien Gardère shows the museography and exhibition design of the Aga Khan Museum collection.

references to Islamic architecture should be abstract in this instance, and the screens we have developed respond to this approach. The choice of cladding materials allows for a certain translucency from the inside, perhaps a bit like the effect created by the marble used in the Beinecke Rare Book Library at Yale designed by Gordon Bunshaft [Skidmore, Owings & Merrill, New Haven, Connecticut, 1963]."[12]

In explaining the interior forms of the Museum's auditorium, Maki makes reference to a specific dome: "The auditorium recalls the domes of Islam—perhaps the Bazaar in Kashan, Iran, for example." The angled skylights introduced into the Museum design by the architect are, of course, abstract, but his own documentation refers to the very subtle windows of the Sheykh Lotfollah Mosque (Isfahan, Iran, 1603–19). On the whole, the architect has sought to carry out the wishes of the client. "In Ottawa and also here," he says, "His Highness wanted a modern building, but once you are inside, there should be a feeling of Islamic architecture. Some of the patterns or screens employed intentionally evoke this spirit."[13]

THE PROCESSES OF CHANGE

The dedication of the Aga Khan to architecture, seen in such ongoing programs as the Aga Khan Award for Architecture in which Maki was an active participant, has to do more with improving the conditions of life of a vast part of humanity than it does with heralding a new architectural style. Pointedly, the Aga Khan refers to architecture as part of "the processes of change"—a terminology that may be at odds with most descriptions of contemporary buildings. When asked if, for him, building is not, in fact, a way of bringing people together, he responds: "Yes, or giving them a sense of individuality. Sometimes they need that also. I think spirituality is not necessarily experienced only in a societal context. It can be very much an individual thing. In the Islamic world we always

The angled skylights introduced into the Aga Khan Museum design by Maki are, of course, abstract, but they were inspired by the very subtle windows of the seventeenth-century Sheykh Lotfollah Mosque in Isfahan, Iran.

look at the fundamental unity of *din* and *dunya*, of spirit and life, and we cannot tolerate that one functions without the other."[14]

It is surely in the evocation of light in the Aga Khan Museum that the talent of Fumihiko Maki is felt, and the connection between the client and the architect is most readily apparent. It is no accident that in describing "light" in his original letter to Maki, the Aga Khan passes directly from an evocation of a sura of the Qur'an to a reference to the European Enlightenment. The light he refers to crosses through civilizations and religions—it is the source of life and art, the two forces being brought together in the walls of the Aga Khan Museum. The ultimate message of pluralism and tolerance conveyed by His Highness the Aga Khan might best be summed up in this instance by his own references to the two sources of light, "natural light emanating from God's creation," and "light ... which emanates from human sources, in the form of art, culture and well-inspired human knowledge."[15]

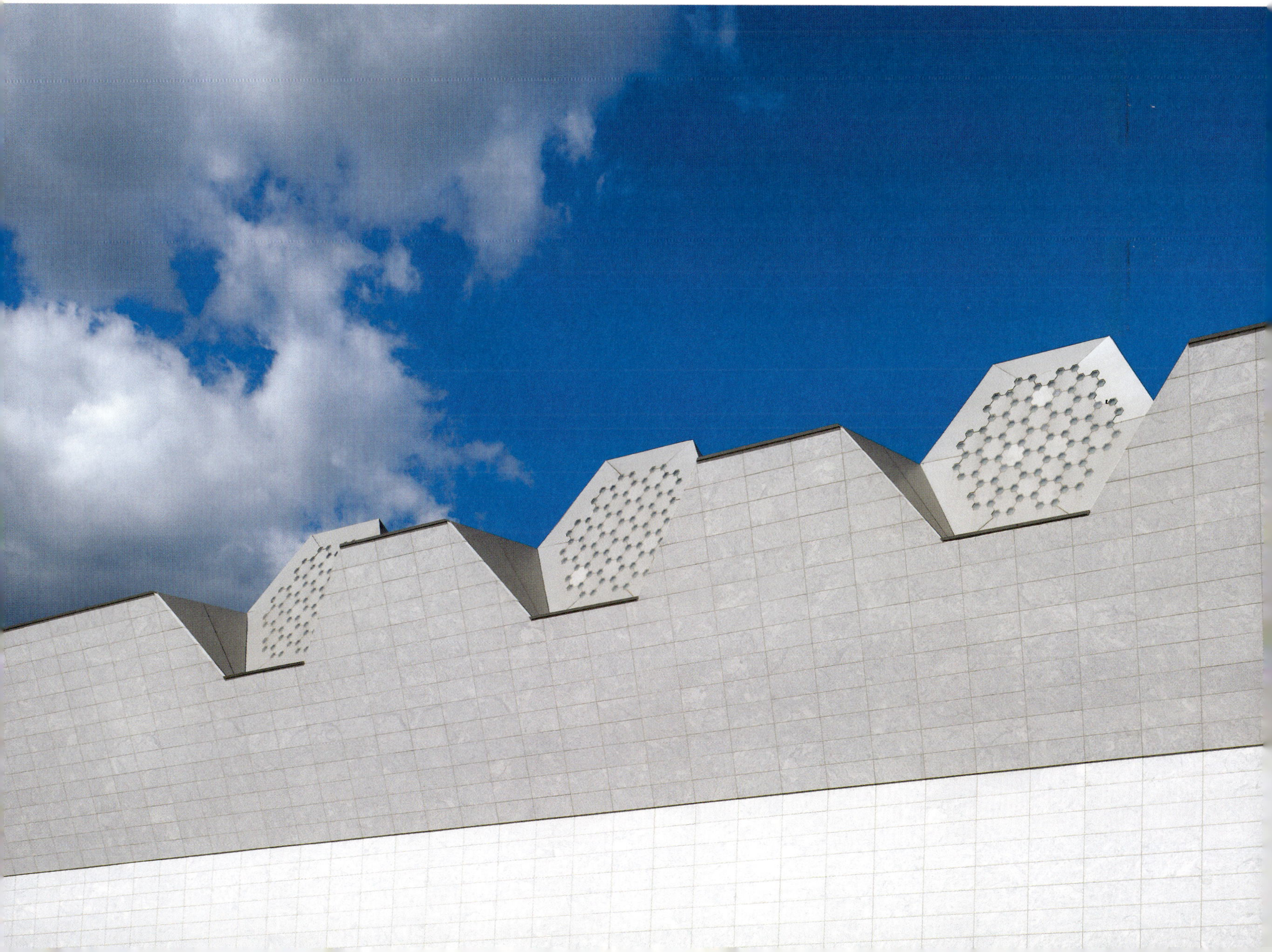

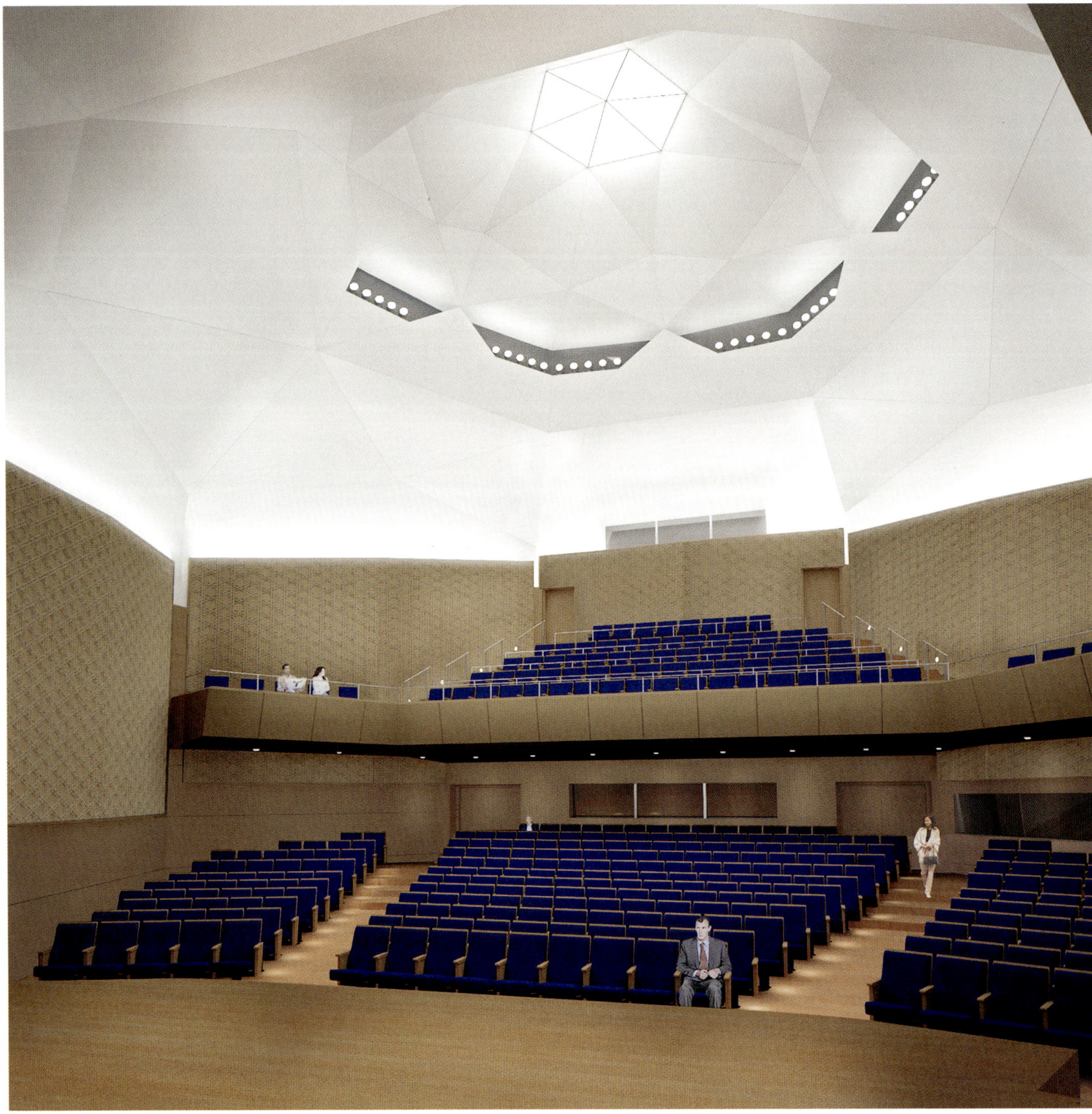

The Aga Khan Museum's auditorium, according to Maki, "recalls the domes of Islam — perhaps the Bazaar in Kashan, Iran, for example.... His Highness wanted a modern building, but once you are inside, there should be a feeling of Islamic architecture. Some of the patterns or screens employed intentionally evoke this spirit."

“The angular facade,” Maki says of the Museum, “is able to refract natural light in quite an interesting way. The cladding of the building, in white granite, assumes different colours according to light conditions.”

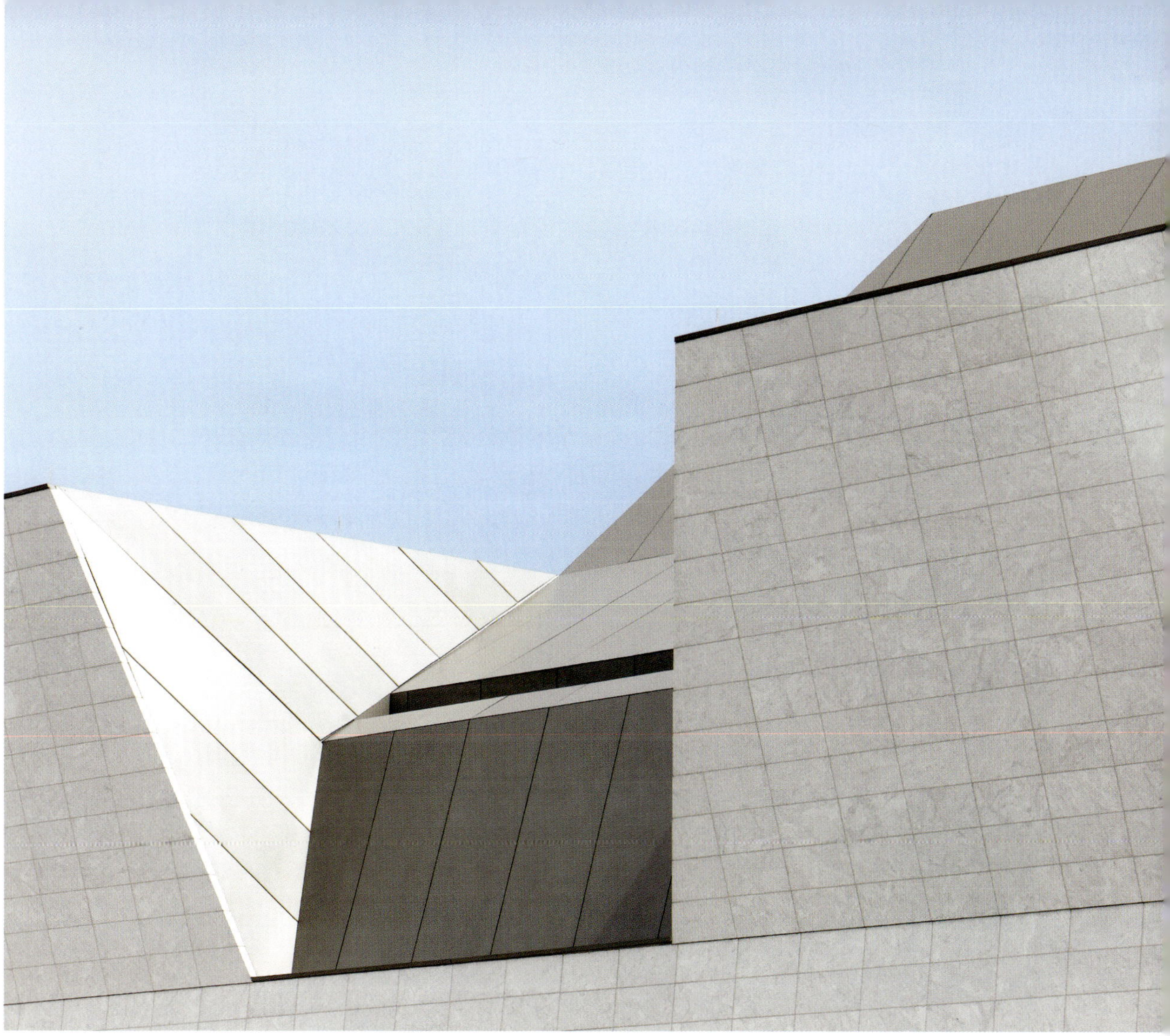

NOTES

1. Design Architects: Fumihiko Maki and Maki and Associates, Tokyo, Japan. Architect of Record: Moriyama & Teshima Architects, Toronto, Canada.
2. Qur’an 24:35: “Allah is the Light of the heavens and the earth. The Parable of His Light is as if there were a Niche and within it a Lamp: the Lamp enclosed in Glass: the glass as it were a brilliant star: Lit from a blessed Tree, an Olive, neither of the east nor of the west, whose oil is well-nigh luminous, though fire scarce touched it: Light upon Light! Allah doth guide whom He will to His Light: Allah doth set forth Parables for men: and Allah doth know all things.”
3. Letter from His Highness the Aga Khan to Fumihiko Maki, January 3, 2006.
4. Accessed at *www.pritzkerprize.com/1993/jury* on January 8, 2013.
5. Fumihiko Maki in conversation with Philip Jodidio, Zurich, October 16, 2012. The jury comment was: “This is a significant addition to Ottawa’s repertoire of diplomatic buildings and puts Canadian architecture firmly on the world stage. Impressively monumental in scale, the project combines a powerful civic presence with a remarkable level of sophistication. Its integration of traditional Islamic motifs such as specially crafted screens and a lush courtyard garden is choreographed with assurance and sensitivity, bringing the building wonderfully to life as a delicate and sensual piece of architecture, while the quality of materials and detailing is outstanding.” Accessed at *www.raic.org/honours_and_awards/awards_gg_medals/2012recipients/ismailiimamat_e.htm* on January 8, 2012.
6. Fumihiko Maki and Maki and Associates, <*Aga Khan Museum 007.02.17.pdf*>. Document provided by Fumihiko Maki to Philip Jodidio.
7. Fumihiko Maki in conversation with Philip Jodidio, Basel, Switzerland, May 13, 2008.
8. Fumihiko Maki in conversation with Philip Jodidio, Zurich, Switzerland, October 16, 2012.
9. *Ibid.*
10. Letter from His Highness the Aga Khan to Fumihiko Maki, January 3, 2006.
11. Fumihiko Maki in conversation with Philip Jodidio, Basel, Switzerland, May 13, 2008.
12. *Ibid.*
13. Fumihiko Maki in conversation with Philip Jodidio, Zurich, Switzerland, October 16, 2012.
14. His Highness the Aga Khan in conversation with Philip Jodidio, London, United Kingdom, March 6, 2007.
15. Letter from His Highness the Aga Khan to Fumihiko Maki, January 3, 2006.

The Aga Khan Park: An Urban Oasis

D. FAIRCHILD RUGGLES

What is an Islamic garden in the twenty-first century? This is the question His Highness the Aga Khan has posed for designers and restorers of gardens and parks projects in Canada and around the world. It is the question that landscape architect Vladimir Djurovic sets out to answer in his stunningly modern design for the Aga Khan Park in Toronto. The Park contains the Aga Khan Museum designed by Japanese architect Fumihiko Maki, as well as the Ismaili Centre and prayer hall designed by Indian architect Charles Correa.

These singular buildings gaze at each other across large formal gardens that capture elements of each building and extend them into the outdoors. In designing a major landscape site such as this, the architect had to consider practical issues such as traffic, pedestrian safety, parking, and water runoff—elements of design that escape notice when they work well, as they do here. But the striking beauty of the design is in its formal gardens at the heart of the Park. They are composed of a series of axial views directed across a tightly controlled series of horizontal ground planes, a visual experience that is enhanced by the sensory experience of scent and sound. In the design competition that led to the selection of Djurovic for this commission, the questions that the landscape architects had to consider were: What kind of Islamic garden is appropriate for Toronto today? And how can a garden designed for today echo the past while looking forward to the future?

The Aga Khan Park in Toronto takes its place in a constellation of twenty-first-century park projects commissioned by the Aga Khan Trust for Culture (AKTC). These include the cultural-ecological park set within a forested reserve on the outskirts of Mali's capital, Bamako, one of the fastest-growing African cities; the restored gardens at the Tomb of the Moghul emperor Homayun

Artist's rendering of the Ismaili Centre (left), the gardens of the Aga Khan Park (centre), and the Aga Khan Museum (right).

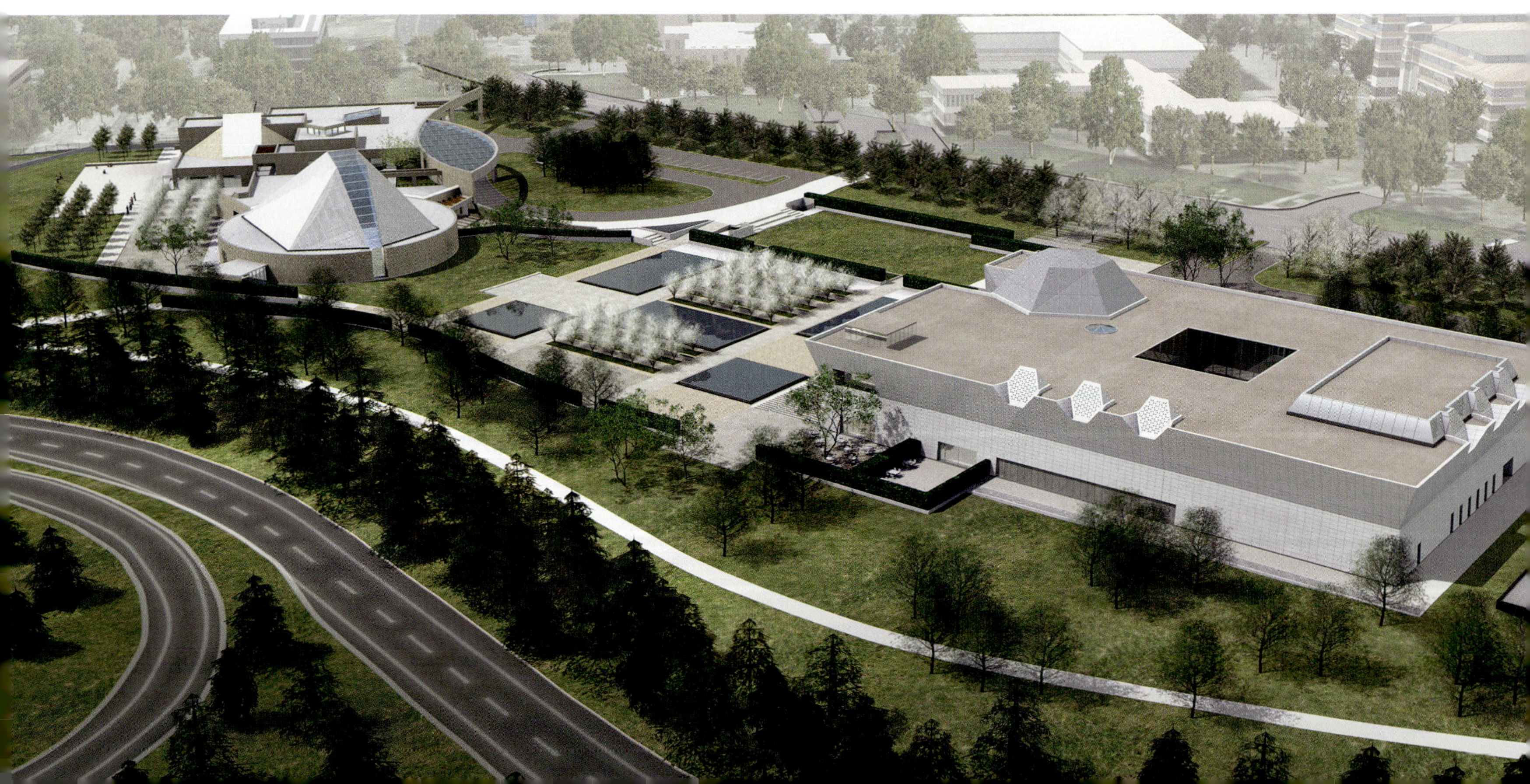

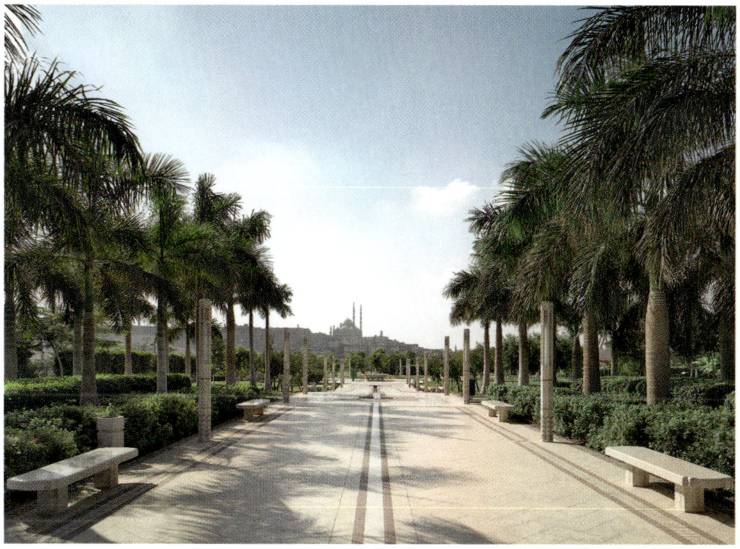

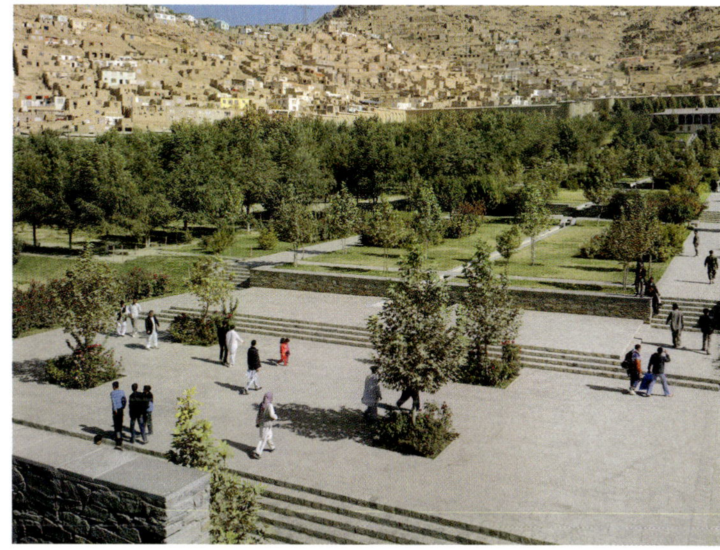

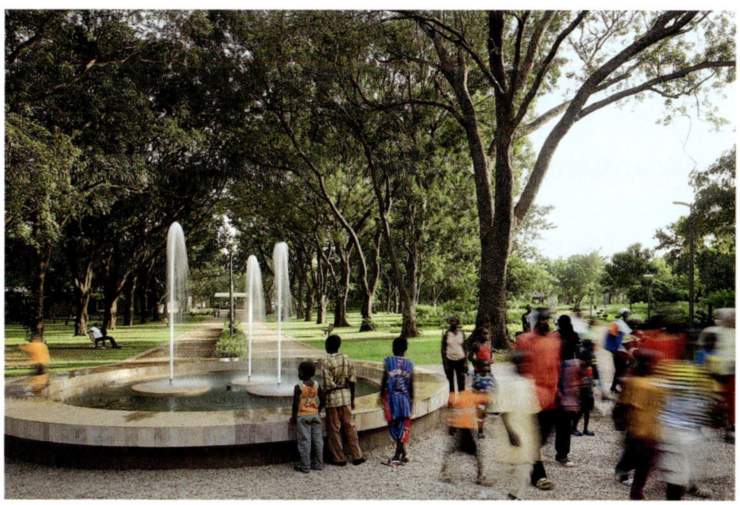

(built in 1571); al-Azhar Park in Cairo, Egypt, built on a former rubbish dump and comprising archaeological excavation, historic preservation, and a revitalization plan for the nearby low-income Darb al-Ahmar neighbourhood, setting a new standard for how such projects could stimulate jobs and improve the living conditions of residents; and in Kabul, Afghanistan, the restoration of the Moghul emperor Babur's sixteenth-century gardens, which combined attention to historic fabric with concern for the well-being of people living there today.

In Toronto the Aga Khan Park likewise has an ambitious goal of providing a place for beauty, culture, and education. The linchpin of the Park is the formal gardens that mediate between the Museum and the Ismaili Centre. Although the gardens stand as an independent design, Djurovic thought carefully about the character of each building and met with the architects personally. The result is coordination between the three-dimensional architectural volumes and the landscape. The formal gardens are laid out with large-scale pools and terraces to match the majestic proportions of the buildings. There are moments when the consonance is striking as, for example, from inside the Museum's entrance hall where a viewer who pauses to look back through the glass wall sees the distinctive pyramidal roof of the Ismaili Centre. The hall flows as a continuous volume out into the gardens where it pauses midway at a rectangular pool in which, from one side, the Centre's pyramidal roof again appears, this time as a reflection, while from the other side, it is the Museum that is caught on the water's surface.

TOP LEFT: Built on a plateau rising above the old city, al-Azhar Park provides splendid views of Cairo, Egypt.

TOP RIGHT: The Bagh-e Babur project in Kabul, Afghanistan, features a restoration of the tomb of the Moghul emperor Babur as well as re-creations of the water channels, terraces, and fruit orchards of the sixteenth-century garden.

BOTTOM: A fountain attracts children on a path leading from the entrance to the National Park of Mali in Bamako, the country's capital.

The effect seems magical, yet it is entirely intentional. For the large pools, Djurovic chose dark granite to better capture reflected images so that, in his words, "everything is there but not there" by virtue of the reflection. He describes the pools as "five pure mirrors to capture the sky, trees, Museum, and the pyramidal roof of the Ismaili Centre's prayer hall."[1]

The formal gardens are laid out as a series of flat planes. The horizontal surfaces of the shimmering pools are divided by broad walkways that pass through stands of serviceberry trees (*Amelanchier laevis*) that themselves have a regular shape and even height. The visual effect is not of casual clumps of vegetation but geometrical blocks of orchard that at maturity will reach a consistent height of nine metres (thirty feet). Despite its consistent appearance, this horizontality is not a natural characteristic of the site; it is achieved by tight control of the natural landscape and paying attention to its contours. Djurovic's previous work reveals his love for the horizontal plane, notably his award-winning, small-scale works in Beirut where pools, and even stepped pools of water, are used to assert horizontality.

There are hidden secrets in the formal gardens. To discover them, one must visit the Park throughout the year to catch the changing displays of colour, texture, fragrance, and even sound. The colours can be dramatic, and they change from season to season. A stand of dogwood trees (*Cornus kousa*) near the Ismaili Centre provides a show of white petals in the spring, brilliant red berries in the summer, and foliage that turns red in the fall. Drifts of flowering bulbs are planted in the understory of the various tree groves to inaugurate the spring season. Plantings of magnolia (*Magnolia* x *soulangiana* and *Magnolia stellata*), burning bush (*Euonumus alatus*), hydrangea (*Hydrangea quercifolia* and *Annabelle Hydrangea*), butterfly bush (*Buddleia davidii*), and weigela (*Weigela florida*) contribute to the constantly changing cycle of colour. Bordering the lawn on the western side, a large bed of roses (*Rosa* spp) has dense foliage and in the late spring and summer bursts into bloom with five-petalled pink and white flowers. In the fall the maple trees that surround the site blaze with colour.

The trees, shrubs, and plants were chosen for their fragrance and multi-sensory appeal. The rose blooms have a lovely scent in the summer, followed by bright orange-red rosehips later in the season, adding fresh colour to the gardens as well as attracting birds, who like the plump, tart seed pods. The rosehips cling through fall and winter, a visible memory of the cycle of flowers-to-fruit. The roses are one of many gestures to Muslim tradition, for historically the scent of the rose was associated with the Prophet Muhammad, whose sanctity caused him to smell sweet.[2]

Similarly, the serviceberry trees in the centre of the formal gardens have a spreading, multi-trunked body with white blooms in the early spring, followed by tasty berries that emerge as pink but darken to deep purple by summer's end. In the fall the leaves turn red, transforming the formal gardens into a tumult of colour. Thyme is planted underneath, an herb that offers both the colour of its tiny white, pink, and lavender flowers as well as the pungent scent of its leaves.

The edible rosehips and fruit of the serviceberry attract birds, whose trills and chirps, in time, will fill the Park. As a constant rhythmic accompaniment to the birds' songs, water splashes from the pools into deep channels that run below and around their edges. The pools were designed to enhance the sound of the water, with the pools' lips bevelled so that the water does not simply slide over the edges but falls noisily into the channels.

When the Museum opened, many of the trees — especially those in the formal gardens at the Park's centre — were already fairly large. The story behind them reveals Djurovic's attention to detail. The design for the Park was accepted by the Aga Khan in 2008 and called for a great many trees. Djurovic had the idea of buying many of them in advance, and North American nurseries had trees on sale in 2008 due to the recession. The strategy had two benefits: first, the trees were purchased at affordable prices when nurseries needed customers; and second, the trees had time to grow and mature on-site during the construction phase. Consequently, when the Park was ultimately built in 2013–14, it had the unusual luxury of featuring large specimens. The fortuitous result is that the Park appears not as an emerging idea but as an already formed garden.

In this modern space of smooth planar surfaces, clean geometry, and sensory delight, what is it that recalls the traditional character of an Islamic garden? And how can a landscape designed today reflect past values in a sensitive manner yet be freed from constraints that such a backward glance might impose? Vladimir Djurovic thought carefully about these questions when he began designing the Park almost ten years before it was completed and open to the public.[3] He could draw on past experience, growing up in Lebanon (the son of a Lebanese mother and a Serbian father) and designing for patrons in the Middle East and North Africa in some of his earlier commissions. In addition to award-winning private residential gardens in Dubai and Lebanon, he won

TOP: In this artist's rendering, the Aga Khan Museum's front facade can be seen as well as part of the formal gardens in the Aga Khan Park.

BOTTOM: The serviceberry trees in the Aga Khan Park, as seen in this artist's rendering, will have white blossoms in the early spring, while the larger honey locust trees to the right of the Aga Khan Museum stand in a circular island of stone mosaic.

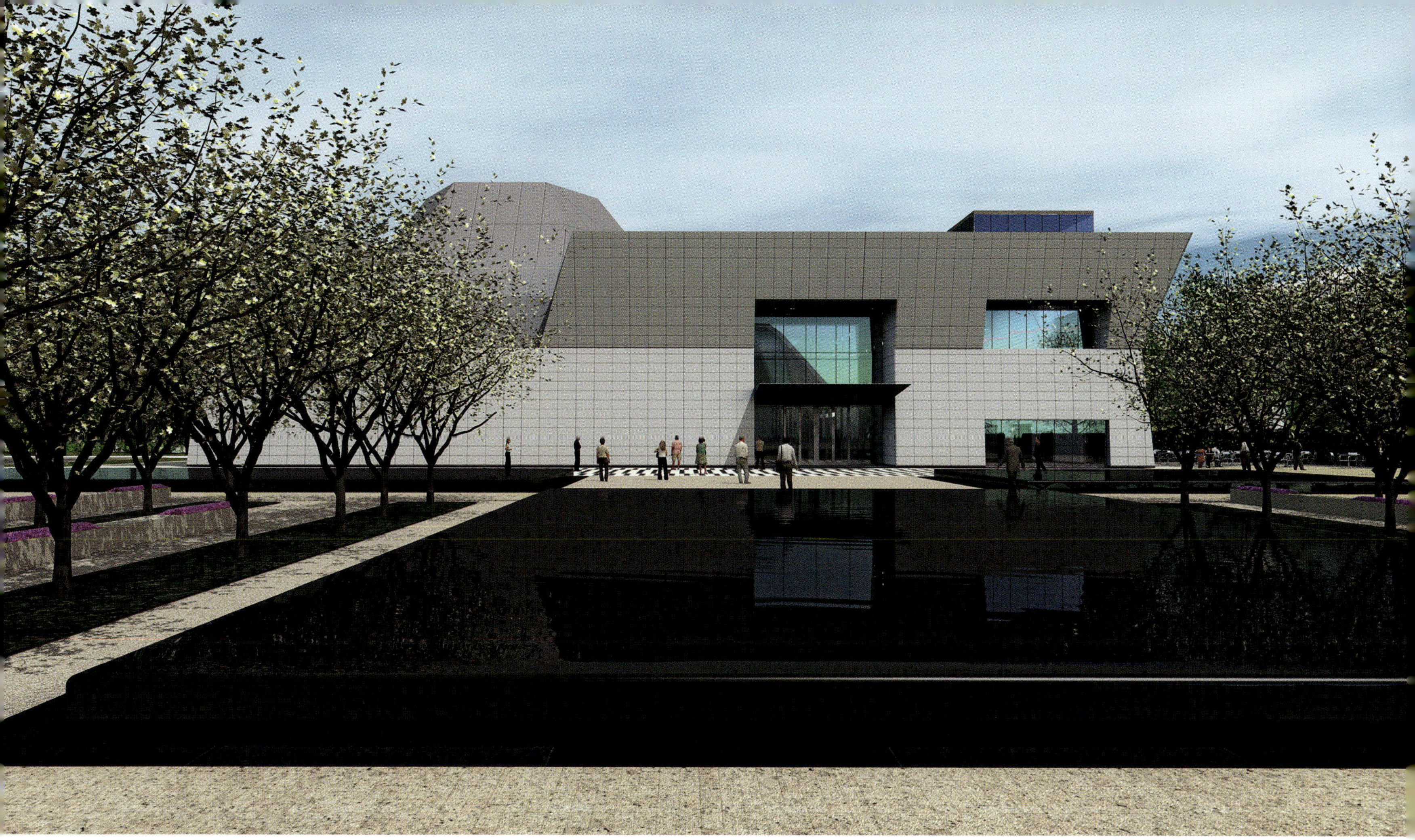

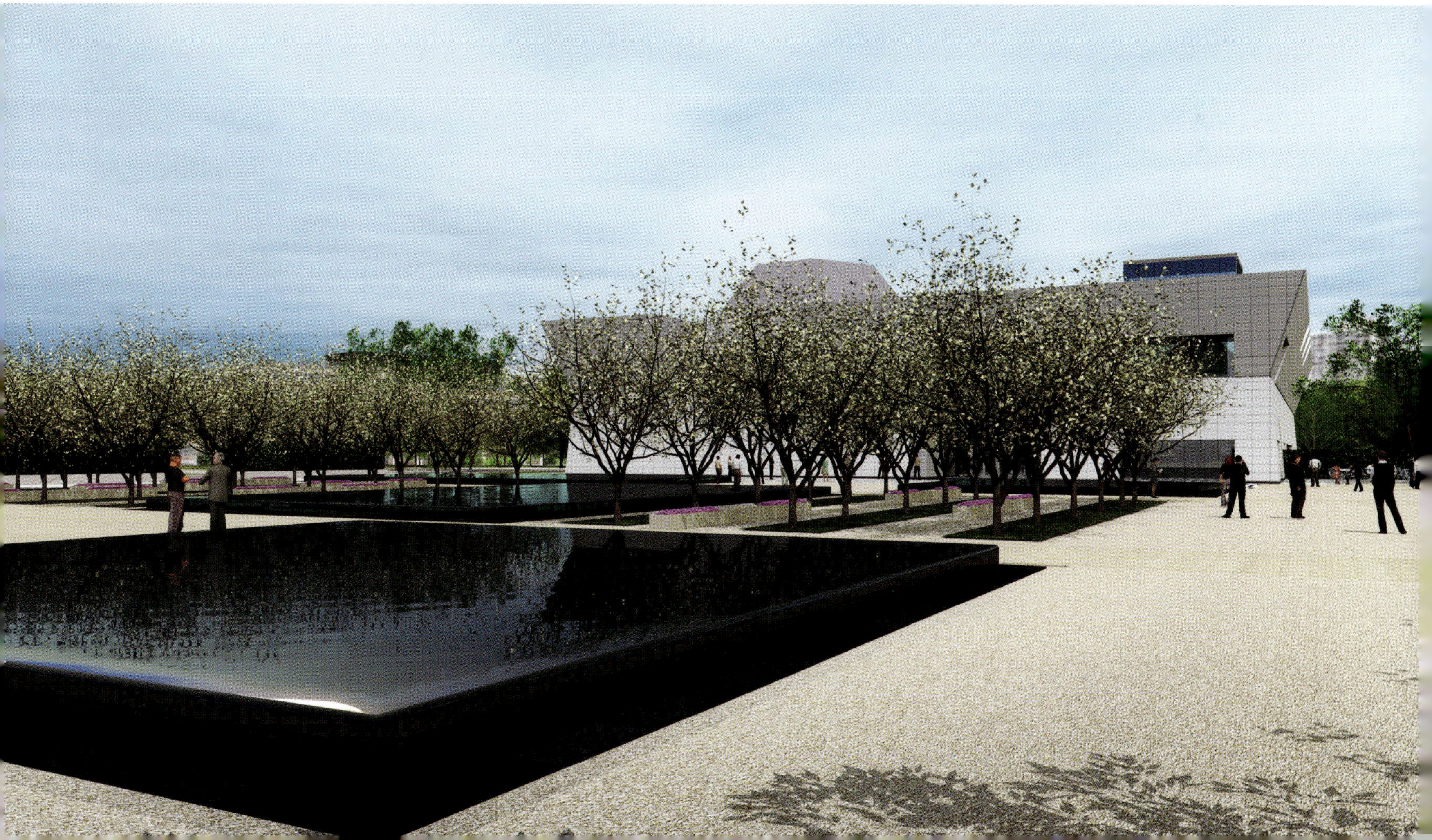

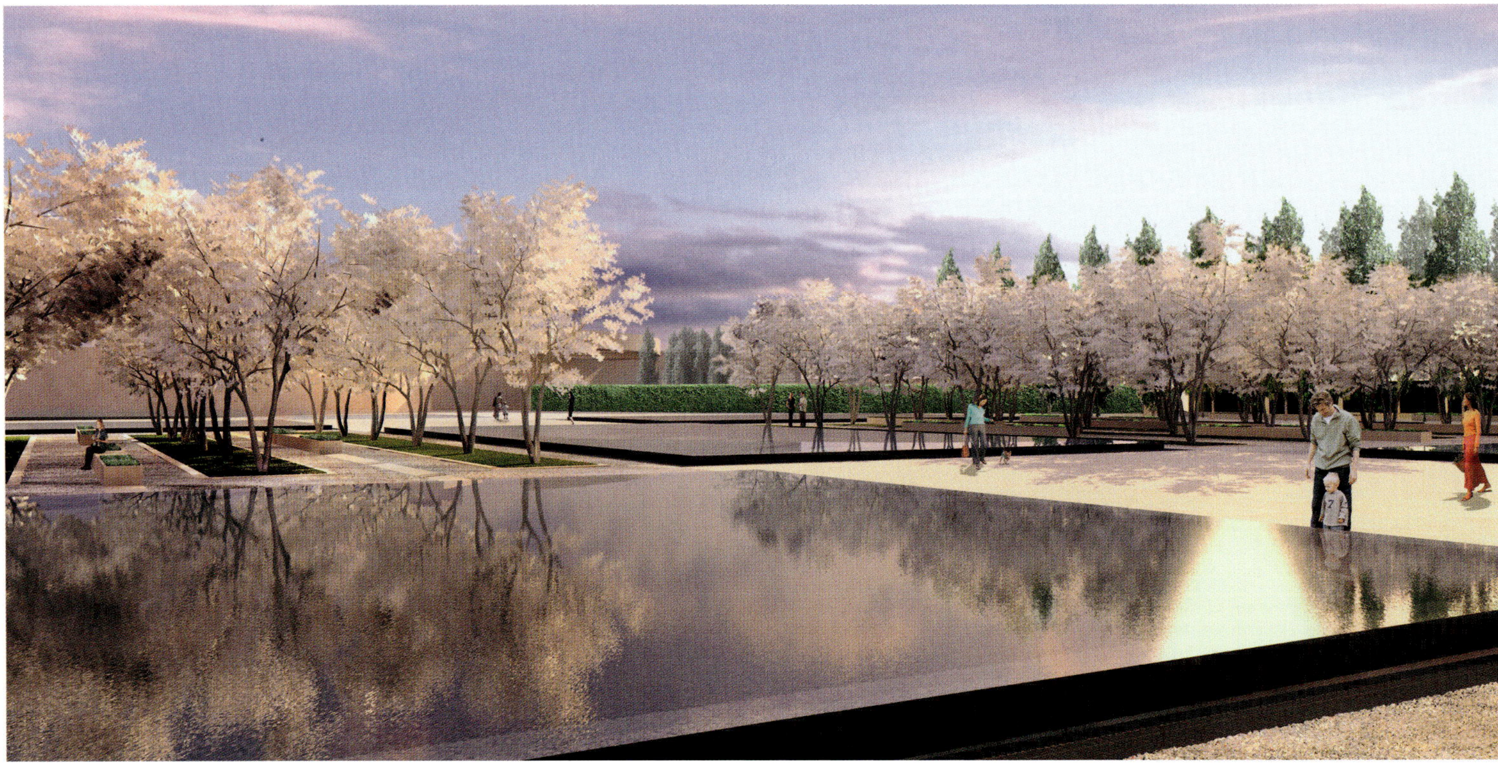

the Aga Khan Award for Architecture in 2007 and an Honor Award from the American Society of Landscape Architects in 2010 for his design of Samir Kassir Square (completed in 2004) in Beirut.

When the Aga Khan encouraged Djurovic to tour major Islamic gardens to deepen and expand his knowledge of history and of his own cultural roots, he visited and was profoundly influenced by two gardens in particular: the Tomb of Homayun in Delhi and the Alhambra's courtyard gardens in Granada, Spain. Each offered him a different kind of inspiration.

Built in the fourteenth century, the Alhambra's Court of the Myrtles is a peaceful courtyard with a large, deep pool of water flanked by rows of myrtle shrubs. The composition is simple, yet its impact is extraordinary: the water's silvery surface reflects the surrounding architecture of delicate stucco and columnar arcades, while at either end of the rectangular pool, round basins contain water jets that leap upward before falling gently into the pool. Djurovic marvelled at the dematerialization of surrounding form and ornament in the Court of the Myrtles where "everything dissolves." He captures the minimalism of water and vegetation and the same wonderment in dematerialized form in his composition of reflecting pools in the Aga Khan Park's formal gardens.

Homayun's Tomb offered a different experience. The sixteenth-century Moghul garden site consists of a huge domed tomb that stands at the centre of an enormous enclosure divided axially into a classic *chahar bagh* (four-part garden). Although largely flat, the ground, in fact, has just enough change in level to allow small water cascades to splash into recessed basins, introducing pleasant sound into the immense space and

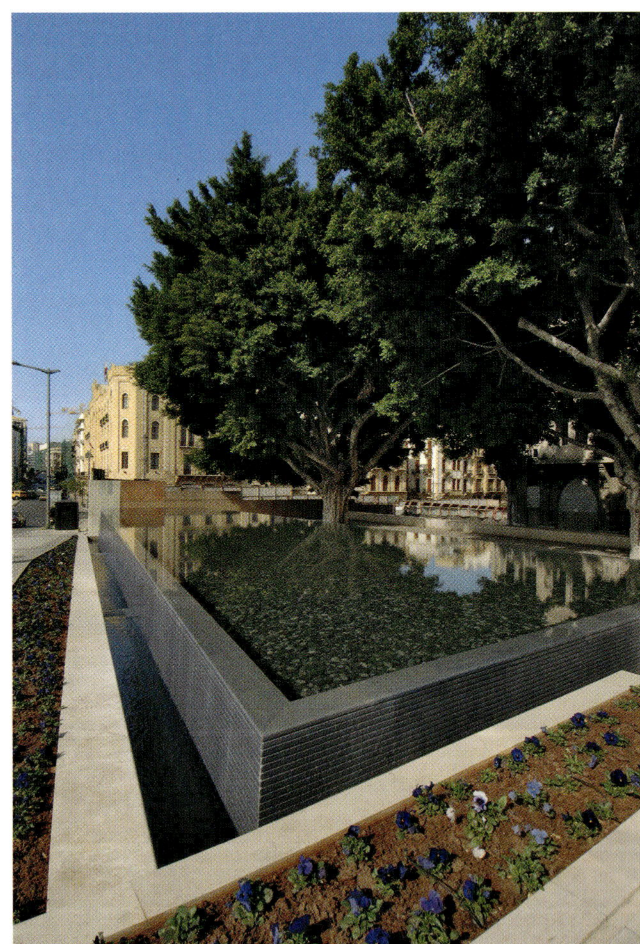

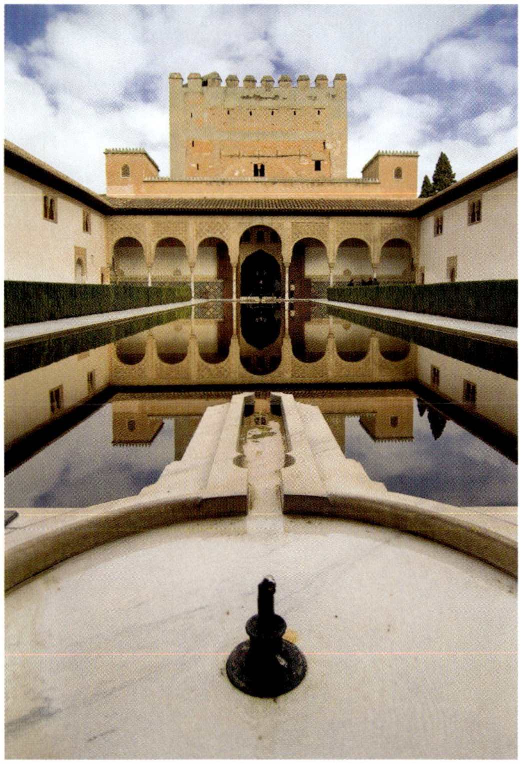

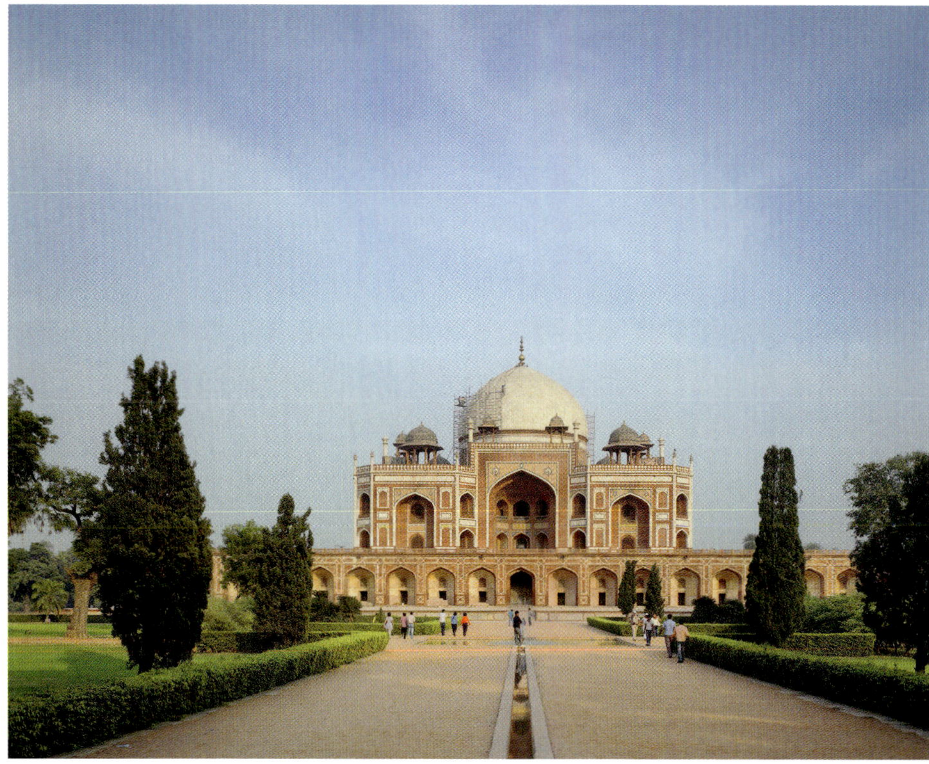

OPPOSITE TOP: An artist's rendering of the reflecting pools in the Aga Khan Park.

OPPOSITE BOTTOM: Vladimir Djurovic's Samir Kassir Square in Beirut, Lebanon, offers a tranquil respite in a city that has known more than its share of strife.

TOP LEFT: In Granada, Spain, the Alhambra's fourteenth-century Court of the Myrtles provides a peaceful environment for contemplation and reflection.

TOP RIGHT: The Moghul emperor Homayun's sixteenth-century tomb in Delhi, India, stands at the centre of an enormous enclosure divided axially into a classic *chahar bagh* (four-part garden).

keeping the water moving and fresh. This grand imperial garden has become a popular park where Delhi residents and visitors seek calm refuge from the busy city. Thus, in its present form, Homayun's Tomb emblematizes one of the challenges that faced Djurovic: how to translate a cultural tradition that was designed for an elite set of patrons into modern terms for modern audiences.

Ever since the earliest palace gardens were wrought from the arid conditions of the deserts of the Middle East in the seventh century, the Islamic garden was a place of lush vegetation, repose, and leisure, as well as an expression in intimate detail of all the processes by which humankind makes the earth hospitable and productive. As gardens evolved, their shade was equated with the promise of paradise, a place of rest and pleasure. The fruit-bearing trees and plants likewise were understood to provide a foretaste of the heaven to come. The water on display and the vegetation were signs of a divine blessing from "He who sends down water from the skies, and brings out of it everything that grows" (Qur'an 6:99). However, it was a blessing conferred on a people who had worked to make the earth habitable and fruitful, the primary signs of which were the well-tended and irrigated agricultural landscape and the refined garden that was a metaphor for that larger landscape.[4]

Basic processes of the working landscape gained special meaning: the well from which water was laboriously lifted by buckets in the desert was represented in the garden as a gushing fountain; the irrigation canal became the ornamental water channel; the organization of the landscape into plots, each cultivated by a different farmer, was abstracted into the four-part garden plan. A landscape of human labour was thus transformed into an ideal place, one that was enjoyed on earth by only a very few, while imagined and desired by the rest. In Islamic history the garden thus became one of its primary art forms, having the combined ability to represent the critically important relationship between humankind and nature, as well as developing as a form that provided a sensory foretaste of the gardens of paradise that awaited the faithful.

Historically, most earthly gardens were places that could be enjoyed by only the most elite members of society who alone had the means to commission them and the leisure to enjoy them.

This is in striking contrast to the twenty-first century, when the garden is more likely to be a public park, a college or hospital campus, a hotel courtyard, or a children's playground open to all. Those gardens, like the Park of the Aga Khan Museum, invite visitors to stroll about, to savour fragrances, to rest and contemplate, to gaze and reflect, or to find a private corner in which to sit quietly and enjoy the sights and sounds of the flowers, water, and birds. Djurovic wanted to create a space that "unifies without alienating or segregating, and a serene environment where contemplation finds spirituality." It is a place for solitude but also conviviality and conversation. In this sense of welcoming everyone, the modern urban park — and in particular Toronto's Aga Khan Park — may be the quintessential built form of the new millennium.

Just as the Islamic gardens of the past had recognizable forms, purposes, and meanings, the modern world is endowing the contemporary Islamic landscape with new forms, purposes, and meanings. Whether built in Cairo, Kabul, or Toronto, these sites present challenges to the designer: how to evoke the style and history of the Islamic gardens and parks without being inextricably bound by their forms and values, and how to create a park in cosmopolitan Toronto that reflects a tradition of royal and imperial Islamic gardens yet serves a new global clientele seeking art, education, and engagement with nature and each other. In the twenty-first century, space matters — especially the public spaces where modern, civil society gathers — and these are important questions.

NOTES

1. Quotations throughout are from an interview conducted by D. Fairchild Ruggles and Ruba Kana'an with Vladimir Djurovic, May 16, 2013.
2. Maria Subtelny, "Visionary Rose: Metaphorical Application of Horticultural Practice in Persian Culture," in *Botanical Progress, Horticultural Innovation and Cultural Change*, ed. Michel Conan (Washington, DC: Dumbarton Oaks, 2007), 13–34 (see n. 25).
3. Philip Jodidio, "A Garden in Toronto: The Design of Vladimir Djurovic," in Philip Jodidio, *The Aga Khan Museum, Toronto* (Munich: Prestel, 2008), 82–101.
4. D. Fairchild Ruggles, *Islamic Gardens and Landscapes* (Philadelphia: University of Pennsylvania Press, 2008), 89–101.

THE COLLECTOR AND THE COLLECTION

Prince Sadruddin Aga Khan: A Collector in an Age of Connoisseurship

ASSADULLAH SOUREN MELIKIAN-CHIRVANI

Do collectors whom life propels far beyond the cultural sphere of their ancestors have a head start when possessed with the urge to acquire the art that these created? Consider the story of Prince Sadruddin Aga Khan who was born in Paris in 1933 into one of the most illustrious princely houses of Iran.

The dazzling hoard of manuscript paintings from Iran and the Persian-speaking courts of Asia that Prince Sadruddin built up over a lifetime, almost until his death in 2003, includes some of the great masterpieces from the world that stretches from Istanbul, the former Ottoman capital, to Golconda deep in the south of the Indian subcontinent. Better still, it brings several revelations, as if some inherited sixth sense had given the prince an insight that made up for his upbringing in the environment of the Parisian elite.

The prince's father, Mohamed Shah Aga Khan III, was the leader of the Ismaili community, a branch of Shia Islam that bears the imprint of the age-old Iranian brand of esoteric mysticism. A descendant of Fath 'Ali Shah who founded the Qajar dynasty of Iran, Mohamed Shah Aga Khan III married Andrée Joséphine Carron, Sadruddin's French mother. Educated in French-speaking *lycées* (high schools) and a graduate of Harvard University, the prince was not just bilingual in French and English. He was bicultural.

Prince Sadruddin Aga Khan and Her Royal Highness Princess Alexandra of Britain discuss a miniature (folio 89v) attributed to Sadeqi Beg from a sixteenth-century *Anvar-e Soheyli* (Lights of Canopus) manuscript (AKM289) at the *Princes, Poets & Paladins* exhibition at the British Museum in January 1998.

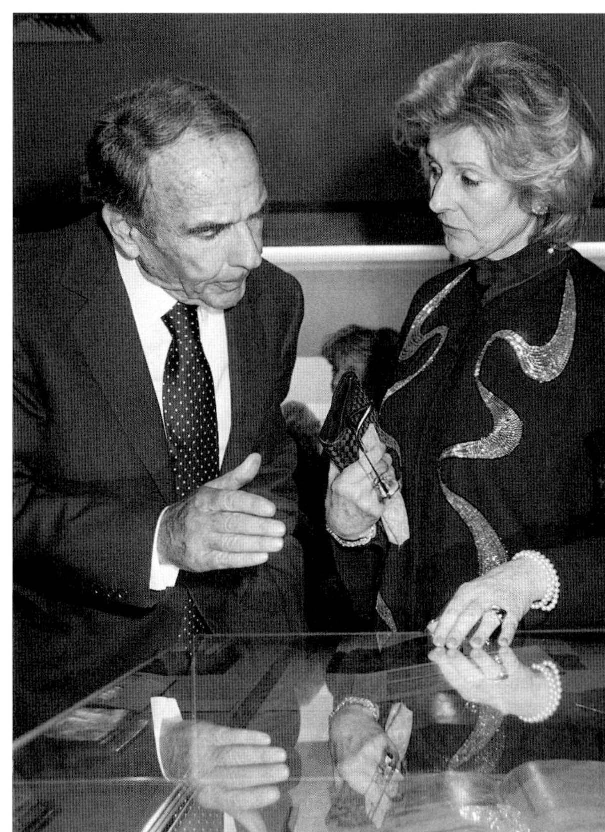

To Western friends, Sadruddin Aga Khan seemed French or English as circumstances required. His sense of irony owed much to the former and his light humour to the latter. Easterners, however, perceived an unmistakable Iranian imprint on his makeup. The prince, who did not learn Persian, had no access to one of the most subtle literatures in the world. But when amused, he had that slight glint, instantly controlled, that lights up the eyes of Iranian literati confronted with drollery. The collector fully mastered the art of dropping hints so indirectly allusive that you might briefly doubt that any real intention prompted them. It made you wonder whether this was the ultimate avatar of the Sufi art of *eshârat* ("allusion," literally, "pointing to"). His urbanity, which owed as much to kindliness as to good breeding, was another trait of the Iranian *nojabâ* ("the great and the good") at their best. A lifetime spent honing an innate diplomatic talent in international organizations, safeguarding cultural relics or protecting refugees in distress, left its imprint on Sadruddin's temperament. A lesser man would have been worn out. Instead, this appears to have deepened the profound sense of relativity that defines the Iranian psyche. Under his Western clothes, the Ismaili prince was remarkably Eastern.

Very discreet in private life about his international commitments as about everything else, Sadruddin Aga Khan could have been cast in the mould of the Shia tradition of mental reserve (*taqiyeh*) and secrecy (*ketmân*) elevated to the level of a fine art by his ancestors. That served him in good stead in his collecting endeavours.

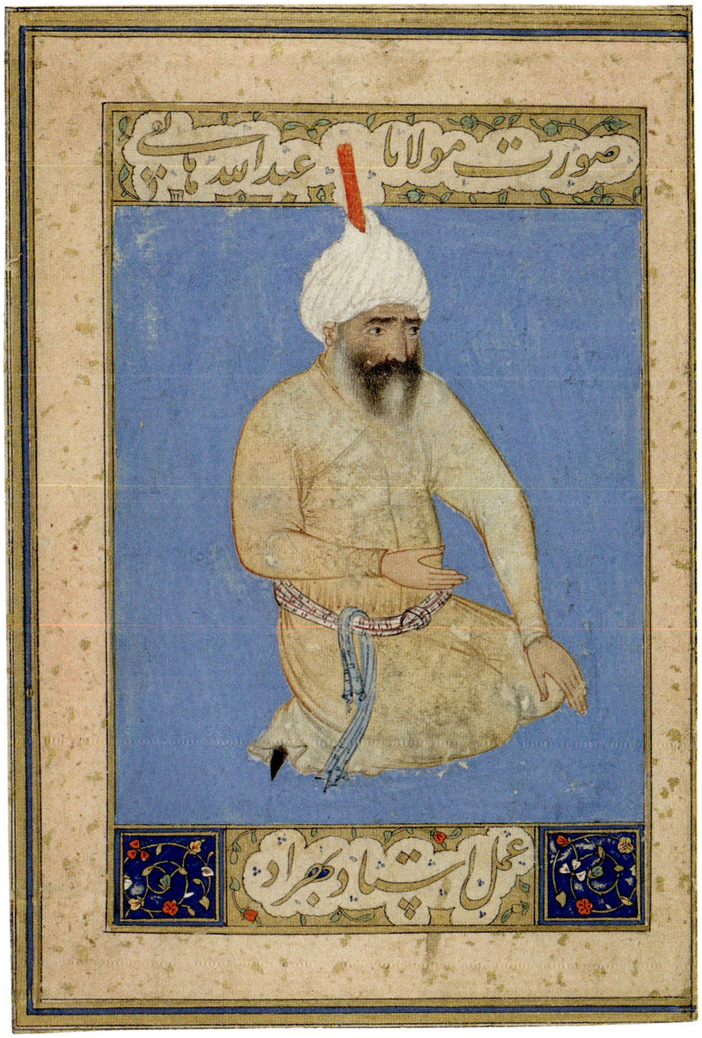

Portrait of Hatefi the Poet, folio from a 1544–45 album assembled for Bahram Mirza, attributed to Behzad, Herat, Afghanistan (Historic Iran), ca. 1511, opaque watercolour, ink, and gold on paper, 11.8 × 7.8 cm (4⅝ × 3⅛ in.), AKM160.

When the art lover began acquiring his first manuscript paintings, buyers did not reveal their hand to others any more than you do at poker. If they wanted an object, they took pains to conceal their intentions, lest less knowledgeable competitors might be inspired to act by their example to go after it or, worse, for fear that dealers should "run up" the price at auction. It was not only bad form to brag about your collection. It was seen as a silly inducement to others to make you pay through the nose, which it still is. Prince Sadruddin was the silent collector par excellence. He left no diary. Typically, when a catalogue of his manuscript paintings and objects was established, he had it printed privately in a set of four volumes to be given away as presents.

One can only speculate about what prompted the young man to make his first acquisitions. Was he eager to explore his ancestors' culture in order to understand the foundations of his own personality? And was he stirred by the example of his nephew, Prince Amyn Aga Khan, whose sharp eye for beauty led him to secure some remarkable painted pages and early ceramics from Iran?

At Harvard Sadruddin Aga Khan rubbed shoulders with two young men who would also be possessed with the irrepressible urge to buy works of art, the Bostonian Stuart Cary Welch and George Ortiz, a scion of the Patiño family from Bolivia who grew up in Paris. Stuart Cary Welch went mostly after the arts of the book with an investor's approach — when the market for Iranian manuscript paintings almost reached its apex, he consigned most of these for sale in order to turn to Moghul India, which was comparatively neglected. George Ortiz, by contrast, bought with a raging passion.

If art lovers ever undergo the influence of their collector brethren, this is through a muted osmosis rather than words. Like others in his generation, Prince Sadruddin started buying with a light heart at a time when speculation played a limited role in the market and prices in his areas of predilection were a fraction of what they are today.

Iranian painted pages torn away from manuscripts and sold piecemeal for greater profit were marketed under the label "Persian miniatures," a misleading expression implying that they are independent works of art standing on their own. They could be bought for a song. I still rue the day in 1962 when I was outbid at the Paris Hôtel Drouot by Welch on a mid-fifteenth-century leaf from Nezami's Quintet (*Khamseh*) accompanying the Iranian poet's passage about "Bahram Gur Slaying the Dragon." The impecunious student that I was conceded defeat as the hammer price reached 300 francs, then about US$60.

When perchance isolated paintings turned up at Drouot jumble sales without a catalogue, a common occurrence, gems could be had for a pittance. In 1962 the portrait of a turbanned man of letters cut out from the same "patchwork" (*moraqqa'*) album as Sadruddin Aga Khan's likeness of the poet Hatefi by the famous fifteenth-century painter Behzad was sold at Drouot for the then equivalent of US$40. It was one of the revelations at the exhibition *Le chant du monde: L'art de l'Iran safavide 1501–1736* that I curated at the Musée du Louvre in 2007 and is a rare discovery among the handful of paintings that can be seriously ascribed to Behzad (the master from Herat is what Leonardo da Vinci is to Florence).

This happy state of affairs, which likewise prevailed at the New York auction house Parke-Bernet, encouraged Prince Sadruddin to collect at a date when his resources still found their limit.

Market conditions were radically modified around the late 1960s when newly wealthy Iranian buyers began entering the market. They bought enthusiastically, if not always with a clear understanding of the art, or of the opaque ways in which the art market worked.

The entry of the Iranian court into the art game intensified competition. Queen Farah Diba dispatched emissaries to buy paintings and *objets d'art* and built up from scratch the collections of the enchanting Muze-ye Reza 'Abbasi in Tehran. Prices shot up. Western dealers responded by putting up selling shows. When Colnaghi of London dispersed in 1976 some of the Iranian and Hindustani paintings kept by the Paris Rothschilds, the Iranians were there. They bought pages from "a large royal manuscript of the Shah-Nama" (equals *Shah-Nameh*), which has consistently been described without verifiable evidence as a commission ordered for or by Shah Isma'il II who mounted the throne in 1576. So did Sadruddin, now able to pay substantial prices. Still intact when shown in 1903 at the Musée des Arts décoratifs by the Paris dealer Georges Demotte, the manuscript was cut up in the following years. The text was lost, as were the opening page that would have named the patron and the end page with the colophon that would have stated the date of execution.

If Prince Sadruddin, who treated manuscripts with utmost respect, agonized in anxious hesitation before buying, he kept his thoughts to himself. It was too late to repair the havoc. All that could be done was to rescue some of the flotsam and jetsam out of the twenty-one painted pages from the destroyed book that were on sale at Colnaghi.

At that point the commercial environment had changed.

A new wave of American buyers had begun to join the fun in the late 1960s. They loved Moghul art of the late sixteenth- and seventeenth-century Hindustan, as the Persian-speaking Moghuls called the Indian subcontinent. The Western European impact on the Iranian foundations of Moghul manuscript painting that culminated under Jahangir (reigned 1605–27) made it feel more familiar. Welch unloaded a big stash of his Iranian holdings at auction when the market was on a high and switched to Moghul painting on a big scale. In Los Angeles the lawyer Ralph Benkaim became a driving force on the Moghul art scene.

In the late 1970s, another factor hugely increased the firepower of commerce in "Islamic Art." Arab buyers from the Gulf jumped in. The pioneering collectors came from Kuwait. Jasem al-Homaizi formed a vast collection, which, after its restitution to the Kuwaiti collector by the state of Iraq following the first Gulf War, was sold to Qatar. The package deal was reportedly worth US$17 million. Sheykh Nasser al-Sabah of the Kuwait ruling family trumped them all. Paying top dollar, he formed one of the most important collections, mostly of Iranian art, currently in private hands. From then on Arab buying shot up ever higher.

Sadruddin judiciously steered his boat in these choppy waters. His ultimate masterpieces, which were acquired when his collection had already reached museum proportions, must have left a man who spent his life trying to safeguard artistic monuments with a taste of ashes in his mouth.

In 1976 Christie's, the London auction house, triumphantly announced that seven pages from a *Shah-Nameh* manuscript commissioned for the ascension of Shah Tahmasp I in 1524 would be up for sale. This signalled the beginning of the dismantling of one of the world's great masterpieces. Probably the most remarkable assemblage of manuscript painting ever produced in Iran with its 248 painted pages, Shah Tahmasp's *Shah-Nameh* remained intact while in the possession of the Paris Rothschilds through much of the twentieth century. In 1959 the New York art gallery Rosenberg & Stiebel acting on their behalf sold the volume for US$259,000 to Arthur A. Houghton, Jr., a collector known until then for his love of rare English books. Soon after, the

Esfandiyar Kills the Simorgh, folio from a *Shah-Nameh* (Book of Kings) produced for Shah Isma'il II, attributed to Siyavosh, Qazvin, Iran, ca. 1576, opaque watercolour, ink, gold, and silver on paper, 40.4 × 29.8 cm (15⅞ × 11¾ in.), AKM103.

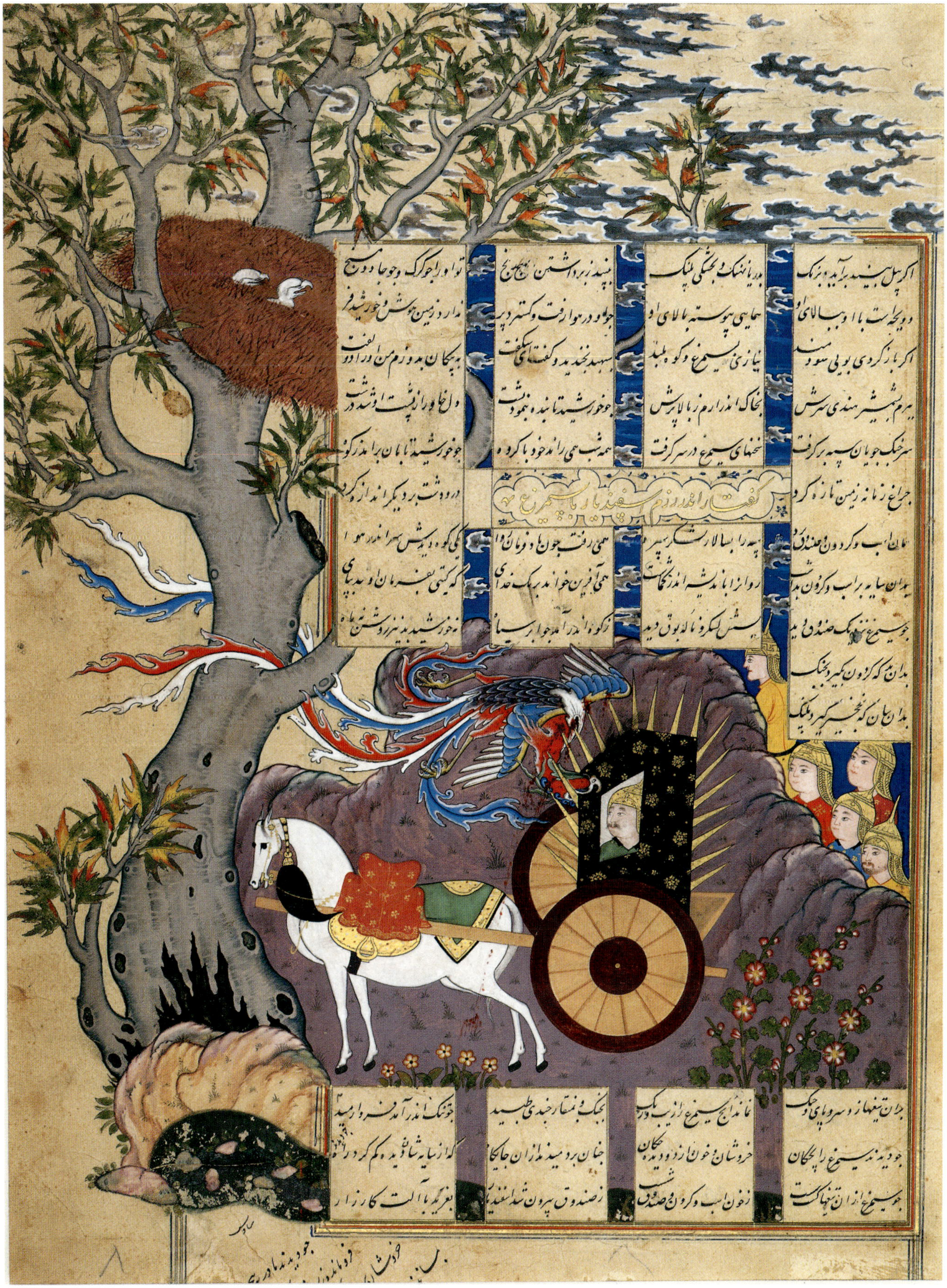

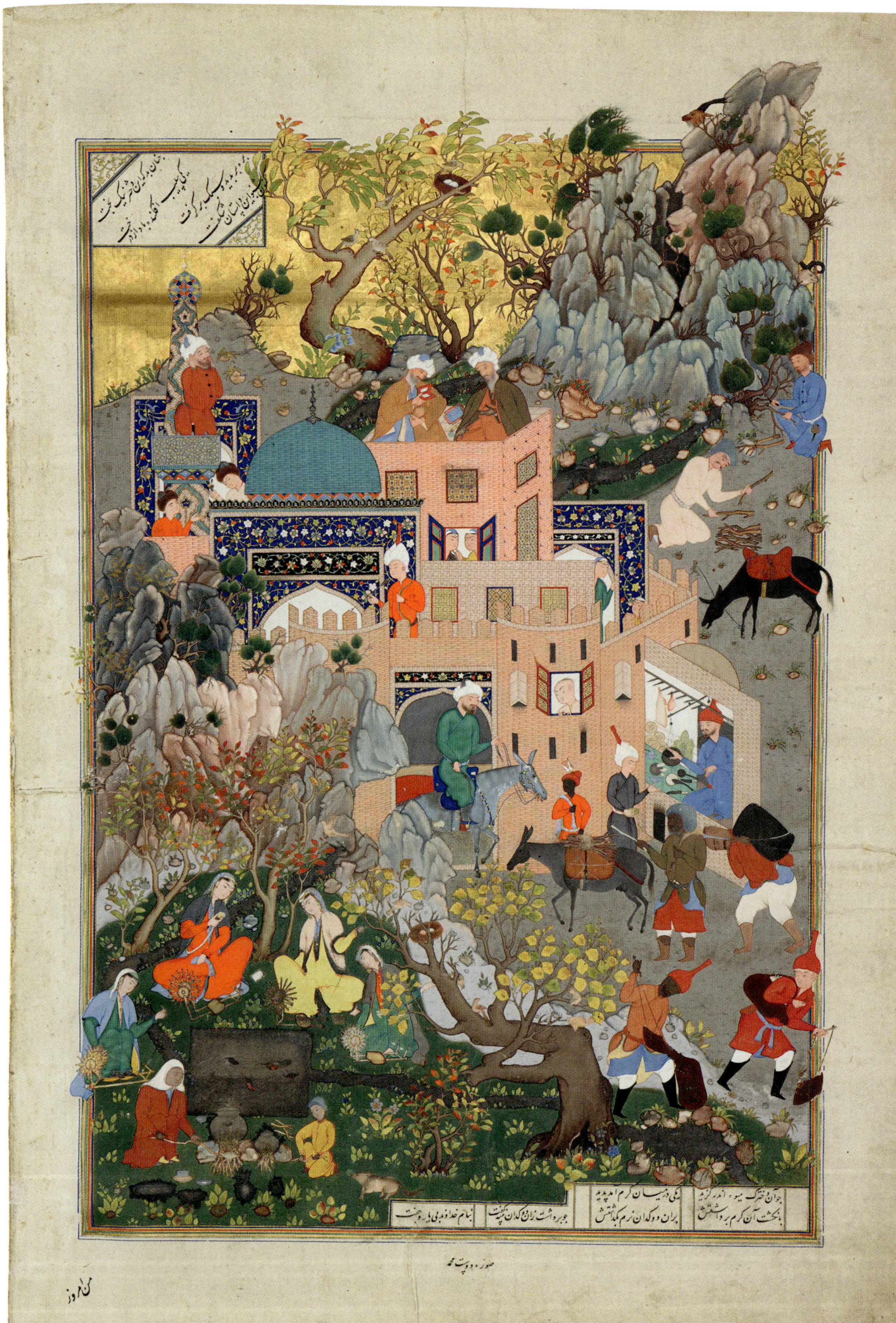

American bibliophile began taking out pages and displaying them at the Grolier Club in New York. He would have been unaware that the composition of each page is ordained in relationship to the layout as well as to the textual content of the facing page, as was his friend Stuart Cary Welch who probably inspired him to buy the book. Welch, who did not read Persian, actually prided himself on the fact that this left his artistic judgment unclouded. At the time of his death the collector is said to have owned six folios.

At the Christie's sale of November 17, 1976, Sadruddin bought two pages from Shah Tahmasp's book. Some years elapsed before the greatest of all (AKM165, see pages 52, 114–15, and 120–21) entered the collection. It relates to the court of the mythical Emperor Keyomars enthroned amid his courtiers. Unlike all the other paintings but one in the *Shah-Nameh* of Shah Tahmasp, the scene can irrefutably be proved to be the work of a known master, the great Soltan Mohammad of Tabriz. Dust Mohammad, who was himself a famous painter and calligrapher, refers to the page in the clearest terms in the Persian preface that he wrote for a *moraqqa'*, specifying that the painter is Soltan Mohammad.

Years later the only page that has an authentic signature in turn entered the collection. It carries the name of Dust Mohammad, who calligraphed his tiny signature in Arabic, as was customary. It cuts across the lower frame of the image and unambiguously reads: *sawwarahu Dust Mohammad* ("Dust Mohammad executed the figural scene").

So it was that the two most precious pages of the greatest manuscript from Safavid Iran came under the safekeeping of the Aga Khan Museum. Seventy-eight others donated by Houghton in 1970 are now in the Metropolitan Museum of Art in New York. The remaining half of the manuscript was acquired from the Houghton estate by the Islamic Republic of Iran in 1993 in exchange for *Woman III* by Willem de Kooning. It saved the volume from further destruction and kept together much of the text. This was a first step toward the establishment of the Safavid "edition" of a poem that originally ran to some fifty thousand couplets but exceeded sixty thousand couplets by the sixteenth century through various interpolations.

Future generations of world curators may want to strive to put back together this monument of humankind's artistic heritage.

Episode from the Story of Haftvad and the Worm, folio 521v from a *Shah-Nameh* (Book of Kings) produced for Shah Tahmasp I, signed by Dust Mohammad, Tabriz, Iran, ca. 1540, opaque watercolour, ink, gold, and silver on paper, 45 × 30 cm (17¾ × 11¾ in.), AKM164.

Discovering Art in the World of Islam

ASSADULLAH SOUREN MELIKIAN-CHIRVANI

Future generations might find it surprising to hear that the first museum highlighting the extreme diversity of the Islamic nations only opened its doors in the twenty-first century. We have tried in the Aga Khan Museum to display works according to the highly distinctive cultures they represent in chronological order as much as was feasible.

In their concepts, as in their visual arts, Islamic nations are farther apart than Western nations with a past rooted in Christianity are from one another.

The two blocks that have been at the heart of the Islamic civilizations since the faith began spreading in the seventh century, the Arab Near East and the Iranian world, differ a great deal more from each other than France does from Germany, or Italy from Britain. Their past goes back at least three millennia earlier, and, if only because of its imprint on their collective consciousness, their evolution widely diverged. Art, the clearest mirror of a culture because the eye takes it in before the intellect interjects its commentary, spectacularly reflects these differences that tend to be swept under the carpet by Western commentators.

When Islam progressed eastward toward the Indian subcontinent, it arrived from Iran, promoted by its dynasties mostly of Turkic stock, from the Ghaznavids in the eleventh century, to the Timurids in the early fifteenth century, to the Moghuls after their victory at Panipat in 1526. Utterly identifying with Iranian culture, the Turkic rulers introduced Persian as the language of literature and polished usage. While the literature read by the Muslim elite of Hindustan, as the Persian-speaking Moghuls called the Indian subcontinent, remained Persian, the art was thoroughly recast according to Indian aesthetics. Whether in the Sultanates of the twelfth to the fifteenth centuries, or under Moghul rule from 1526 to 1858, the art of Hindustan, even when Persianate, is further removed from the art of Iran than German Medieval or Renaissance art is from its Italian sources.

In Anatolia, the land now called Turkey, the story of artistic evolution is equally complex. It was home to different nations with different languages — Armenian and Kurdish in the East; Greek among the Hellenized populations of the centre and the Greeks of Ionia along the west Mediterranean shores of Anatolia; Arabic in the Syrian areas of the southeast. The Turkic

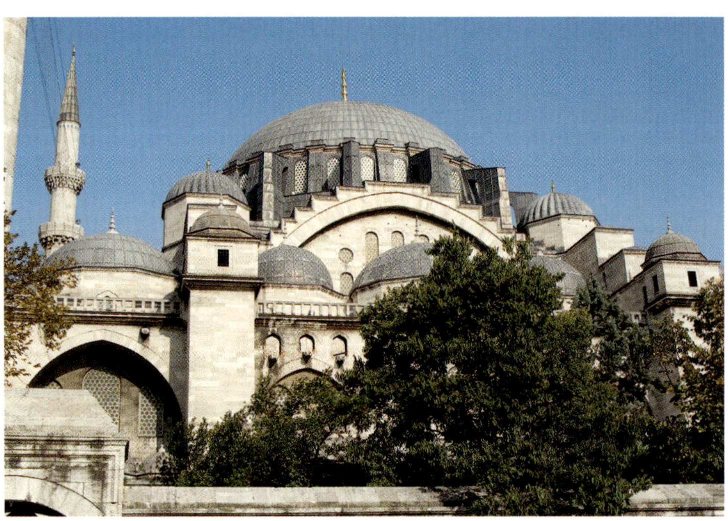

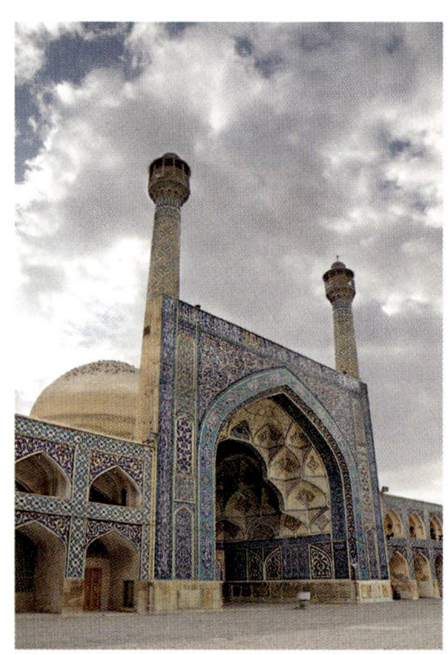

LEFT: The Süleymaniye Mosque in Istanbul, Turkey, was built between 1550 and 1558, blends Islamic and Byzantine architectural elements, and is the largest mosque in the city.

RIGHT: The Masjid-e Jami' in Isfahan is one of the oldest mosques still standing in Iran. Shown here is the southwest iwan, one of four added in stages by the Seljuqs. The four-iwan style eventually became common in Iran and the rest of the Islamic world. The two minarets were added later by the Safavids.

Seljuqs who invaded Anatolia from Iran wrested it from Byzantine domination in the eleventh century. As in India, the Turkic sultans imposed Persian as the official language. A much-quoted saying assures that dogs started barking in Persian on entering the city of Konya, as ancient Iconium now became known. The vast territory called the Sultanate of Rum became independent in the thirteenth century. Linguistic turkicization took centuries. Incessant shifts in population and cultural orientation led to an exceptionally complex succession of art forms, often unrelated to each other. Except for brief periods, the architecture and objects of Islamic Turkey bear no remote resemblance to those of Iran. Even at the height of close cultural contacts with Safavid Iran, Ottoman bronze and ceramic wares of the sixteenth century share no common ground with Safavid objects of the same period (see AKM687 and also page 85).

Add to all this, artistic developments in parts of the world where Islam prevailed for a while before vanishing in the wake of ethnic cleansing operations. Art thrived for seven hundred years in so-called "Arab Spain" between the eighth and fifteenth centuries and more briefly in Arab Sicily. It also did among the Islamic communities of China. A mosque was erected in a Beijing neighbourhood in the thirteenth century, and blue-and-white porcelain inscribed with Persian verses was made as early as the fourteenth century.[1] The art of porcelain for Chinese Muslims culminated under Emperor Zhengde (1505–21), reported by a Turkish traveller to have converted to Islam (see AKM722 and also page 86).

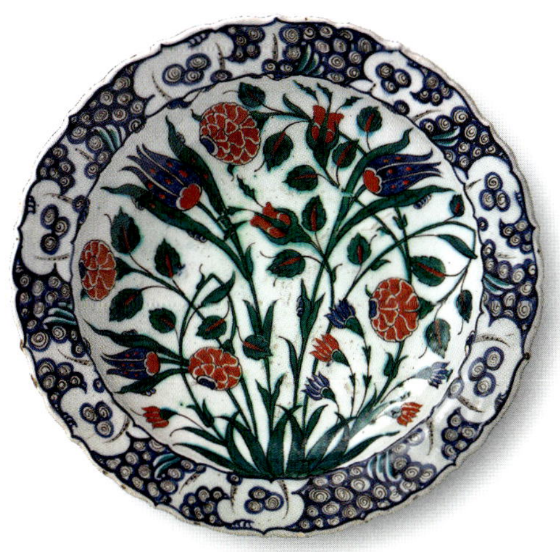

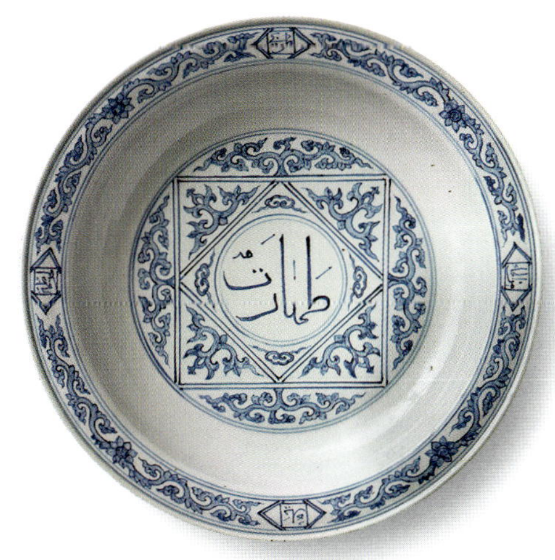

LEFT: Dish, Iznik, Turkey, 1570–80, fritware, underglaze-painted, diameter 34.3 cm (13½ in.), height 7.4 cm (2⅞ in.), AKM687.

RIGHT: Ablution Basin, Jingdezhen, China, 1506–21, porcelain, underglaze-painted, diameter 41.8 cm (16½ in.), height 7.5 cm (3 in.), AKM722.

To group all these artistic expressions under the artificial construct of "Islamic Art," devised by nineteenth-century Orientalists, is intellectually misleading and visually confusing.

To cover even superficially the span of so many artistic cultures exceeds the ability of any institution. The holdings of the Aga Khan Museum make up an anthology, not a comprehensive survey. They allow viewers to catch insights into privileged aspects of the art created at various periods over a space that stretches from the Atlantic shores to the China Sea.

The three-dimensional works, whether bronze and ceramic vessels or architectural pieces, were not acquired by the Aga Khan Museum as part of a preconceived plan. They entered the collection as market opportunities allowed. Regarding *objets d'art*, the possibility of enlarging our holdings is limited by our determination to respect the criteria of legitimate ownership defined in the UNIDROIT Convention put forward by UNESCO. Our aim is to initiate visitors to the cultures of the Islamic nations, not to help in destroying their artistic heritage. Where possible, we resort to private loans.

The display, which reflects the makeup of the collection, largely dwells on important moments in the evolution of the Arab Near East and historic Iran.

Two stone capitals that once topped engaged columns somewhere in Syrian lands convey the sculptural feel of architectural ornament in the palaces of the seventh-century Umayyad caliphs. The thrust of the stylized leaves metamorphoses the distant loan from the Hellenistic phase of the Arab Near East, and it does so with a sense of rhythm alien to Greece.

A storage jar in glazed pottery, on loan from a European collection, was acquired by a Paris dealer before the First World War. It bears witness to the continuity of the Pre-Islamic tradition of monumental pottery in Iran. The wavy lines impressed on the body are inherited from the Sassanian period (224–651 CE), but the deep glaze veering from purplish red to olive green points to Islamic times, even if dating it precisely remains problematic.

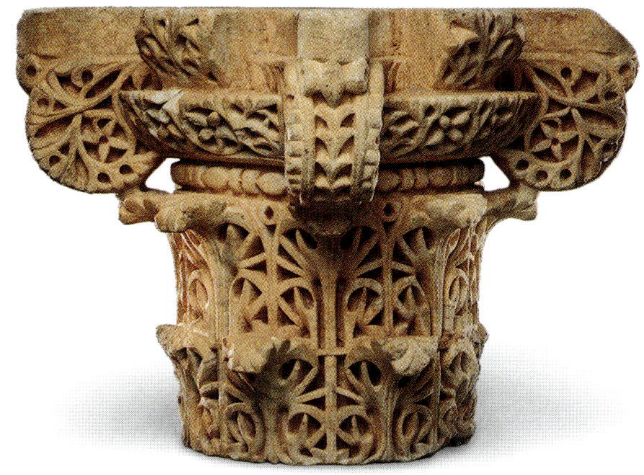

Capital, Spain (Historic al-Andalus), 10th century, carved marble, height 28 cm (11 in.), AKM663.

Visitors discover the calligraphic pottery of the Iranian world where Neyshabur and Samarqand, both cradles of early Persian literature, created its greatest masterpieces. The lapidary precepts that dispense behavioural advice in Arabic are occasionally peppered with mocking irony. Standing out in ivory white against the sepia brown ground of a late ninth- or tenth-century bowl (AKM545), these words would have leaped to the reveller's eyes as he drank the last drop of wine: "Beware of the imbecile: do not socialize with him; and of the woolly-headed admirer: do not get near him."[2]

A bowl from the same workshop in the Victoria and Albert Museum carries a precept in the same vein that also stands out in white against the sepia brown ground: "the imbecile is not to be blamed, but the intelligent one if he seeks his company."[3] Made in Neyshabur where characters were depicted on other vessels in Picasso-like fashion, such as the royal rider on a bowl painted in yellow, green, and sepia brown,[4] these calligraphic bowls are a reminder that great calligraphy did not arise as a substitute for figural art, as is so often maintained. It thrived alongside figuration.

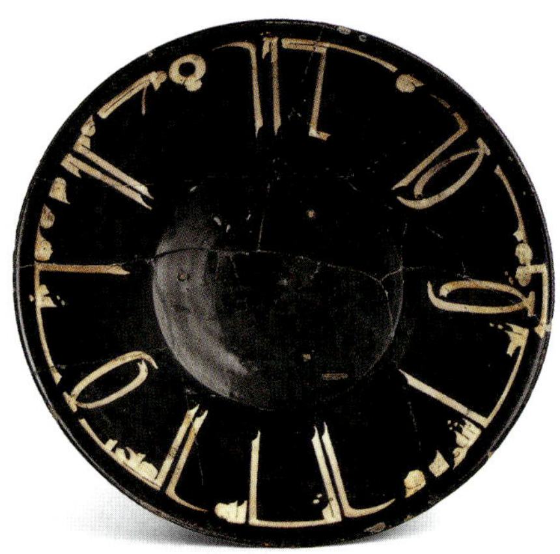

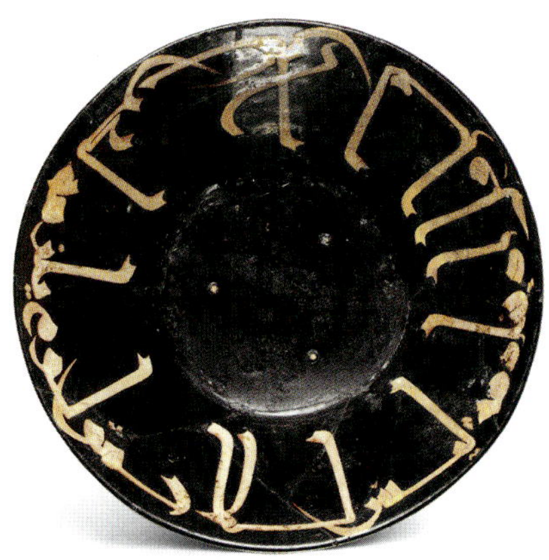

LEFT: Dish, Iran or Central Asia, 10th century, earthenware, slip-painted and glazed, diameter 33.5 cm (13¼ in.), height 10.3 cm (4 in.), AKM545.

RIGHT: Bowl, eastern Iran or Uzbekistan, 10th century, earthenware, slip-painted and glazed, diameter 27 cm (10⅝ in.), height 8 cm (3⅛ in.), Victoria and Albert Museum, London, C.131-1963.

Isolated rarities displayed at intervals highlight some cultural trends with a power of persuasion that the best art historical essays cannot match.

A bronze oil lamp stand (AKM593) from the tenth-century Arab emirate of Spain preserves the memory of vanished architectural structures and has horseshoe arches resembling those of the Visigoths who dominated Spain before semi-Arabized Berbers pouring in from North Africa invaded the peninsula in the eighth century. The birds, on the other hand, recall those seen on Neyshabur bronzes. Clearly, exchanges took place between the then westernmost and easternmost extremities of the Islamic world in an age of indefatigable travellers. They left traces in societies that otherwise immensely differed.

A bronze decanter (AKM735) of the fifteenth century reveals how far the art of Arabized Spain had departed from its erstwhile Syrian models. Like the Alhambra that bears no connection

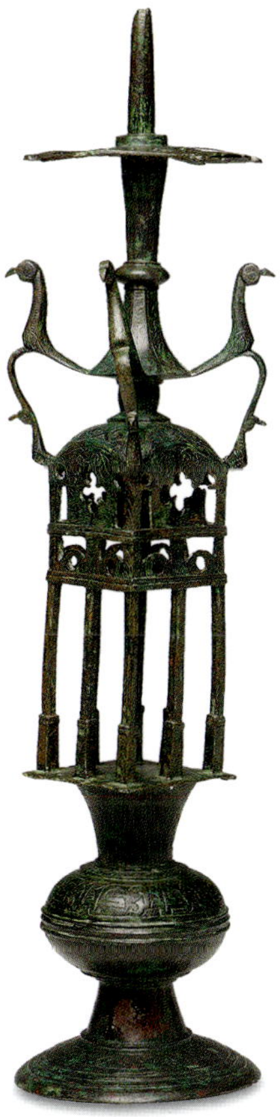

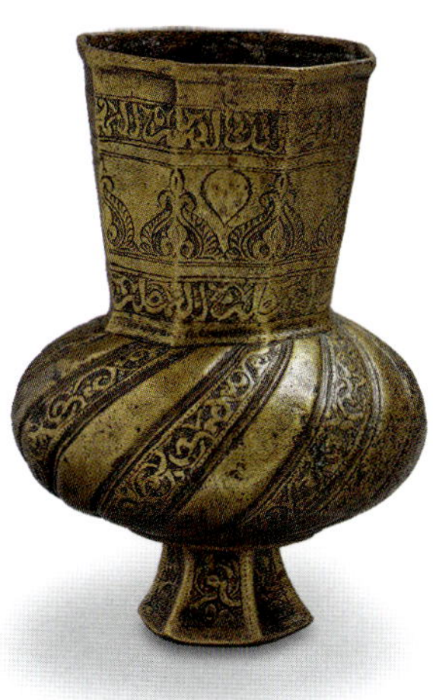

TOP: Oil Lamp Stand, Spain (Historic al-Andalus), 10th century, cast and engraved bronze, height 52.5 cm (20⅝ in.), AKM593.

BOTTOM: Goblet, signed by Yahya ibn Yusuf, Spain (Historic al-Andalus), 15th century, cast and engraved bronze, height 14.5 cm (5¾ in.), diameter 10 cm (4 in.), AKM735.

to the architecture of Syria or Egypt, it belongs to a thoroughly independent culture despite a shared literary language with the Arab East. That did not prevent it from being uprooted in one of the most drastic campaigns of ethnic cleansing in human history ordered by the Catholic monarchs at the end of the "Reconquista."

An ivory horn (AKM809, see also pages 16–17 and 132–33) illustrates one of the unresolved enigmas linked with another vanished outpost of Arab culture in Western Europe. Animals and stylized plants are carved in a manner pointing to contacts with eleventh- or twelfth-century Syria and Egypt. Horns of this type, and caskets with related decoration, which have essentially survived in Western church treasuries, are considered by Ernst Kühnel to have originated in southern Italy or Sicily.[5]

Seen from a historical perspective, the case for Sicily is perhaps stronger. The island, overrun by the Arabs in the ninth century, remained under the control of the Fatimids ruling Egypt and Syria until the early twelfth century. For a while, a syncretic culture blending loans from Medieval Europe and a Fatimid input prevailed. After the Normans conquered the island, the new Christian monarchy donned the mantle of Arab civilization. Literally so.

The famous silken cope, circa 1133–34, woven for the Christian ruler Roger II "in the Sicilian Capital (*Bi-madinat Siqilliya*)" that is preserved in the Kunsthistorisches Museum in Vienna, associates Near Eastern iconography and Western dress code.[6] The inscription in plaited Kufic that runs on the hem wishes the Norman monarch God's graces in rhyming prose (*saj'*), suitable for a patron well versed in Arab language and literature.

So deep was the imprint of Arab art in Sicily that the ceilings of the Cappella Palatina built for Roger II in 1140 were decorated in Fatimid style by artists trained in the Arab tradition.[7] That the sculptor of the horn related to Fatimid art may have been Sicilian seems plausible enough.

Far less known is the fact that literature of a high order was written in Arabic by Sicilians into the Christian period. Whether these were Arabs, or Europeans adhering to Islam and educated in the mould of Arab culture, is impossible to tell. Its masterpiece, *Kitab Sulwan al-Muta' fi 'Udwan al-Atba'* (The Comforts of Those Who Are Obeyed When Faced with the Hostility of Their Followers), was written by Ibn Zafar al-Siqilli ("the Sicilian").[8] He composed his exemplary parables in 1140, partly inspired by the model of *Kalila wa Dimna*, the first major work of Arabic prose ever, penned in eighth-century Basra by the Iranian Ruzbeh under the name Ibn al-Muqaffa'. Ibn Zafar's work was admired long after the writer was driven out of Sicily by a wave of anti-Muslim persecution that started in the mid-twelfth century, and eventually sought refuge in Syria where he died in 1156. It survives in a few manuscripts of which one royal example, as demonstrated by the frontispiece, was painted in the 1320s in Damascus.[9]

Brought to Europe in the twentieth century by a Syrian dealer, the volume suffered the fate meted out in the West to royal manuscripts with painted pages from Islamic lands. The opening folio, on which the right-hand half of the frontispiece is painted, was ripped off, and so were two more folios now in the Freer Gallery of Art in Washington, D.C.[10] When the right-hand half was consigned to a Paris auction by the dealer's heir, the volume from which it had been torn off was not identified. Prince Sadruddin Aga Khan bought the painting, and soon after, I published the title of the work and the author's name, written on the back, in the July-August 1974 issue of the French art monthly *L'œil*.[11]

The powerful image depicts court officials looking toward the sultan depicted on the left-hand half of the diptych, which remains in the volume, now in Doha, Qatar. The ruler takes part in an Iranian-style wine banquet traditionally held after the hunt. One attendant extends his wrist on which a cormorant, trained to catch fish, is perched. Next to him, the Royal Falconer (*Bazdar*) stands with the female hawk trained to hunt game. Far left, the Master of the Hunt (*Amir Shekar*) clutches three arrows in one hand and the royal bow in the other.

All have the round faces and slit eyes of the "Moon-Faced Buddha" (*bot-e mahruy*), the literary archetype of ideal beauty in early Persian literature,[12] overlaid here by the stylized rendition of Mongol features. These were still familiar to painters a century after Genghis Khan's invasion of the Near East. The type assigned to some characters by Syrian painters in the thirteenth and early fourteenth centuries acknowledges the Turkic identity of the Mamluk rulers, because the Mongols were classified among Turkish groups by Middle Eastern historians.[13]

A similar merger of archetype and stylized real life had taken place more than three centuries earlier in Iran. It occurs on bronze vessels from tenth-century Khorasan,[14] on a mural from an unknown location now in Tehran, possibly of the tenth century,[15] on a later fresco from an eleventh-century Ghaznavid palace in Lashkari Bazar (in modern Afghanistan),[16] and on a great many vessels painted with figural scenes in Western Iran between the late twelfth century and the mid-fourteenth century. A group of vessels painted in golden (so-called "lustre") colour reportedly began to turn up in Gorgan after the First World War, stashed in enormous storage jars according to Mehdi Bahrami.[17] The spoofy touch and the poor quality of the inscriptions reproducing Persian verses on a number of the vessels published by Bahrami[18] suggest that the find — if a single find — far from yielding a precious hoard, may simply represent the stock of a workshop concealed in fear of the advancing Mongol hordes that devastated Iran from 1217 until the mid-1220s.

The Moon-Faced Buddha archetype with a Mongoloid overlay gradually evolved. It can still be recognized in Iranian painting well into the fifteenth and sixteenth centuries, of which the Aga Khan Museum preserves a number of masterpieces. These will be shown in rotations because works on paper cannot be exposed to light for long periods. The Museum will thus offer at intervals a new display of paintings and calligraphy.

Instantly attractive to laymen for its intense colours, in particular the carmine red and lapis blue that dazzled the twentieth-century French painter Henri Matisse, the Iranian art of the book is still poorly understood.

The nature of the connection between calligraphy and figural scenes has been overlooked by Western commentators, the best known of whom could not read Persian. This meant that they had no access to sources that say something about the art, and, worse, missed the precise wording of the texts in which the paintings are inserted. Some technical links have been ignored. A magisterial essay written by the Iranian art historian Chahryar Adle in 1975 establishing the use of modules and of complex proportion calculations in composing paintings in relationship to the proportions used in the calligraphy has been ignored.[19]

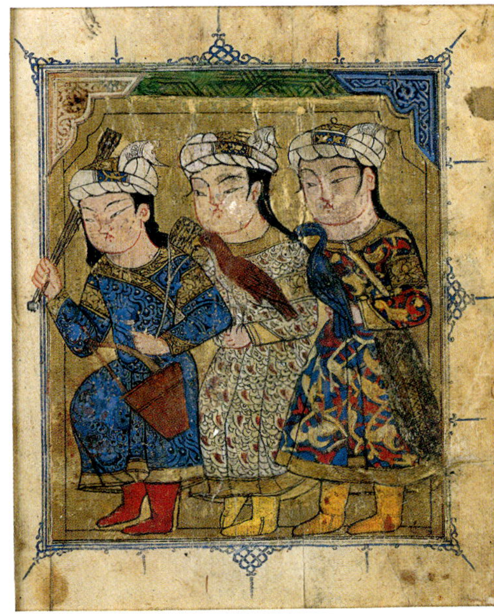

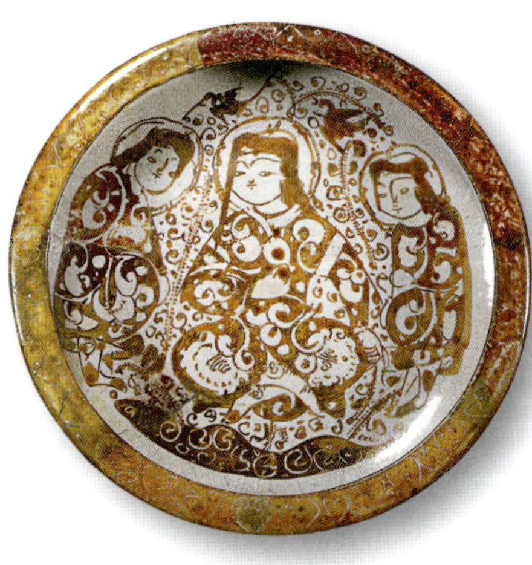

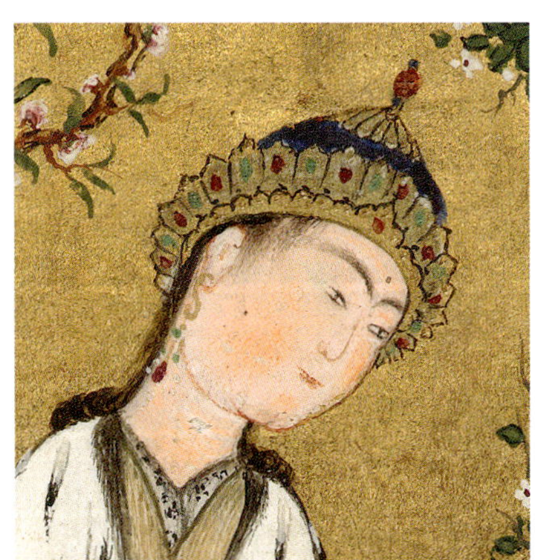

ABOVE: *Three Court Officials*, frontispiece from a dispersed *Sulwan al-Muta'* (The Comforts of Those Who Are Obeyed) by Ibn Zafar al-Siqilli (d. 1170), Egypt, ca. 1325, opaque watercolour and gold on paper, 24.5 × 17.2 cm (9⅝ × 6¾ in.), AKM12.

BOTTOM LEFT: Dish, Iran, early 13th century, fritware, lustre-painted, diameter 17 cm (6¾ in.), height 4 cm (1⅝ in.), AKM559.

BOTTOM RIGHT: Detail of *The Court of Keyomars*, folio 20v from a *Shah-Nameh* (Book of Kings) produced for Shah Tahmasp I, painting by Soltan Mohammad, Tabriz, Iran, ca. 1522, opaque watercolour, ink, gold, and silver on paper, 47 × 32 cm (18½ × 12⅝ in.), AKM165.

Most Orientalists writing about "Persian Miniatures" seem unaware that the layout of a manuscript painting is conceived within the framework of a double page and that it often relates to the text on the facing page. Thus, the head of the main character in the passage with which the image deals can be precisely at the level of the line mentioning him.

Most importantly, in assessing the aesthetics of figural scenes, commentators miss the metaphorical nature of Iranian art. From the late fourteenth century on, paintings in manuscripts of the *Shah-Nameh*, the Persian Book of Kings, and other narratives do not "illustrate" the subject of the text, the word still used by an American art historian as recently as 2007.[20] The Iranian painter considerably adds to the text by inserting multiple details that visually transcribe metaphors. These are obvious to Persian viewers/readers who know the corresponding expressions in poetry.

In a famous image painted by Soltan Mohammad in the *Shah-Nameh* commissioned for the library of Shah Tahmasp I (reigned 1524–76), the colours match the literary images, as is invariably the case. The grass is green like an emerald, as it is in the spring according to Persian poets.[21] This signifies that the rule of Keyomars, sung as the first king of Iran in the Book of Kings, is the spring of Iranian kingship. The sky is painted in gold because gold is the colour of the sun, and therefore, of the light of glory shining upon the monarch. That age-old Iranian concept is conveyed in earlier times by the halo of gold that frames the heads of Sassanian monarchs on parcel-gilt silver phiales.[22]

Other literary metaphors underlie some important details of the scene showing Keyomars and his court. The courtiers stand in a circle, because the circle is the symbol of the sky in Persian thinking, and the sky in turn symbolizes the universe. The courtiers standing in a circle send two messages. One is that Emperor Keyomars is the king of the universe, a standard eulogy, and the other is that the courtiers represent the emperor's celestial court — Shah Tahmasp is referred to as "The Shah of the Paradisiac Court" by Qazi Ahmad Monshi Qommi in the *Golestan-e Honar* (The Rose Garden of Art).[23] The does shown reclining next to peaceful felines transcribe a traditional literary image celebrating the just rule of the king that leads to universal harmony and safety for all.

The principles of Iranian painting were adopted in part by the Islamic courts of India, but the creative gifts of Indian artists led them to recast whatever they borrowed into highly original art forms.

When Homayun, the heir to the throne of the Moghul dynasty, returned from a seven-year exile at the Iranian court, it seemed for a brief period that painting in purely Iranian style would spread in Hindustan. Two Iranian masters, *Mir* Sayyed 'Ali and 'Abd os-Samad, set up the new court atelier. In a self-portrait now in Los Angeles, Sayyed 'Ali, whose signature appears in the form of a Persian couplet composed by him and calligraphed on a scroll, is seen in Hindustani attire.[24]

But the Iranian style soon underwent marked changes. A manuscript page that has been attributed to 'Abd os-Samad on supposed stylistic similarity and dates from the 1580s probably is from an Iranian hand (see AKM122, page 53).[25] Awareness of Western painting makes itself felt, if very discreetly, in the composition of the scene. It is determined by the diagonals of the rectangular format, a fundamental rule in Western pictorial art of the mid-sixteenth to seventeenth centuries that was beginning to reach the Moghul court. The plane tree rises from the point at the imaginary crossing of the diagonals. Touches of shading may be seen in the rocky hillocks rising above the three standing characters, and a relative sense of perspective can be detected in the rockery in the bottom corner right. Even the horse's robe with its white flecks on pale beige and the tail that veers from dark beige to white heralds the soon-to-be trend toward the adoption of a certain degree of naturalism.

The Iranian style of Homayun's court was about to be radically transformed. Emperor Akbar (reigned 1556–1605), a deeply religious Muslim, laid emphasis on the theme of "God's

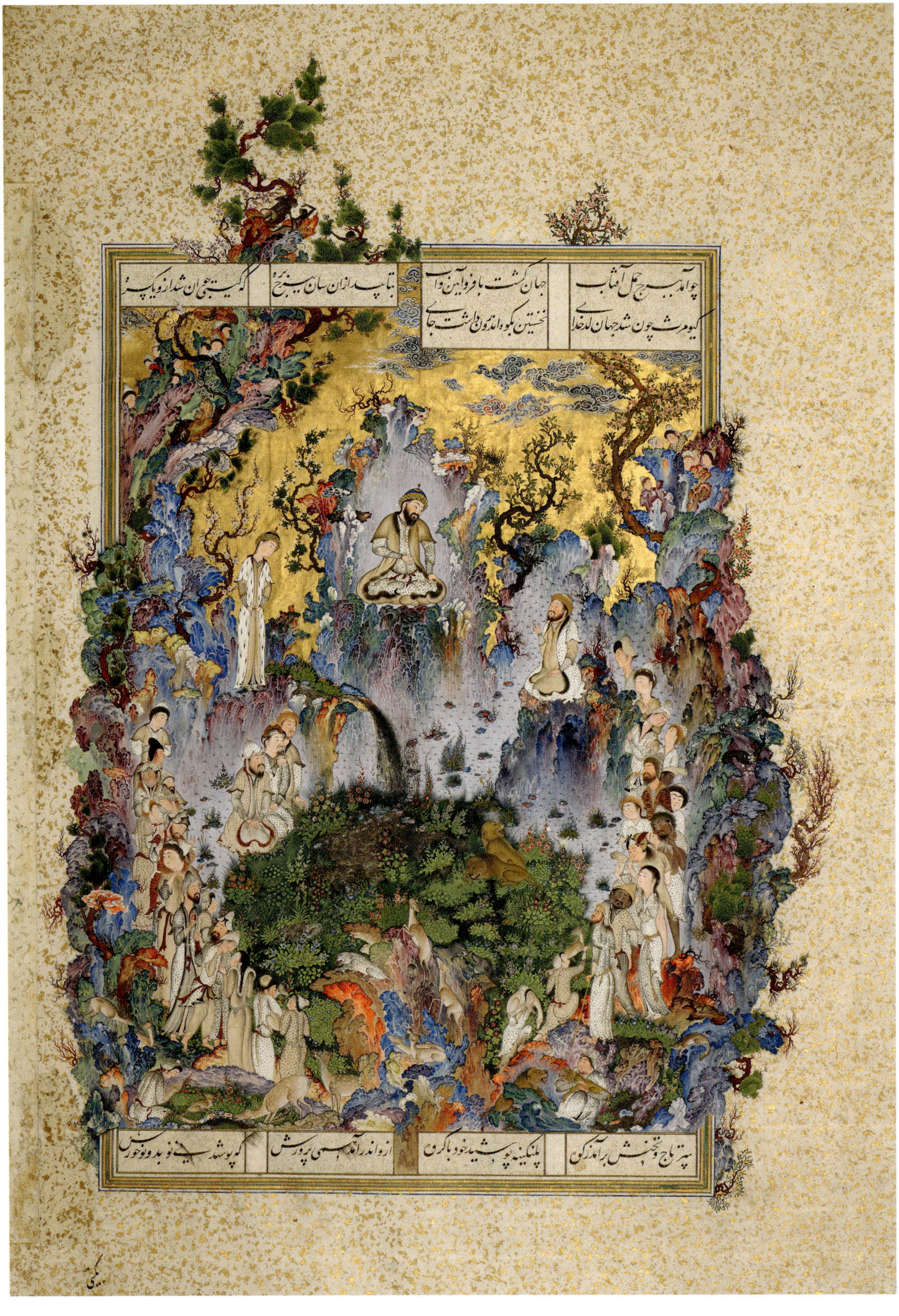

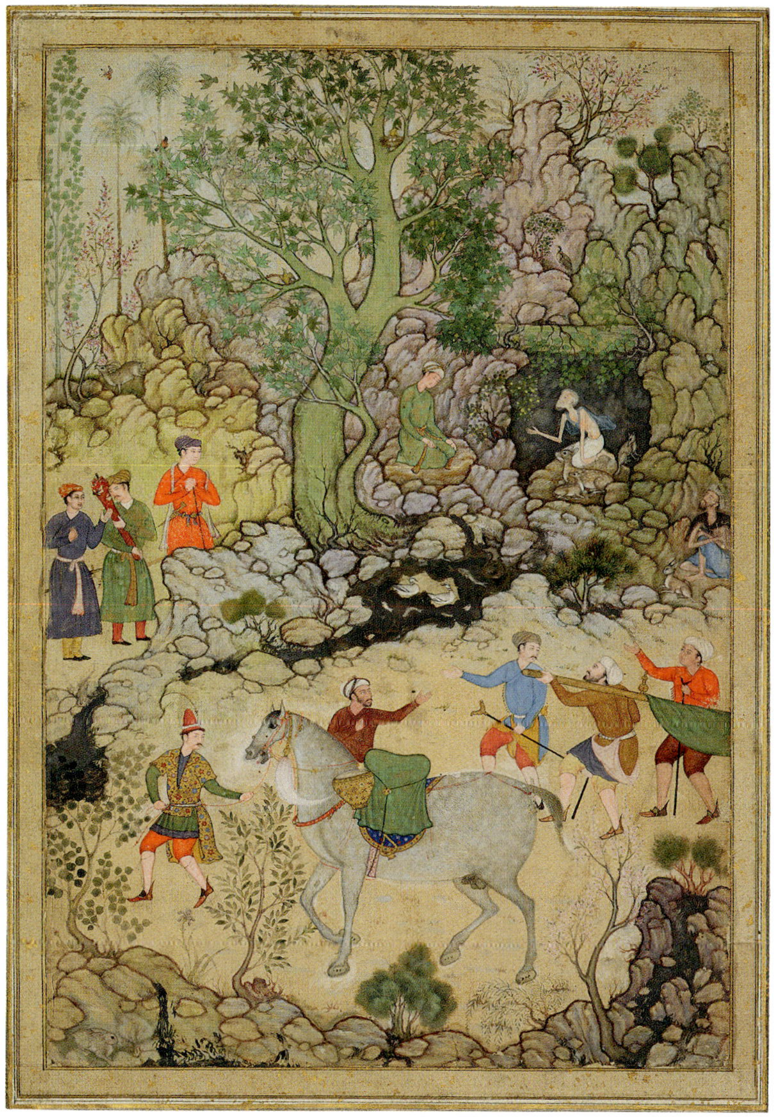

OPPOSITE: *The Court of Keyomars*, folio 20v from a *Shah-Nameh* (Book of Kings) produced for Shah Tahmasp I, painting by Soltan Mohammad, Tabriz, Iran, ca. 1522, opaque watercolour, ink, gold, and silver on paper, 47 × 32 cm (18½ × 12⅝ in.), AKM165.

ABOVE: *A Prince Visits a Hermit*, Fatehpur Sikri, India (Historic Hindustan), ca. 1580, opaque watercolour, silver, and gold on paper, 39.7 × 31.4 cm (15⅝ × 12⅝ in.), AKM122.

Religion" (in Arabic *Din Allah*) that resonates in the Qur'an and is a cornerstone of the Islamic faith.[26] It is rendered in Persian grammatical construction by the words *Din-e Elahi*, "The Divine Religion."[27]

The inherent universalism of the Qur'anic revelation that transcends time and space made Akbar curious of other faiths. He welcomed Europeans to his court. Among them, Jesuit missionaries from Portugal and northern Europe brought volumes of the Bible as well as numerous religious engravings. While the priests failed to make the hoped for conversions, they aroused considerable curiosity at the most international-minded court that ever existed in Asia.

By the early years of Jahangir's reign (1605–27), a thoroughly syncretic school of painting merging the Iranian tradition and European features such as shading and a certain sense of perspective had emerged. It produced, among others, astonishing copies of crucifixion scenes of which one of the finest done around 1605–10 is in the Museum collection (AKM117).[28]

A couple of decades later or so, Iran in turn showed increasing evidence of Western influence in painting. The presence of Catholic missionaries in Iran trying from around the 1620s to proselytize among the Armenian Christians residing in the land who were of the Orthodox Monophysite persuasion may have played a part. Hindustani influence reaching Iran through the comings and goings of thousands of Iranian literati between the two countries is likely to have been more important. Last but not least, Georgians whose land was under Iranian sovereignty, and who were present at the Safavid court, almost certainly played a major role. A famous painter in the service of Shah Tahmasp, Siyavosh Beg, was Georgian: Qazi Ahmad Monshi Qommi says so in his treatise on painters and calligraphers.[29]

The oil portraits of the mid-seventeenth century in the Museum share distinctive characteristics with Georgian manuscript painting (see AKM499).[30] A picture from the same group shows a roast piglet on a tray.[31] The animal, considered unclean food, is banned in Islamic countries. The portrait cannot have been executed by an Iranian painter, nor can it have been intended for an Islamic abode. It is probably the work of a Georgian artist, explaining, among other things, the Georgian outfits. A distinguished American scholar nevertheless feels that the group is Iranian.[32]

A profound break with ancient tradition took place in Iranian painting around the mid-eighteenth century. In the early nineteenth century, Qajar Iran (1785–1925) cultivated a style incorporating European influence while reverting to its tradition of stylization. Both are illustrated by two outstanding pictures of princely characters in the Museum collection (AKM503 and AKM506).

As if possessed with a yearning for the glory of yore, Qajar Iran also indulged in a curious form of Revivalism. Works carrying dates and signatures of much earlier periods are executed in typical Qajar style. These were not meant to deceive any more than the poems composed by Rezaqoli Khan Hedayat in the style of the early eleventh-century Farrokhi Sistani, the late eleventh-century Amir Mo'ezzi, or the twelfth-century Khaqani pretend to be by these ancient poets.[33]

Attempts were made to revive the style of the Safavid shahs in the late seventeenth and early eighteenth centuries. A few were brilliant. A steel shield on loan from a private collection made for commemorative representations carries the name "Shah Soltan Hosayn" overlaid in gold. It is surrounded by an *eslimi* (arabesque) pattern, also overlaid in gold, which is based on the design of the mosque within the Madrase-ye Madar-e Shah built by Shah Soltan Hosayn in Isfahan between 1704 and 1716. But the hand in which the Persian verses running along the rim are written, and the handling of the royal riders engaged in hunting and jousting, unambiguously point to the early nineteenth century.

Chance finds from the distant Pre-Achaemenid past began to be treated like precious treasures. A first millennium BCE burnished earthenware vase dug up in Damghan was thus enshrined in an openwork silver case exquisitely wrought in Neo-Safavid style in 1872–73. It is in the Muze-yi Melli-e Iran (The National Museum of Iran).

This was the time when Iran was discovering photography with a passion. Thus did the modern era with its new cultural self-awareness begin.

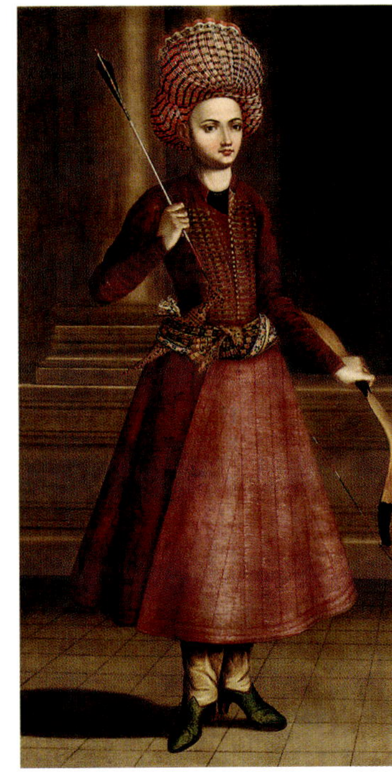

Portrait of a Safavid Nobleman, Iran, second half of the 17th century, oil on canvas, 160 × 85 cm (63 × 33½ in.), AKM499.

Notes

1. As proved by the highly important discovery of wasters, including a footed bowl executed between 1323 and 1336 in Jingdezhen, by Huang Qingua, a researcher at the Shenzhen Archaeology and Cultural Relics Institute. My gratitude goes to my colleague Regina Krahl, who kindly drew my attention to it. See Regina Krahl, "Shanghai Exhibition and Symposium on Yuan Blue-and-White," in Oriental Ceramics Society *Newsletter* 21 (May 2013), 12–15. On the role of the Iranians in the transmission of shapes and motifs in blue-and-white, the presence of an Iranian calligrapher and designer in a workshop producing blue-and-white in Yuan times is described by A.S. Melikian-Chirvani, "On Some Underglaze Persian Inscriptions in Yuan Period Blue and White Porcelain," in *Fiftieth Anniversary Exhibition: Twelve Chinese Masterworks* (London: Eskenazi, 2010), 26–29, where four trays (*tabaq*), complete or fragmentary, carry the name of an Iranian calligraphed underglaze.
2. Sophie Makariou, ed., *Chefs-d'œuvre islamiques de l'Aga Khan Museum* (Paris: Musée du Louvre, 2007), 178–79, cat. 63.
3. Victoria and Albert Museum inventory number: C.131-1963. The aphorism is slightly misunderstood in the translation posted on the Web where it reads: "The fool never receives the reproaches he deserves but the wise man does who keeps him company." The Arabic *lawm* means "blame" rather than "reproach."
4. *Chefs-d'œuvre islamiques de l'Aga Khan Museum*, 16–17. The headdress misunderstood as *une sorte de toque plate* is the rendition in profile of the crown. The *sorte d'oie* is the Iranian "court partridge" (*kabk-e dari*), and this tells us that the royal rider is in the hunting field. It rules out the "warrior, polo player" mentioned as possible representations by Carine Juvin.
5. Ernst Kühnel, *Die Islamischen Elfenbeinskulpturen: VIII–XIII Jahrhundert* (Berlin: Deutscher Verlag für Kunstwissenschaft, 1971). See 19–20 where the German scholar observes that "'the oliphants' (the ivory horns) and caskets ... display several details that are not only utterly alien to Fatimid but to Islamic art." The horns closest to the Aga Khan Museum piece are ascribed to "Southern Italy" (plates 71–81). So is, for example, a casket in Berlin (plate 82) that offers stylistic analogies in its handling of animals with the Aga Khan Museum's horn.
6. Janine Sourdel-Thomine and Bertold Spuler, *Die Kunst des Islam* (Berlin: Propyläen-Verlag, 1973), 265, cat. 199, reproduced in colour. The inscription was recorded in Étienne Combe, Jean Sauvaget, and Gaston Wiet, eds., *Répertoire chronologique d'épigraphie arabe* (Cairo: Institut français d'archéologie orientale du Caire, 1931–), 7, 1845sq.
7. On which see latterly the monumental monograph by Ernst J. Grube and Jeremy Johns, *The Painted Ceilings of the Cappella Palatina*, Islamic Art, Supplement 1 (Genoa: Bruschettini Foundation for Islamic and Asian Art, 2005).
8. A.S. Melikian-Chirvani, *Sulwan al-Muta' fi 'Udwan al-Atba': An Art Historical Essay* (Kuwait: TRI Publishing Company, 1985), where the painting (AKM12) now in the Aga Khan Museum is studied at length as are the other paintings from the manuscript.
9. The Damascus School of Manuscript Painting in the first half of the fourteenth century is identified for the first time in *Sulwan al-Muta*, 97sq, on the basis of three manuscripts. They include a *Maqamat* in the British Library, in which a painter, Ghazi b. 'Abd ar-Rahman ad-Dimashqi, has signed his work within the frame of the painting. The painter was famous as a calligrapher — the two arts being inseparably interwoven in Syria as in Iran.
10. Esin Atil, *Art of the Arab World* (Washington, DC: 1975), 112–14, publishes the two pages, reproducing my identification of their provenance in *L'œil* without mentioning my essay "Ils ont peint."
11. A.S. Melikian-Chirvani, "Ils ont peint," *L'œil* 228–29, 56–59 and 57, figure 4 (Paris: July–August 1974).
12. Described in A.S. Melikian-Chirvani, *Le roman de Varqe et Golšâh: Essai sur les rapports de l'esthétique littéraire et de l'esthétique plastique dans l'Iran prémongol. Arts Asiatiques* 22 (Paris: École française d'Extrême-Orient, 1971), 43–46. Analyzed extensively in relation to Buddhist monuments and rites cited by the Persian poets in A.S. Melikian-Chirvani, "L'évocation littéraire du bouddhisme dans l'Iran musulman," *Le monde iranien et l'Islam* 2 (Geneva and Paris: 1974), 1–72.
13. Rashid ad-Din Fazlollah, *Jame' ot-Tavarikh I: Az aghaz-e peydayesh-e qabayel-e Moghol ta payan-e dowre-ye Teymur-Qa'an* (*World History I: From the First Appearance of Mongol Tribes to the End of the Period of Teymur Qa'an*). Ed. Bahman Karimi (Tehran, 1362/1983 second edition), 27: "These Mongols were one of the Turkish peoples" (*In Moghol yek qowm bude and, az aqvam-e Atrak*).
14. A number of these have come to light. At the time of writing, the only published reproduction may be found in A.S. Melikian-Chirvani, "The Buddhist Heritage in the Art of Iran," in William Watson, ed., *Mahayanist Art After A.D. 900: Colloquies in Art & Archaeology in Asia No. 2* (London: Percival David Foundation of Chinese Art, 1972), 56–63. See 117, plate 13b, and 104, for a brief characterization: East Iran, late tenth or first half of the eleventh centuries.
15. *An Illustrated Souvenir of the Exhibition of Persian Art* (London: Burlington House Exhibition Catalogue, 1931), 101, where a tenth-century date is put forward.
16. Daniel Schlumberger, "Le palais ghaznévide de Lashkari Bazar," *Syria* 29 (Paris, 1952): 251–70. See 261–67 and plate XXXII for murals from what the archaeologist calls "the audience hall."
17. Mehdi Bahrami, *Gurgan Faiences* (Cairo: Le scribe égyptien, 1949), 13, plate I, showing a Turkmen, shovel in hand, standing next to a jar. There is no way of being sure that this is not a *mise en scène* for the purpose of a picturesque shot, supporting the claim of a find in Gurgan.
18. For example, a decanter, called a "bottle" in Bahrami, plate XL; a jar in plate XLI; a footed bowl in plate XLIII; a jug in plate XLIV. Other pieces are of decidedly superior quality, e.g., plate LXXIII.
19. Chahryar Adle, "Recherche sur le module et le tracé correcteur dans la miniature orientale I: La mise en évidence à partir d'un exemple," in *Le monde iranien et l'Islam* 3 (Paris and Geneva, 1975): 81–105.
20. Sheila Canby, "Six illustrations du *Shahnameh* de Shah Tahmasp,"in *Chefs-d'œuvre islamiques de l'Aga Khan Museum*, 73–87.
21. A.S. Melikian-Chirvani, *Le chant du monde: L'art de l'Iran safavide 1501–1736* (Paris: Musée du Louvre/Somogy, 2007), 214–15, cat. 36.
22. See colour plate in Prudence Oliver Harper, *Silver Vessels of the Sasanian Period* (New York: The Metropolitan Museum of Art, 1981), plate XII.
23. Qazi Ahmad Monshi Qommi, *Golestan-e Honar*. Ed. Ahmad Soheyli Khwansari (Tehran, 1352/1974), 148.
24. A.S. Melikian-Chirvani, "*Mir* Sayyed 'Ali: Painter of the Past and Pioneer of the Future," in Asok Das, ed., *Mughal Masters: Further Studies* (Mumbai: Marg Publications, 1998), 30–56. See 30 (image), 36–37, where the poem that identifies the sitter as Sayyed 'Ali is transcribed in Romanized letters and its correct meaning is restored. The signature is given below, in part in Arabic and in part in Persian at the bottom of the tablet: *sawwarahu Sayyed 'Ali Nader ol-Molk-e Homayunshahi*, "rendered in figural manner by Sayyed 'Ali, the Rarity of the Homayunid reign."
25. Benoît Junod, *Treasures of the Aga Khan Museum: Arts of the Book & Calligraphy* (Istanbul: Sakıp Sabancı Museum, 2010), 326, cat. 141, with earlier bibliography.
26. Qur'an 3:83: "Do they want [any faith] other than God's Religion [*Din Allah*]?" Qur'an 29:65: "They call unto God, proclaiming in purity 'The Religion is His.'" Qur'an 31:32: same verse. Qur'an 39:2: "Verily We sent to you the Scripture to Truth, so worship God, proclaiming in purity 'The Religion is His.'" Qur'an 39:3: "Is not the Religion His?" Qur'an 40:14: "Call unto God, proclaiming in purity: 'The Religion is His,'" and further verses.
27. Almost every Western art historian dealing with Akbar's time trots out the myth of Akbar's attempt "to create a syncretic religion (*Dîn-i-Ilâhî*) indifferently borrowing from different creeds," in the words of Amina Okada, *Miniatures de l'Inde impériale: Les peintres de la cour d'Akbar* (Paris: Éditions de la Réunion des musées nationaux, 1989), 16.
28. *Chefs-d'œuvre islamiques de l'Aga Khan Museum*, cat. 34–35.

29. A different view is held by Eleanor Sims, "Five Seventeenth-Century Persian Oil Paintings," in *Persian and Mughal Art* (London: Colnaghi & Co., 1976), 243, and plate 140.
30. See *Persian and Mughal Art*, 223–58, where they are considered Iranian. The same view is maintained by the author, Eleanor Sims, with nuances and numerous additions, in "Six Seventeenth-Century Oil Paintings from Safavid Persia," in Sheila S. Blair and Jonathan Bloom, eds., *God Is Beautiful and Loves Beauty: The Object in Islamic Art and Culture* (New Haven and London: Yale University Press, 2013), 341–63, where groups of paintings that, in my view, do not have the same provenance and display blatantly different aesthetics and iconography, are all ascribed to an Isfahan school.
31. *Ibid.*, plate 140. A woman in Georgian costume holds a wine horn in her right hand and a quince in her left hand according to Iranian custom in wine banquets with a difference: only men are seen taking part in Iranian wine banquets. The roast piglet is laid in an oval bowl at her feet. The landscape reveals a sense of perspective, and the clouds, a sense of naturalistic observation that point to far greater familiarity with European art than is ever seen in Iranian painting.
32. Put forward in the two essays cited in note 30.
33. Rezaqoli Khan Hedayat, *Majma'al-fosaha* (The Assembly of the Polished Ones, literally, those speaking a pure and eloquent language), ed., Mazaher Mosaffa (Tehran: Amir Kabir, 1957–61, 6 vols.), vol. 6, 1262–63: the ode is headed "Following / on the model of an ode by the Wise Farrokhi Sistani"; another ode, *ibid.*, 1266, headed "On the model of Amir Mo'ezzi Samarqandi (*Dar Tattabbo'-e Amir Mo'ezzi Samarqandi*)." But some odes following the model of Khaqani, for example, do not acknowledge their model, and there was certainly no intention of deceiving Persian leaders who would instantly recognize the Khaqani-like voice.

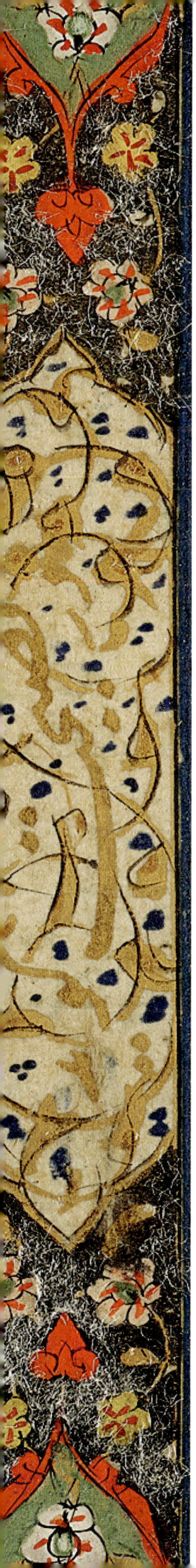

HIGHLIGHTS IN THE PERMANENT COLLECTION

RUBA KANA'AN

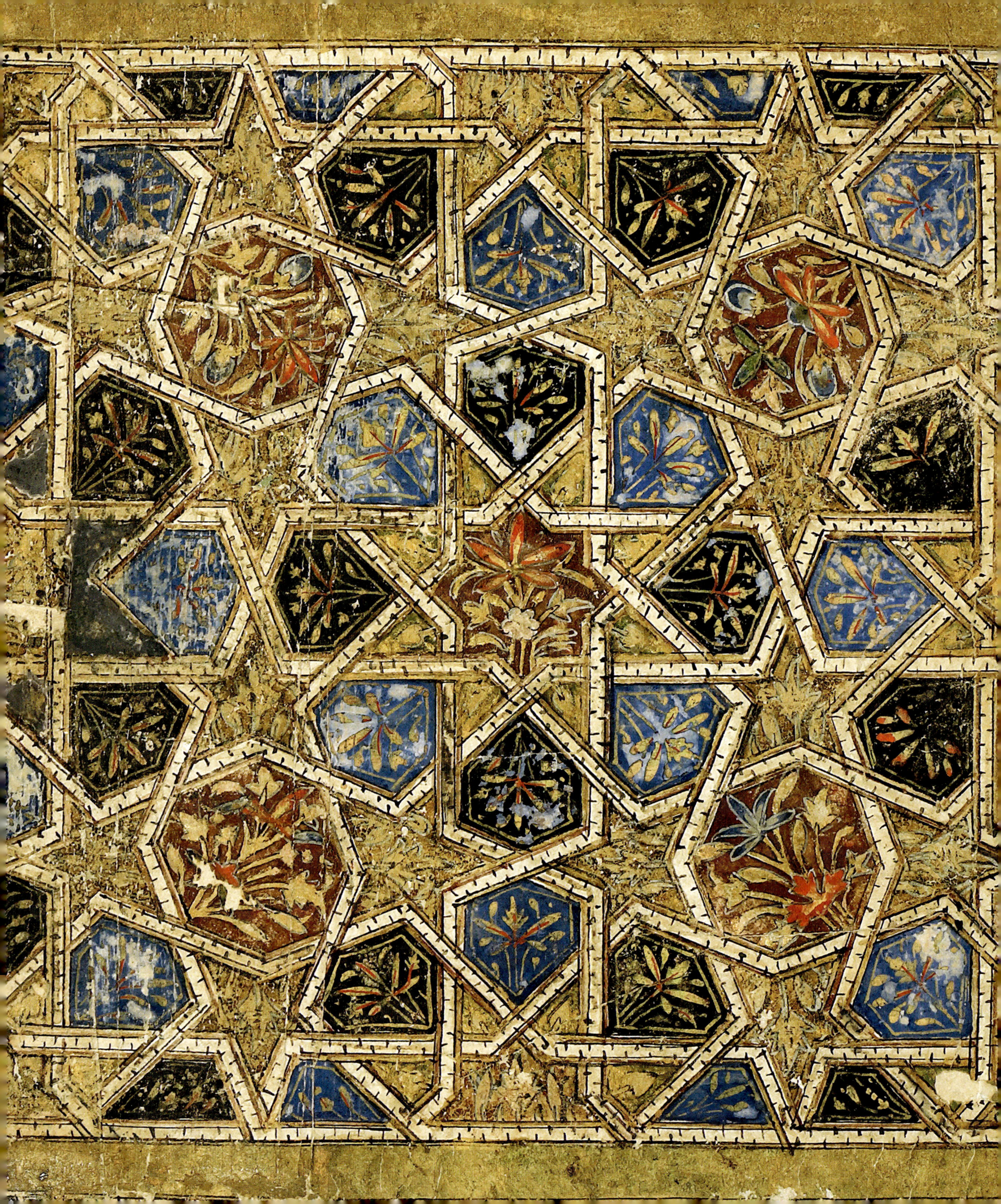

QUR'ANS

THE QUR'AN IS REGARDED BY ALL MUSLIMS as the Word of God—the sacred text that serves as the foundation of their faith and practice. It was revealed in Arabic to the Prophet Muhammad (died 632) through the Archangel Gabriel. During the lifetime of the Prophet, verses of the Qur'an were transmitted orally and written down on various materials such as parchment, bone, and stone. The compilation of the Qur'an into the current codex took place under the direction of 'Uthman (died 656), the third caliph. The shift to copying the Qur'an on paper came much later, with the earliest surviving paper copy dating to the end of the tenth century. The transition from parchment to paper is also reflected in the format of the codex, since parchment Qur'ans were usually smaller in size and copied horizontally, while paper allowed for a variety of sizes and vertical formats.

The Qur'an has 114 chapters, known as suras, each dealing with a number of topics. In addition to its central message of faith and ethics, the Qur'an also contains histories, parables, and stories that have inspired the arts. The suras of the Qur'an are arranged according to their length: the longest suras appear at the beginning of the Qur'an, whereas the shortest appear at the end. Muslims copied the Qur'an in single volumes (AKM281) or designed the copy to be bound in several volumes or divisions known as *juz's*. The most common divisions were seven or thirty *juz's* (AKM279 and AKM829).

This section illustrates some of the Aga Khan Museum's finest Qur'an manuscripts, focusing on two interconnected aspects of the art of the Qur'an: the evolution of the Arabic script used for copying Qur'ans and the ensuing importance of the art of calligraphy (see pages 142–53); and the evolution of the art of decorating Qur'ans with geometric and floral designs, known as illumination.

Early Qur'ans were written in an angular script known as Kufic, characterized by an emphasis on horizontal lines and short vertical strokes. Additional markers, mostly in the form of dots, were used above and below the text line to indicate vocalization. By the tenth century, new styles of cursive script that were faster to write and easier to read evolved. These standard styles include the six canonical scripts of Arabic calligraphy: *naskh*, *thuluth*, *muhaqqaq*, *tawqi'*, *riq'a*, and

Detail of Qur'an (see page 67)
Copied by Mahmud Sha'ban
Gwalior Fort, India (Historic Hindustan), 1399
Ink, opaque watercolour, and gold on paper
Folio: 28.9 × 22.2 cm
(11⅜ × 8¾ in.)
AKM281

rayhan. Unique regional variations on these cursive scripts were used in China (AKM824) and the Indian subcontinent (AKM281).

Copies of the Qur'an were commissioned by benevolent rulers and gifted to mosques locally and in faraway regions (AKM475). Rulers and patrons considered the endowment of beautifully copied Qur'an manuscripts with state-of-the-art decoration and magnificent leather binding as an act of piety. The art of decorating the Qur'an with intricate borders of geometric and floral designs thus became a prominent art (AKM256). These illuminations reveal changes of style over time; they also reflect regional artistic traditions in which Muslims chose to copy and decorate their sacred text (AKM488).

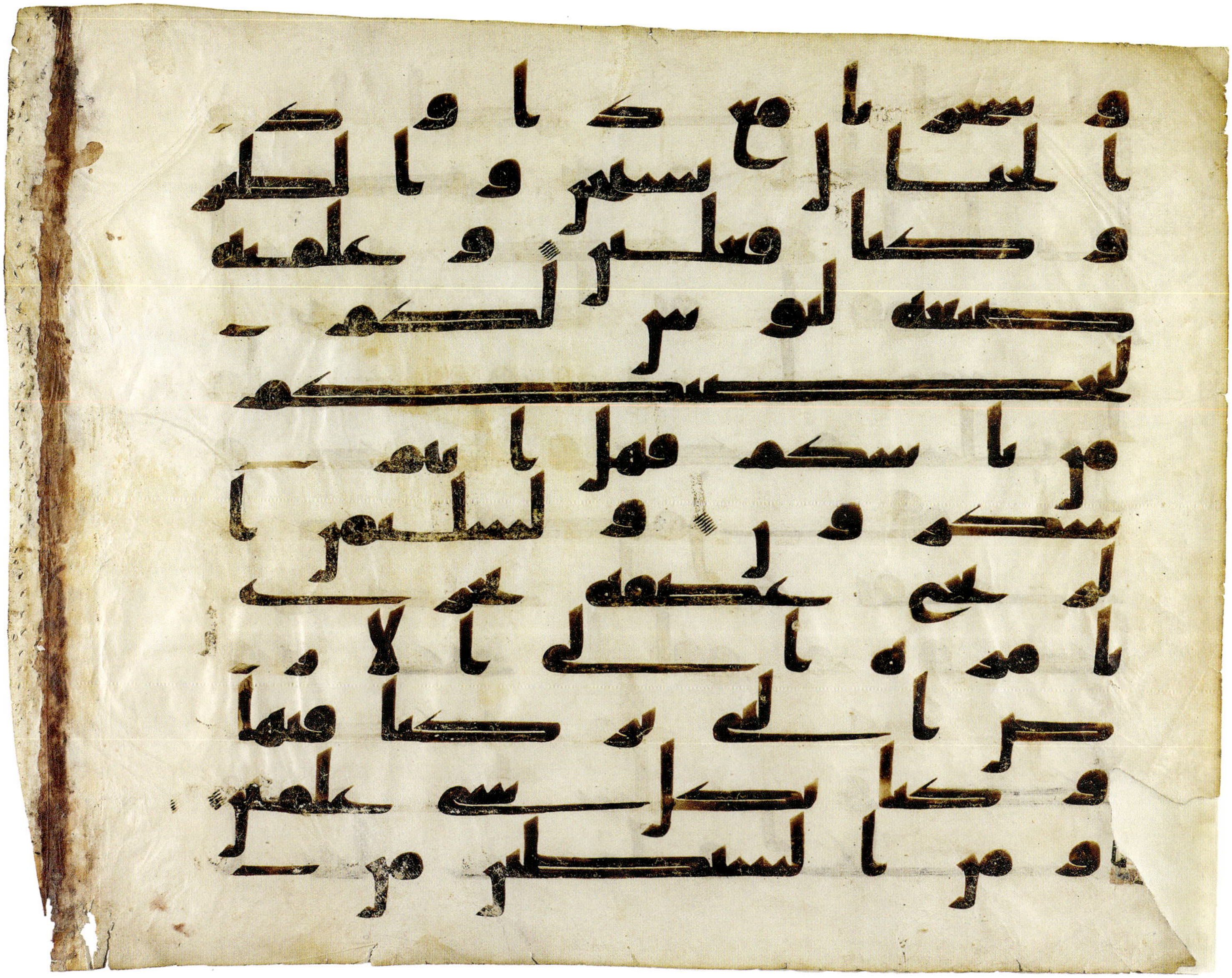

With the spread of Islam out of Arabia, Muslim rulers sent copies of the Qur'an to new urban centres of Muslim congregation. This gesture was meant as a symbolic reference to the caliph's role as the custodian of faith, as well as to impress the receivers with the beauty and monumentality of these Qur'ans. Here, the text appears quite simple and unadorned. The Kufic script is evenly spaced using horizontal elongation of letters (*mashq*) and dashes at the end of the line (on the left) to achieve a justified text block. Indeed, the whole of the fifth line is a single word. What would have been most impressive for the eighth-century community to which this Qur'an was sent, however, is the fairly large size of the parchment (see AKM238, page 62) on which it is copied and the number of its folios. This monumental Qur'an, most of which is now in Tashkent, Uzbekistan, was probably one of the most expensive to be produced in the second half of the eighth century.

Qur'an Folio
(Q21: 76–82)
North Africa, 8th century
Ink on parchment
58.5 × 71.5 cm (23 × 28⅛ in.)
AKM475

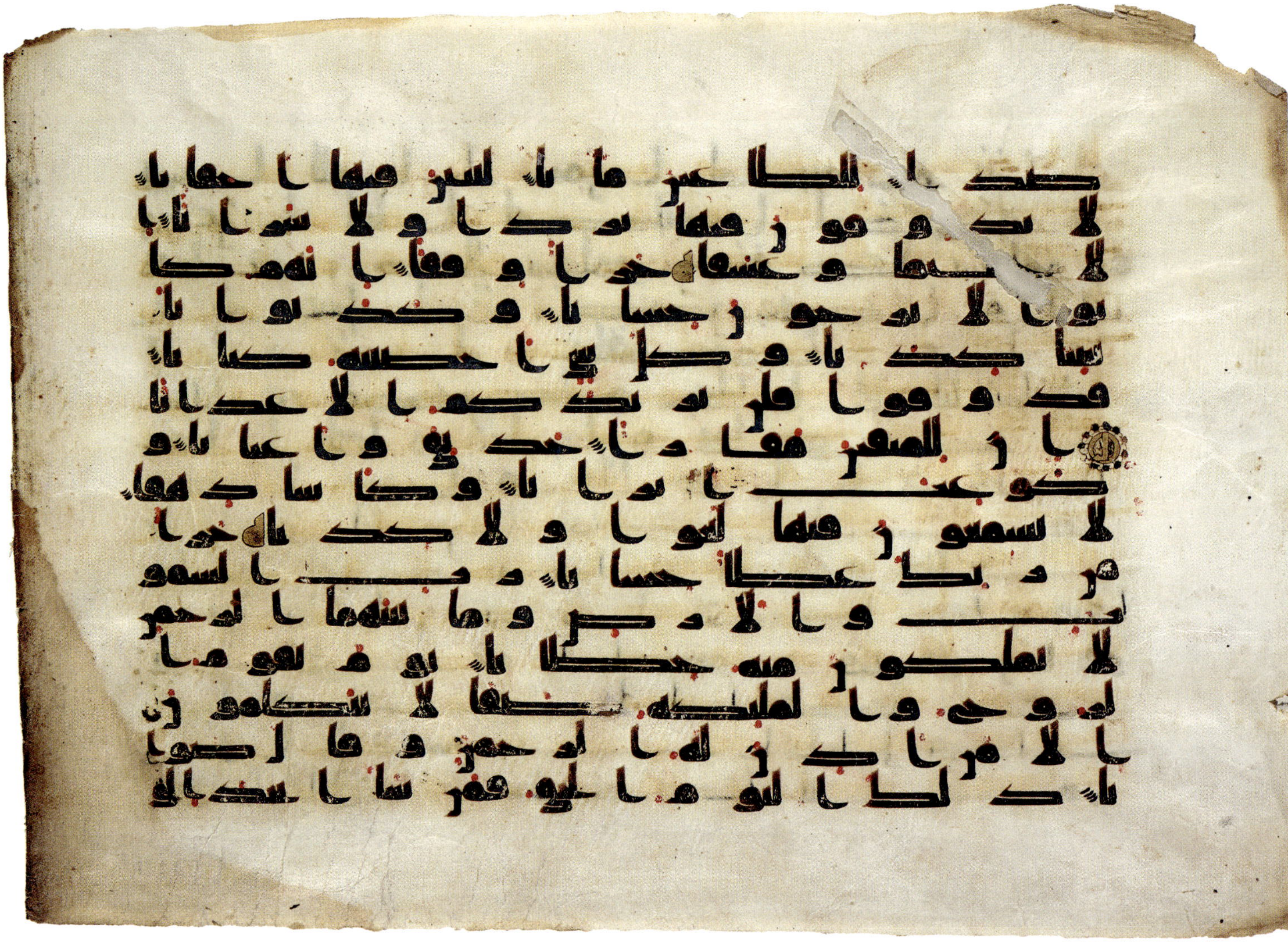

Qur'an Folio
(Q78:1–38)
Iran or Iraq, 850–900
Ink and gold on parchment
61 × 45.6 cm (24 × 18 in.)
AKM238

Muslims discovered the secret of papermaking after the Battle of Talas in 751 when the Abbasids (750–1258), ruling from Baghdad in present-day Iraq, and the Tang dynasty (618–907), ruling from Xi'an in China, battled for control of Central Asia. Their first use of paper, however, was reserved for administrative documents. Until the end of the tenth century, Qur'ans, like this ninth-century folio, were still being copied on parchment, an animal skin that is stretched, limed, and scraped to produce a uniform writing surface. The fifteen lines of Kufic script in this folio are interrupted by four oblique strokes that indicate the end of each verse, with a letter marker filled with gold after each fifth verse. The diacritical marks are indicated with red ink dots that add a pleasant decorative element to the uniform black ink of the text.

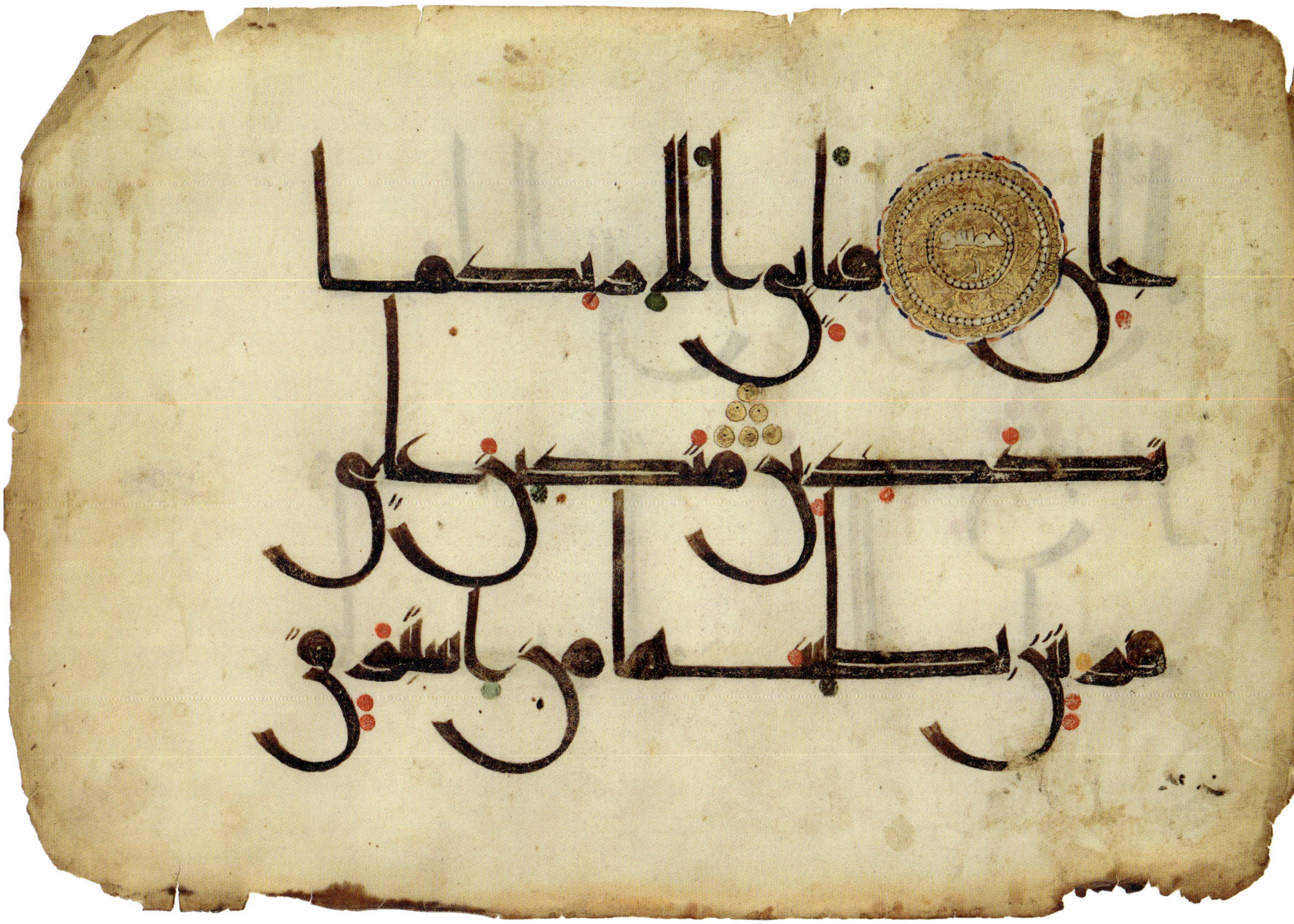

Qur'an Folio
(Q55:52–54)
North Africa, 10th century
Ink and gold on parchment
23.8 × 33.1 cm (9⅜ × 13 in.)
AKM482

This elegant folio is from a dispersed Qur'an manuscript that must have been magnificent to see and costly to produce. Each side of the parchment has three lines only, suggesting that the complete manuscript was enormous. The text is written in a Kufic script with distinctive features such as the emphasis on the vertical letters and the swooping tails of the final curved letters that later became a hallmark of the *maghribi* script known from Spain and North and West Africa. The red and green dots in the text are early examples of vocalization markers, mostly indicating *hamzas* and long vowels. The end of each verse is signified by six gold dots in the form of a triangle, with each fifth verse marked by a decorative circle.

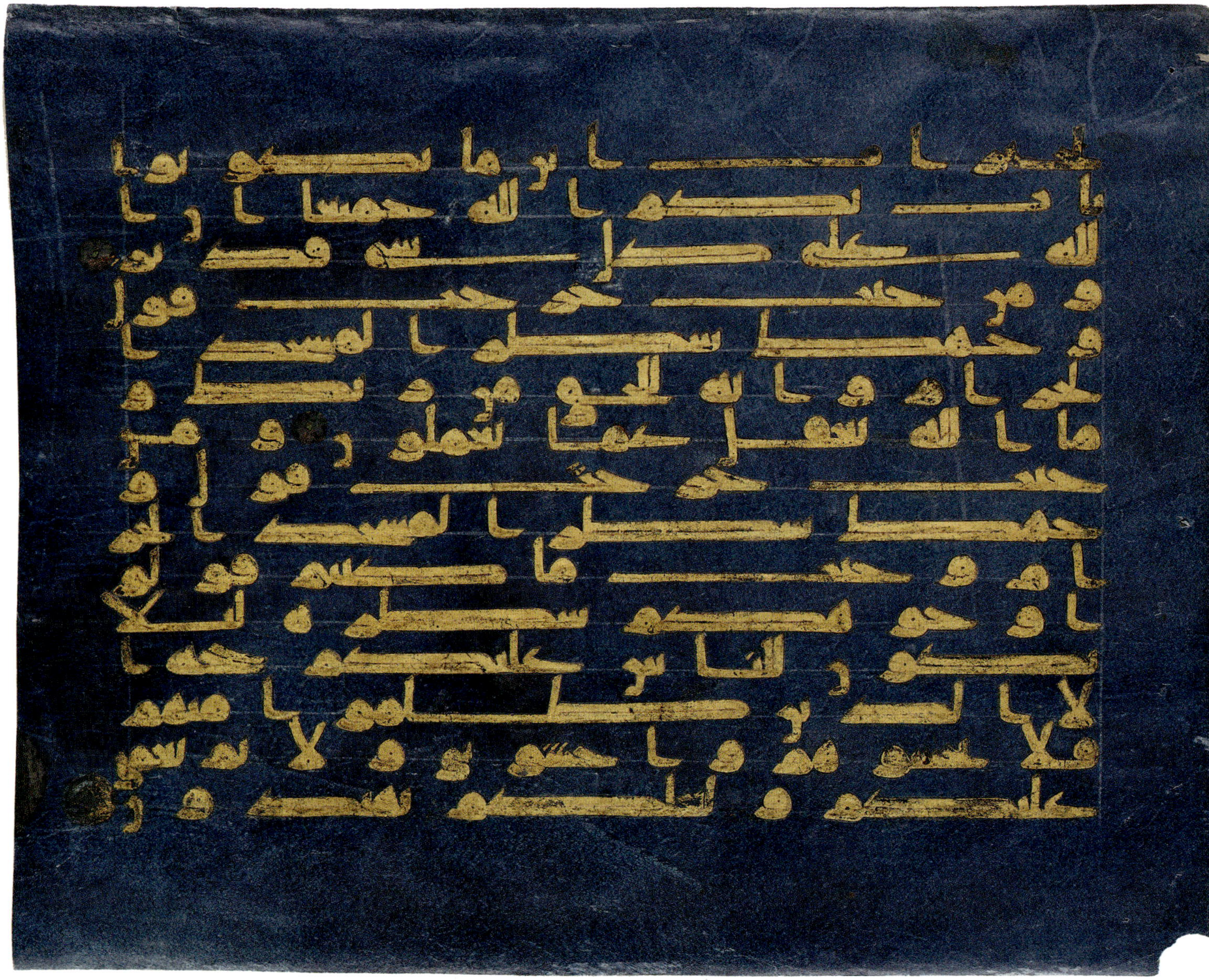

Qur'an Folio
(Q2:148–150)
North Africa, Iraq, or Iran, 9th–10th centuries
Gold and silver on blue-dyed parchment
28.5 × 35.3 cm (11¼ × 13⅞ in.)
AKM248

The dispersed "Blue Qur'an" to which this folio belongs is one of the most famous surviving Qur'an manuscripts. The text of this outstanding Qur'an is copied in gold ink outlined in black on a deep indigo-blue parchment. Small silver rosettes (now oxidized) punctuate the flow of the text at the end of each verse and add a decorative element to an already spectacular folio. Although rare in Qur'an manuscripts, the gold-on-blue aesthetic was used in royal manuscripts in the courts of the Abbasids (750–1258) and the Fatimids (909–1171). It can also be seen in the mosaic inscriptions of the Dome of the Rock in Jerusalem, dating to 692, and known from the literary descriptions of the mosaic inscriptions in the earliest mosques in Medina and Damascus. Around a hundred leaves from this Qur'an are known from museum and private collections, including a section in Mashhad, Iran, and sixty-seven pages in a museum near Qayrawan, Tunisia.

Qur'an Folio
(Q5:44–45)
Iran, mid-12th century
Ink, opaque watercolour, and gold on paper
31 × 20.8 cm (12¼ × 8¼ in.)
AKM256

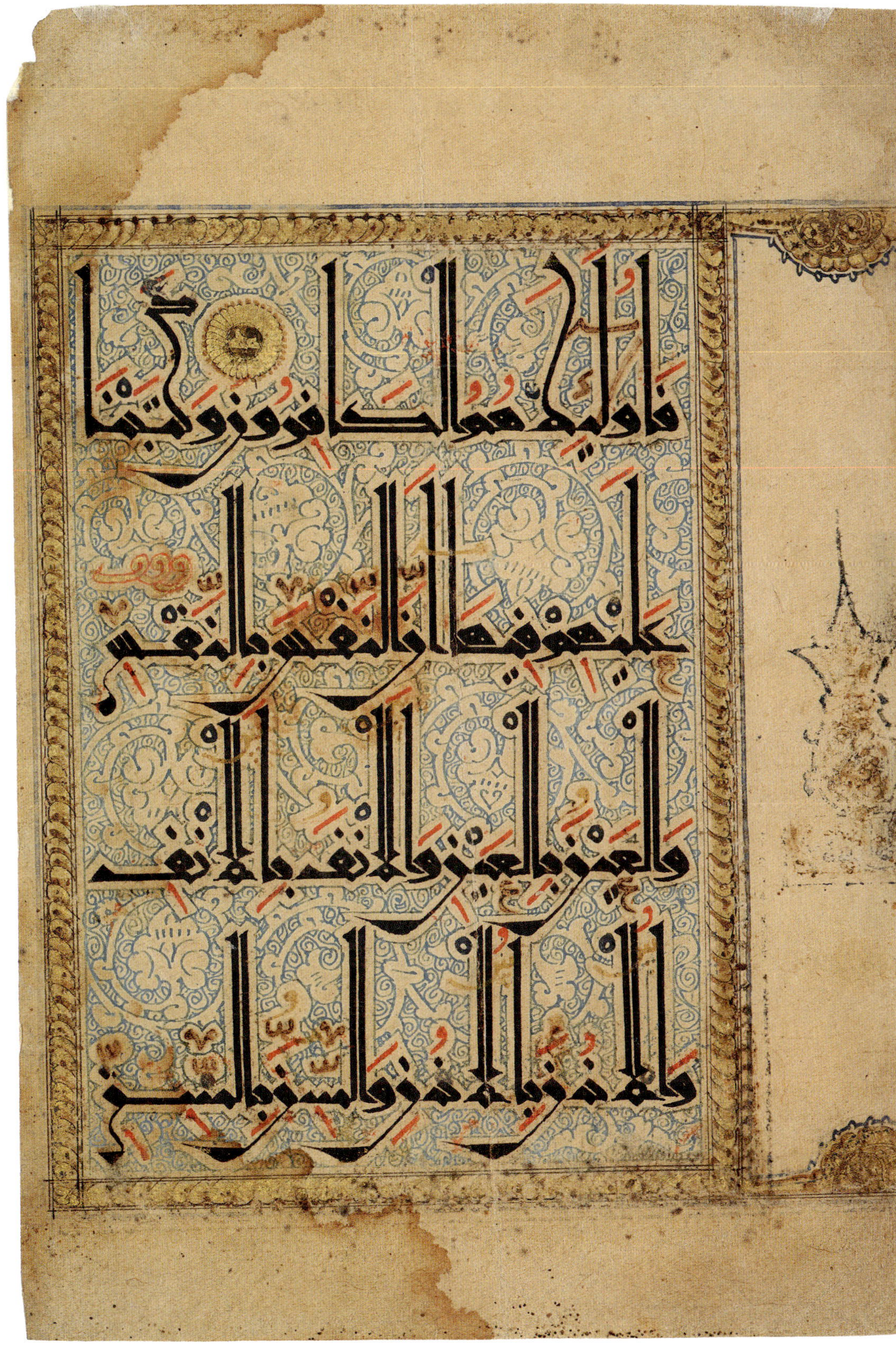

By the time this magnificent folio was copied in eastern Iran, the use of paper in a vertical format and the full pointing and vocalization of the text were already established standards (except in Spain). Here, all pointing and diacritic marks are written in the same ink and hand as the letterforms, while the vocalization is rendered in red, most probably after the text was copied. However, it is the design and layout of the folio that are most magnificent. The generous spacing between the lines and the graceful verticality of the uprights of the letters create a rhythm for the full decoration of the background. An ornamental palmette-scroll (arabesque) outlined in blue surrounds the text and takes pride of place on the page, with a miniature tight scroll filling the space in between. The gilded braid framing the page and the marginal finials give it a sophisticated finished look. It would have been an elaborate undertaking by a wealthy patron to commission and complete this thirty-volume dispersed Qur'an. Scholars have estimated that this Qur'an would have had approximately 4,500 pages, some of which are in prominent museum collections.

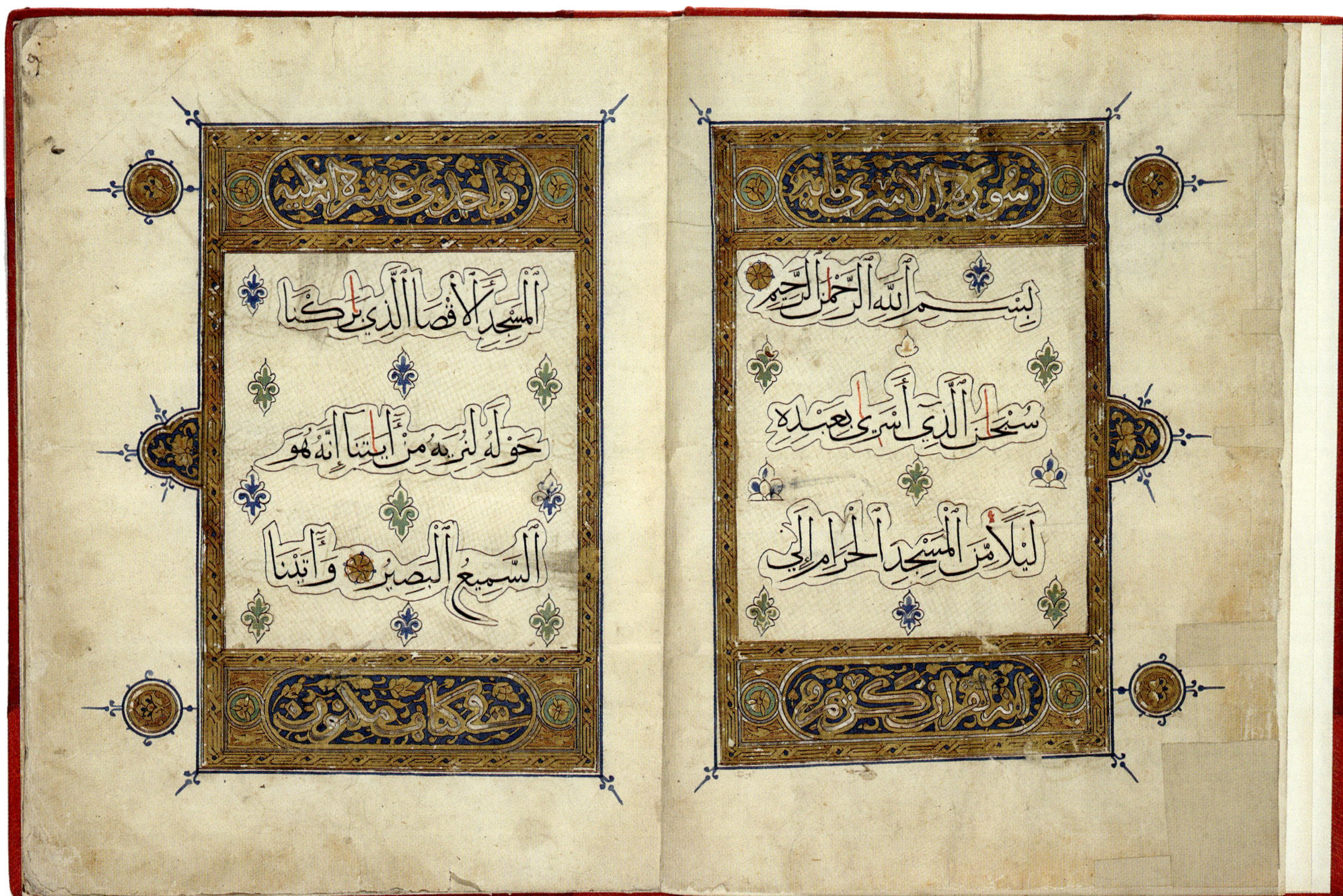

Qur'an *Juz'*
Cairo, Egypt, 14th century
Ink, opaque watercolour, and gold on paper
Folio: 37.2 × 27.3 cm
(14⅝ × 10¾ in.)
AKM279

Qur'ans copied under the Mamluks, who ruled in Syria and Egypt between 1250 and 1517, were mostly commissioned by sultans or their officials as endowments (*waqf*) given to elaborate architectural complexes that were established to house religious and charitable foundations. Some of these Qur'ans, like this section (*juz'*), were copied in multiple volumes. This *juz'* from a late fourteenth-century Qur'an demonstrates a typical layout with a lavishly illuminated opening page followed by simpler text pages where the decoration is limited to verse markers. The gold-filled elaborate braid that frames the three-part division of the opening pages indicates a wealthy, if not royal, patron. An inscription on the leather binding suggests that this Qur'an was copied for the religious complex of the Mamluk Sultan al-Zahir Barquq, who ruled intermittently between 1382 and 1399.

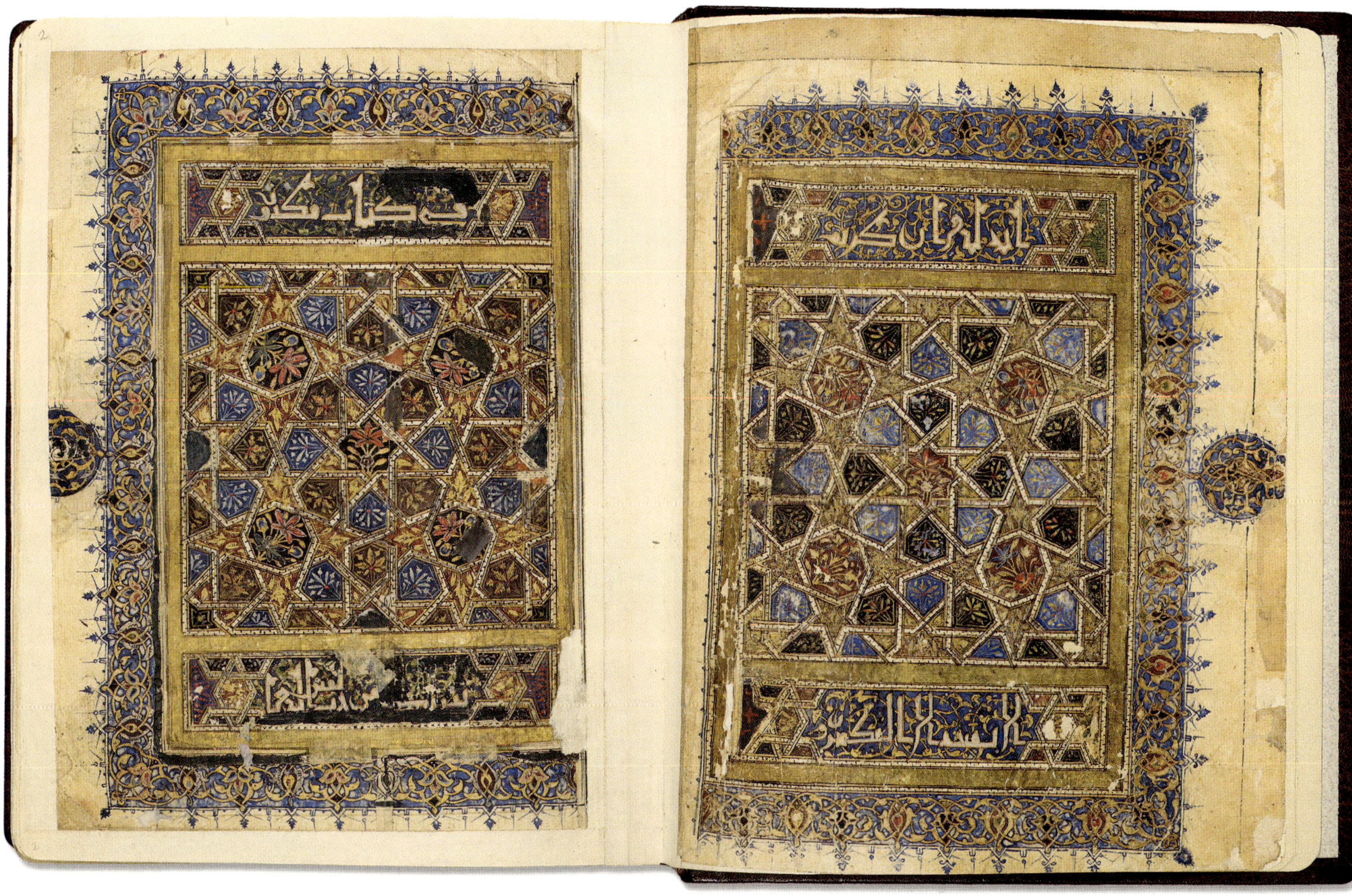

Qur'an
Copied by Mahmud Sha'ban
Gwalior Fort, India (Historic Hindustan), 1399
Ink, opaque watercolour, and gold on paper
Folio: 28.9 × 22.2 cm (11⅜ × 8¾ in.)
AKM281

Copied under the Tughluqs (1320–1414) who ruled parts of present-day India and Pakistan before the Moghuls (1526–1858), this unique Qur'an is one of the earliest surviving manuscripts in the *bihari* script. Known as the Gwalior Qur'an after the Gwalior Fort where it was copied, this Qur'an is testimony to the active diplomatic networks and cultural and economic interactions in the fourteenth and fifteenth centuries. Although the *bihari* script, which was common in pre-Moghul India, is a unique variation on *naskh*, the decorative features of the Gwalior Qur'an bring together elements from Mamluk (1250–1517) and Ilkhanid (1256–1353) layouts and illuminations as well as the exuberance of Indian painting conventions. The strapwork design of this spectacular opening page, for example, recalls the elaborate Qur'an illumination celebrated under the Mamluks. Also significant is the use of interlinear translation where verses in the original Arabic in which the Qur'an is copied, memorized, and recited are translated into Persian in a smaller *naskh* script.

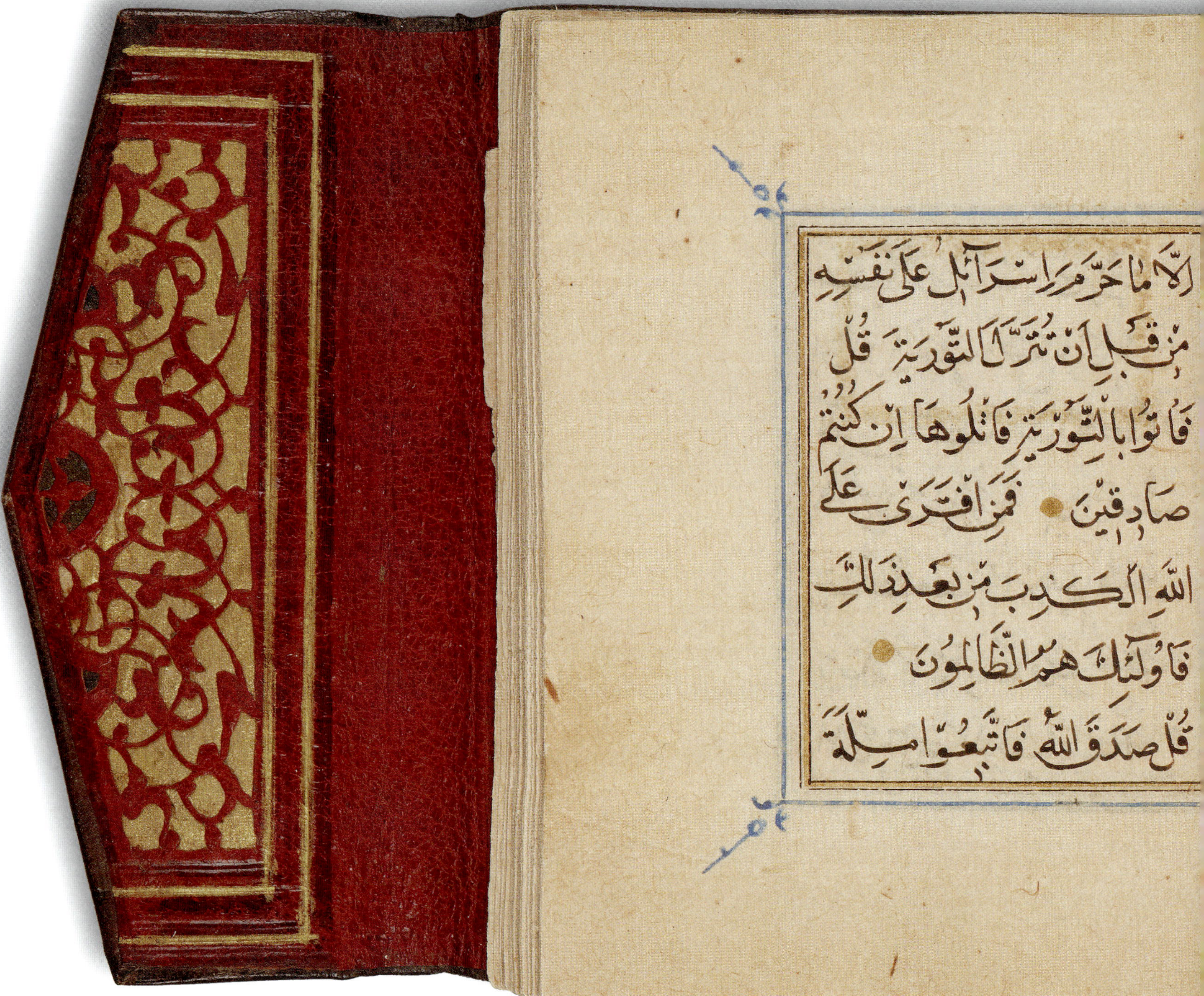

الا ما حرم اسرائل على نفسه
من قبل ان تنزل التورية قل
فاتوا بالتورية فاتلوها ان كنتم
صادقين • فمن افترى على
الله الكذب من بعد ذلك
فاولئك هم الظالمون •
قل صدق الله فاتبعوا ملة

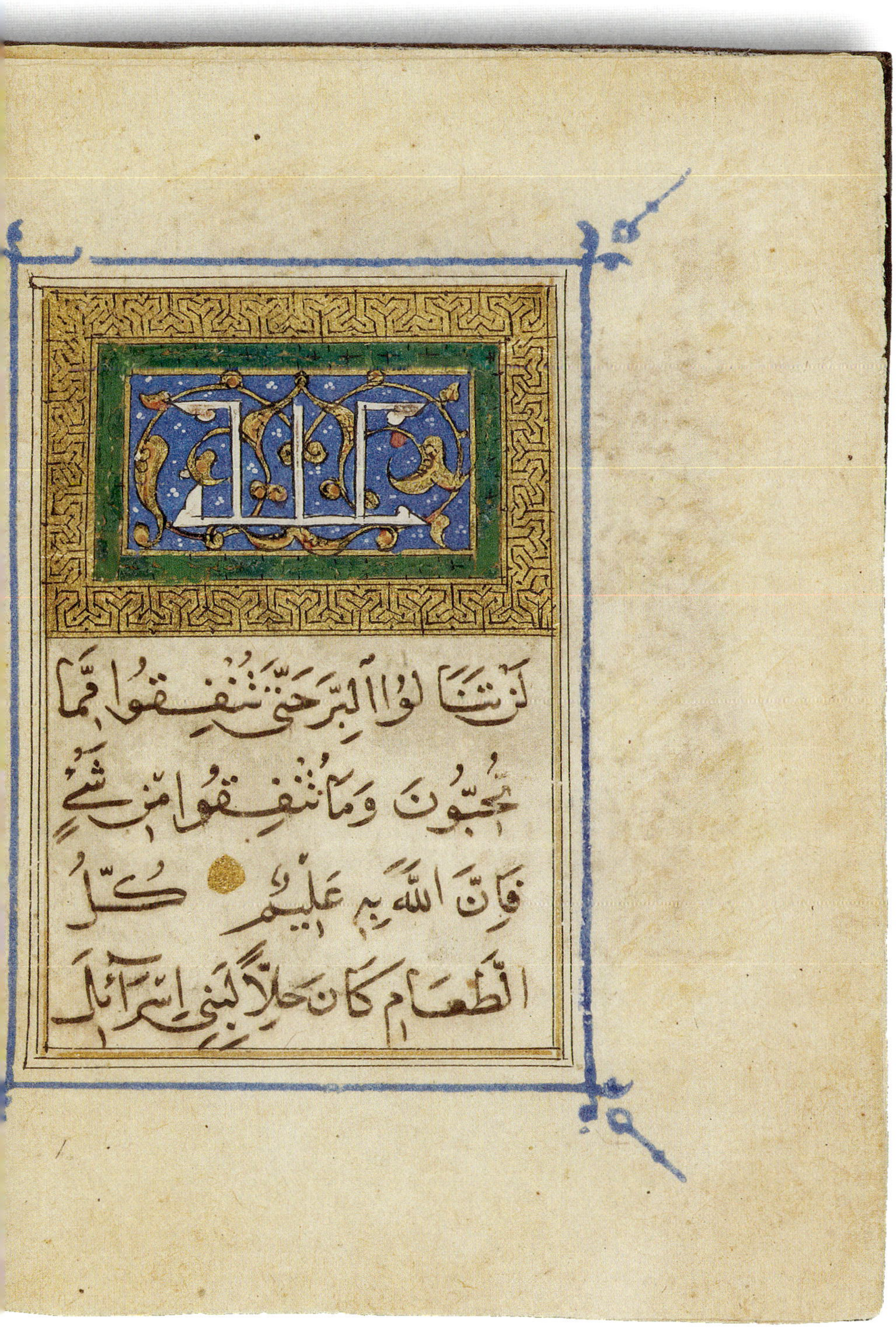
لن تنالوا البر حتى تنفقوا مما
تحبون وما تنفقوا من شيء
فإن الله به عليم كل
الطعام كان حلا لبني إسرائيل

Qur'an *Juz'*

Iran, mid-15th century
Ink, opaque watercolour, and gold on paper, leather binding
Folio: 6.6 × 4.7 cm (2⅝ × 1⅞ in.)
AKM829

Dividing the Qur'an into thirty sections enabled Muslims to memorize or recite an individual section each day, especially in the fasting month of Ramadan. Each section, called *juz'*, was a separate volume, as is the case in this *juz'* that was copied under the Timurids, who ruled in Iran and Central Asia between 1370 and 1507. This palm-size Qur'an *juz'* got the full attention that would have been given to a large, elaborate manuscript. Its forty-two pages, each with seven lines, are written in a crisp cursive *naskh* script, the text is outlined with a simple decorative border, and the heading is intricately illuminated. The quality of the leather binding, however, is what is most remarkable about this small Qur'an. The binding has cartouches with gilt and stamped designs on the outside and cut filigree on the inner face of the binding (doublures), rendering this Qur'an truly exceptional.

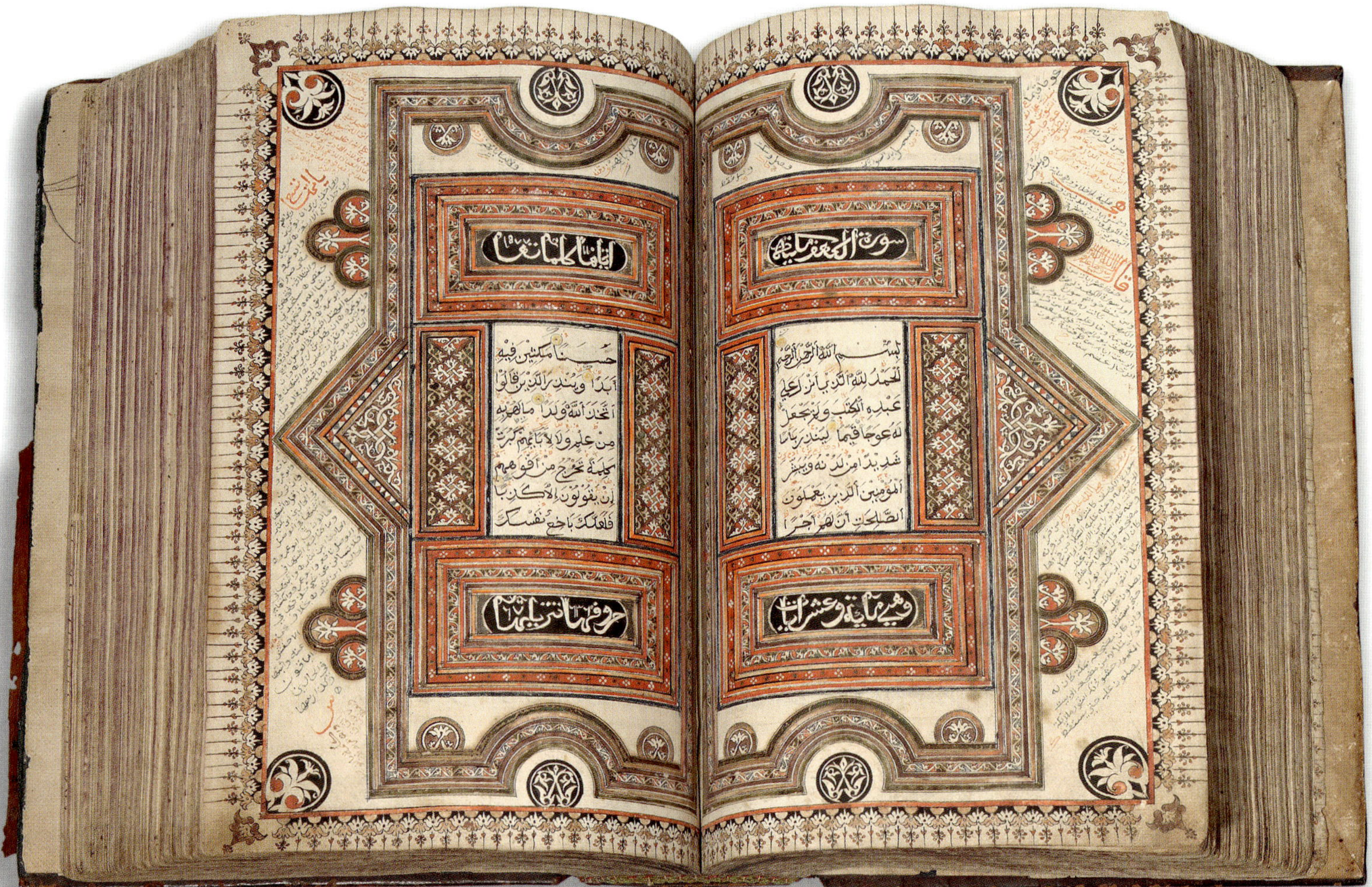

Qur'an
Copied by Isma'il b. 'Abdallah Makassar
Sulawesi Island, Indonesia, 1804
Ink, opaque watercolour, and gold on paper
Folio: 34.5 × 21.5 cm
(13⅝ × 8½ in.)
AKM488

This rare example of a complete and finely illuminated Qur'an from Sulawesi Island in Indonesia is a magnificent example of the localized artistic traditions in which Muslims chose to copy and decorate their sacred text. The Qur'an has three fully illuminated spreads with complex geometric illuminations in red, black, brown, ochre, and reserved white. What is most interesting here, though, is that in addition to the usual markers at the end of each verse, and the distinctive marker on every fifth verse, this Qur'an has marginal markers in a variety of circle and rosette forms to indicate other points of interest, including the middle of the Qur'an and the beginning of each *juz'*. It also includes an extensive amount of marginalia on recitation variances, grammar, and interpretation.

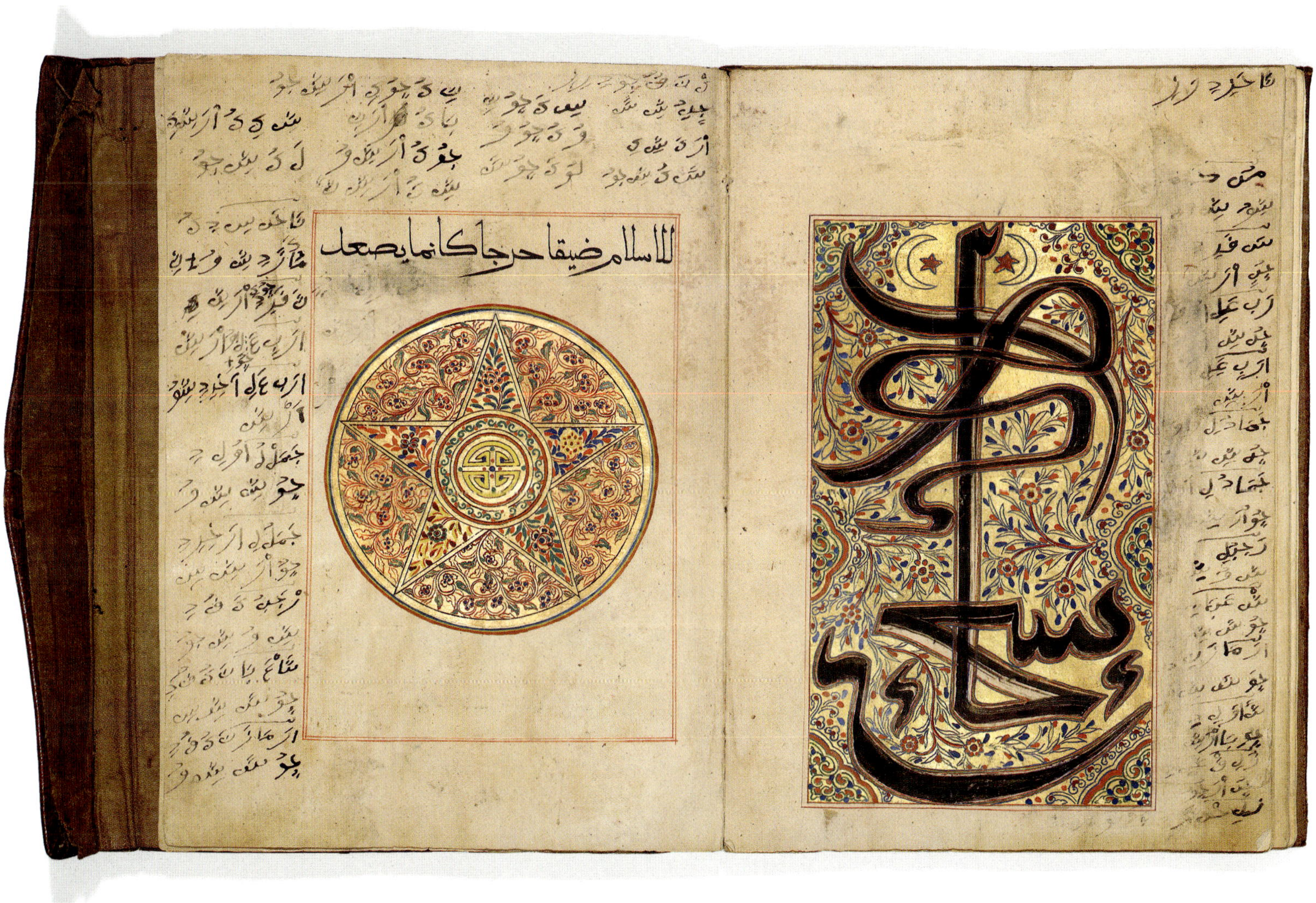

Qur'an Anthology
China, second half of 18th century
Ink, opaque watercolour, and gold on paper
Folio: 27.5 × 20 cm (10⅞ × 7⅞ in.)
AKM824

The fluid brushlike strokes of this calligraphic composition are written in the striking *sini* script developed in China by Muslim calligraphers. The folio on the right has the Qur'anic phrase *subhan Allah* ("glorious is God") set in a background floral spray. The sweeping letterforms and particularly thin uprights seem to derive from a monumental *thuluth* script that was clearly adapted to a Chinese visual aesthetic in its *sini* form. The manuscript contains a compilation of Qura'nic suras and illuminations, including the decorative roundel, on the left, with a Chinese symbol of good luck at its centre. Islam spread to China from the middle of the seventh century mainly through trade and diplomatic exchanges.

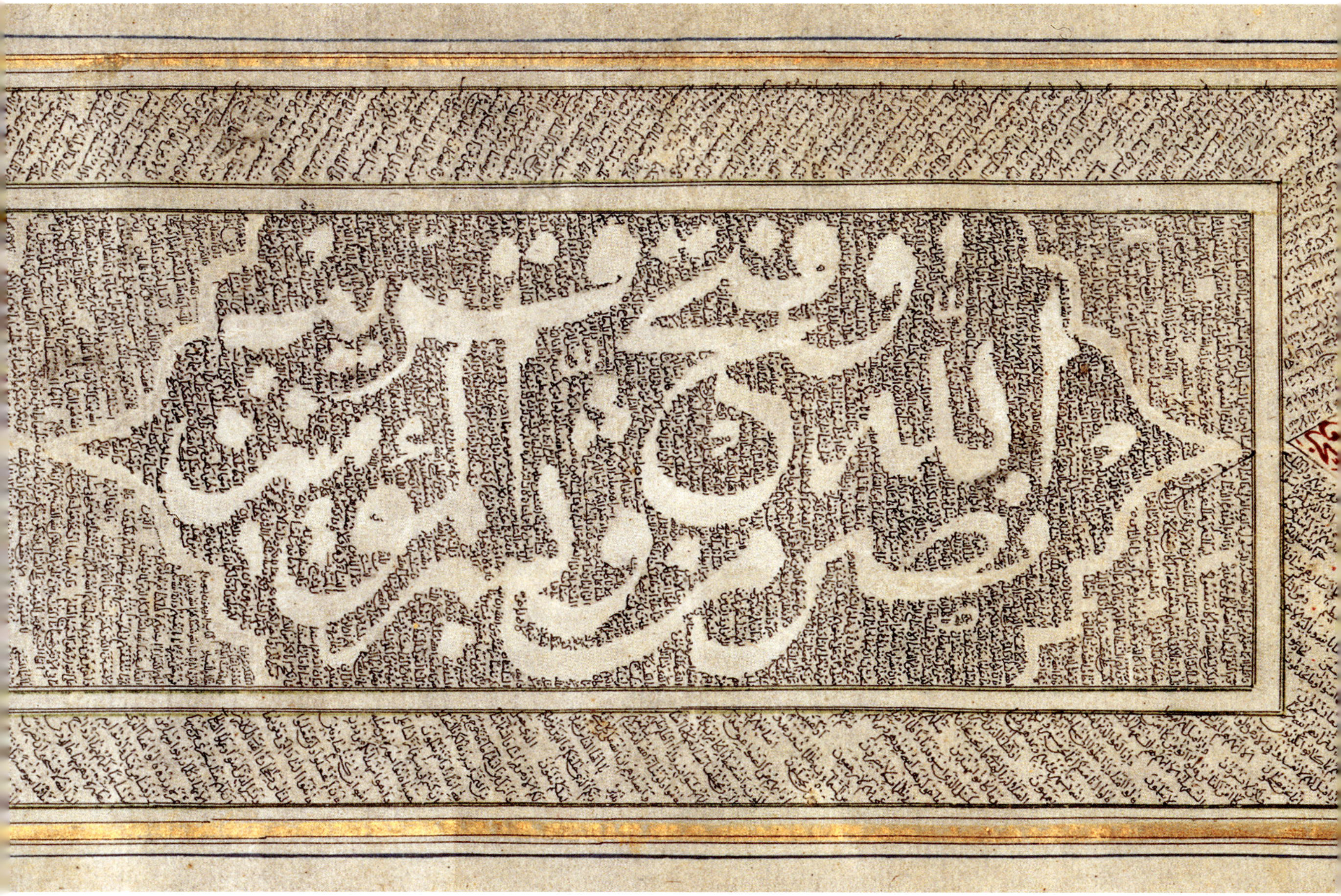

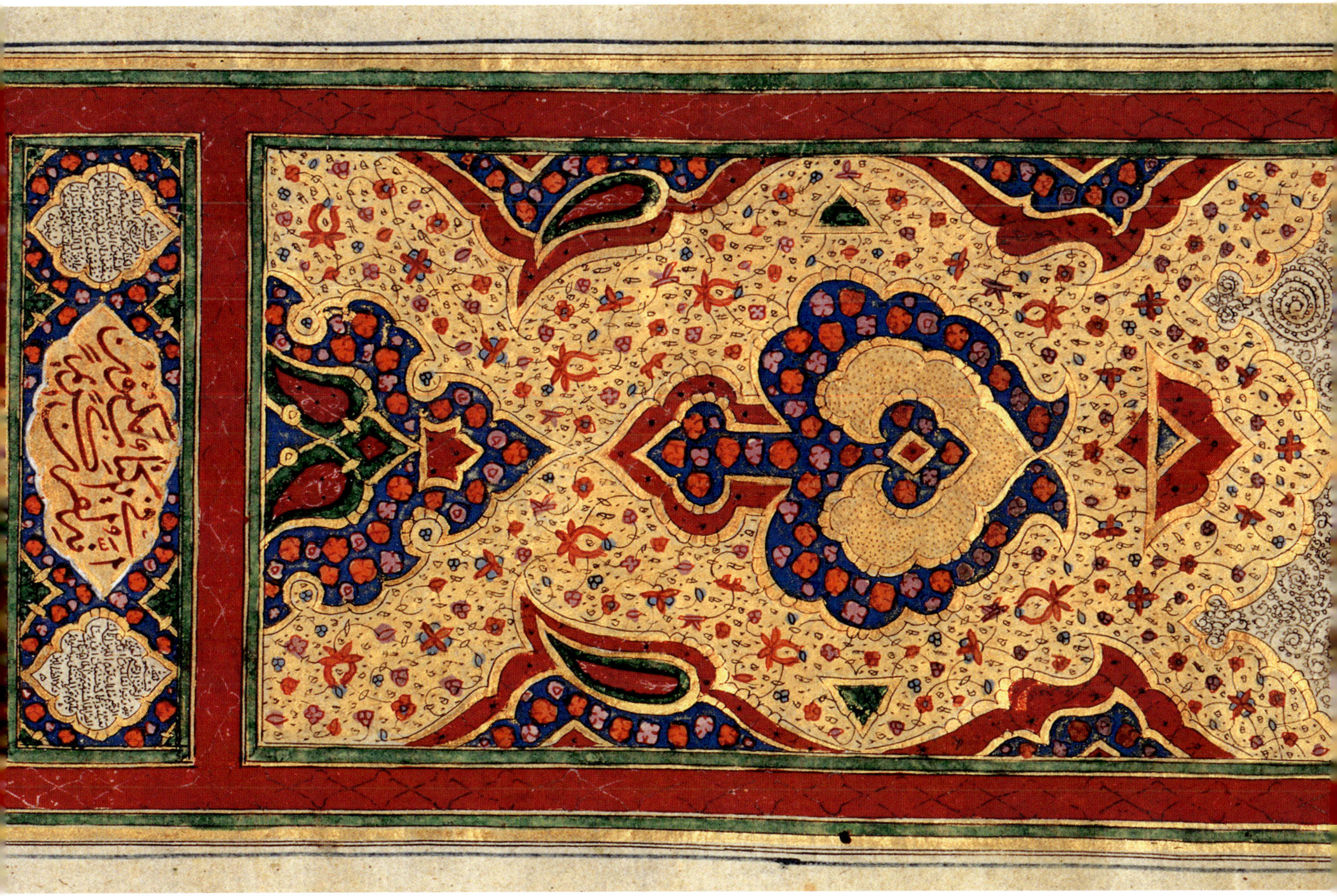

Qur'an Scroll
Copied by Zayn al-'Abidin Isfahani
Iran, 1847
Opaque watercolour, gold, and ink on paper
575 × 12.5 cm (226⅜ × 4⅞ in.)
AKM492

This magnificent Qur'an was copied in 1847 on a narrow paper scroll that is more than five metres (sixteen feet) long. The minute script employed here is known as *ghubar* (literally, "dust"). It is a miniature form of *naskh* that seems to have originally developed to transcribe messages transferred by carrier pigeons. Employing *ghubar*, in this case, provides the opportunity to copy the whole Qur'an in an easily portable form while creating a pleasing visual effect. The text is copied in a manner that leaves a pattern of cartouches in reverse, some forming Qur'anic verses in a larger script. An elaborate decorative panel, to the right, and a simple blue-and-gold outline, frame the whole composition.

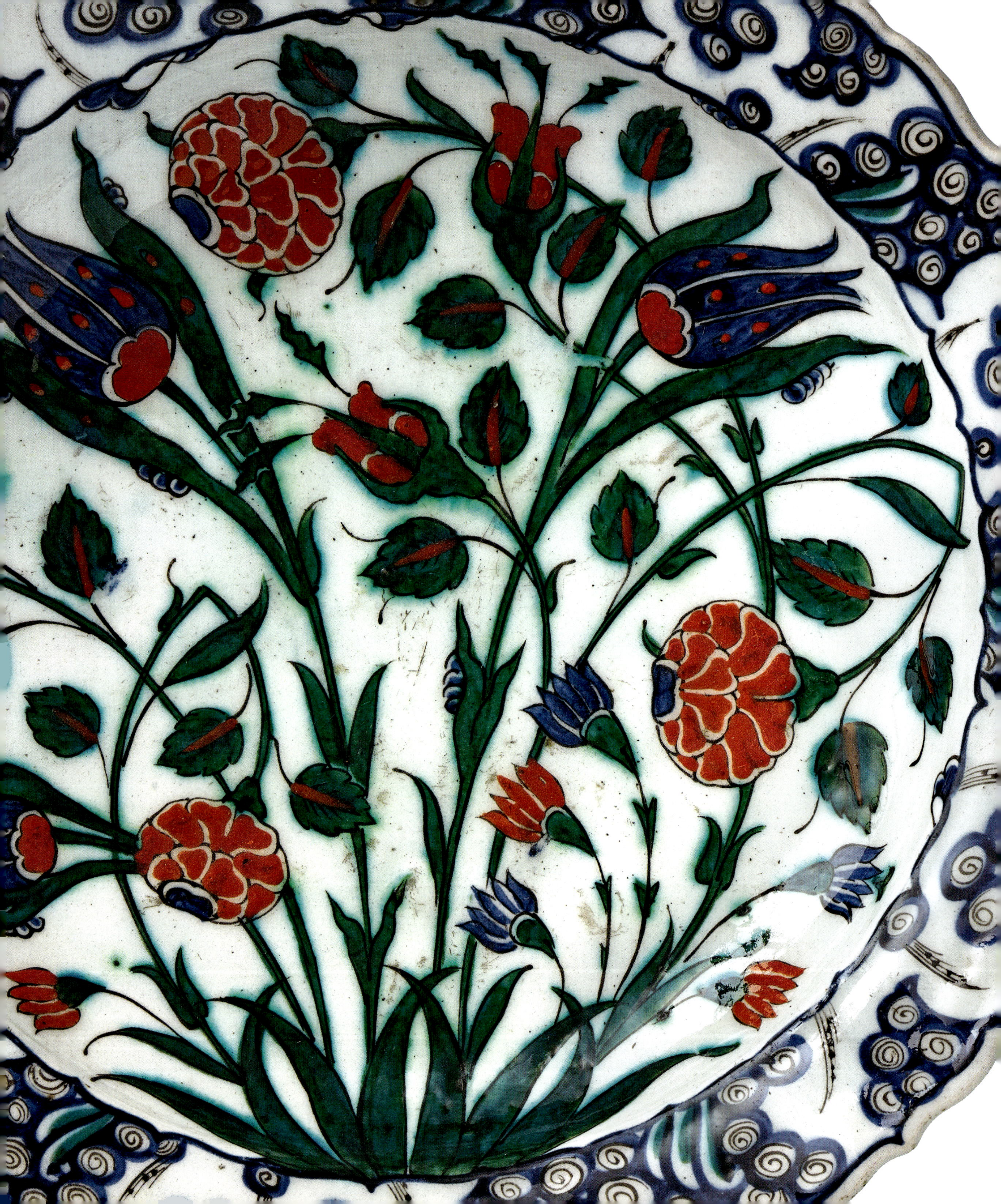

CERAMICS

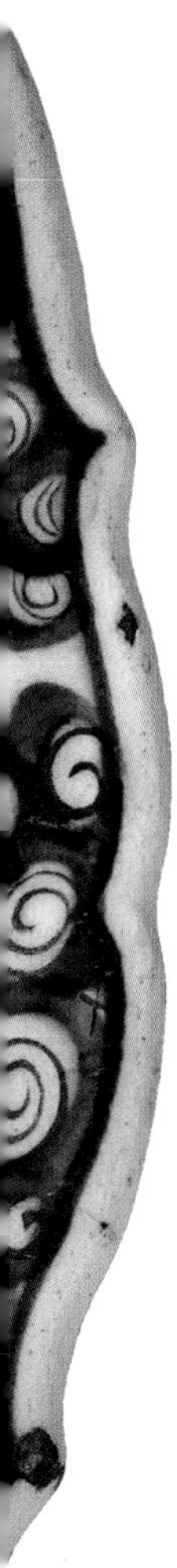

The thousand years of ceramic history represented here from the Aga Khan Museum collection demonstrates the creative efflorescence of Muslim artists and craftsmen and their ability to adapt to new styles and techniques. This selection purposefully illustrates the diversity of ceramics produced throughout the various regions of the Islamic world during different historical periods. The methods range from minimal calligraphy that stands boldly against a contrasting background (AKM546) to an assortment of figural styles (AKM557) and floral sprays (AKM687) depicted in various degrees of creative naturalism.

The development of glazing techniques rendered the body of the earthenware object impervious, but it was also a catalyst for human creativity. Whether clear or coloured (AKM562), transparent or opaque, these glazes opened up the possibilities of turning everyday ceramic objects into art canvases. In some cases, glaze formed a background for an elaborate decorative style that utilized minerals with a golden lustrous sheen (known as lustre ceramics) to create intricate compositions (AKM556 and 684). Clay itself was also used as part of the decorative process when thin layers of coloured clay, known as slip, were employed to create bold designs (AKM541) under clear glaze.

The production of a broader variety of ceramic forms and decorative styles from the eleventh century onward owed a large debt to the use of fritware (also known as stonepaste) as the chosen material for ceramic objects in Egypt, Syria, and Iran. Fritware was suitable for a number of creative opportunities such as the application of moulds for objects with complex forms. Its whitish colour and dense body allowed for intricate renditions of images and inscriptions on these ceramics reflecting the refined literary sensibility of patrons (AKM557).

Both pottery makers and their patrons responded to evolutions in style that were either reactions to local changes in tastes and trade patterns or the result of new imported fashions and motifs. The trade and diplomatic relations between China and the Muslim world, for example, had a major impact on the ceramic industry. Since the white clay (kaolin) of Chinese porcelain with its compact body and translucency was not available in Muslim centres of ceramic production, potters adapted the Chinese technique to create a whitish layer on their earthenware that emulated the visual effect of porcelain, then used this background as a canvas for their own designs (AKM546). Later encounters with Chinese imports led to the introduction of new motifs (AKM786) and new designs (AKM588).

Detail of Dish (see page 85)
Iznik, Turkey, 1570–80
Fritware, underglaze-painted
Diameter 34.3 cm (13½ in.), height 7.4 cm (2⅞ in.)
AKM687

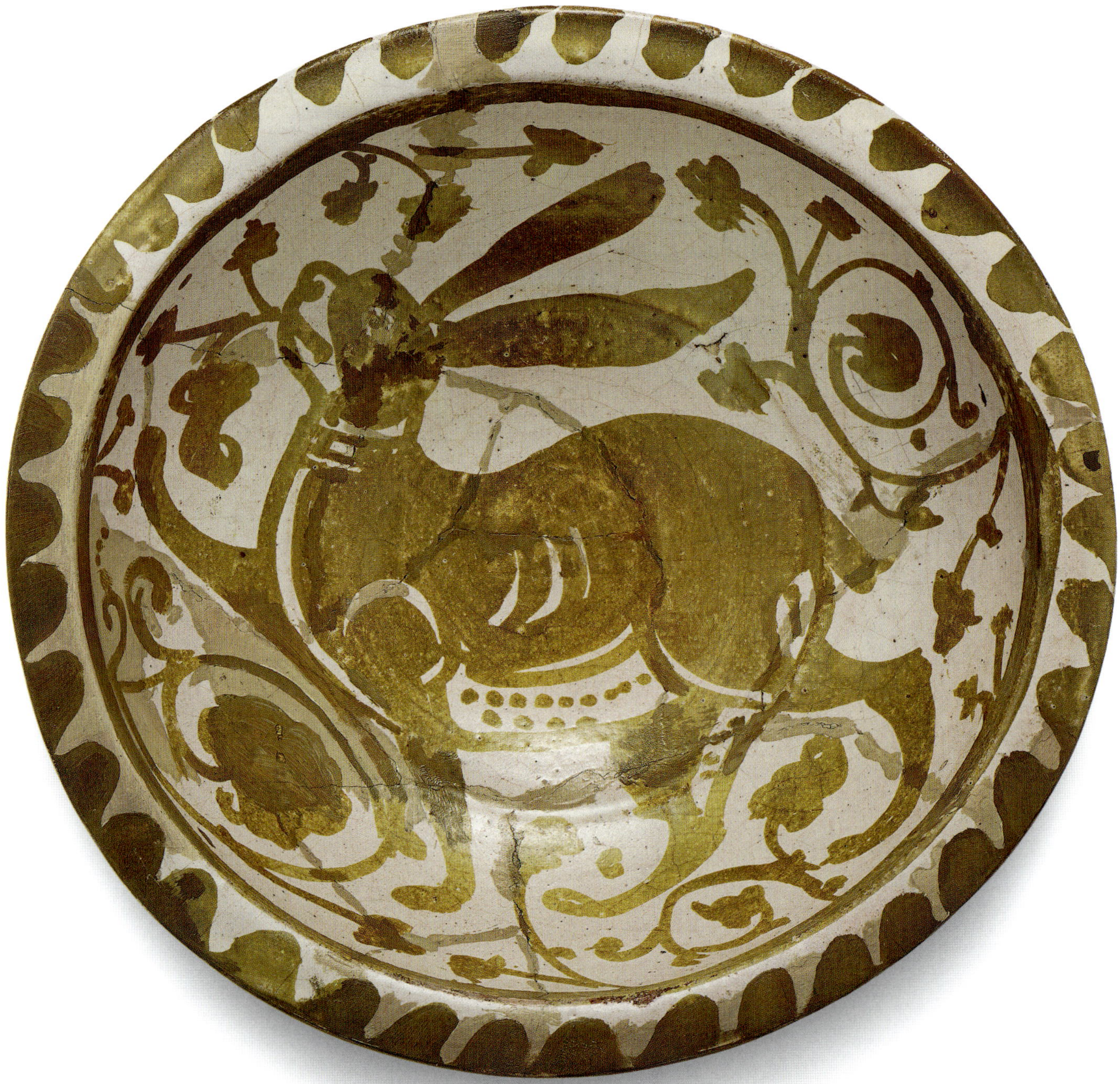

Bowl
Egypt, 11th century
Fritware, lustre-painted
Diameter 19.4 cm (7⅝ in.),
height 6.6 cm (2⅝ in.)
AKM684

By the tenth century, the Fatimid capital of Cairo became the centre of production for ceramics that were decorated in a metallic paint that had a golden lustrous sheen (known as lustre ceramics). The striking visual compositions on these ceramics portray men and women, animals, and acrobats painted in fluid lines and lively naturalism. The jovial long-eared hare in the centre of this bowl is one of the many animals that appear on textiles, wood, ivory, and ceramics from the Fatimid period. The everyday nature of the depicted scenes and the golden tone of the lustre sheen set them apart from the earlier lustre ceramics in Iraq and later examples from Iran, both of which are represented in this selection from the Aga Khan Museum's collection. This type of Fatimid lustre bowl was highly appreciated as an export product throughout the Mediterranean, and several bowls can still be seen decorating the exterior walls of churches in Pisa, Italy, from the late eleventh and early twelfth centuries.

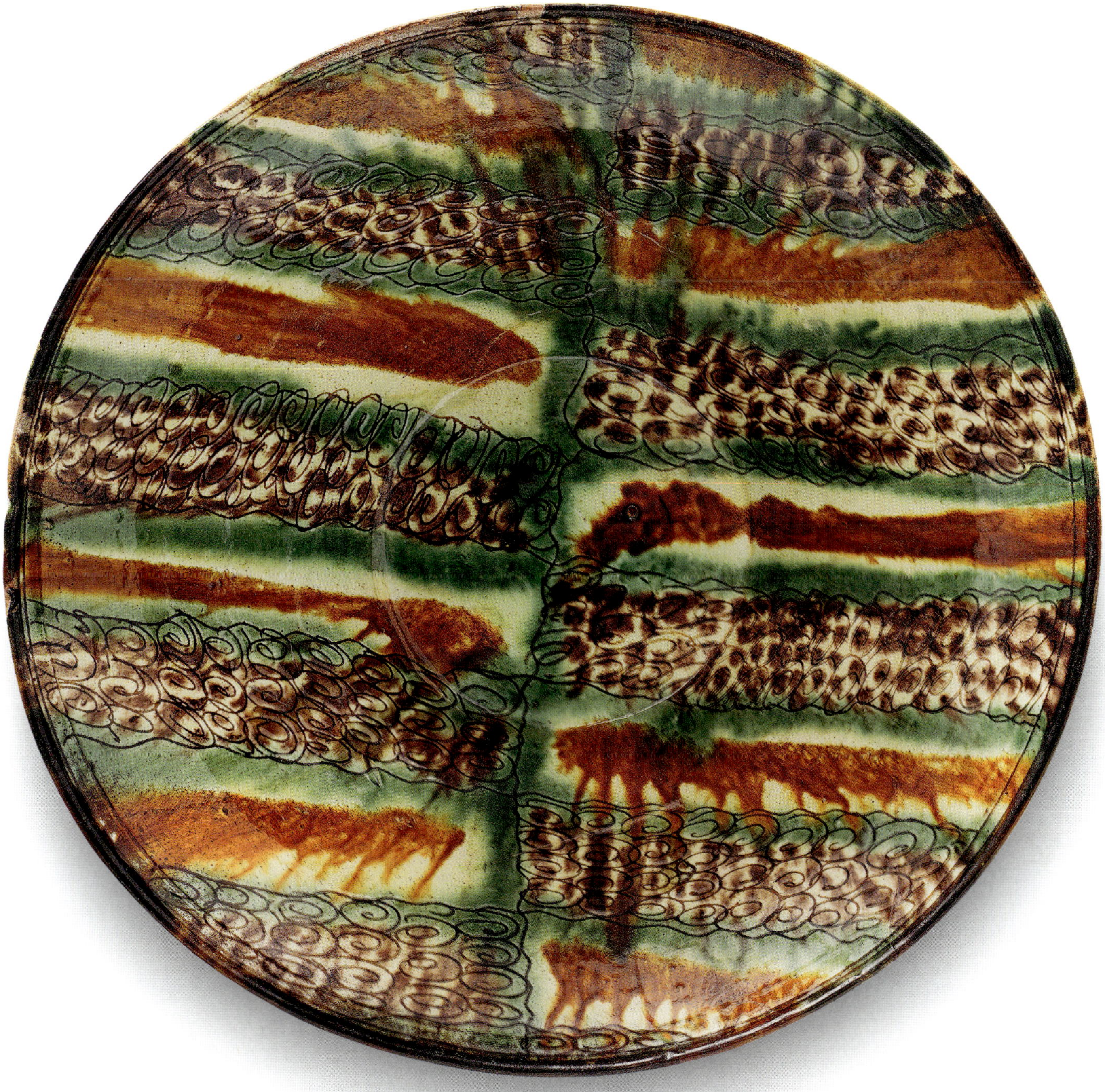

Dish

Neyshabur, Iran, 10th century
Earthenware, underglaze slip-painted
Diameter 35.6 cm (14 in.), height 12.7 cm (5 in.)
AKM740

This exceptional dish with its broad splashes of ochre, green, and brown glazes over a white background with an incised pattern is as pleasing to the eye as it is probing to the intellect. The similarity of its splashing effect and colours to the splash-painted wares (*san-ts'ai*) of the Tang dynasty (618–907) led to the assumption that this style was directly influenced by imports from China into the Abbasid realms of Iraq and Iran. Indeed, there is ample evidence that during the ninth century, potters in Abbasid Iraq tried to emulate the forms and visual effect of imported Chinese porcelain, which led them instead to use tin glaze to create a white background on earthenware. The Chinese splash-painted ceramics, however, were mainly developed as figurines and tomb goods and were not utilized in daily life. There is also no evidence they were ever exported to Iran where this intriguing dish was made. Could this be a case of exchange of ideas for which we have lost the evidence, or could it be the result of simultaneous development in design and glazing techniques?

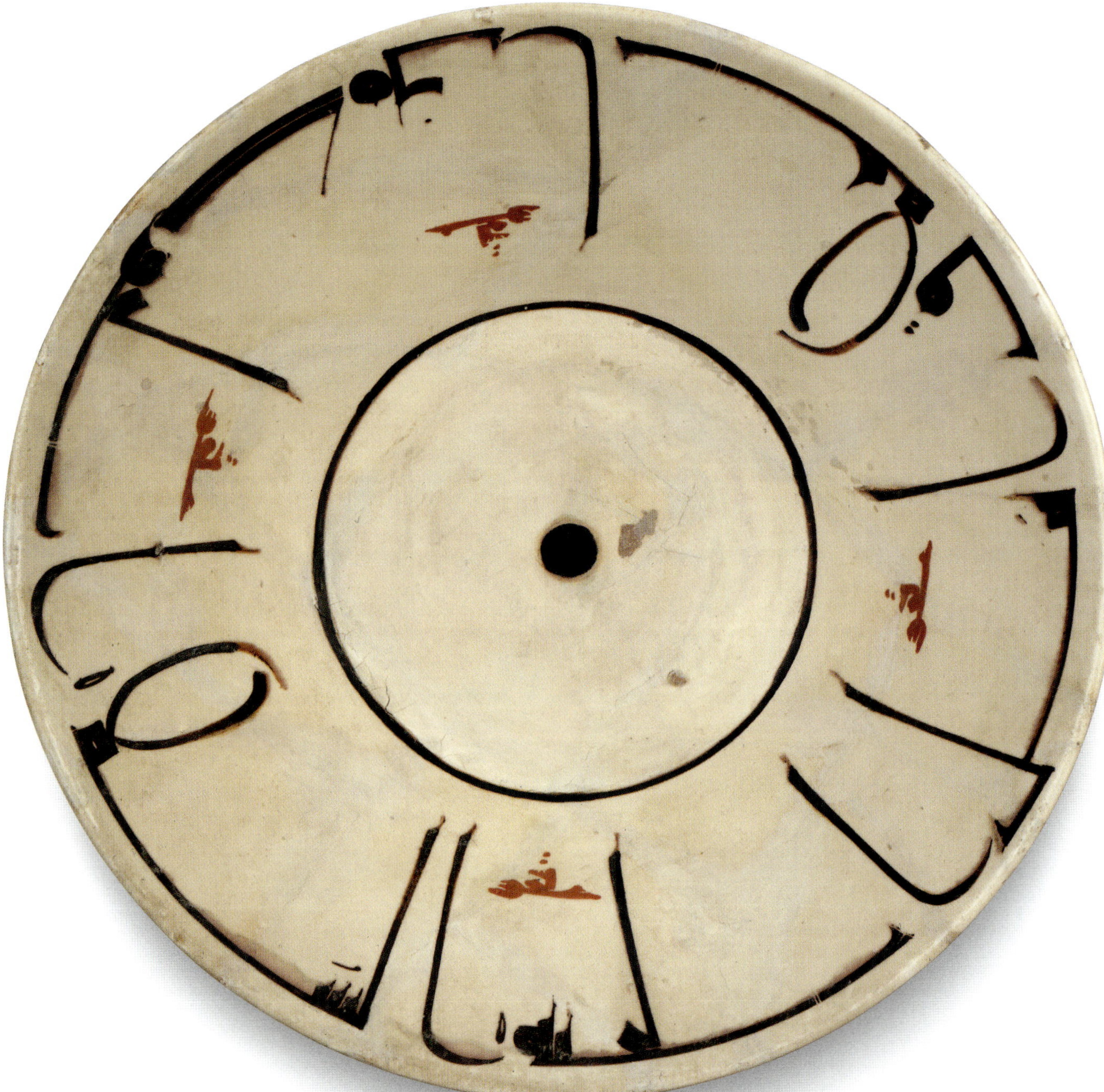

Dish
Iran or Central Asia, 10th century
Earthenware, underglaze slip-painted
Diameter 34.9 cm (13¾ in.)
AKM546

The graceful design on this dish displays two aspects of the arts of Iran and Central Asia in the historical context of the tenth century: the prominence of literature and artistic creativity. The survival of objects, such as this dish, that are decorated with poetic and literary inscriptions both in Persian and Arabic coincided with the blossoming of Persian literature in Iran and Central Asia, including the works of great poets such as Rudaki (died 940) and Ferdowsi (died 1020). The aphorism, inscribed here in Arabic, reminds the viewer that "Generosity is the disposition of the dwellers of Paradise." This style of calligraphic pottery decorated with blessings, quotations from Hadith, and general aphorisms represents a most creative use of design and techniques. The placement of the inscription with its elongated letters on the sides or cavettos of the pottery and the striking contrast between the inscription and the background provide a pleasing rhythm and balance to the decorative composition. Both the white background and the black and red colours are layers of thin clay that were used to paint the composition under a layer of transparent glaze.

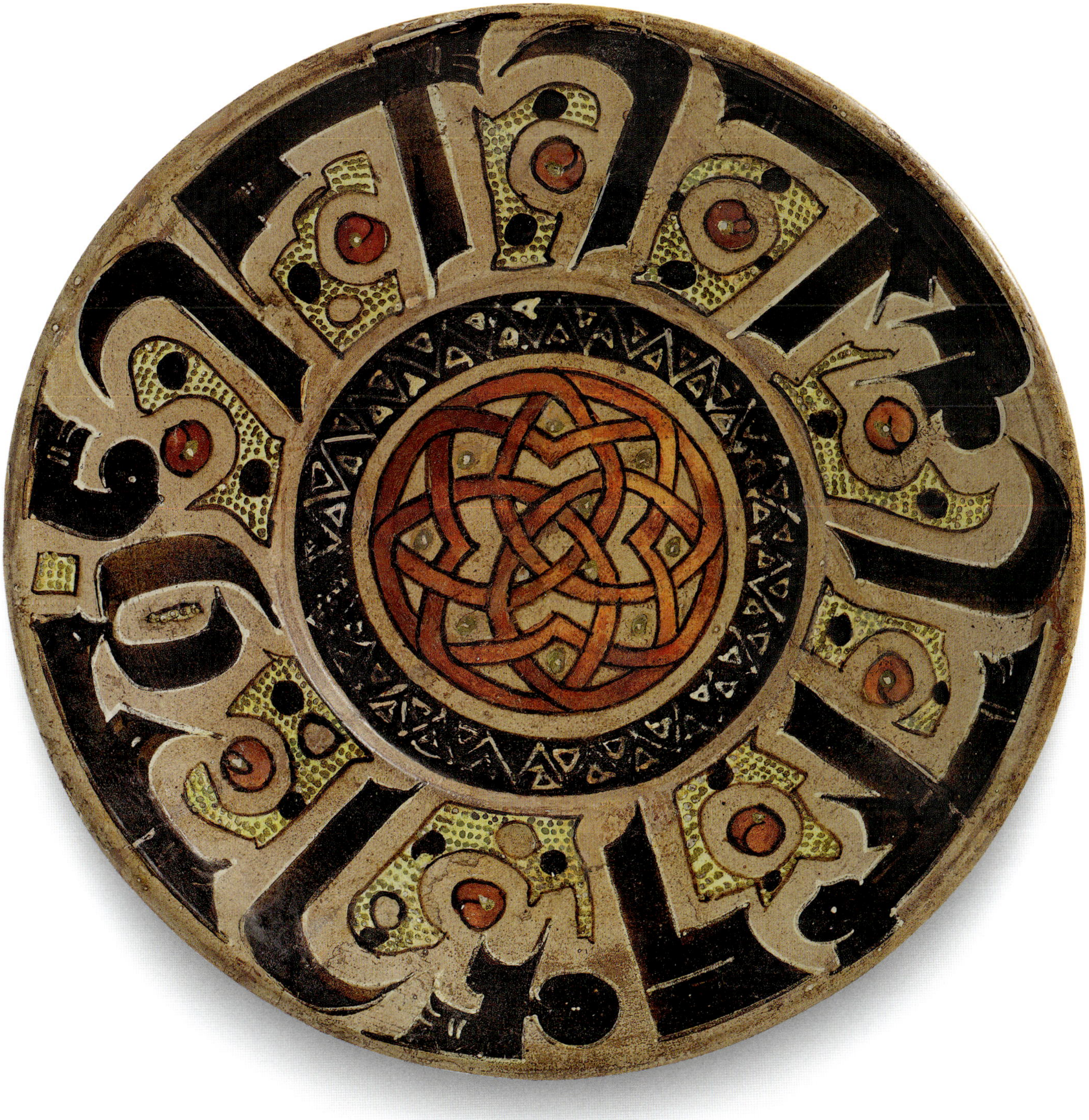

Dish
Northeast Iran, 10th century
Earthenware, underglaze slip-painted
Diameter 32.8 cm (12⅞ in.)
AKM541

Similar to the aphorism on AKM546, the one decorating the rim of this dish also reads "Generosity is the disposition of the dwellers of Paradise." Also comparable is the method in which the dish is made and decorated with thin layers of coloured clay. But here the similarities end. The calligraphic composition on this dish is painted on a coloured background in a broad brush and fluid lines, and the space between the letters is filled with circles and abstract forms. The most significant aspect of this dish, however, is the sophisticated interlace at the centre of the dish with interweaving strapwork in the form of an eight-pointed star. This motif is the inspiration for the Aga Khan Museum logo.

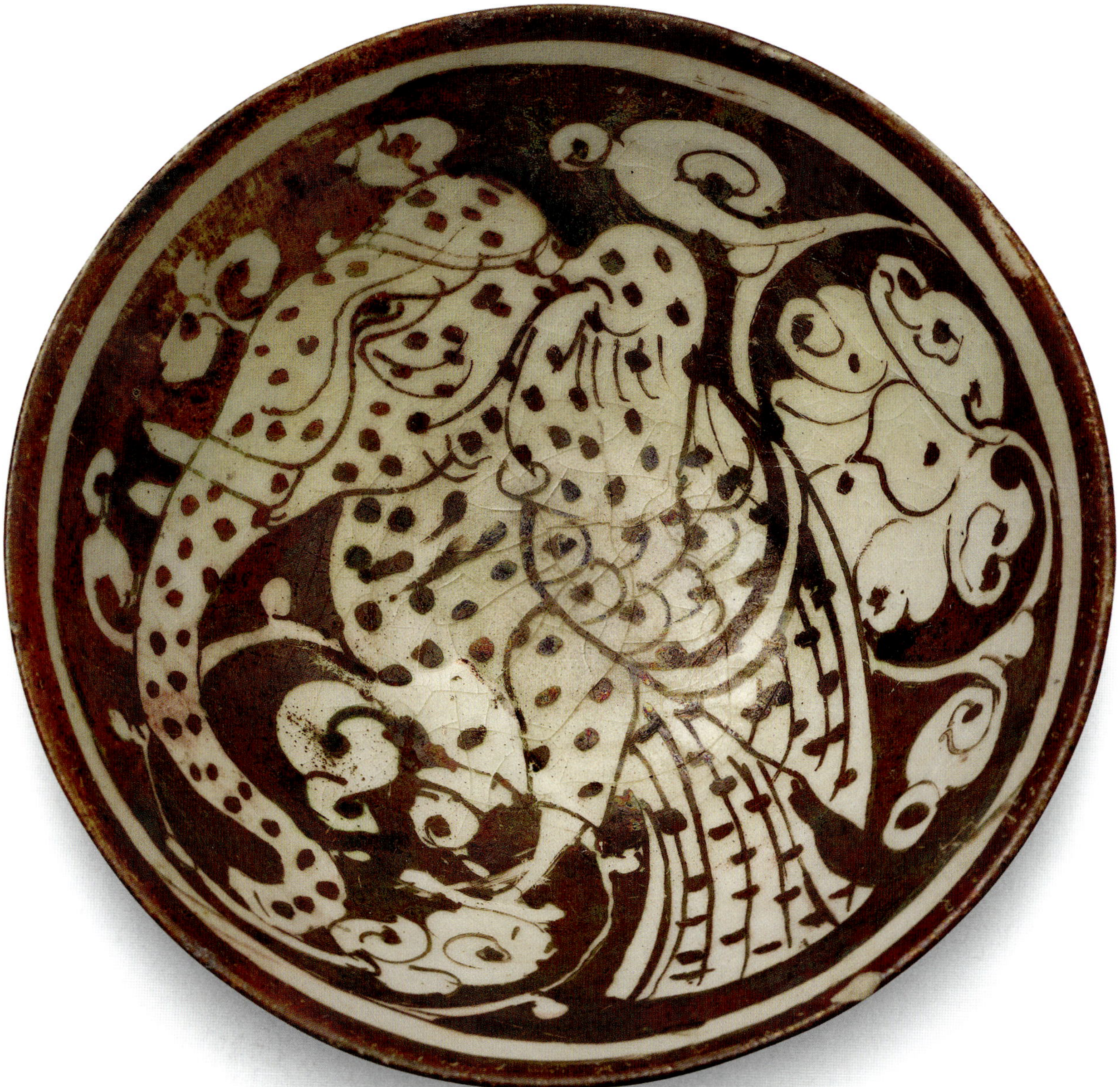

Bowl
Iran, 13th century
Fritware, lustre-painted
Diameter 15.2 cm (6 in.)
AKM556

While the depiction of mythical creatures is common throughout Islamic civilizations, the elephant-bird image on this bowl is quite unique. This creature has the head of an elephant with a piercing look and flapping ears, and the body of a large bird with wings and talons perched on a vine scroll filling the bowl's background. While clearly mythical, it is possible that this depiction is inspired by oral narrations of a roster of mythical birds, including the *simorgh* of Attar's *Conference of the Birds* (twelfth century) and Ferdowsi's *Shah-Nameh* (994–1010), the roc (*rukh*) of *One Thousand and One Nights* (eighth to ninth centuries), and the bird carrying off an elephant from the Sanskrit *Mahabarata* (fourth century BCE) and *Ramayana* (fifth to fourth centuries BCE). It could have also been inspired by the now-extinct species of a giant flightless elephant bird native to Madagascar. This beautifully drawn image provides evidence of the craftsman's creative imagination and the folk traditions of the diverse cultures of the region.

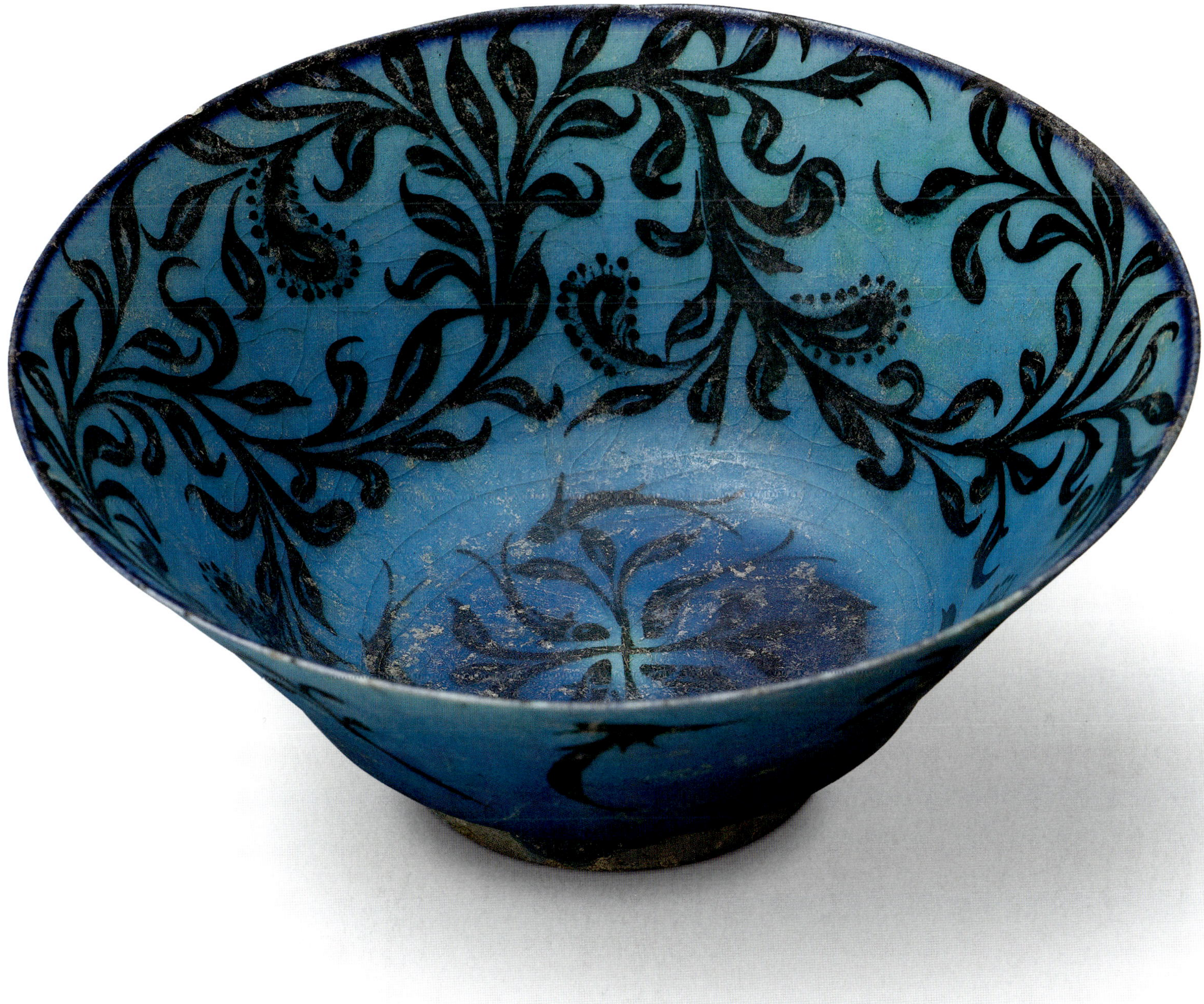

Bowl

Iran, early 13th century
Fritware, underglaze-painted
Diameter 21.9 cm (8⅝ in.), height 10 cm (4 in.)
AKM562

The development of a fritware ceramic (also known as stonepaste) in eleventh-century Iran revolutionized ceramic production, since it presented the opportunity to create a thinly potted white body that could easily be shaped and decorated. The new fritware ceramics could also be moulded into complex objects such as this conical bowl with its straight walls that are more suited to metalwork production. An early medieval recipe left by Abu'l-Qasem Kashani, a member of a family of potters, informs us that fritware is made out of ten parts ground quartz, one part ground glass, and one part fine white clay. The white body of this bowl is a perfect background for the combination of black-painted decoration and transparent turquoise glaze. The undulating stems of the water-weed motif on the sides of the bowl surround a school of fish painted in a thin brush, allowing for finer lines and elaborate flourishes.

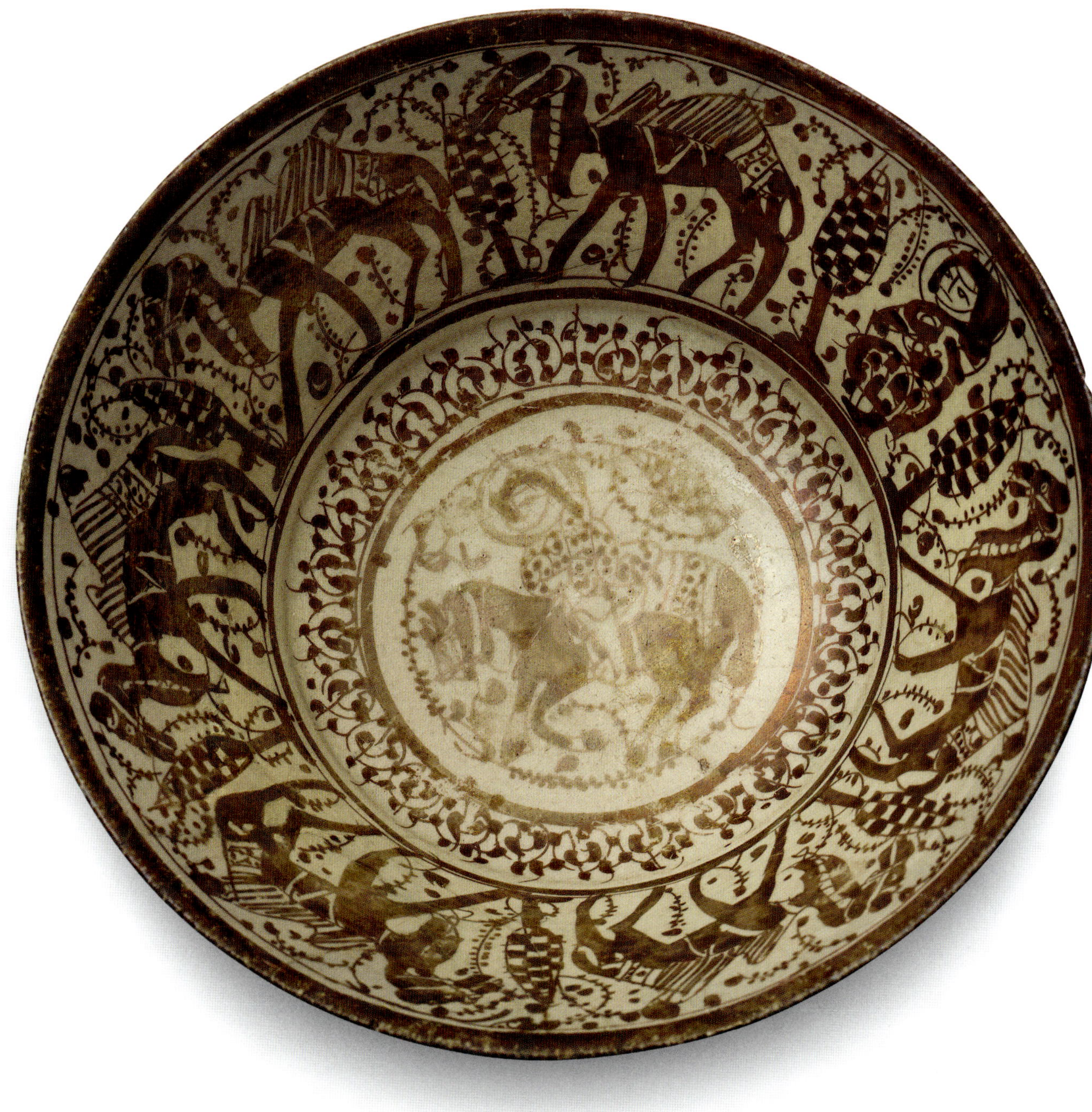

Bowl

Iran, 13th century
Fritware, lustre-painted
Diameter 17 cm (6¾ in.), height 8 cm (3⅛ in.)
AKM557

The mounted horseman — whether prince, hero, or warrior — remains one of the most common visual motifs in works of Islamic art. Here, the figure of a horseman is depicted at the centre of a conical bowl surrounded by a superb depiction of a merchant caravan. The sides of the bowl are decorated with six camels laden with bags led by an attendant. The artist has given the caravan a lively sense of animation, with the camels stepping forward to provide a feeling of motion that suits the circular nature of the vessel. The figures are rendered in metallic enamel paint that offers a golden lustrous sheen against the white background. Trees with a checkerboard pattern and branches with small leaves complete the landscape setting for the caravan. This style of fine depiction on thinly potted fritware ceramics was common in Kashan, Iran, in the late twelfth and early thirteenth centuries. There are many surviving examples, including a similar bowl in the Aga Khan Museum's collection, where the central mounted figure is encircled by horses instead of the camel caravan.

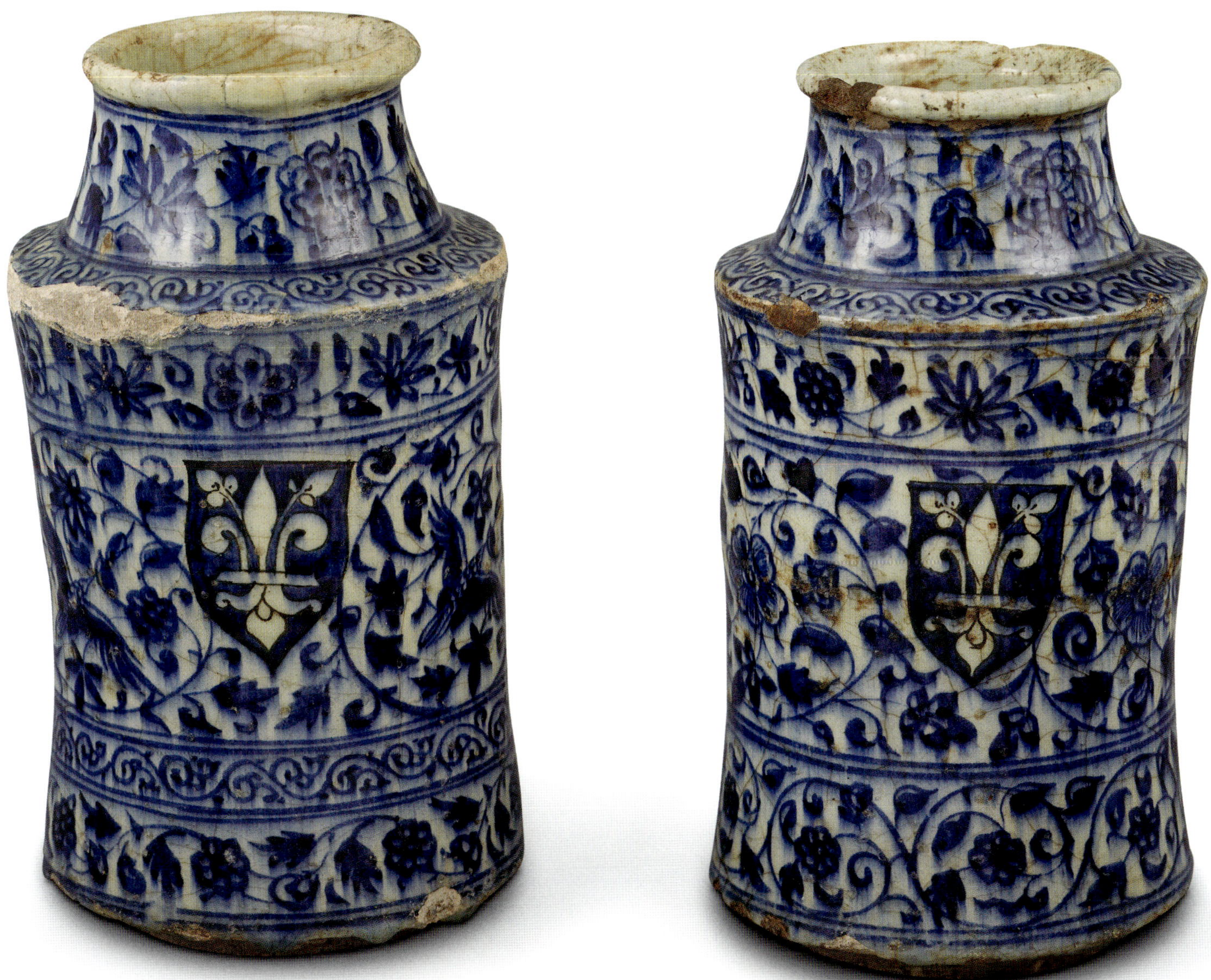

Pharmacy Jars (*Albarelli*)
Syria, 15th century
Fritware, underglaze-painted
AKM567: diameter 49.4 cm (19½ in.), height 32 cm (12⅝ in.)
AKM568: diameter 49.4 cm (19½ in.), height 30.7 cm (12⅛ in.)

Ceramic vessels were historically traded for their aesthetic value or as containers of valuable cargo. These two pharmaceutical jars, known as *albarelli*, are among a group of four magnificent examples from the Aga Khan Museum's collection, ranging in date between the thirteenth and fifteenth centuries and used for trading valuable pharmaceutical substances. Collectively, they highlight the active trade between the Mamluks (1250–1517) and Italian city-states such as Venice and Florence. This unique pair of *albarelli* is typical of the form, style, and design of ceramics made in Syria and Egypt in the fifteenth century, with the decorative motifs organized in clearly defined registers of intricate foliage painted in cobalt blue under a clear glaze. The fleur-de-lys heraldic shield in the central band of each of the *albarelli* is most probably the coat of arms of Florence associated with the merchants who commissioned the precious cargo held in them or the city in which the lucrative trade was based (see also page 18).

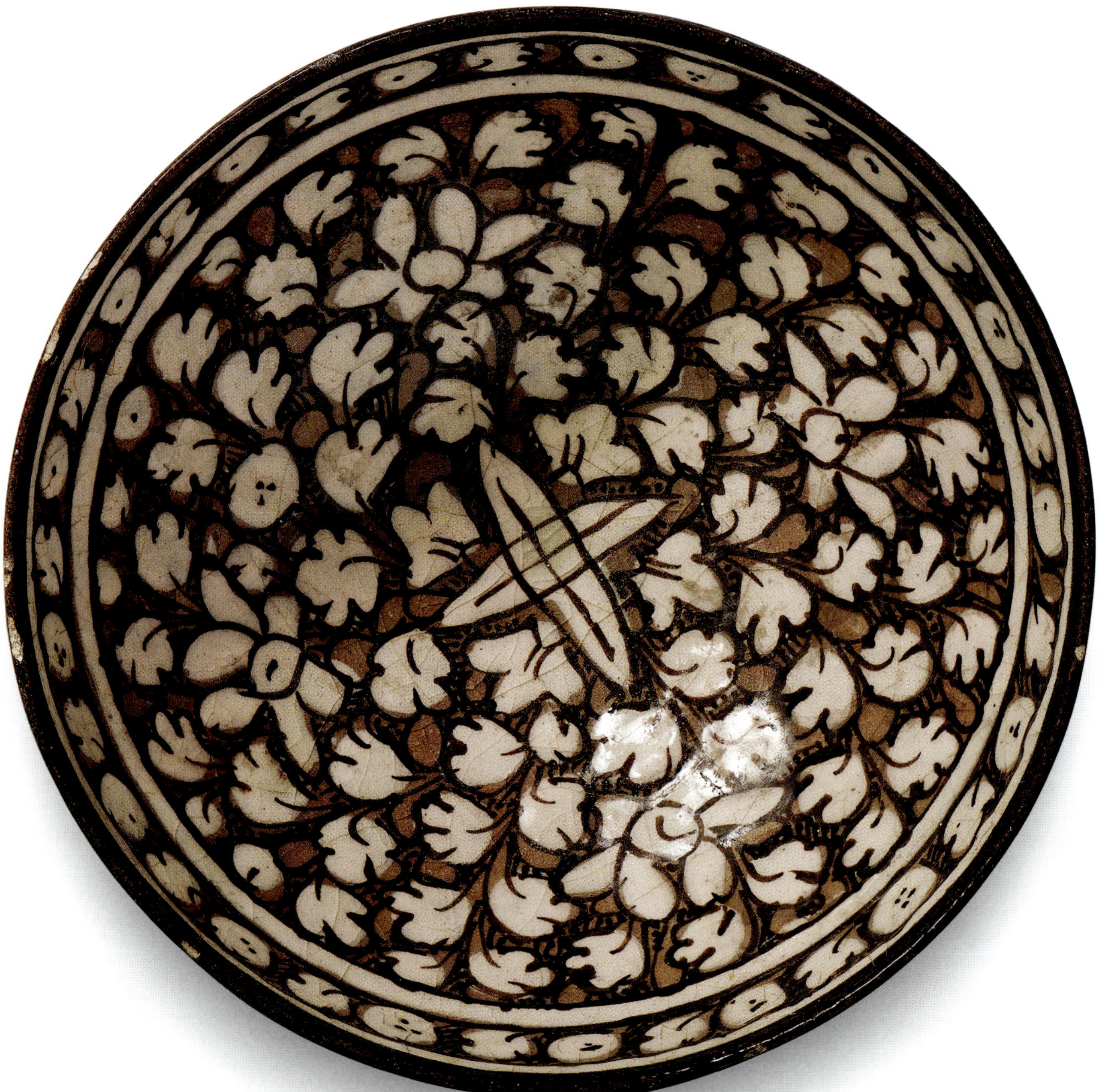

Bowl

Iran, early 14th century
Fritware, underglaze slip-painted
Diameter 17.8 cm (7 in.),
height 8.3 cm (3¼ in.)
AKM786

Textiles that were traded along the Silk Route were the most common way in which ideas and decorative motifs such as lotuses, dragons, and sphinxes were transferred between China and Iran. With the Mongol conquests of the thirteenth century, and the conversion of the Mongol Ilkhanid dynasty to Islam, Iranian potters began using these imported motifs in their designs. Here, the bowl is decorated with a mass of leaves surrounding lotus flowers. The bowl draws its influence from green-glazed stoneware known as celadon that was imported from China during the fourteenth century. The painted arcade panelling on the exterior of the bowl is a local rendition of the moulded form of the Chinese origin. This bowl, along with several other exquisite examples in the Aga Khan Museum's collection, is attributed to the city of Sultanabad in western Iran.

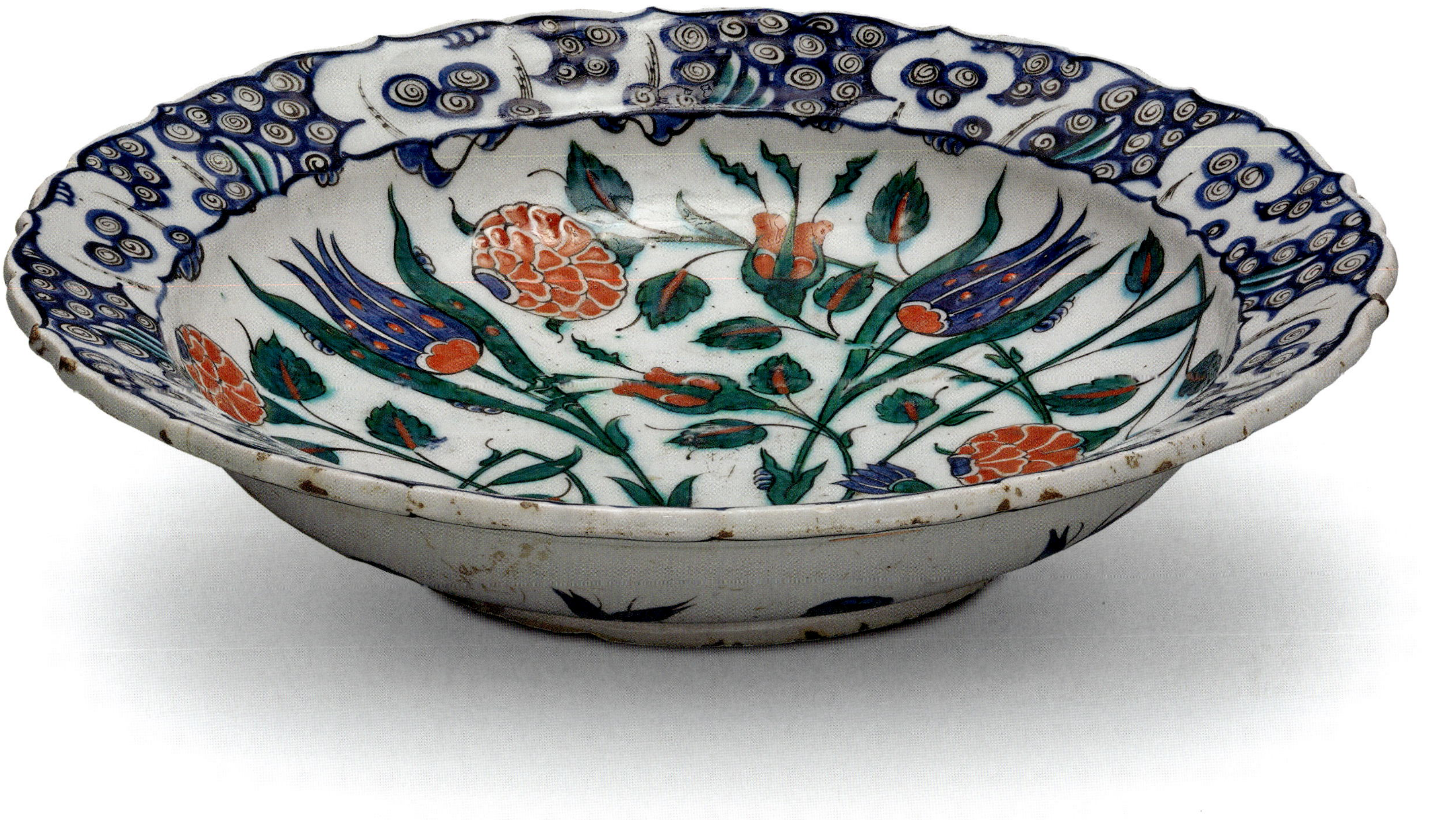

Dish

Iznik, Turkey, 1570–80
Fritware, underglaze-painted
Diameter 34.3 cm (13½ in.),
height 7.4 cm (2⅞ in.)
AKM687

During the first half of the sixteenth century, artists of the royal design atelier of the Ottoman court developed a new decorative style characterized by its bright colours and naturalistic depiction of flowers. The floral composition on this dish with its tulips, carnations, and roses in red and blue on a white background is typical of the production of the Ottoman imperial kilns in the city of Iznik. Similar patterns of floral designs were used on textiles, carpets, book illuminations, and tiles, including some splendid examples in the Aga Khan Museum's collection. The consistency of the Ottoman floral style helped establish a distinctive and singular visual brand for the Ottoman Empire and its arts. It is during this period that tulips caught Europe's attention when they were first introduced there by Ogier Ghiselin de Busbecq, the Austrian ambassador to the Ottoman court (see also page 47).

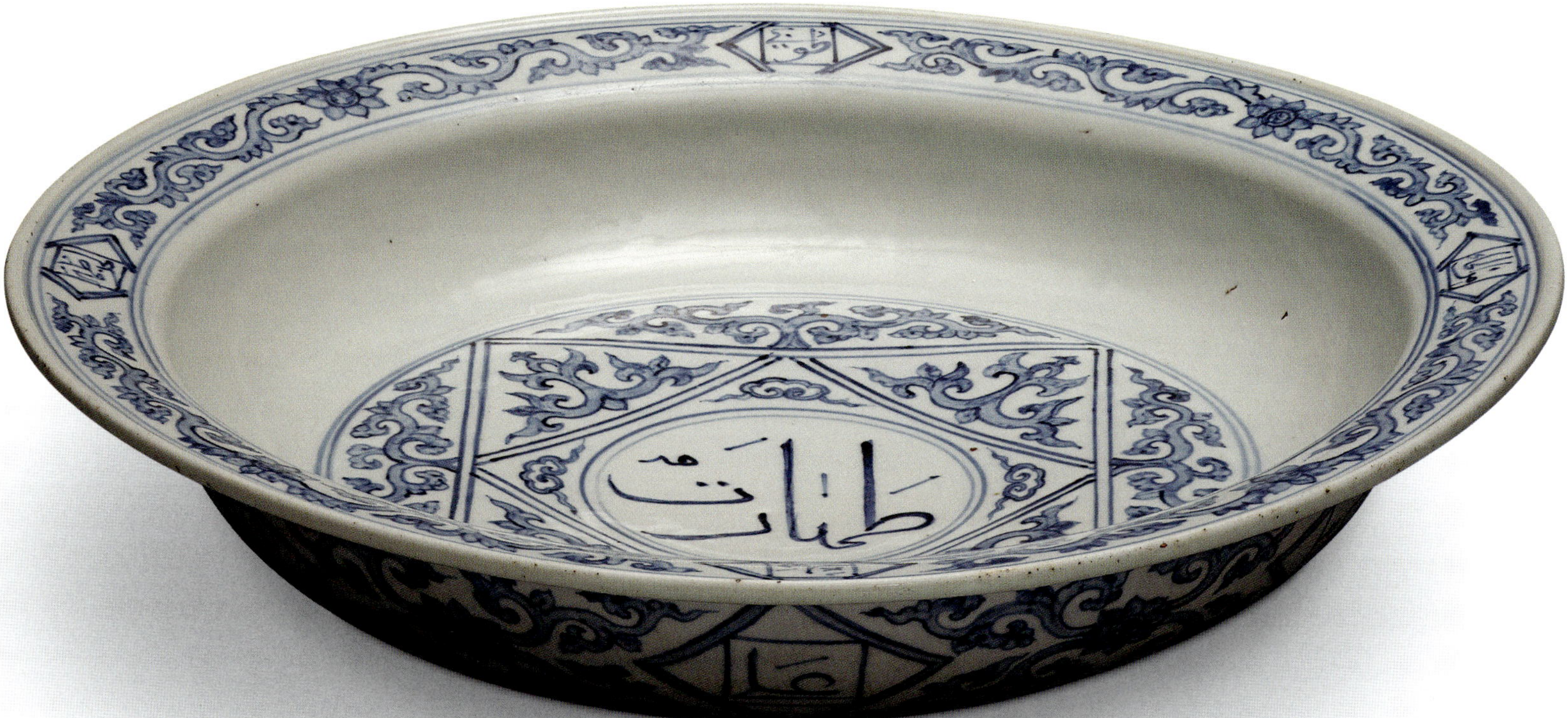

Ablution Basin

Jingdezhen, China, 1506–21
Porcelain, underglaze-painted
Diameter 41.8 cm (16½ in.),
height 7.5 cm (3 in.)
AKM722

The multiple examples of sixteenth-century Chinese porcelain with Arabic inscriptions are testimony to the presence of an established Muslim community in China during that period, as well as the close and continuous contact between China and the Muslim world. This large dish (see also page 47) was made in the porcelain kilns of the province of Jingdezhen in China for a Muslim patron, most probably a member of the close circle of Emperor Zhengde (reigned 1505–21) whose mark can be seen on the back of the dish. The word *taharat* ("purity") is inscribed in Arabic in the central medallion of the dish, implying that it was meant for use in ablution, a basic requirement of Muslim prayer. The Chinese-style floral meander on the rim of the dish and its back frames several inscriptions that further evoke the concept of ritual purity and specifically mention ablution (*al-wudu'*).

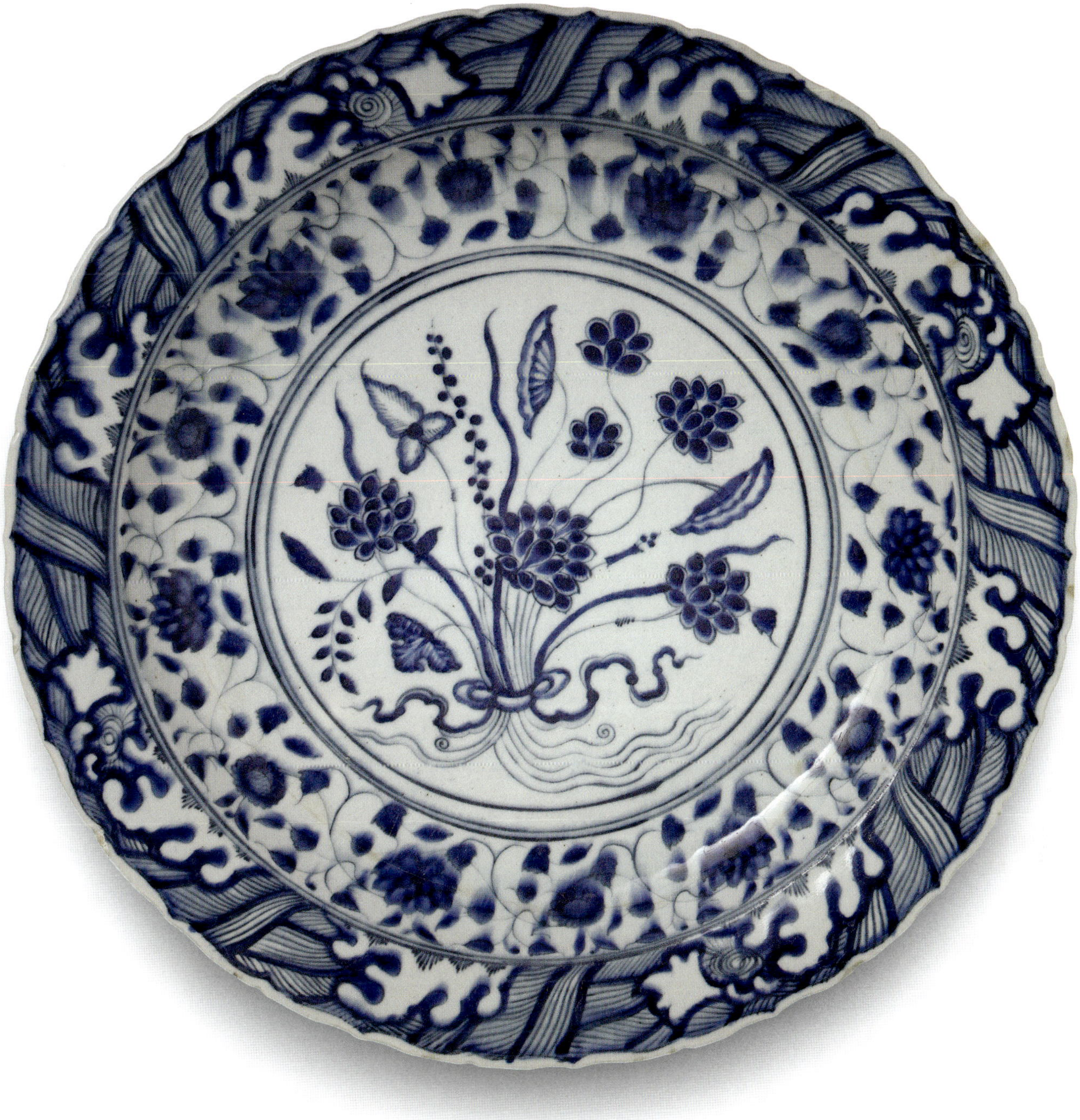

Dish

Iran, 17th century
Fritware, underglaze-painted
Diameter 46.6 cm (18⅜ in.)
AKM588

The bouquet of blossoming lotus stems tied with a cloud-band ribbon at the centre of this large dish, the floral spray that surrounds it, and the wave pattern on its foliated rim are faithful copies of fifteenth-century motifs popular on Chinese porcelain in the Ming dynasty (1368–1644) almost two centuries before its manufacture. In the Safavid period (1501–1722), Chinese Ming porcelains were highly coveted for their beauty and translucency, and many were given as gifts to shrines, including the one in Ardabil dedicated to Sheykh Safi al-Din, after whom the Safavid dynasty was named. Iranian potters developed this style of blue-and-white ceramic employing a dense white fritware body and cobalt blue painting under a transparent glaze to evoke these superb gifts.

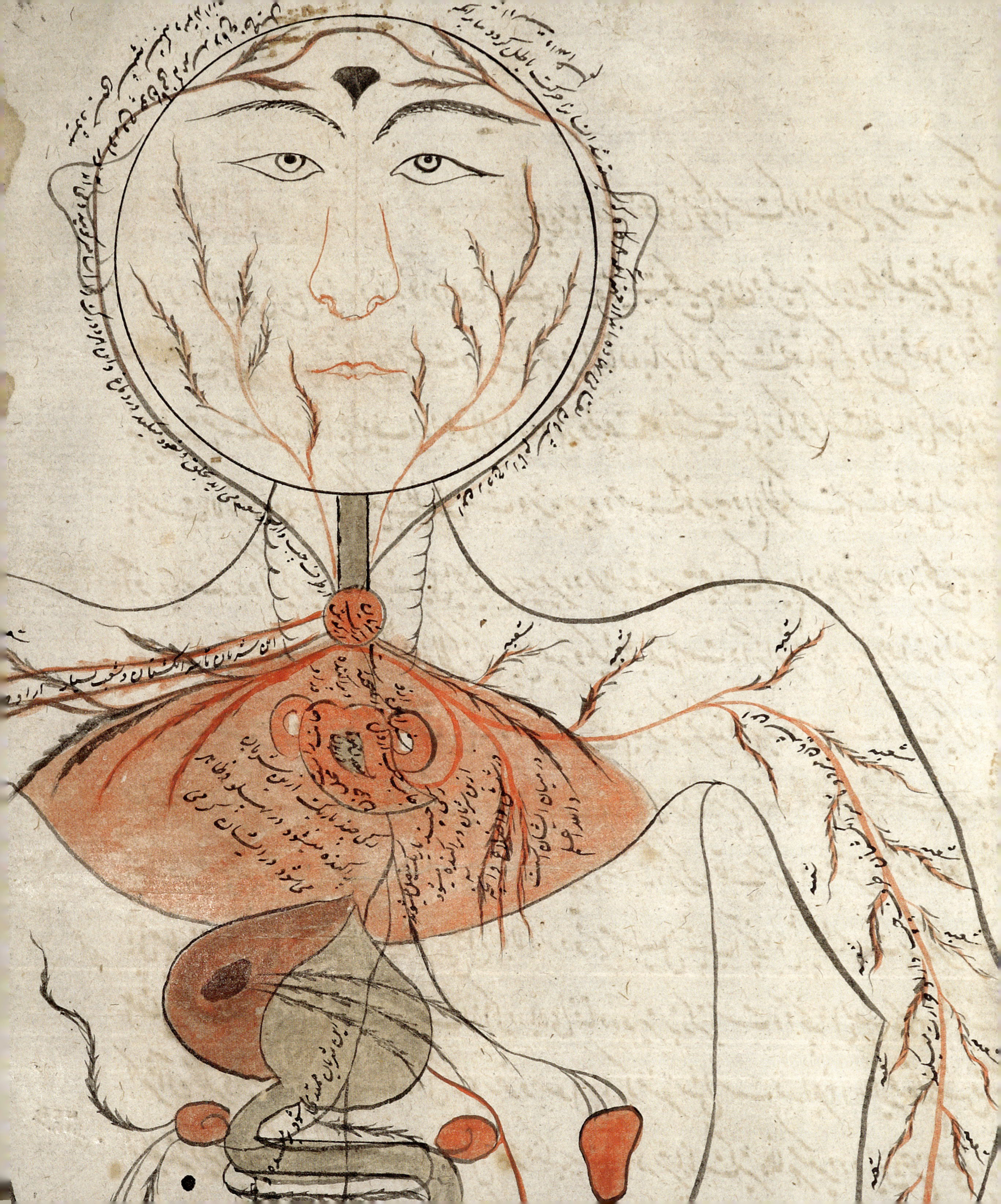

SCIENCE AND LEARNING

WITH THE EXPANSION OF MUSLIM RULE into the eastern Mediterranean regions and western Asia, the diverse Pre-Islamic science and learning traditions of the Greeks, Persians, Indians, and Chinese came into creative contact under the patronage of the ruling Muslim courts. A vast movement of translation, development, and innovation took place in the Abbasid courts of Baghdad between the eighth and tenth centuries where scientists and scholars from various religious and ethnic backgrounds worked together and achieved significant advances. Their creativity and innovations in the fields of science and philosophy were later transmitted to Europe and Asia and formed an important link in humanity's modern intellectual achievements.

Important pharmaceutical (AKM9) and medical (AKM510) manuscripts continued to be produced in multiple copies that were later translated into Latin in Toledo, Spain (AKM510), and Palermo, Sicily (AKM516), during the thirteenth century. The quality of the illustrations of some of these manuscripts (AKM83) suggests the high status in which they were held and perhaps the taste of their patrons.

The development of astronomical sciences (AKM266) and the increase in the precision of astronomical instruments were part of a traditional approach to practical science that evolved in close relationship with religious institutions of learning. The predominant function of astronomical knowledge in Muslim civilizations, however, was determining the direction of prayer (the *qibla*) and establishing prayer times. Scientific instruments such as astrolabes (AKM611) reflect the close relationship among the continuous discoveries in geography, descriptive geometry, and decorative styles.

Detail of *Tashrih-e Mansuri* (Anatomy by Mansur) (see page 97)
Mansur ibn Ilyas
Iran, mid-17th century
Ink and opaque watercolour on paper
Folio: 28.8 × 19.5 cm (11⅜ × 7⅝ in.)
AKM525

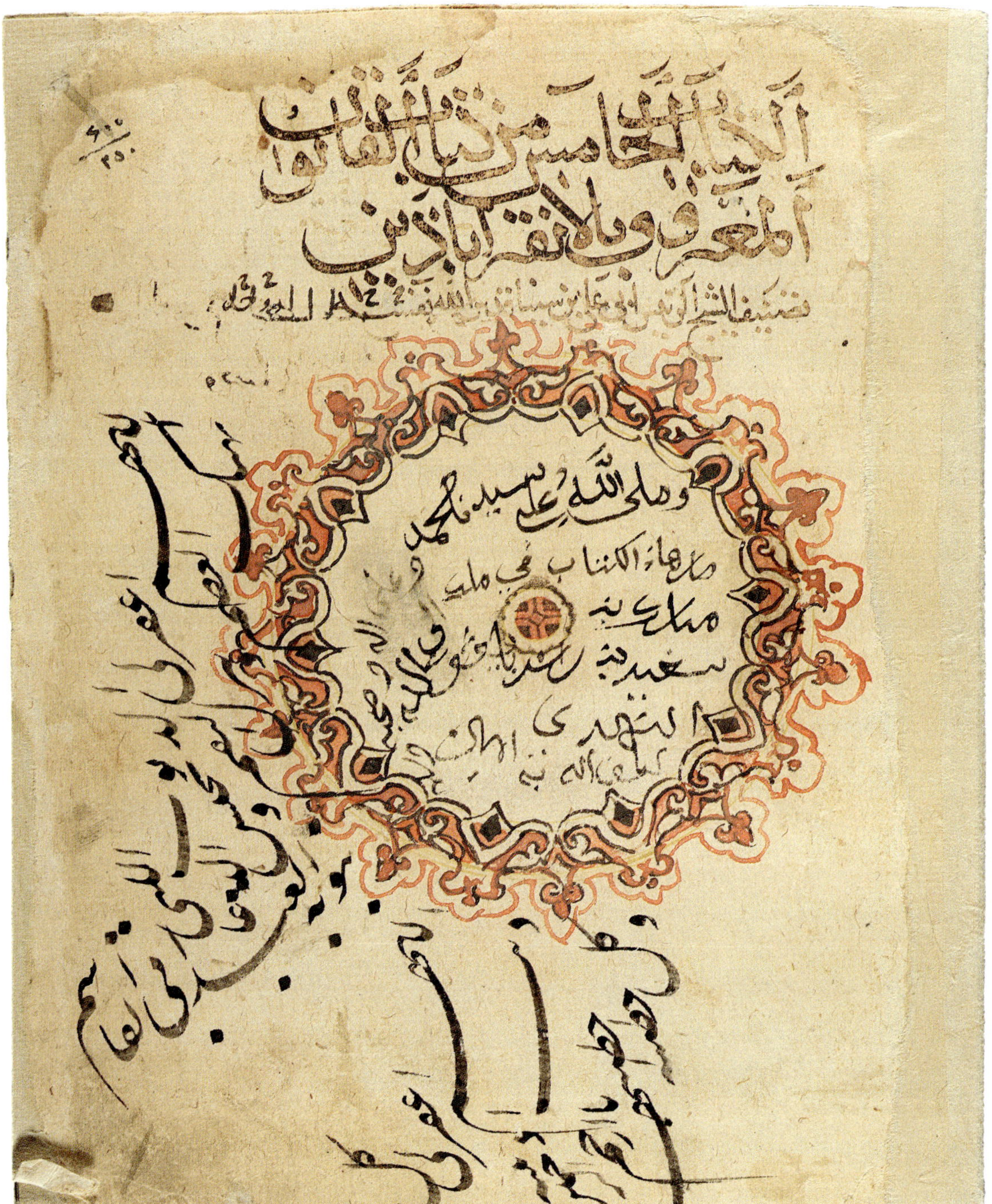

Written within fifteen years of the death of its author, this manuscript is one of the earliest surviving copies of volume five of the *Qanun [fi'l-tibb]* (Canon [of Medicine]) by the Persian scholar Ibn Sina or Avicenna (died 1037), as he is known in the West. Ibn Sina wrote a five-volume encyclopedia that brought together the Greco-Roman medical knowledge of Aristotle (died 322 BCE) and Galen (died circa 216 CE) with the advances in Chinese medicine of his time. Avicenna's *Qanun* was translated into Latin in Toledo, Spain, in the thirteenth century. It then became the most influential medical encyclopedia and was taught in European universities well into the eighteenth century. The Aga Khan Museum's collection also contains volume 4 of this rare copy of the encyclopedia (see also page 17).

Qanun [Fi'l-Tibb] (Canon [of Medicine]), Volume 5
Ibn Sina (d. 1037)
Iran or Iraq, 1052
Opaque watercolour and ink on paper
Folio: 21.2 × 16.4 cm (8⅜ × 6½ in.)
AKM510

This illustration of a poppy plant is part of a pharmaceutical tradition that identifies plants and herbs and explores their medicinal qualities. It is based on a treatise known as *De Materia Medica*, written in the first century by the Greek physician and botanist Dioscorides (died circa 90 CE) and translated into Arabic in Baghdad during the ninth century. In this folio, Dioscorides identifies three varieties of poppy seed, two of which are wild species and one that is cultivated (*thylacitis*) for its general health-inducing benefits. The treatise suggests baking the poppy seeds with bread or mixing them with honey, two practices still common today. Because the main function of this painting is scientific illustration, the watercolour depicts the root, stems, leaves, flowers, and pods of the poppy plant simultaneously.

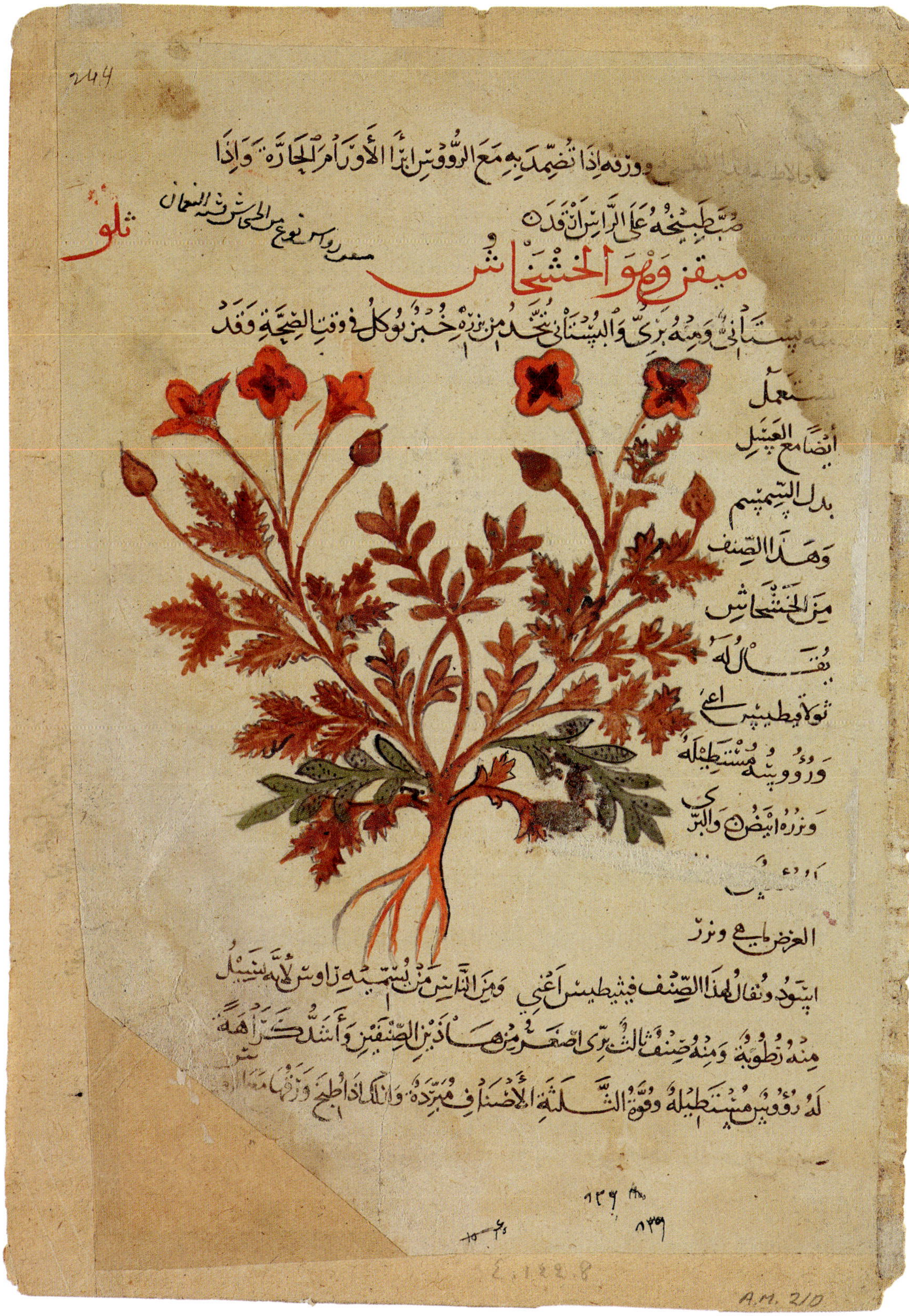

Al-Khashkhash (The Poppy)
Folio from a dispersed *Khawass Al-Ashjar* (*De Materia Medica*)
Iraq, 13th century
Opaque watercolour and ink on paper
29.8 × 20.5 cm (11¾ × 8⅛ in.)
AKM9

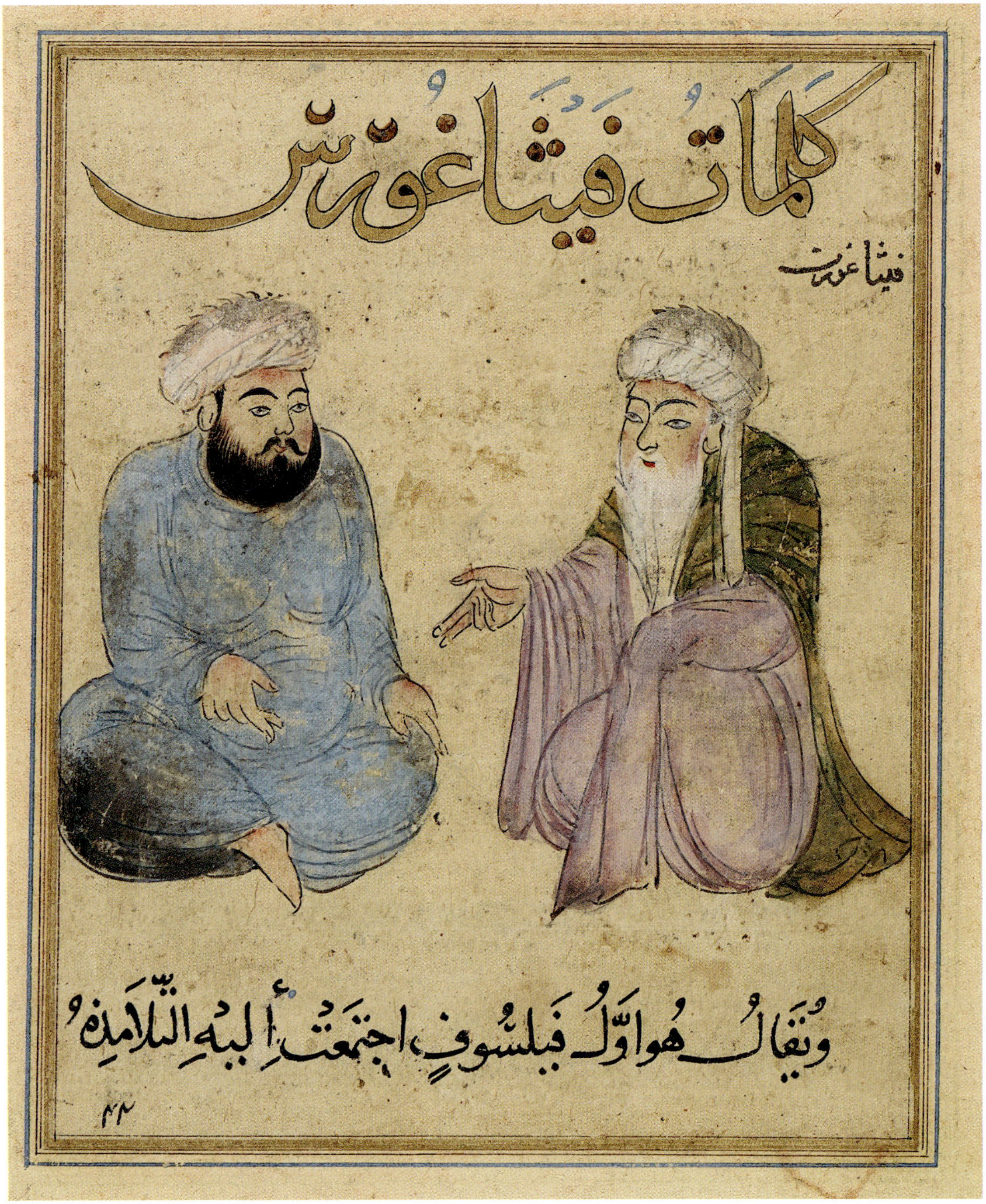

This image represents the didactic interaction between master and disciple or teacher and student as a traditional mode of transmission of knowledge and learning. In this manuscript, various images of the putative sources of Islamic philosophy are placed in direct contact with students whose questions result in the Greek philosophers' wise sayings. The teacher, in this case the Greek philosopher Pythagoras (died circa 495 BCE), is depicted as a turbaned older man talking possibly to a student. The anonymous author of this manuscript continues this didactic practice by passing its content on to the reader who becomes a participant in a venerable humanistic chain of knowledge.

Sayings of Pythagoras
Folio 21v from *Al-Kalimah Al-Ruhaniyah wa Al-Hikmah Al-Yunaniyah* (The Spiritual Word and the Greek Philosophy)
Iraq or Syria, 13th–14th centuries
Opaque watercolour, ink, and gold on paper
Folio: 20.6 × 15 cm (8⅛ × 5⅞ in.)
AKM283

The eleventh-century Persian physician Ibn Bakhtishu (died 1058) wrote the bestiary *Manafi' al-Hayawan* (The Usefulness of Animals) following the Aristotelian tradition that lists and describes animal species while highlighting their benefits. This folio is from a dispersed late thirteenth-century Persian copy of Ibn Bakhtishu's Arabic text. Other folios from the same manuscript are now in major museum collections, including that of The Metropolitan Museum of Art in New York. The painting style seen in this folio also brings together various artistic traditions. By the end of the thirteenth century, book painting under the Ilkhanids (1256–1353) demonstrated strong influences of Chinese-inspired elements seen here in the depiction of twisted trees and the introduction of foreign plant species, including the lotus. One of the benefits mentioned for the magpie (*shiqraq*) shown here is that boiling its droppings in fat is a good treatment for darkening grey hair.

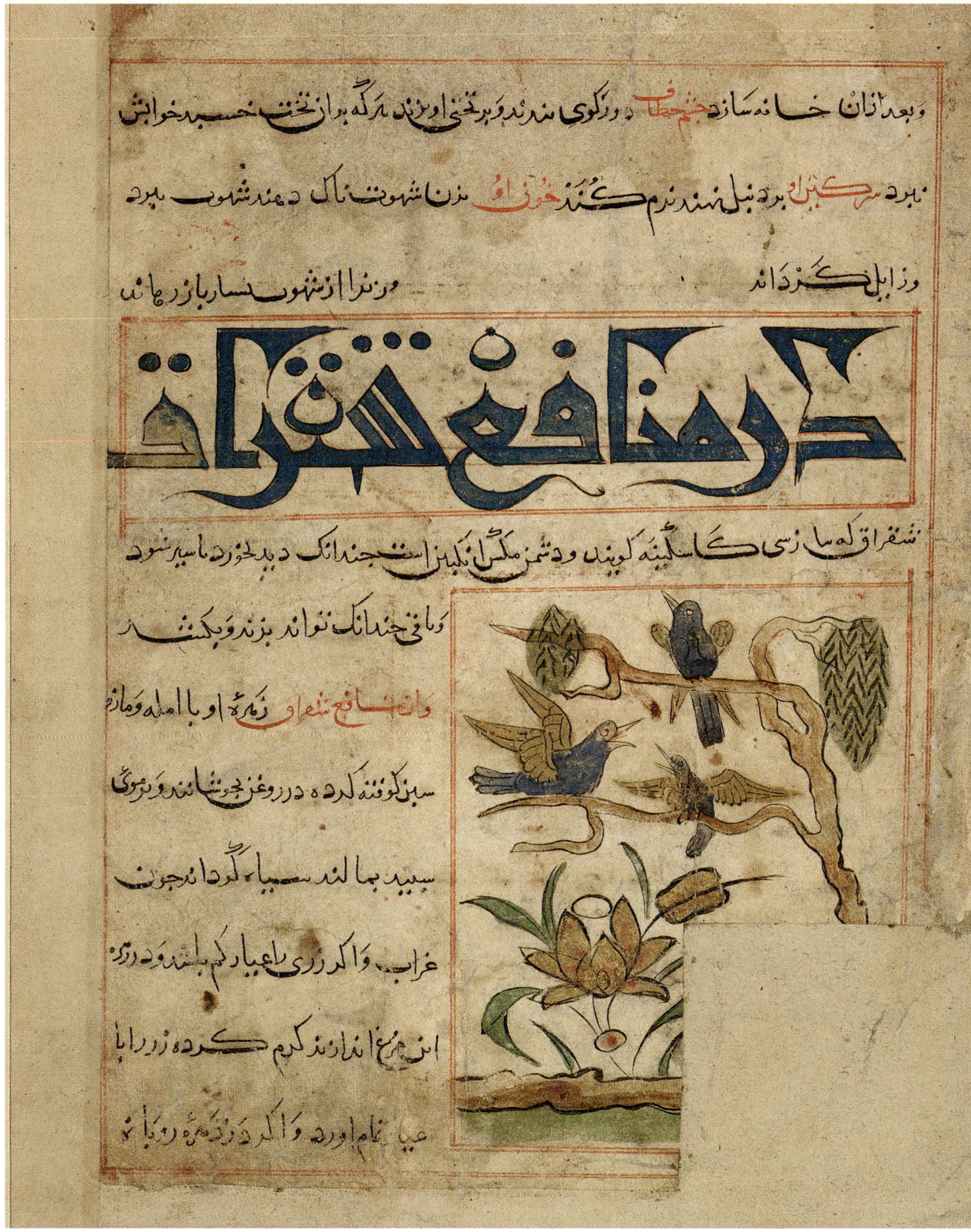

Shiqraq (Green Magpie)
Folio from a dispersed *Manafi' al-Hayawan* (The Usefulness of Animals)
Ibn Bakhtishu (d. 1058)
Iran or Iraq, ca. 1300
Opaque watercolour, ink, and gold on paper
25.7 × 20.5 cm (10⅛ × 8⅛ in.)
AKM83

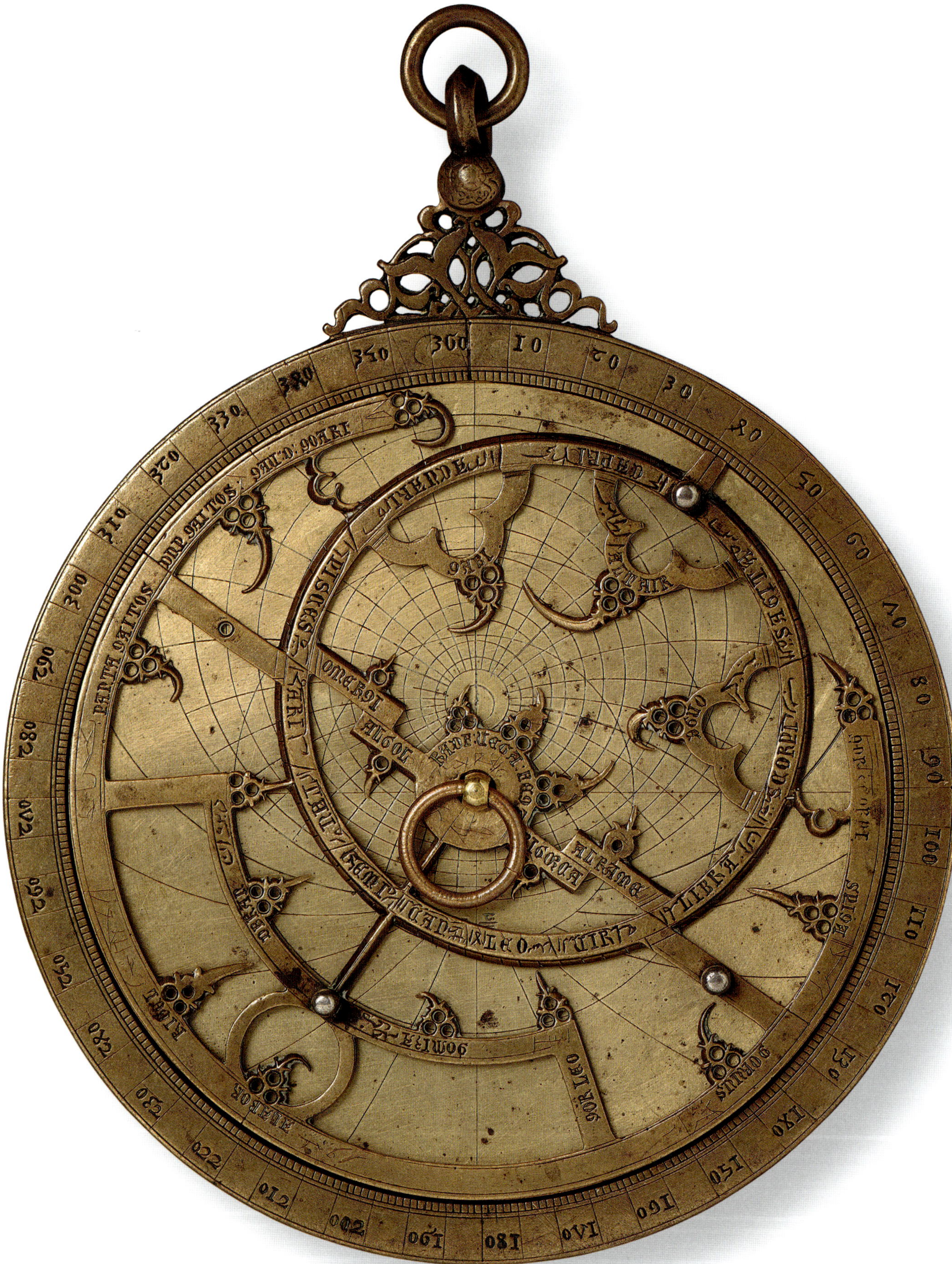

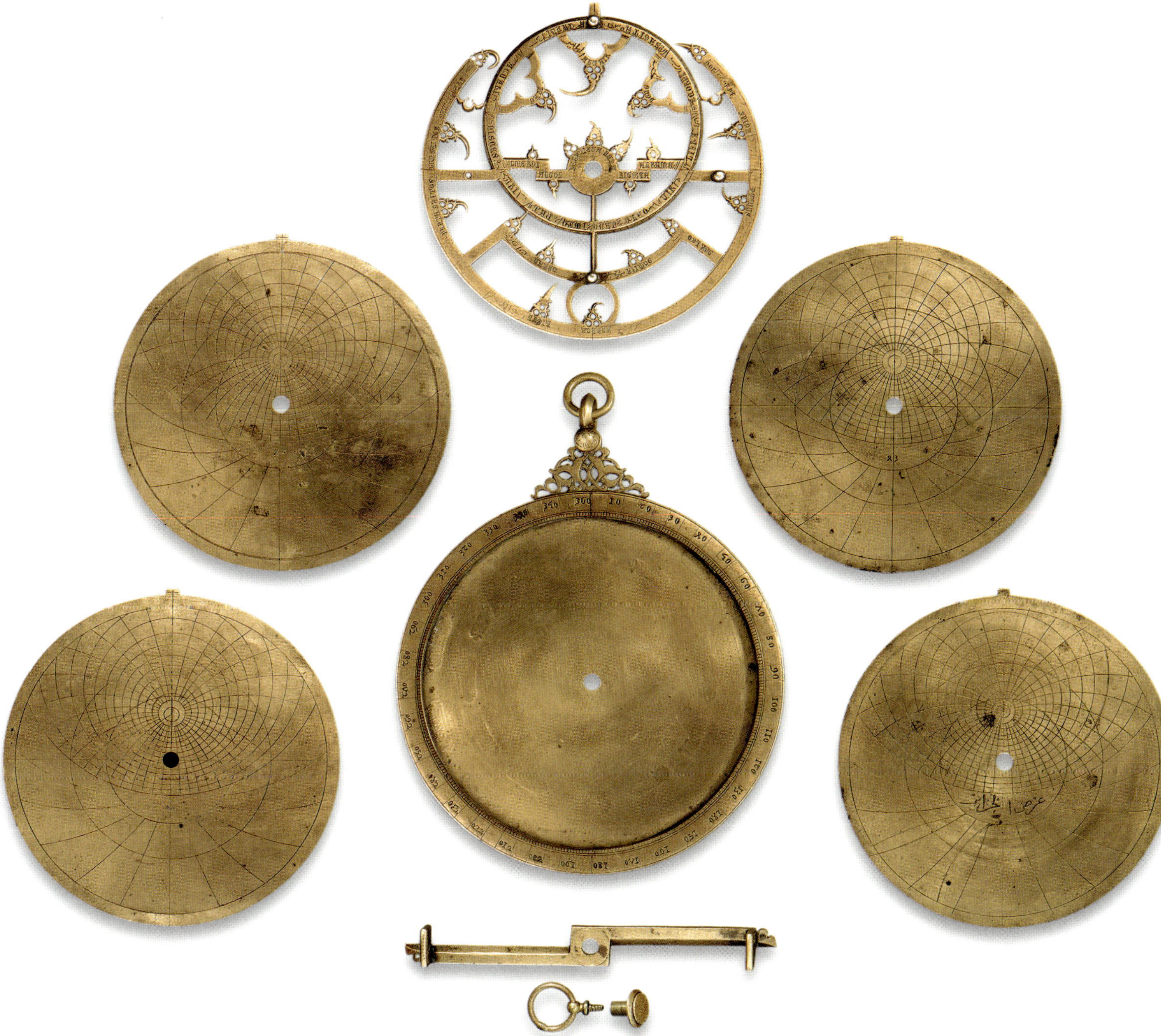

Planispheric Astrolabe
Spain (Historic al-Andalus), 14th century
Bronze inlaid with silver
Diameter 13.5 cm (5¼ in.)
AKM611

Centuries of Muslim rule in Spain (al-Andalus) saw the scientific knowledge inherited from Hellenistic and Indian traditions expanded by Muslim scientists and augmented by Christian and Jewish counterparts working together to translate and transmit this knowledge to Europe. This astrolabe was probably made in Toledo, Spain, then a major centre of scientific translation. The inscriptions on the astrolabe bear the names of constellations in both Arabic and Latin, with additional inscriptions in Arabic and Hebrew. The plates inside the astrolabe include projections for different geographical latitudes and represent different phases of use, confirming that the practical life of this astrolabe extended beyond the place and time of its initial manufacture. The predominant function of the astrolabe in Muslim civilizations was to determine the direction of prayer toward Mecca (the *qibla*) and to establish the times of prayer. This is usually achieved by using a plate with the precise celestial projections for Mecca on one of the plates inside the astrolabe's body, as indeed is the case for this unique astrolabe (see also pages 17–18).

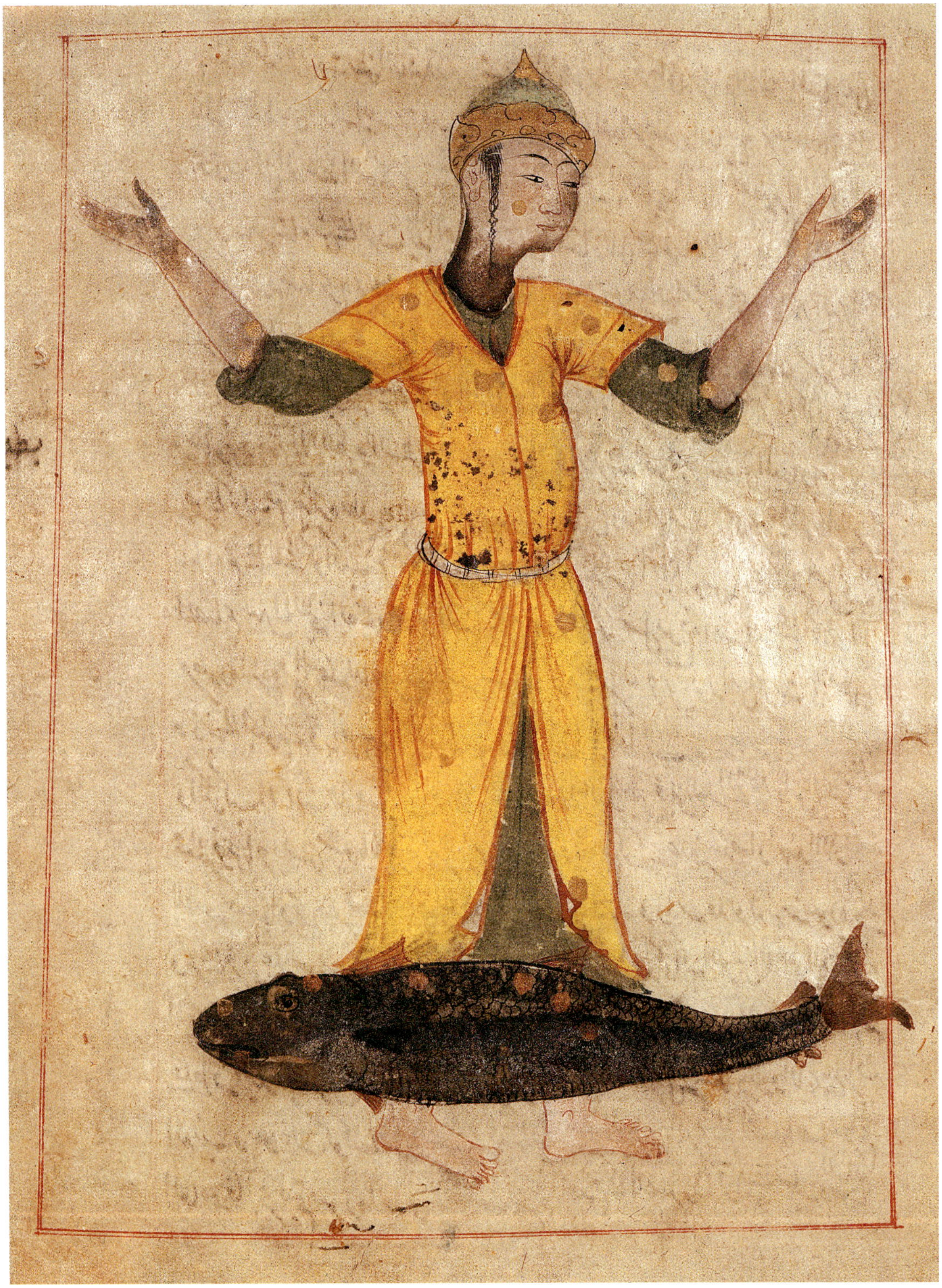

The lady in this saffron-coloured robe and crown-like helmet is a personification of the constellation Andromeda, which was identified by the second-century CE astronomer Ptolemy and continues to be considered a major constellation. With the translation of Ptolemy's *Almagest* in the court of the ninth-century Caliph al-Ma'mun in Baghdad, astronomers working under the patronage of the Muslim rulers in modern-day Iraq and Iran adopted the Greco-Roman astronomical knowledge and expanded on it from the indigenous Arab (*Anwa'*) and Indian astronomical traditions, in this illustration combining Andromeda with Pisces. The most prominent example of this tradition is Images of the Fixed Stars written by the Iranian astronomer 'Abd al-Rahman al-Sufi (died 986), which contained two representations of each constellation, one looking up at the constellation from Earth and the other looking down on it from above. Al-Sufi's work continued to be in broad circulation, and various copies exist in major museum collections.

The Constellations Andromeda and Pisces
Folio from a dispersed *Kitab Suwar al-Kawakib al-Thabita* (Images of the Fixed Stars)
'Abd al-Rahman al-Sufi (d. 986)
Iran, ca. 1450
Opaque watercolour, ink, gold, and silver on paper
21.3 × 14.7 cm (8⅜ × 5¾ in.)
AKM43

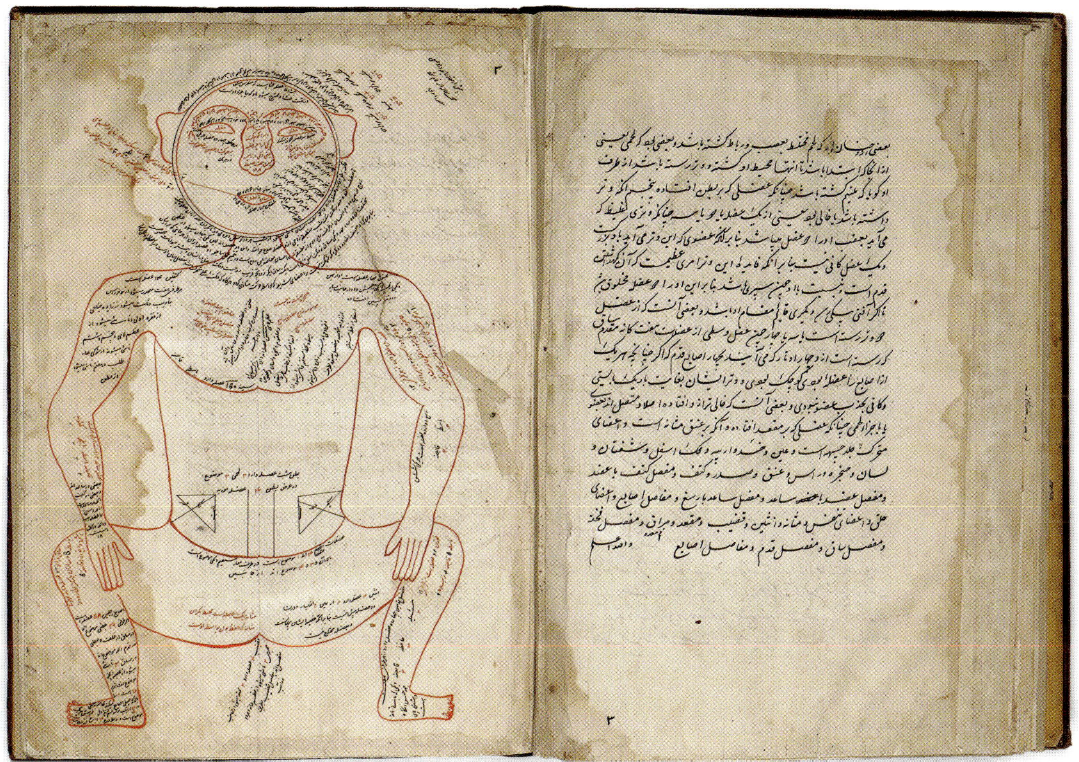

Tashrih-e Mansuri (Anatomy by Mansur)
Mansur ibn Ilyas
Iran, mid-17th century
Ink and opaque watercolour on paper
Folio: 28.8 × 19.5 cm
(11⅜ × 7⅝ in.)
AKM525

This anatomical manuscript was originally written in the fourteenth century by Mansur ibn Ilyas for his patron, the ruler of Fars in Iran. The seventeenth-century copy seen here has five full-page anatomical illustrations of various systems of the body, including the nervous system, skeleton, muscles, veins, and arteries. The anatomical knowledge portrayed in these paintings illustrates the Greco-Roman inheritance and its expansion under Muslim scientists and physicians.

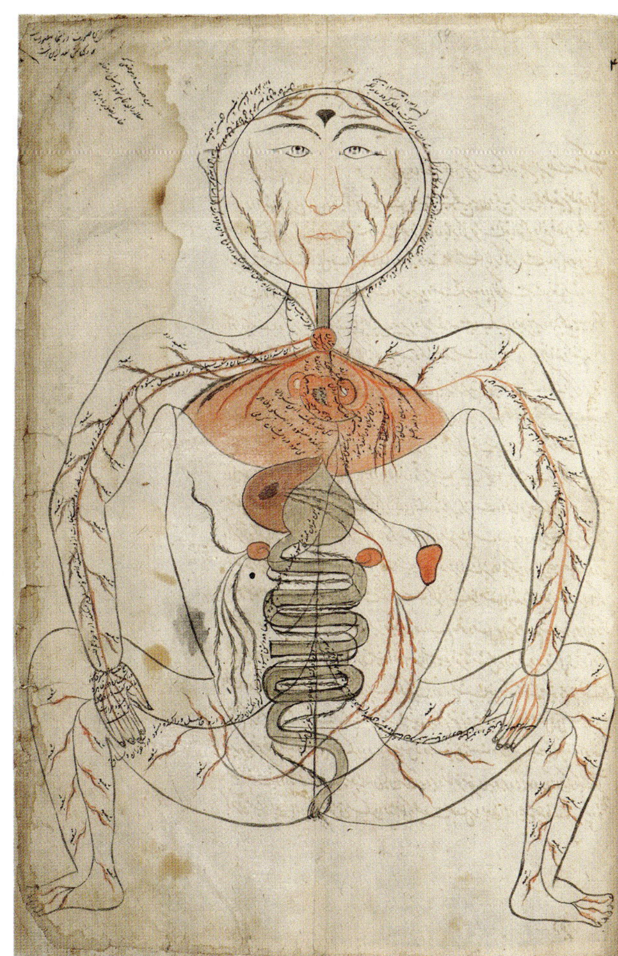

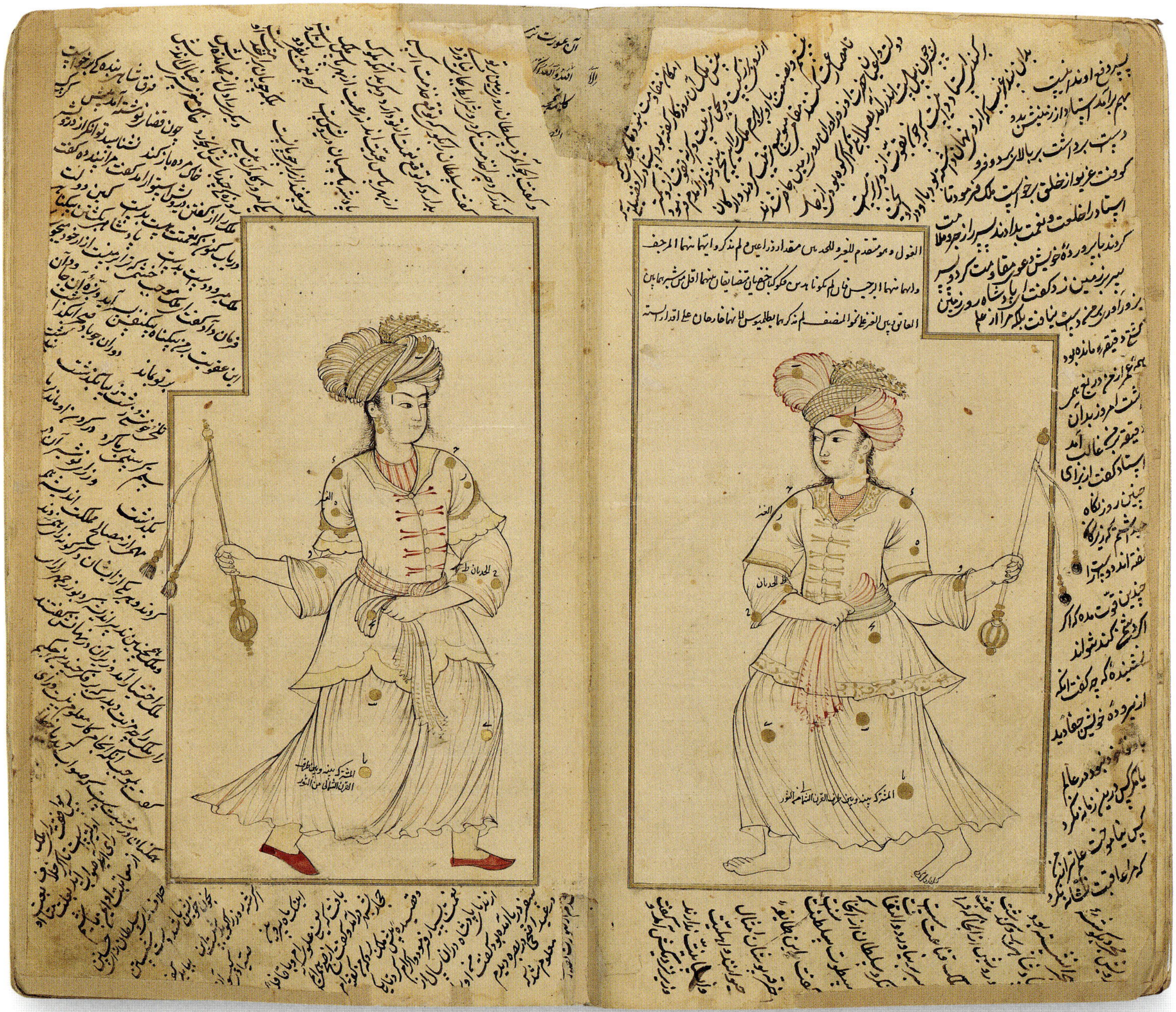

The Constellation Auriga

Folio 48v–49r from a *Kitab Suwar al-Kawakib al-Thabita* (Images of the Fixed Stars)
ʻAbd al-Rahman al-Sufi (d. 986)
Isfahan, Iran, 1640s–1650s
Ink, opaque watercolour, and gold on paper
Folio: 31.4 × 18.3 cm
(12⅜ × 7¼ in.)
AKM266

Although ʻAbd al-Rahman al-Sufi's Images of the Fixed Stars was originally designed to depict accurate longitudes for the constellations for the year 964, it continued to be copied for centuries after that. Considering that the main focus of the treatise is the astronomical description and depiction of constellations, the representations in this manuscript, including that of Auriga (the charioteer) seen here, faithfully follow the painting style of seventeenth-century Iran. The thick, connected eyebrows of Auriga, the round cheeks, small red mouth, and feathery hair, as well as the magnificent attention to the folds of the figure's turban and knotted sash, are typical of the elegant courtiers depicted by a school of painters that painted in the style of Iranian artist Reza-e ʻAbbasi (died 1635).

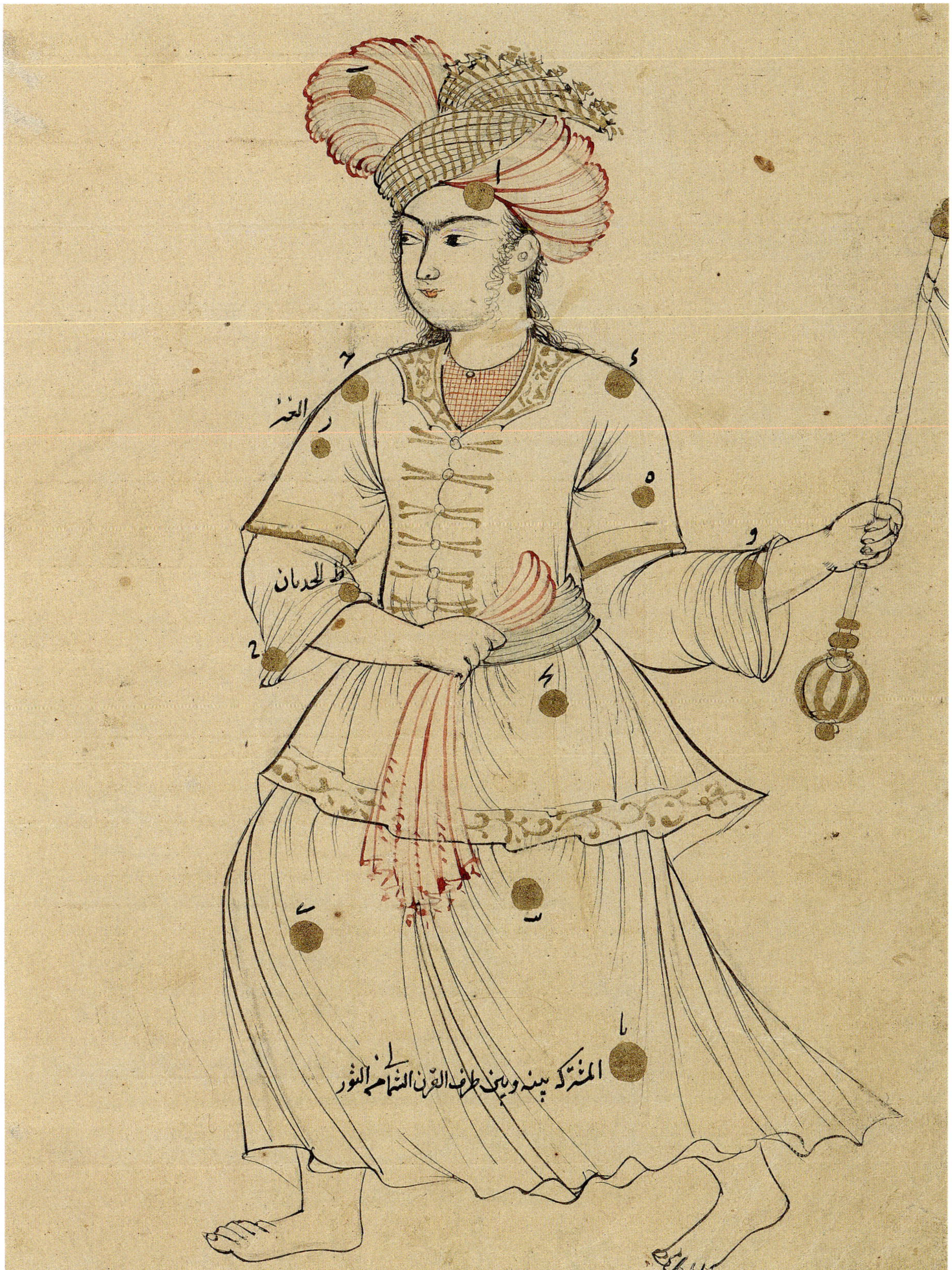

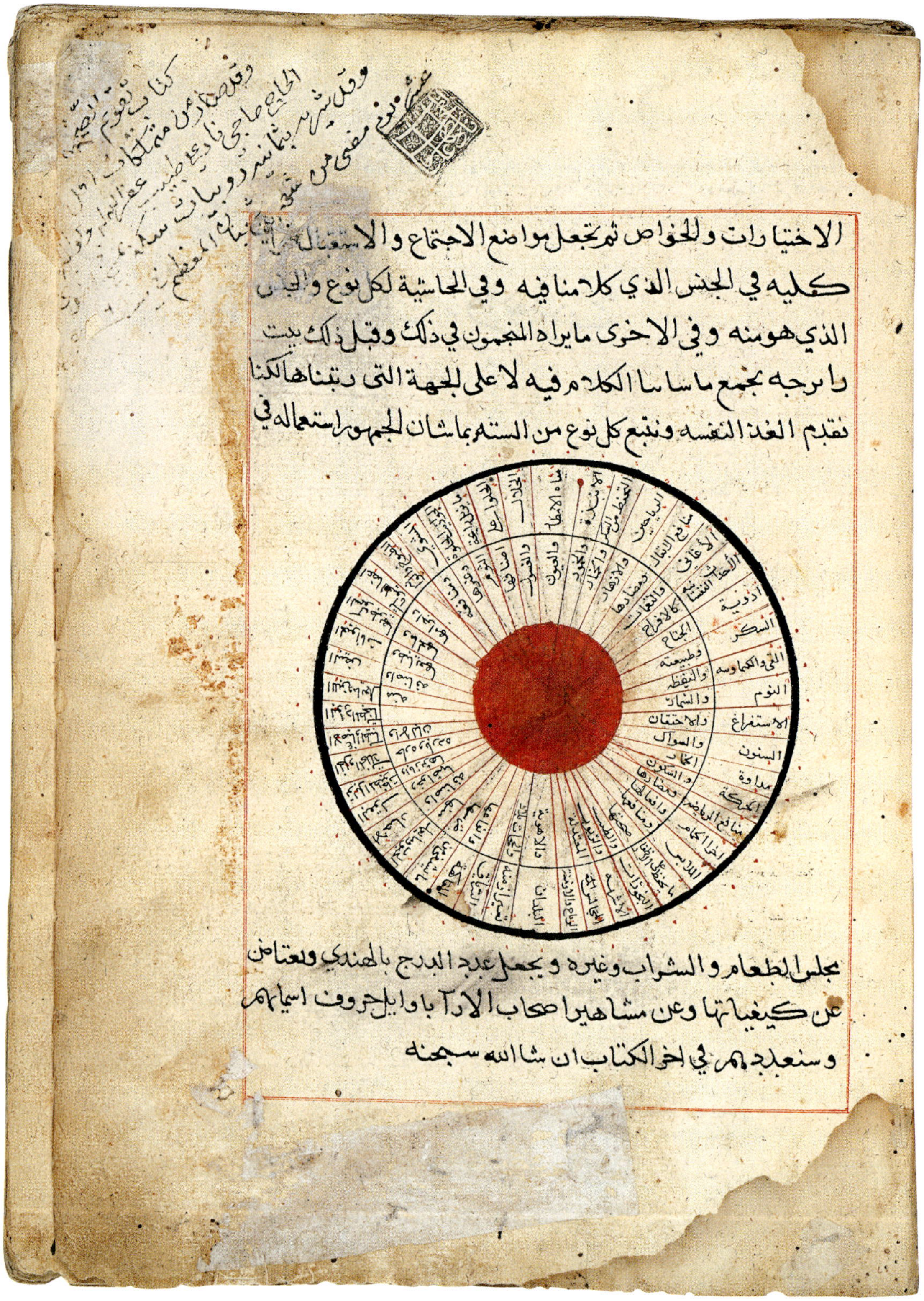

According to Ibn Butlan's *Taqwim al-Sihhah*, the maintenance of good health is dependent on six elements: the quality of air; healthy eating and drinking habits; exercise and rest; sleep; the balance of the humours; and the moderation of joy, anger, fear, and distress. While the theory of humours inherited by Muslim scientists from the Greek physician Hippocrates (died 370 BCE) was discredited by medical discoveries in the nineteenth century, Ibn Butlan's reasoning for health and hygiene based on a moderate lifestyle still resonates today. His treatise includes various tables that list types of habits, environments, drinks, and foodstuffs and links them to physiological effects on the body. *Taqwim al-Sihhah* was translated into Latin in Sicily in 1266 under the title *Tacuinum Sanitatis* and from there became popular in Europe.

Taqwim al-Sihhah bi'l-Asbab al-Sitta (Maintenance of Health Through Six Methods)
Ibn Butlan (d. 1066)
Iraq or Syria, 1344
Ink, opaque watercolour, and gold on paper
Folio: 30.1 × 20.5 cm (11⅞ × 8⅛ in.)
AKM516

This painting comes from a popular treatise on mechanical devices and automata written in 1206 and copied continuously in the following centuries. Al-Jazari, the author of *Kitab al-Hiyal al-naficah* (The Book of Knowledge of Ingenious Mechanical Devices), included descriptions of more than a hundred devices in his treatise, one of which can be seen here. This fascinating device builds on two scientific ideas: bloodletting as a medical treatment and the use of simple machines to create complex automata. The treatment of various ailments through bloodletting was common until the nineteenth century, and it clearly did not need such a complex device. Here, the patient puts a cut finger into a hole in the basin and blood falls through channels into a lower chamber, displacing a float. The float is attached to one end of a rod that, on its other end, attaches to the pen in the hand of the scribe on the upper left. As the level of the blood in the basin rises, it pushes the float up, moving the scribe's pen and indicating marks on his writing board.

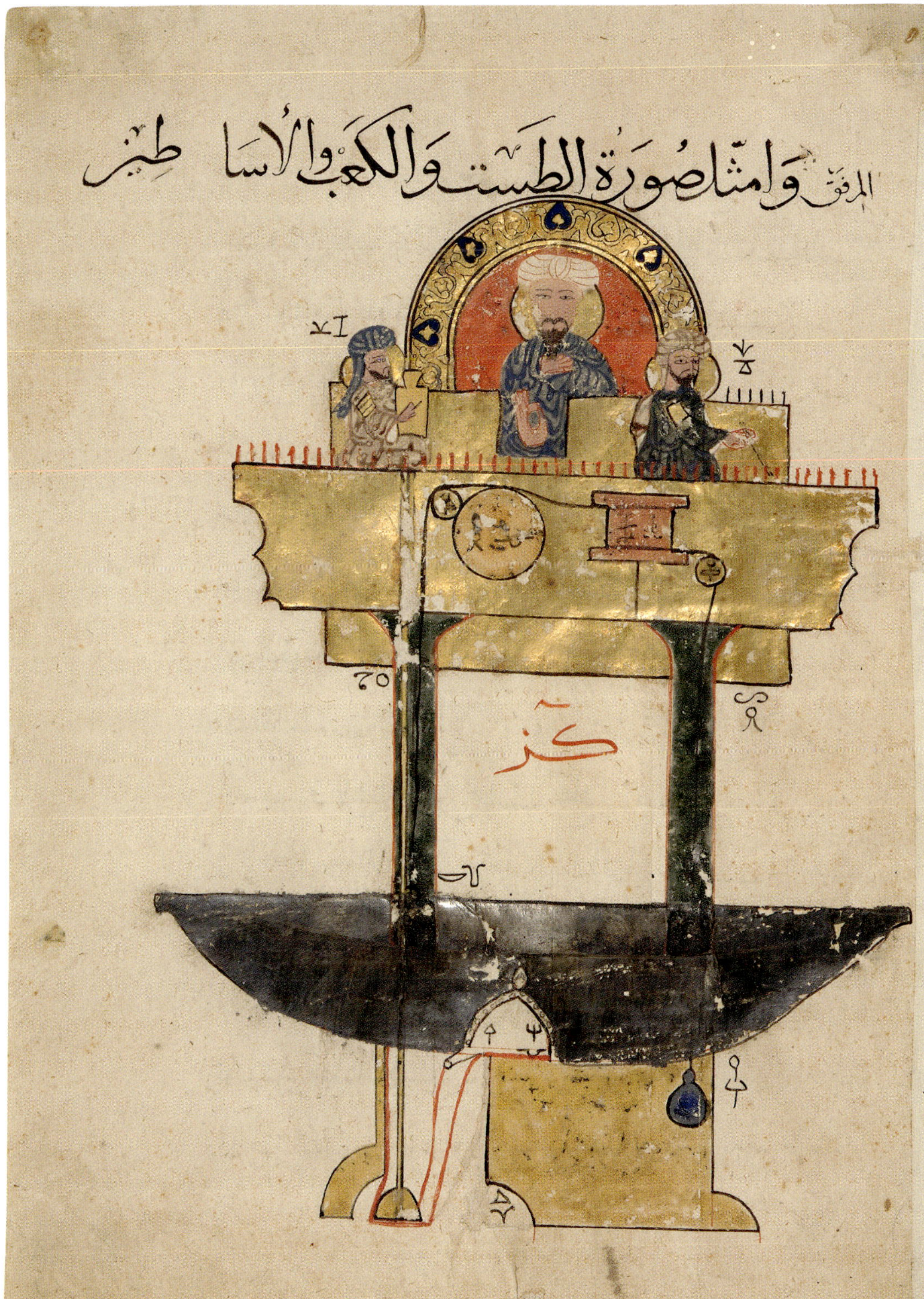

A Blood-Measuring Device
Kitab al-Hiyal al-naficah (The Book of Knowledge of Ingenious Mechanical Devices)
Al-Jazari (d. 1206)
Cairo, Egypt, 1354
Opaque watercolour, ink, gold, and silver on paper
27.3 × 39.1 cm (10¾ × 15⅜ in.)
AKM11

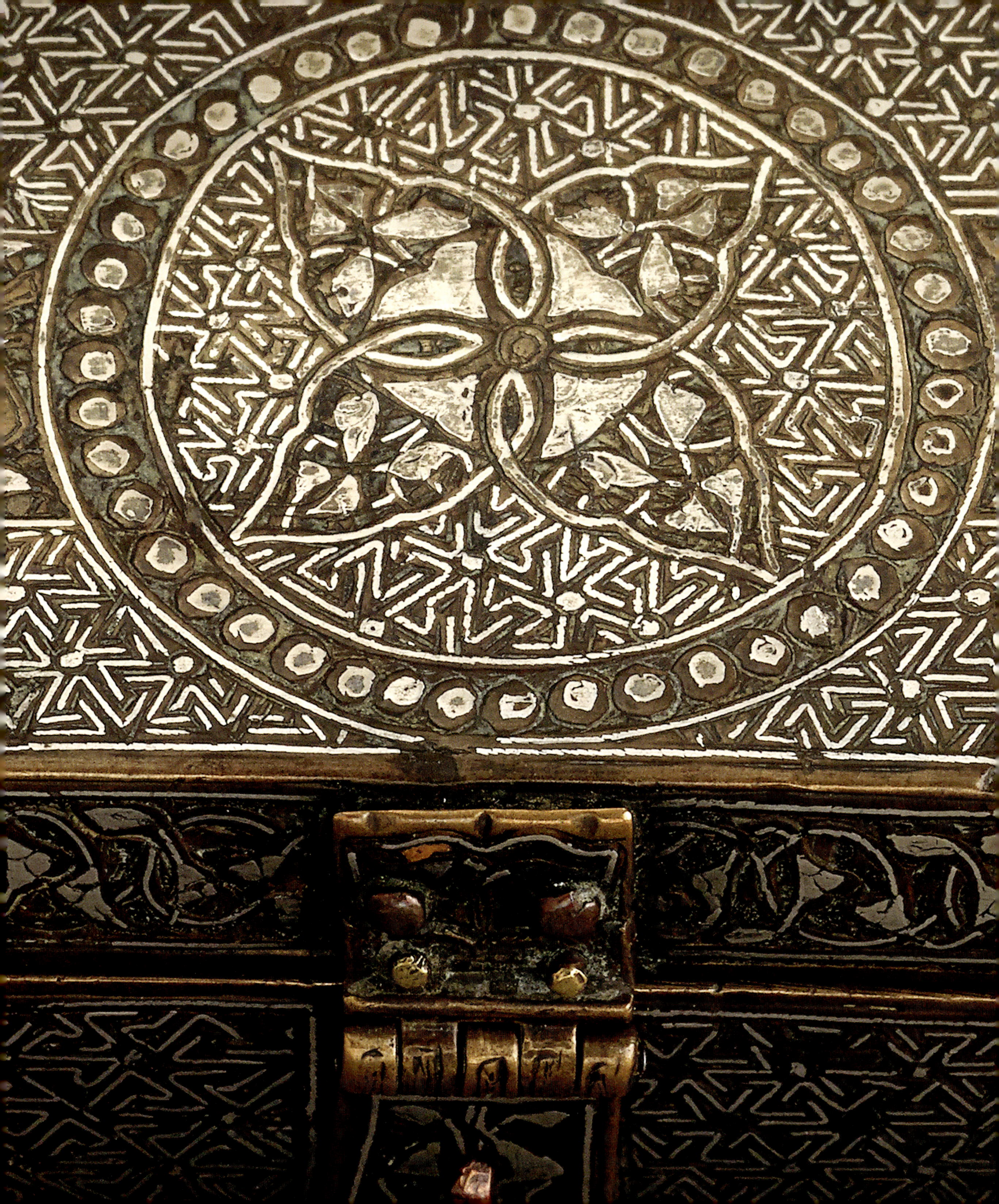

METALWORK

THE SUBSTANTIAL NUMBER OF METALWORK OBJECTS from the Islamic world surviving in museum collections reflects a rich variety of shapes and forms with increasingly complex decorative programs and distinctive styles. The examples from the Aga Khan Museum collection presented here are chosen for their artistic value as well as for the questions they raise and the insights they provide on the metalwork industry and the Muslim societies within which these objects were produced.

Most of the objects presented here are made of variations of brass or bronze alloys, and only scientific analysis can confirm their exact chemical compositions. When these objects were inlaid with silver (AKM610) or gold (AKM609) or worked in repoussé (AKM884), they became objects of considerable beauty, and probably significant value. Another important material for metalworking was crucible steel, which was used for weapons, grilles, screens, and decorative plates (AKM616 and AKM679). Gold and silver were also employed to create objects for the court and for wealthy patrons, but those were regularly melted down and the metal repurposed, especially for minting coins. The most common form in which they survive is gold jewellery (AKM618, see page 132).

Metalwork objects had utilitarian purposes and served the everyday requirements of their owners (AKM726). Yet a few also had highly symbolic roles (AKM612 and AKM679). In all cases, surviving objects from the tenth century onward display a range of creative solutions in decorating metalwork and turning simple objects into works of art (AKM602).

Detail of Pen Box (see pages 106–07)
Western Iran, late 13th century
Brass inlaid with gold and silver
Length 19.4 cm (7⅝ in.), width 4.5 cm (1¾ in.)
AKM609

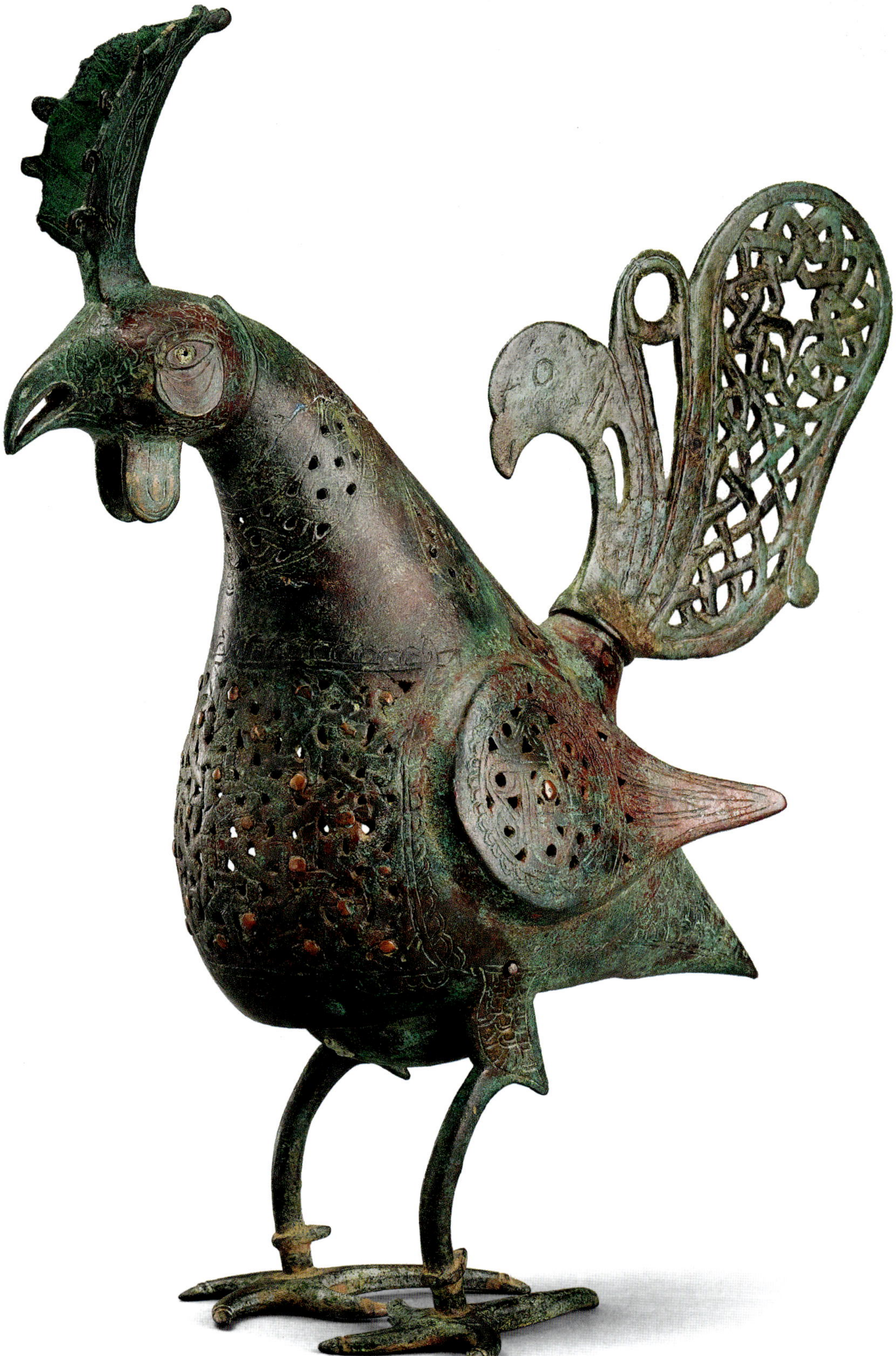

The use of incense in the pre-modern period was believed to have health benefits. Through fumigation and vaporization, scents produced by burning aloe wood (*'ud*), frankincense, or ambergris were believed to expel and neutralize spirits and the illnesses they brought. Incense burners were also appreciated for the pleasant smell they generated. Although metalwork incense burners were made in a variety of shapes, including some birds, this cockerel- shaped incense burner with its magnificent tail and high crest is quite unique. The body of the bird is decorated with pierced interlace that allows the perfumed smoke to escape from the interior receptacle.

Incense Burner
Eastern Iran, 11th century
Copper inlaid bronze
28 × 28 cm (11 × 11 in.)
AKM602

This candlestick is one of a group of related candlesticks in major museum collections that were made out of hammered brass in the late twelfth or early thirteenth centuries in Khorasan (present-day northeast Iran and Afghanistan). Although the candlesticks have variations in size and decorative details, they all have a wide band of hexagonal bosses flanked by repoussé animal friezes on the top and bottom, sometimes extending into the candlestick's shoulder. The same style of low-relief sculptural lions protruding from a brass object is known from a ewer now in the National Museum in Tbilisi, Georgia, with an inscription linking it to eastern Iran and present-day Afghanistan.

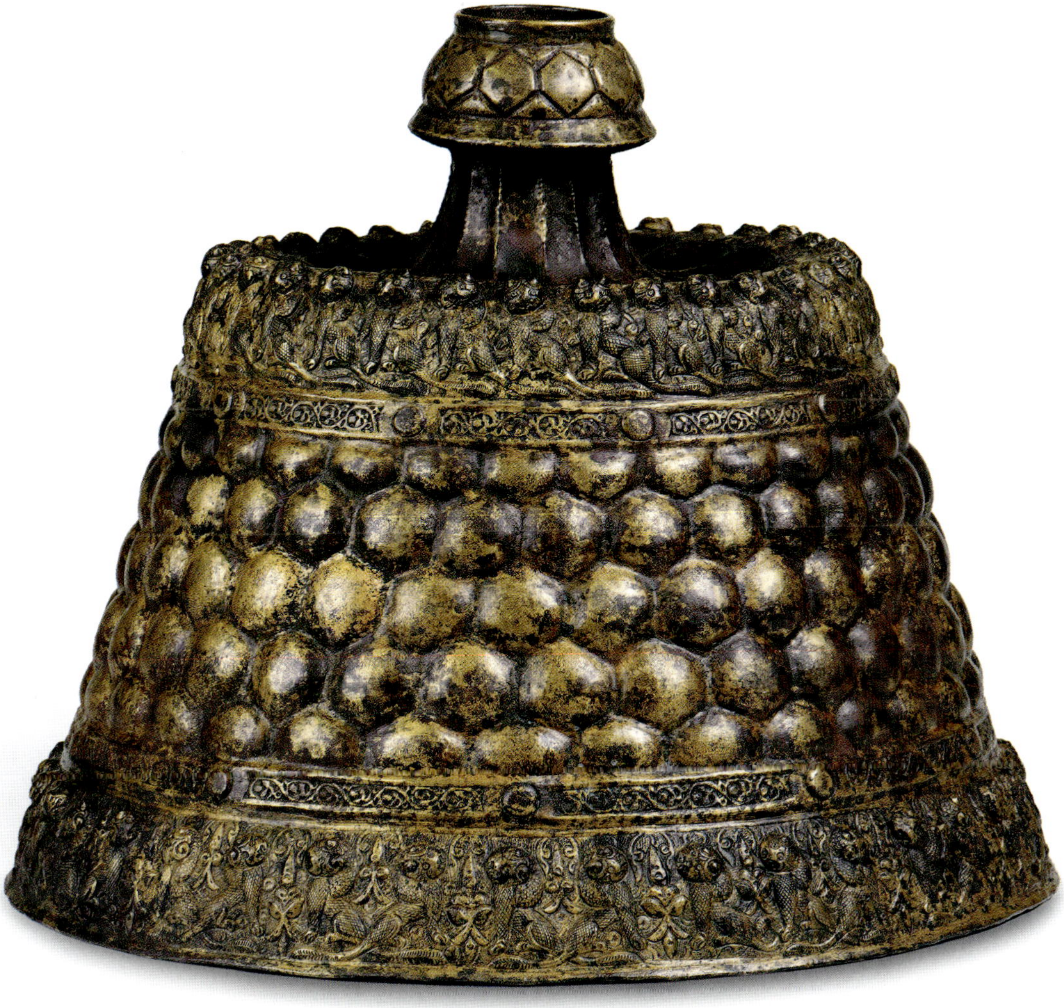

Candlestick
Eastern Iran, 12th century
Embossed and repoussé bronze
Diameter 46.5 cm (18¼ in.),
height 35 cm (13¾ in.)
AKM884

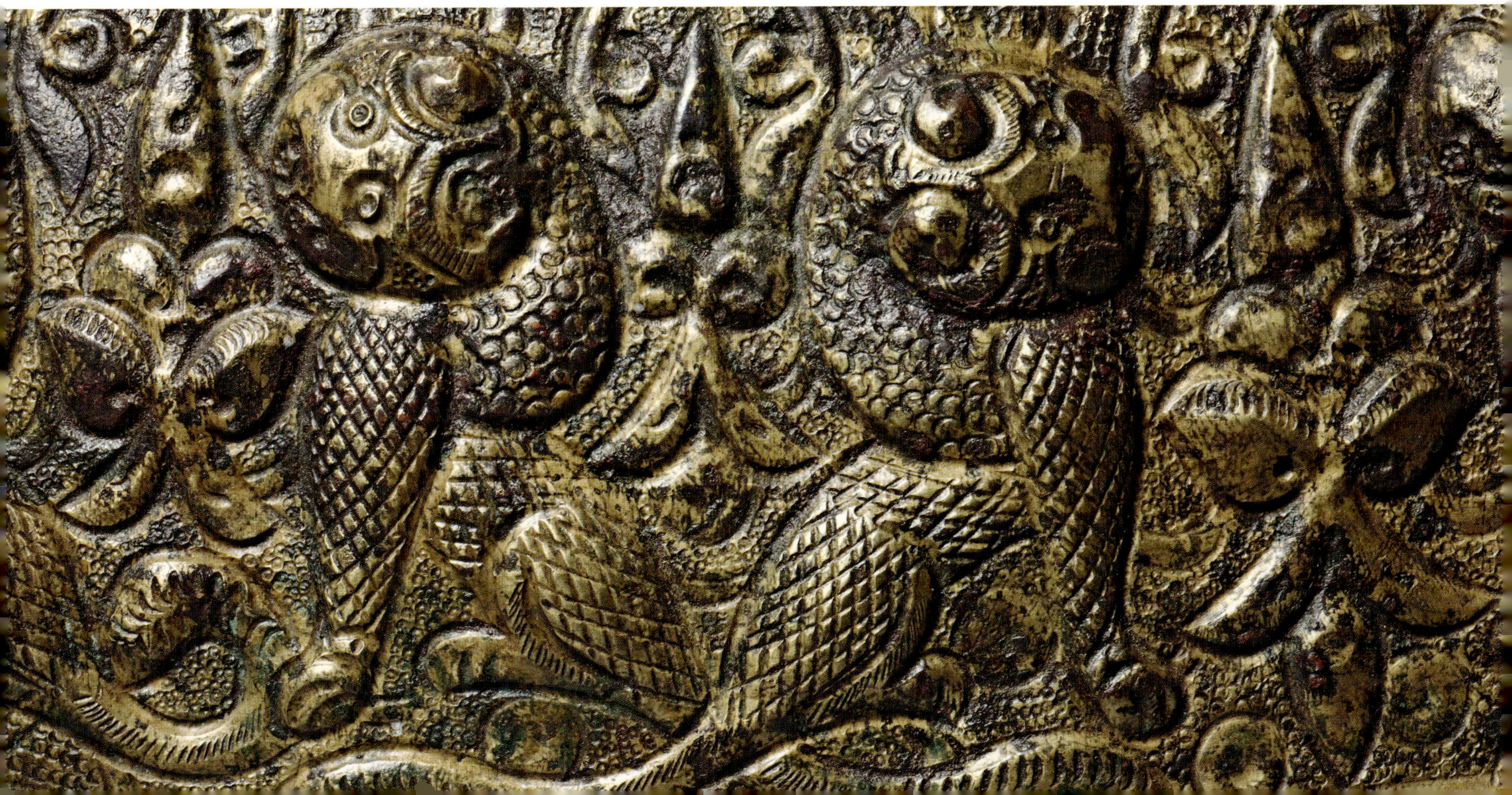

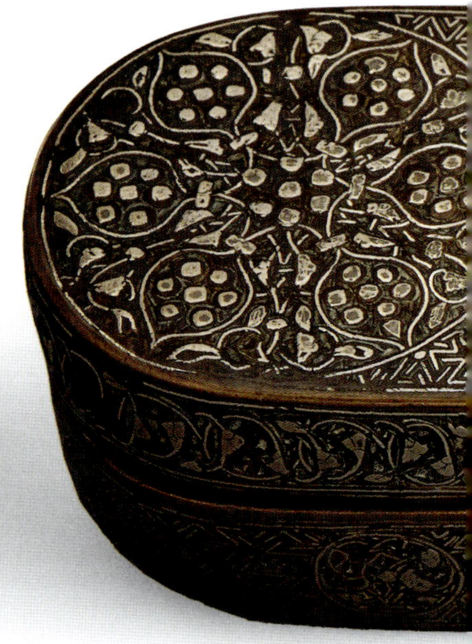

Basin

Probably Iran, 13th century
Cast and engraved white bronze
Diameter 55 cm (21⅝ in.),
height 25 cm (9⅞ in.)
AKM607

This exceptionally beautiful basin is covered with an overall engraved decoration that brings together figural images, calligraphic compositions, and complex geometric patterns over a bed of floral scrolls. The upper band shows a style of interlaced and animated script that is predominantly used on metalwork. All the uprights are interlaced midway, most ending with a human head in a style that made its early appearance in eastern Iran during the eleventh century. The bottom row has representations of the twelve signs of the zodiac, also typical of metalwork from Khorasan. This bowl demonstrates how some metalworking techniques, like high-tin bronze (known as bell metal), and styles such as human-headed calligraphy, moved from their places of origin during the thirteenth century through the migration of artists and the exchange of objects.

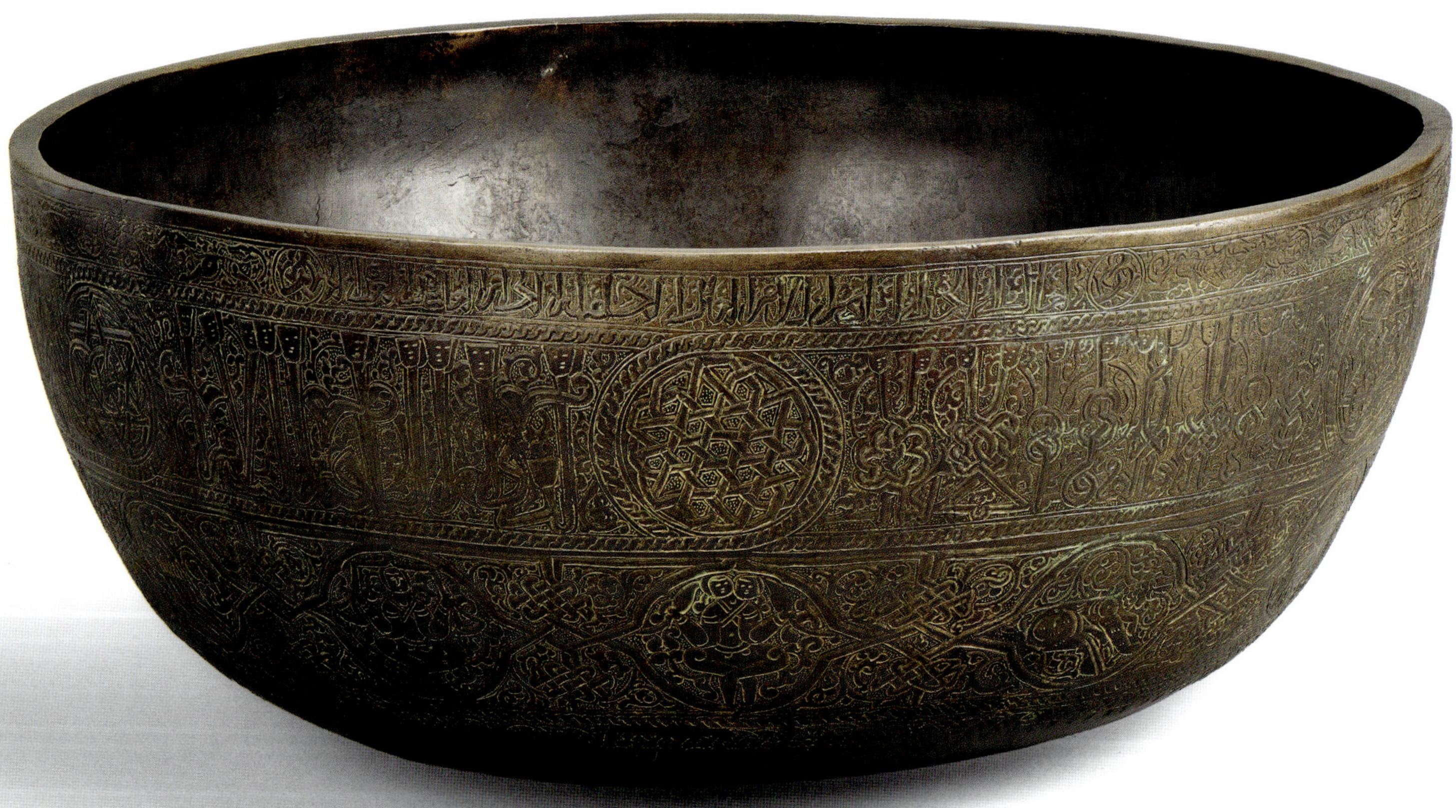

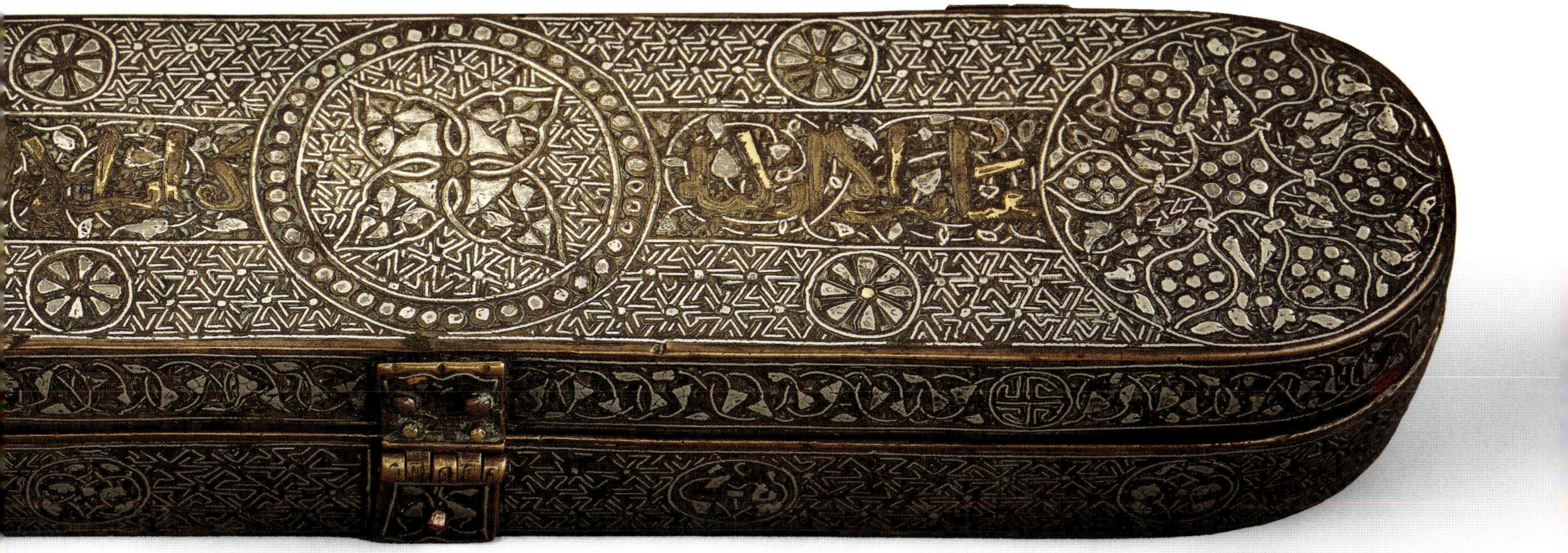

Pen Box

Western Iran, late 13th century
Brass inlaid with gold and silver
Length 19.4 cm (7⅝ in.), width 4.5 cm (1¾ in.)
AKM609

Historians of the thirteenth and fourteenth centuries considered pen boxes and inkwells as part of the insignia of high-ranking government officials. They are also associated with men of knowledge and wisdom in poetry and in painted manuscripts. It is no wonder then that the Aga Khan Museum pen box, seen here, is so intricately and richly decorated. The overall design is outlined with silver wire hammered into the brass box, forming discreet areas mostly filled with floral and geometric silver inlay. As the most visible part of the pen box, the lid is decorated with larger pieces of silver in three elaborate roundels, with intricate rosettes and an inscription inlaid in gold running between them.

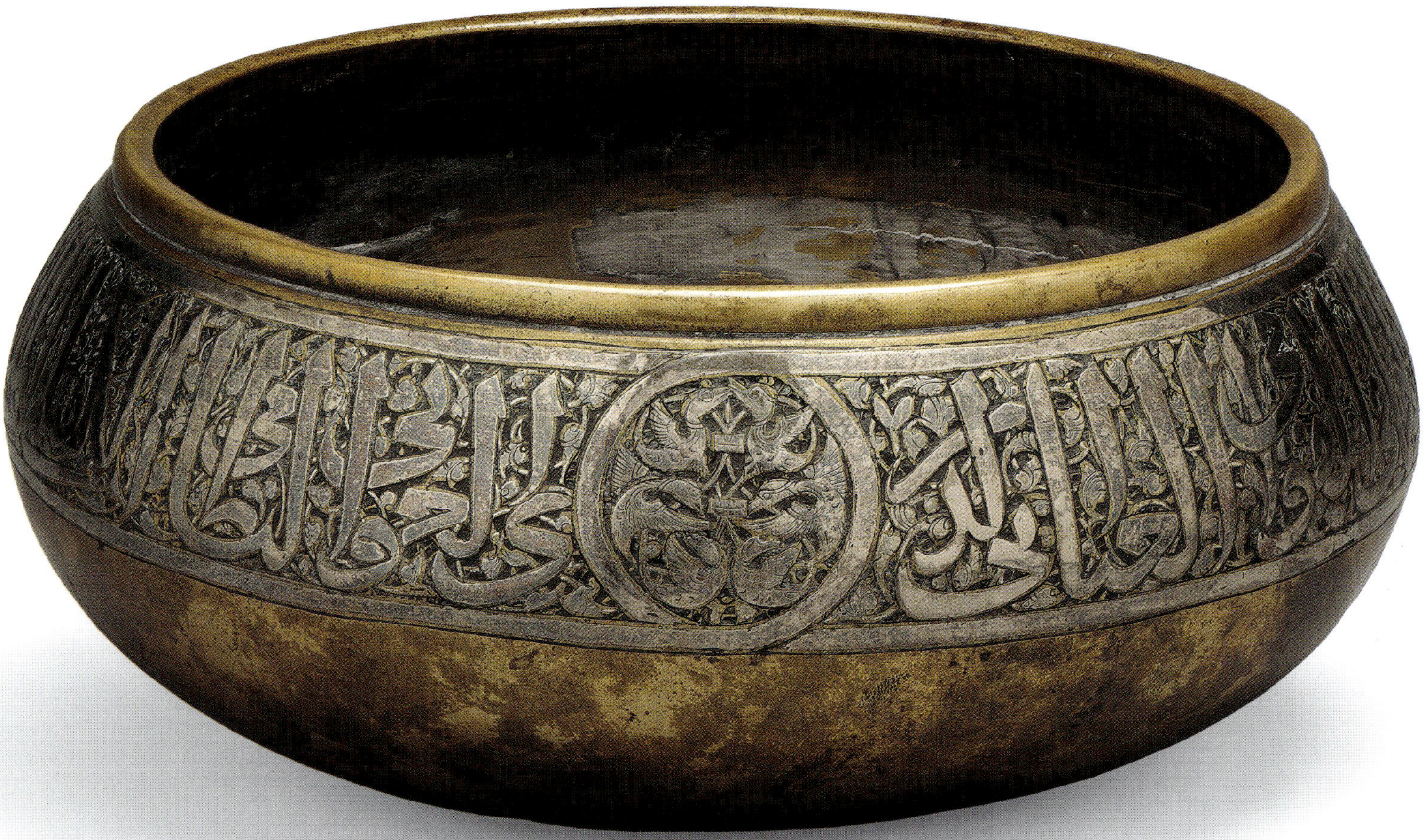

Bowl

Egypt or Syria, 1293–1341
Brass inlaid with silver
Diameter 20 cm (7⅞ in.), height 9 cm (3½ in.)
AKM610

This striking brass bowl is both a feast to the eye and a window into the world of the Mamluks, who ruled Syria and Egypt between 1250 and 1517. The wide band of silver inlay carries a long inscription with the names and titles of a high-ranking official of the Mamluk sultan al-Malik al-Nasir Muhammad (died 1341). Here, the inscription in a bold *thuluth* script is the main decorative element, superseding the small figurative roundel in position and prominence. By the 1320s, the rhythmic tenor of letter uprights in calligraphic compositions became the main feature of Mamluk art. Inscriptions on Mamluk art, including metalwork, reflect the dynasty's concerns with power and self-representation, where individual sultans and high officials perpetuated their memory for posterity by having their names and titles inscribed on buildings and objects.

In the pre-modern world where most architectural spaces were multifunctional, tray stands and trays transformed any room into a temporary place of dining and feasting. This magnificent stand is decorated with an elegant combination of calligraphy and floral motifs. The bold *thuluth* inscription with exaggerated uprights eulogizes the official whose name it carries. The floral arabesques are used here in two different ways, achieving the layered effect typical of Mamluk metalwork. A floral scroll forms the background motif to the monumental inscription, and flowers are also employed as a main decorative element in the roundels punctuating the calligraphic bands. In these roundels the main floral motif is the lotus flower, which saw a revival under the Mamluks through the closer political and trade relationships with the Mongol Ilkhanids (1256–1353).

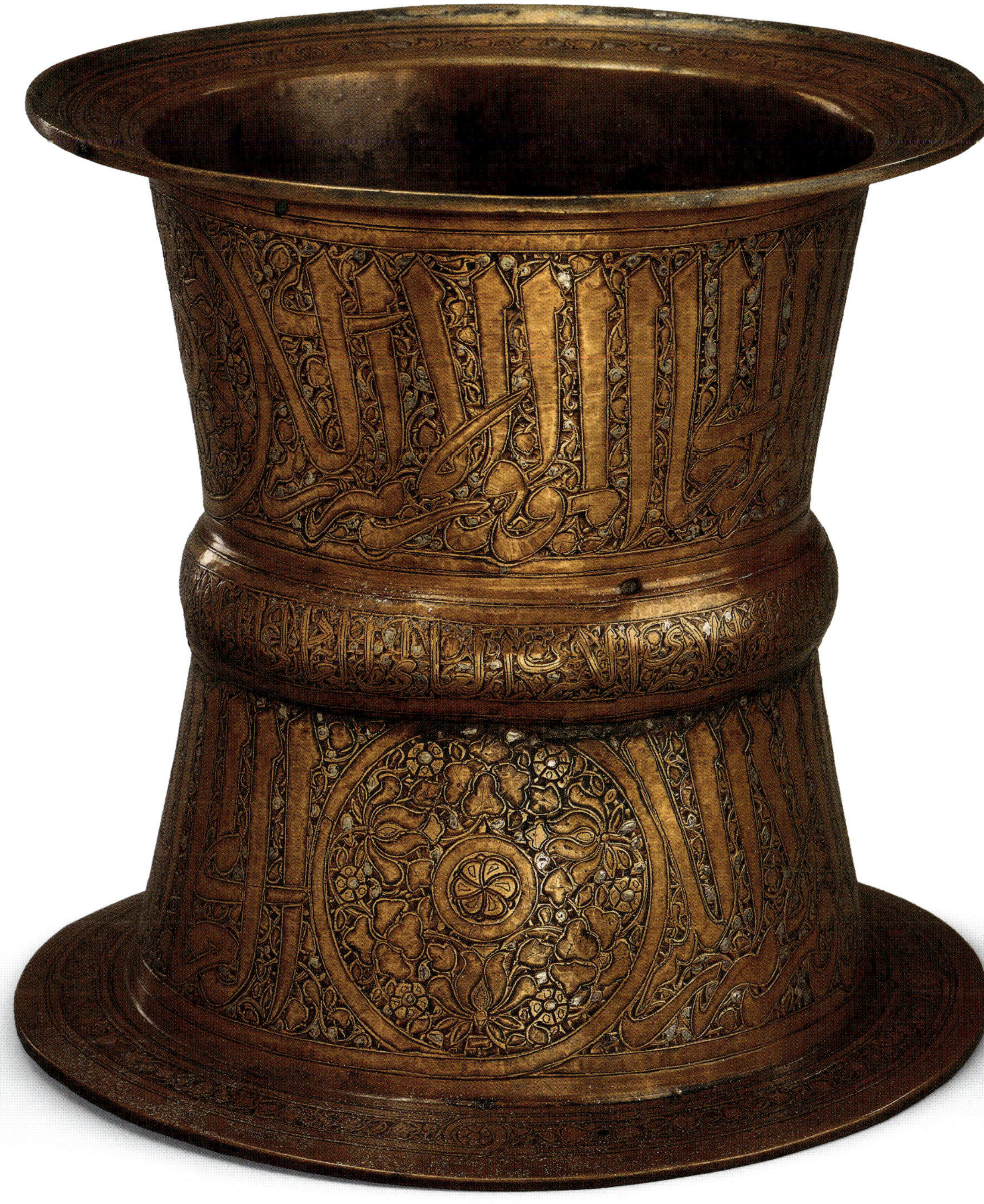

Tray Stand
Egypt or Syria, first half of the 14th century
Brass inlaid with silver
Diameter 18.5 cm (7¼ in.), height 19.5 cm (7⅝ in.)
AKM726

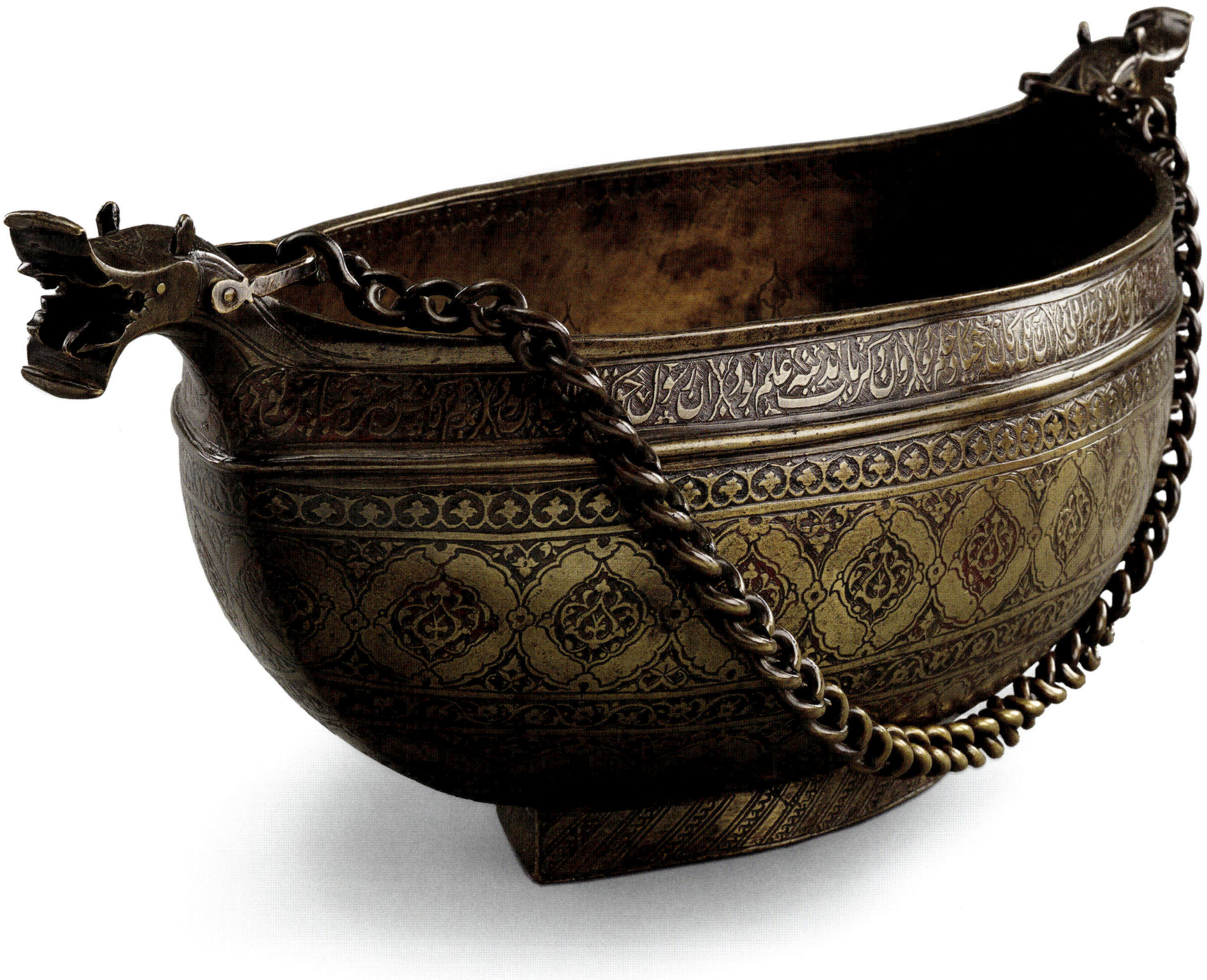

Beggar's Bowl (*Kashkul*)
Iran, late 16th century
Engraved brass
Length 61 cm (24 in.)
AKM612

This beautifully engraved beggar's bowl (*kashkul*) is a ceremonial object that would have had pride of place in a Sufi lodge (*khanqah*). *Kashkuls* were used by wandering mystics who renounced their worldly possessions and subsisted on collecting alms. The bowl's elongated form and its related symbolic function derived from the Pre-Islamic Iranian tradition's wine boat. The *nasta'liq* inscription below the rim contains allegorical Persian verses about the Prophet Muhammad, 'Ali, and the friends of God, generally referring to the Sufi mystics.

"I remember one night as my eyes wouldn't close
I heard the butterfly tell the candle
I am stricken with love, if I burn it is but right
But you why do you weep, why burn yourself out?"

The above verse from a poem by the famous Iranian poet Sa'di (died 1291–92) is commonly found on candlesticks (*sham'dans*) of the Safavid period (1501–1722), including the upper band of the Aga Khan Museum candlestick shown here. The symbolic comparison between the mystic lover seeking the Divine and the moth yearning for the flame finds a natural home decorating lighting devices. Also typical of candlesticks from the Safavid period is split-palmette design on a cross-hatched background, here in an overall pattern that seems to rise along the ridges of the body. The overall floral scroll is interrupted by a six-lobed cusped arch chevron, which seems hidden in the densely engraved foliage.

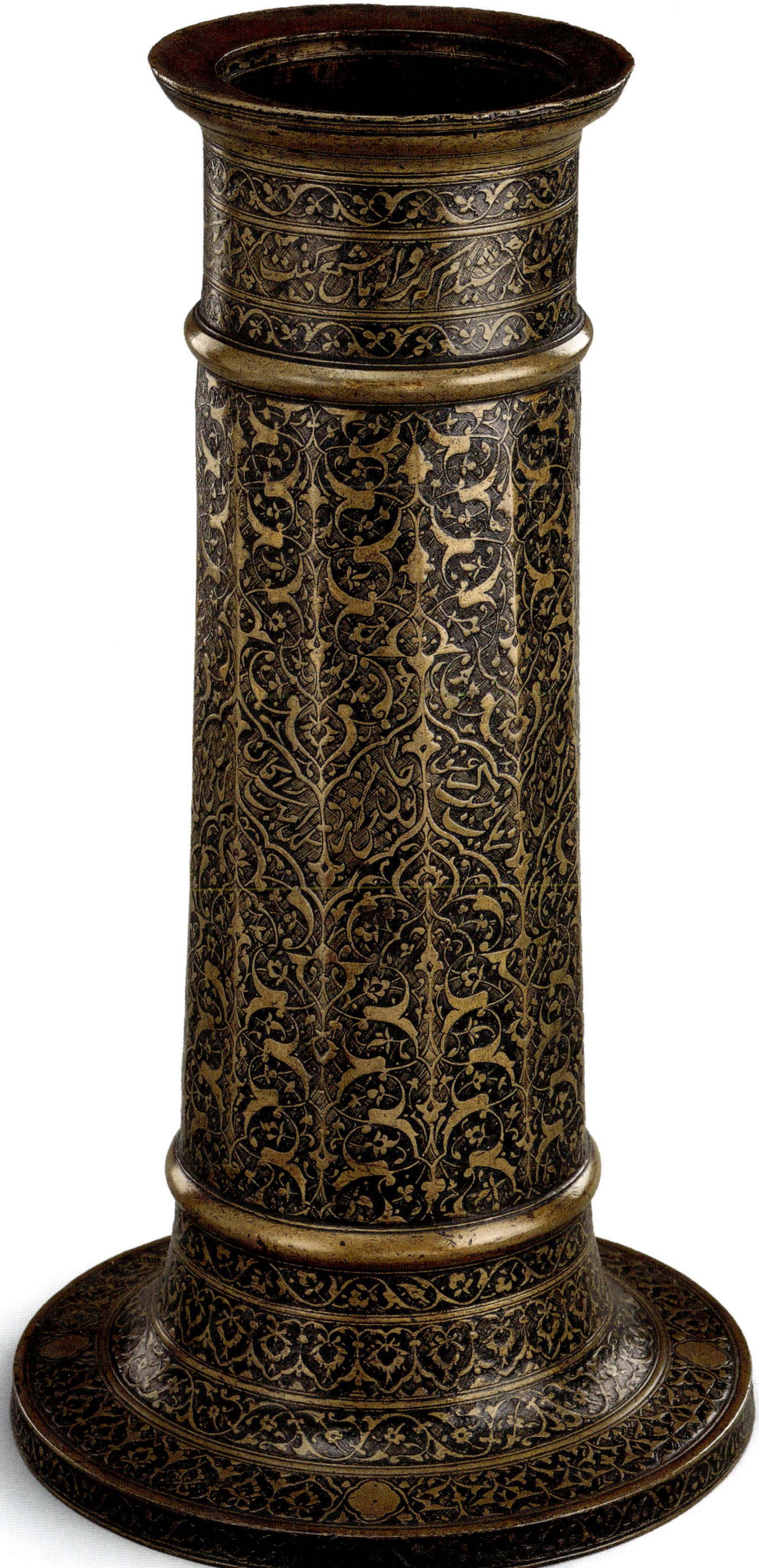

Candlestick (*Sham'dan*)
Iran, ca. 1560
Engraved brass
Height 37.9 cm (14⅞ in.)
AKM613

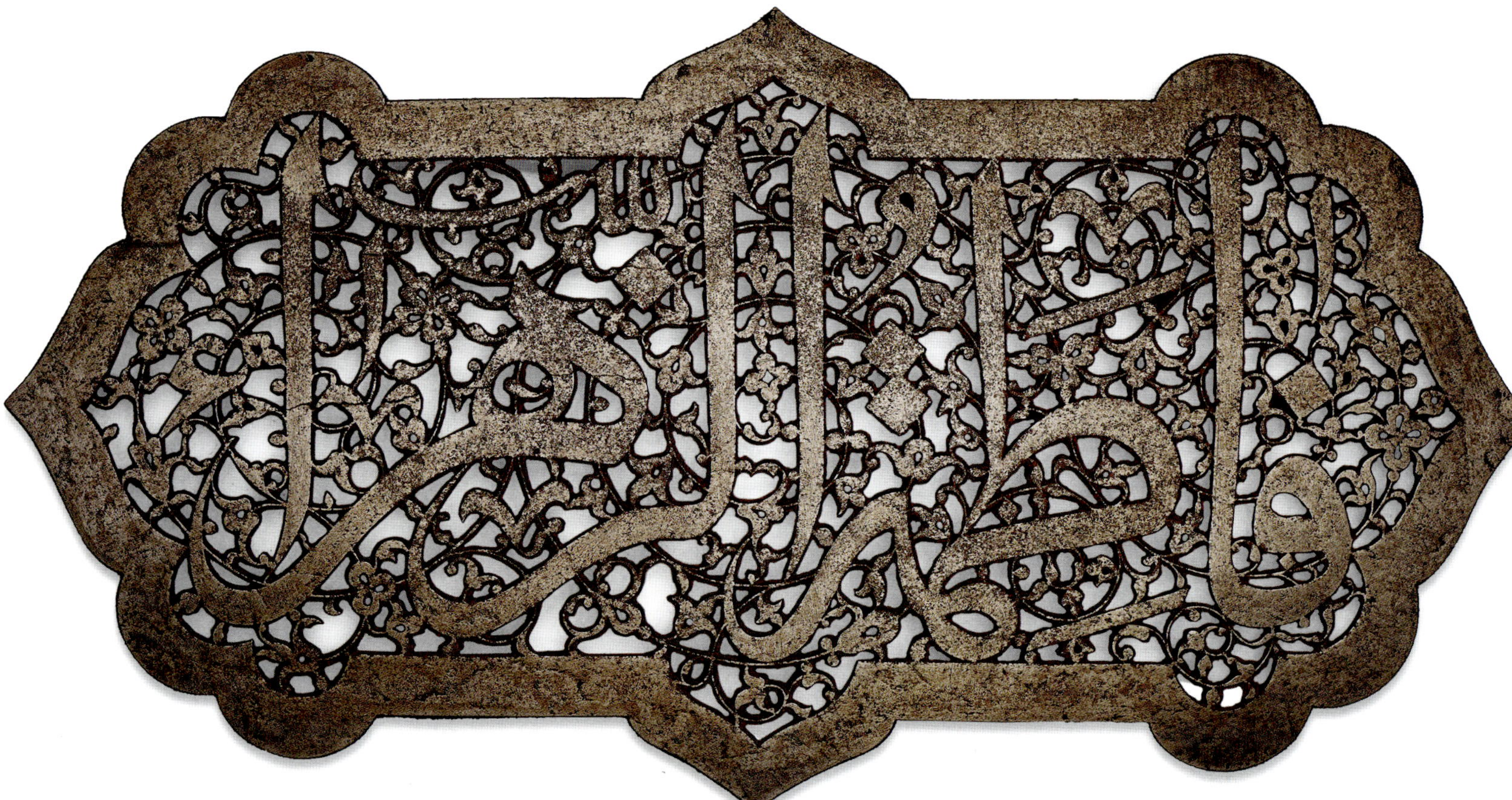

Plaque
Iran, late 17th century
Pierced steel
22.7 × 12 × 1 cm (9 × 4¾ × ⅜ in.)
AKM616

Openwork steel screens and doors are mentioned in the historical annals as special gifts that were given by rulers and powerful individuals to shrines, especially those of the twelve Shia imams and their descendants. Steel was first extensively used as an architectural decorative element in the tomb of the Ilkhanid ruler Oljeitu, built between 1307 and 1314 in Sultaniyya, Iran, and prior to that mostly employed in arms and armour. From that time onward, elaborate screens, doors, and grilles were added to shrines. This steel plaque, for example, would have been part of the openwork components of a shrine door or decorative frieze with the names of the Shia *imams*. The inscription *Fatima al-Zahra'* ("Fatima the Radiant"), the name of the Prophet's daughter and her epithet, is carved out in an elegant contrast between the solid lines of the magisterial *thuluth* script and the intricately carved floral spiral that forms its background.

Processional standards (*'alams*) are used in Shia processions, particularly on the day of 'Ashura, the tenth day of the month of Muharram, to commemorate the martyrdom of the Prophet Muhammad's grandson, al-Husayn, the son of 'Ali, in the seventh century in Karbala', Iraq. In this openwork *'alam*, the form, decorative elements, and function are closely intertwined. The bifurcated blades on the top of the pear-shaped body of this beautifully carved *'alam* are a symbolic reference to the first Shia imam, 'Ali, the Prophet's son-in-law, who is known by the epithet *dhu'l-fiqar* in reference to his bifurcated sword. 'Ali is also referred to by name in the mirror-image inscription on the central field of this *'alam*: *ya Allah ya Muhammad ya 'Ali*, calling upon God, Muhammad, and 'Ali for support. The symmetrical formation of the invocation *ya 'Ali* in the inscription is usually seen as depicting the stylized face of a lion, another symbolic reference to the first imam.

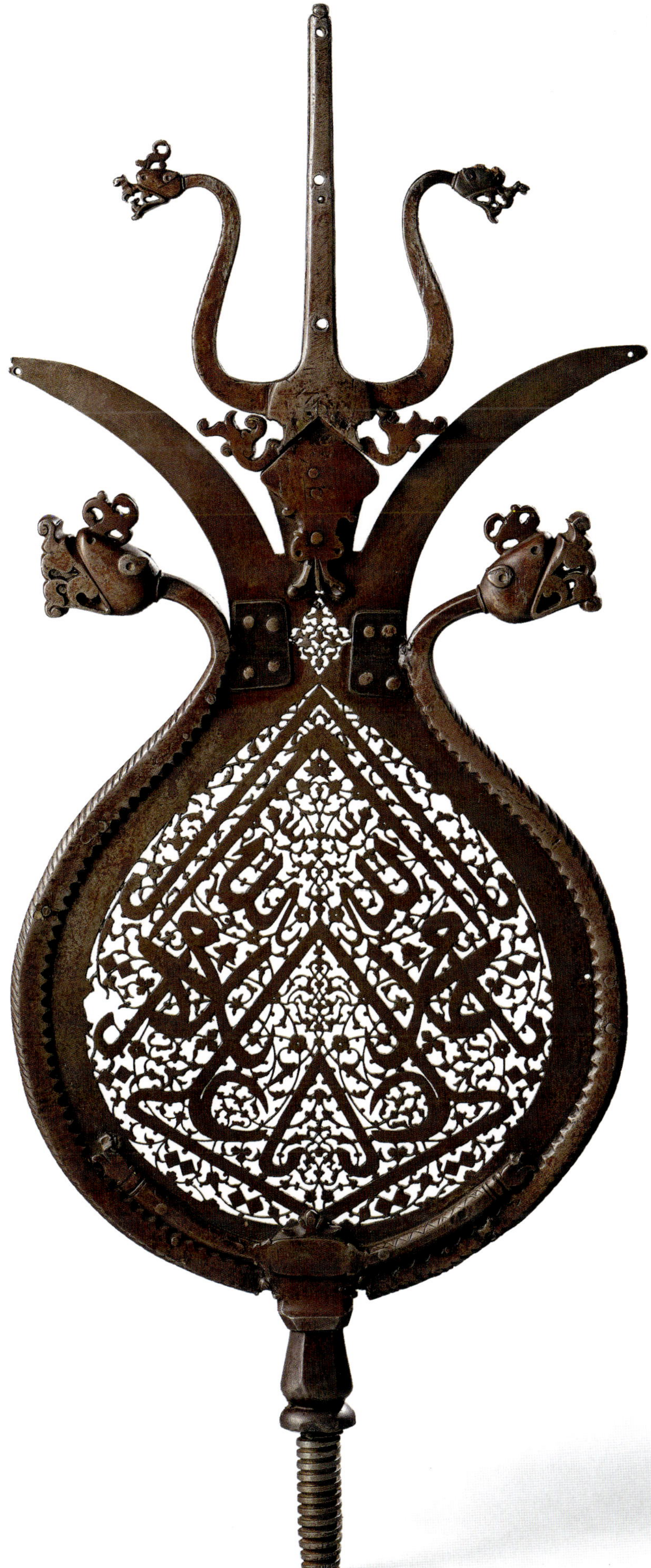

Processional Standard (*'Alam*)
Iran or India (Historic Hindustan), 16th century
Pierced steel
82 × 32.5 cm (32¼ × 12¾ in.)
AKM679

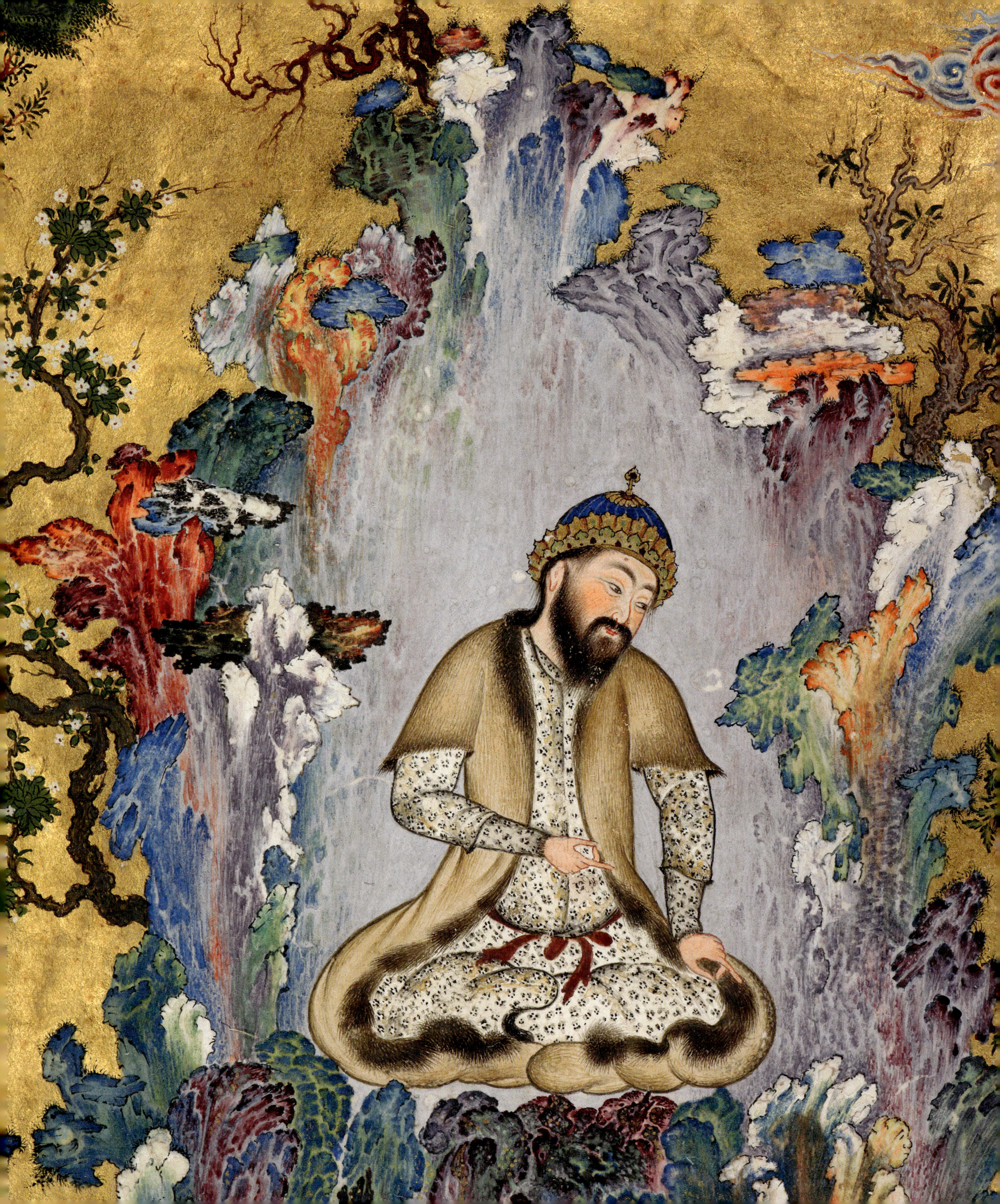

PAINTED MANUSCRIPTS

In Iran, Central Asia, and Moghul India, figural art found its predominant medium in painted manuscripts. Most paintings, as a result, were on paper and small in scale, hence the appellation "miniature." Yet the variety of topics and magnificent sense of detail defy their size and make this art truly unique. No detail was too small to include, from the patterns on textiles to the inscriptions on buildings and their decorative tiles.

In addition to the illustration of historical narratives and lyrical love poems with their traditional subjects of feasting, hunting, and fighting, artists produced single-page paintings that were later collected in albums containing paintings and calligraphic compositions collated together to the tastes and whims of their owners. The Safavids (1501–1722) and Moghuls (1526–1858) also developed an interest in portraiture (AKM124) that was heavily influenced by European prints as well as political and trade encounters.

Few artists are known by name before the sixteenth century, since most manuscripts were products of a group of artists and single paintings were usually a collaborative work by various specialists, some designing and outlining while others painted faces, illuminated borders, or coloured the painting. By the sixteenth century, artists started producing single-page paintings for the open market and signing their names. Some artists' names were also recorded in contemporary sources, including the prefaces for albums that acted as concise narratives for the historical context for the development of Iranian painting.

The rising power of the Timurids (1370–1507) in Iran and Central Asia brought with it scholars and artists who were taken to Samarqand and became responsible for a new beginning to manuscript painting. After the death of Timur (also known as Tamerlane) in 1405, regional centres of patronage were established in other cities, including Herat, Shiraz, Tabriz, and Baghdad, each with its subtle stylistic variations. This painting style is represented in a battle scene (AKM92), where space and depth are created through raising the horizon line and placing figures and landscape in the foreground. In the last part of the sixteenth century, painters in Herat, including Behzad (circa 1450–1535), started developing their

Detail of *The Court of Keyomars*
(see pages 120–21)
Folio 20v from a *Shah-Nameh* (Book of Kings) produced for Shah Tahmasp I
Painting by Soltan Mohammad
Tabriz, Iran, ca. 1522
Opaque watercolour, ink, gold, and silver on paper
47 × 32 cm (18½ × 12⅝ in.)
AKM165

own styles and depicting new topics with expressive narratives such as his *Portrait of Hatefi the Poet* (AKM160). Behzad continued his work under the Safavids and became head of the royal atelier in Tabriz, Iran, in 1522.

When the Safavids took control of Iran in the early sixteenth century, they inherited painting workshops and styles that were characterized by brilliant colours, lush vegetation, elaborate architectural compositions, and fantastical rock formations. *The Court of Keyomars* (AKM165) from the now-dispersed *Shah-Nameh* commissioned about 1525–35 by Shah Tahmasp I in Tabriz is perhaps the most celebrated example of the Safavid style with its exceptional quality of painting and composition. The Safavid artists' elaborate use of architecture to create a complex sequence of events within the picture — indicating inside/outside, before/after, et cetera — and their great attention to detail in depicting architectural decoration are at their most sumptuous in *Sindukht Brings Gifts to the Court of Sam* (AKM496).

Single drawings and paintings independent of a narrative text began appearing toward the end of the fifteenth century. As a result of the loosening grip of the conventional copying of set paintings that accompanied the illustration of literary texts and the rise of album collections, a new style of painting based on direct observation and lyrical imagination developed in Iran, Central Asia, and India. A remarkable example of this individual style is *A Resting Lion* (AKM111) by the prolific artist Mo'in Mosavvir (active circa 1630–97).

The Moghul dynasty, which ruled parts of India and Pakistan for more than three centuries, also followed Timurid examples in its patronage of the arts of the book. Moghul painting, however, combined Timurid artistic heritage with local Indian traditions and the influence of European prints. When the Moghul emperor Homayun (reigned 1530–40 and 1555–56) returned to India after a period of exile in the Safavid court, he brought back with him artists and tastes that infused Moghul art with a fresh wave of Iranian painting influence. Under Akbar the Great, who reigned from 1556 to 1605, Iranian painters along with Hindu and Muslim artists worked to establish magnificent works of art such as the paintings of the *Akhlaq-e Nasiri* (Ethics of Nasir) (AKM288). The Moghuls were specifically interested in naturalism and were avid patrons of animal and botanical studies. This interest varied from individual studies to the sumptuous floral borders surrounding Moghul paintings and calligraphic compositions.

Bahram Gur at the House of Mahyar the Jeweller is a folio from one of the earliest surviving illustrated manuscripts of the *Shah-Nameh* (Book of Kings), the Iranian epic poem. The painting is placed in a rectangular frame occupying the full width of the six-column text of the epic. All the figures are in a row at the lower edge of the work, thus rendering the painting flat and two-dimensional. The lack of depth, however, is compensated by the lavish details of the work. In the story of the charming Prince Bahram Gur and Arzu, the beautiful daughter of Mahyar the jeweller, the sumptuously dressed group is being entertained in a house decorated with luxurious textiles. The richness and variety of textile types and patterns and the opulence of the golden shades of the painting reflect the importance of gold as a symbol of wealth and a store of value. This came at a time of prosperity in which the peace under the Ilkhanids (1256–1353) created a fertile ground for trade in gold-embroidered brocade textiles along the Silk Route.

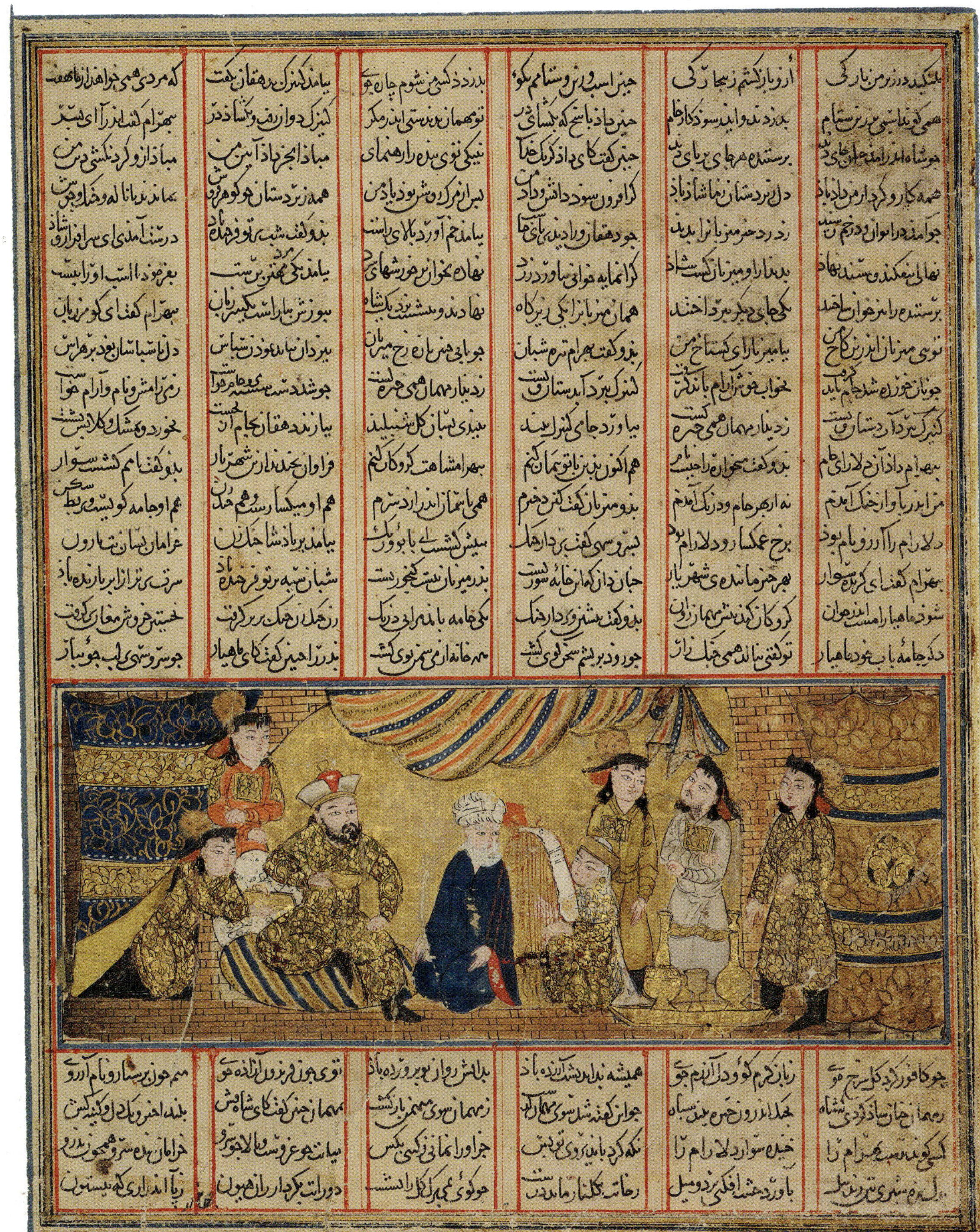

Bahram Gur at the House of Mahyar the Jeweller (Detail)
Folio from a dispersed *Shah-Nameh* (Book of Kings)
Iran or Iraq, ca. 1300
Opaque watercolour, ink, and gold on paper
24 × 19.2 cm (9½ × 7½ in.)
AKM16

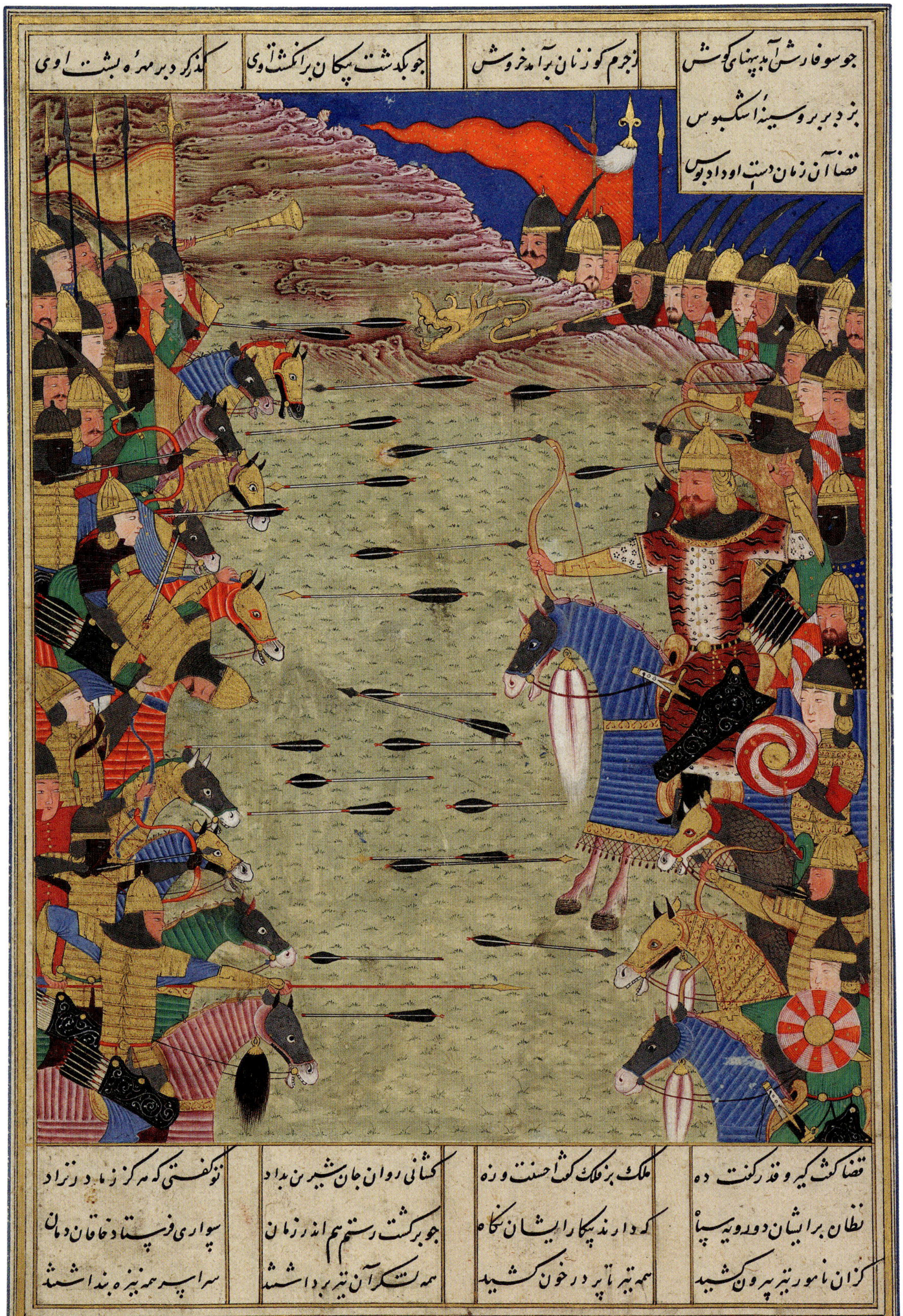

The cascade of arrows hurtling back and forth between the two warring parties in this painting is symbolic of one of the recurring themes of the *Shah-Nameh*: the war between the Iranians and the Turanians, their Central Asian opponents. Advancing from the right is an Iranian army led by the mythical warrior Rostam on his loyal blue-armoured horse Rakhsh. As always, Rostam is identified by his tiger-skin clothes and by his prominent position in the painting. Not only is he larger in size than all the other characters but he alone has the courage to lead into battle on the open field. Rostam's valour and forward movement are contrasted on the left by the reticence of the Turanian army and the fall of their leader, Ashkabus, pierced by Rostam's flying arrow. By raising the horizon line to the top of the painting, the artist managed to create a large battle scene in the confined space of the paper.

Rostam Shooting the Turanian Hero Ashkabus (Detail)
Folio from a dispersed *Shah-Nameh* (Book of Kings) produced for Sultan 'Ali Mirza
Lahijan, Iran, 1494
Opaque watercolour, ink, and gold on paper
23.3 × 15.2 cm (9⅛ × 6 in.)
AKM92

The painter Behzad, whose work we see here, was celebrated as one of the most renowned painters in Herat and Tabriz in Historic Iran during the late fifteenth and early sixteenth centuries. By that time, Behzad was responsible for some of the most magnificent Iranian paintings, two of which are in the Aga Khan Museum's collection. Behzad's painting style is characterized by remarkable fine details and natural gestures that project an expressive narrative and intense individuality of the painted subject. Here the Iranian poet Hatefi (died 1520) is depicted with a greying beard and finely lined face, indicating his old age. The purposefulness of his hand gesture, however, implies an ongoing conversation or perhaps a poetry recital.

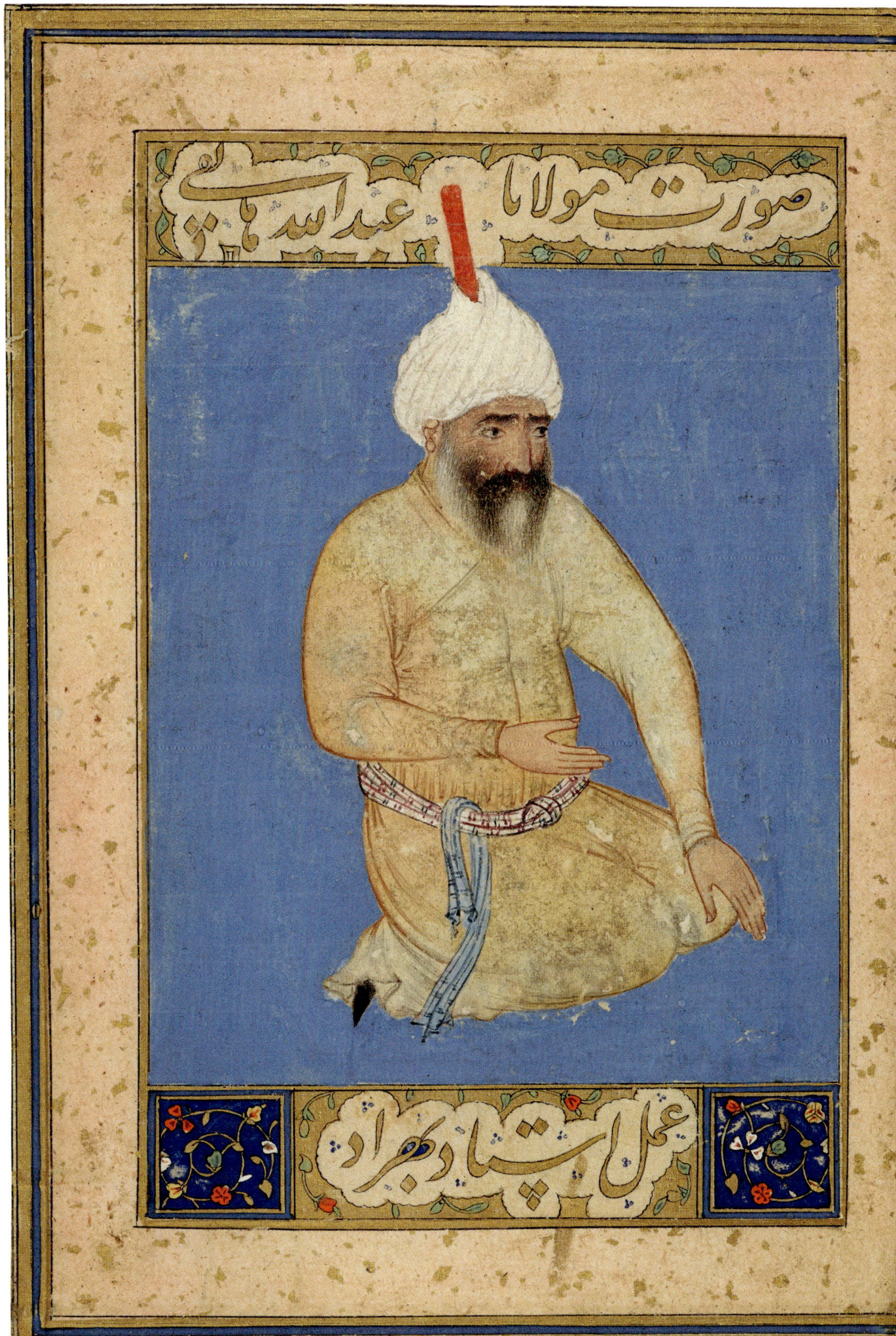

Portrait of Hatefi the Poet
Folio from a 1544–45 album assembled for Bahram Mirza
Attributed to Behzad
Herat, Afghanistan (Historic Iran), ca. 1511
Opaque watercolour, ink, and gold on paper
11.8 × 7.8 cm (4⅝ × 3⅛ in.)
AKM160

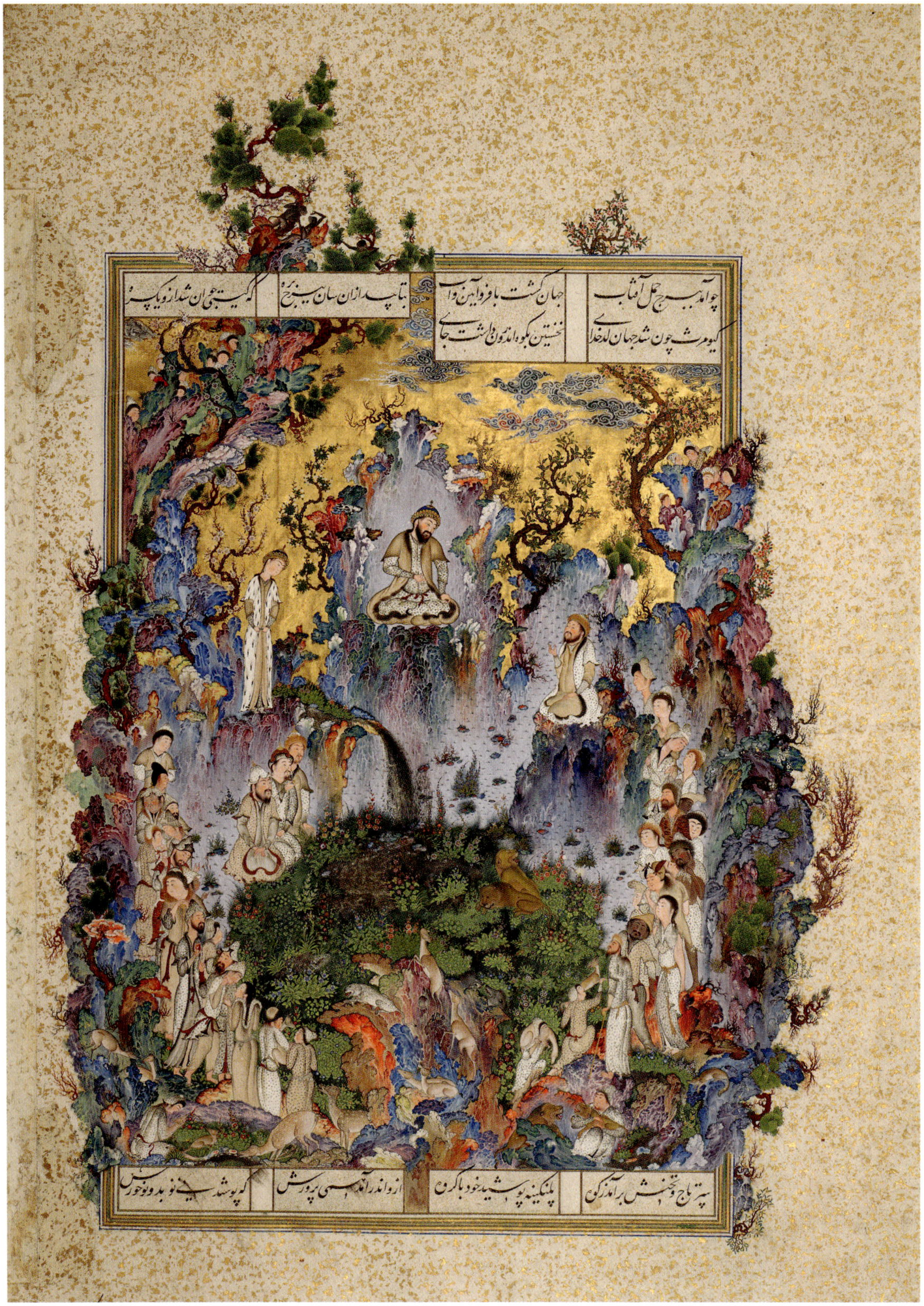

Described in the sixteenth century as a masterpiece and acknowledged to this day as one of the most important works of Iranian painting, *The Court of Keyomars* from the Shah Tahmasp I *Shah-Nameh* remains truly exceptional. The composition of the painting places the mythical King Keyomars at the centre of the narrative and at the apex of the oval composition. Surrounded by his son and grandson, the king pronounces news to all the creatures below him: human, animal, and the myriad of faces depicted in the rocks. The jewel-like intensity of the painting's colours and their variety and balance demonstrate the painter Soltan Mohammad's exceptional mastery. The impeccable details and minute scale suggest the use of such fine brushes at times made of a single squirrel hair. No wonder it took Soltan Mohammad three years to paint this masterpiece for his royal patron Shah Tahmasp I (see also pages 50–53).

The Court of Keyomars
Folio 20v from a *Shah-Nameh* (Book of Kings) produced for Shah Tahmasp I
Painting by Soltan Mohammad
Tabriz, Iran, ca. 1522
Opaque watercolour, ink, gold, and silver on paper
47 × 32 cm (18½ × 12⅝ in.)
AKM165

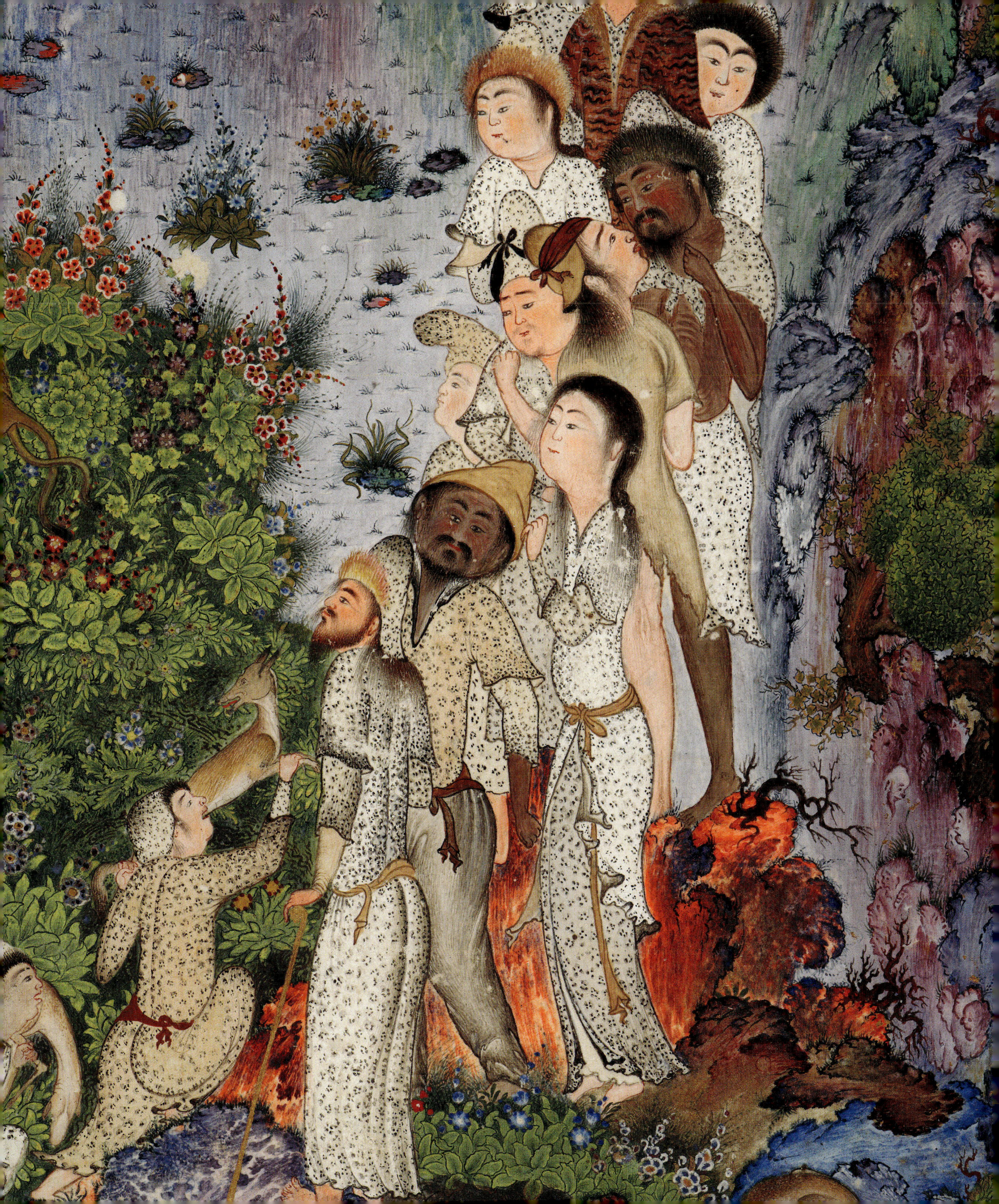

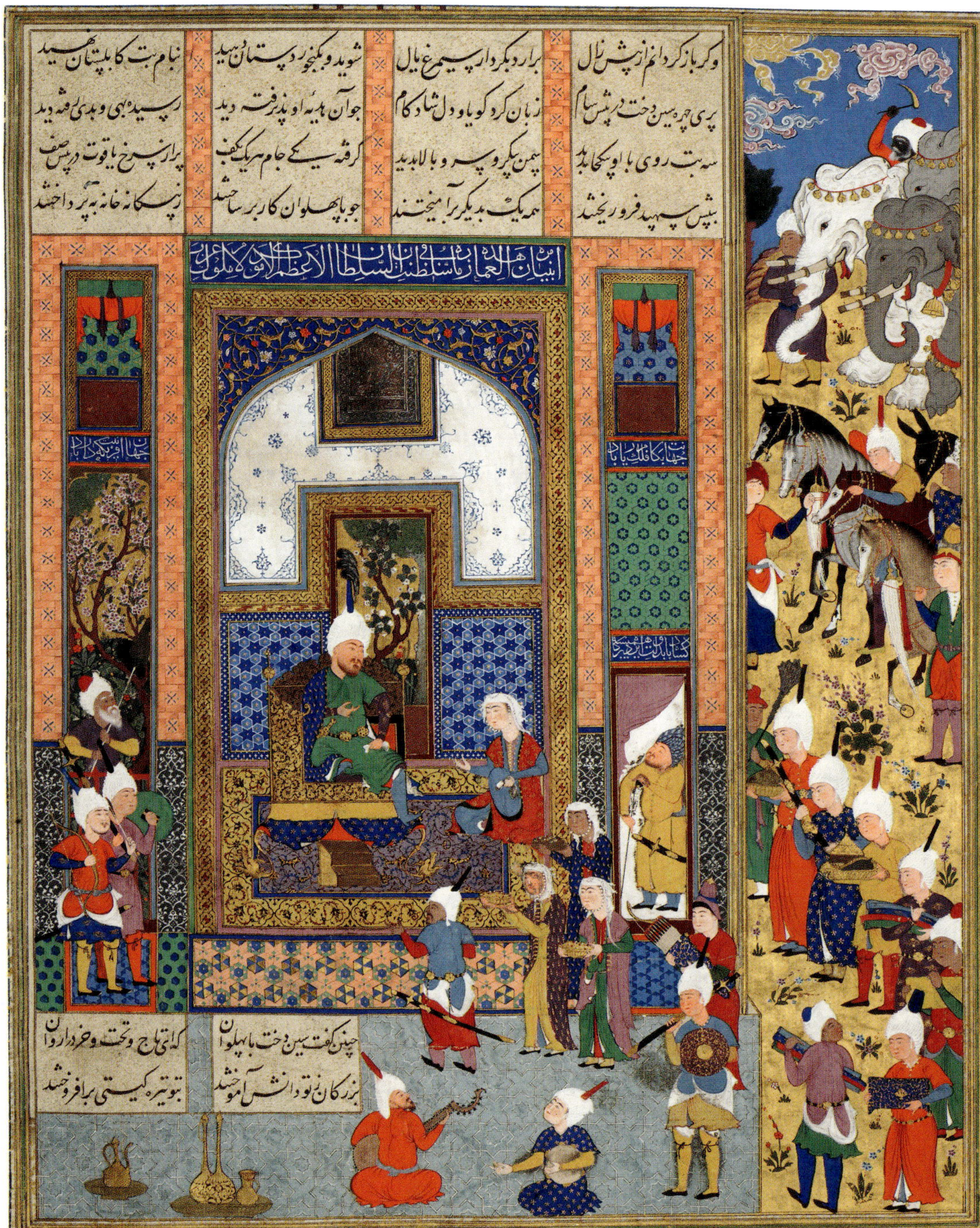

Of the various female heroes in the Iranian poetic tradition, none is more beguiling than Sindukht. Seen in this painting lavishing magnificent gifts and treasures on the mighty warrior Sam, Sindukht uses the old tradition of gift giving to invoke a social obligation that behooves the ruler to listen to her story and respond to her request. Her diplomacy convinces Sam to allow the marriage of his son, Zal, to her daughter, Rudabeh — a union that begets Rostam, the ultimate hero of the Iranian epic *Shah-Nameh*. This painting, which captures Sindukht's reception at Sam's palace, was made for Shah Tahmasp I and is from one of the greatest illustrated *Shah-Nameh* manuscripts. The scene is designed to capture the narrative on multiple levels and from different perspectives. The indoor sequence, on the left, reveals the palatial reception hall in the form of a raised central recess (*iwan*) that is richly decorated with glazed tiles, painted walls, and inscriptions. Meanwhile, outside the palace gate waits a caravan of attendants laden with gifts and accompanied by horses and mighty elephants.

Sindukht Brings Gifts to the Court of Sam (Detail)
Folio 84v from a *Shah-Nameh* (Book of Kings) produced for Shah Tahmasp I
Tabriz, Iran, 1522–35
Opaque watercolour, ink, and gold on paper
46.5 × 31.2 cm (18¼ × 12¼ in.)
AKM496

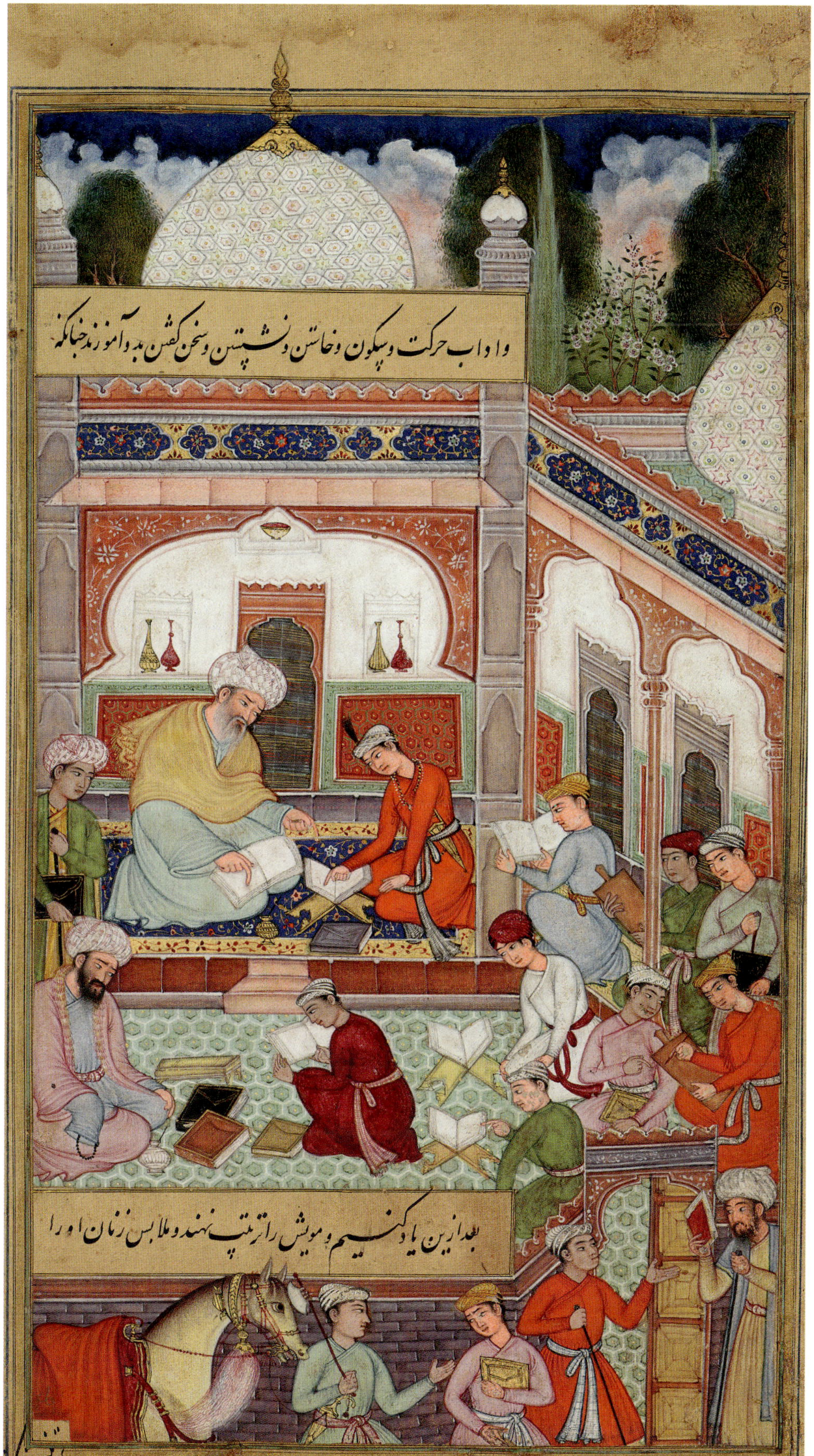

The school courtyard depicted here is one of seventeen paintings from a unique manuscript produced in the court of the Moghul emperor Akbar the Great (reigned 1556–1605) of the thirteenth-century philosophical work *Akhlaq-e Nasiri* (Ethics of Nasir) that was composed by the Iranian philosopher and scientist Nasir al-Din Tusi. At the centre of the painting is a youth reading under the masterful eye of his teacher while other students study independently in the building's courtyard. The scene is set in a red stone building, perhaps a madrasa, with two large domes on either side of the courtyard. The text incorporated in the painting is from the section of Tusi's treatise on the etiquette of learning and the correct behaviour of students, thus giving context to this scene. The disproportionate size of the teacher and his elevated position on the carpeted platform are meant to convey his authority and the importance of his role in the transmission of knowledge and learning.

School Courtyard with Boys Reading and Writing (Detail)
Folio 149v of the *Akhlaq-e Nasiri* (Ethics of Nasir) by Tusi (d. 1274)
Northern India (Historic Hindustan), ca. 1590–95
Opaque watercolour, ink, and gold on paper
23.9 × 14.2 cm (9⅜ × 5⅝ in.)
AKM288

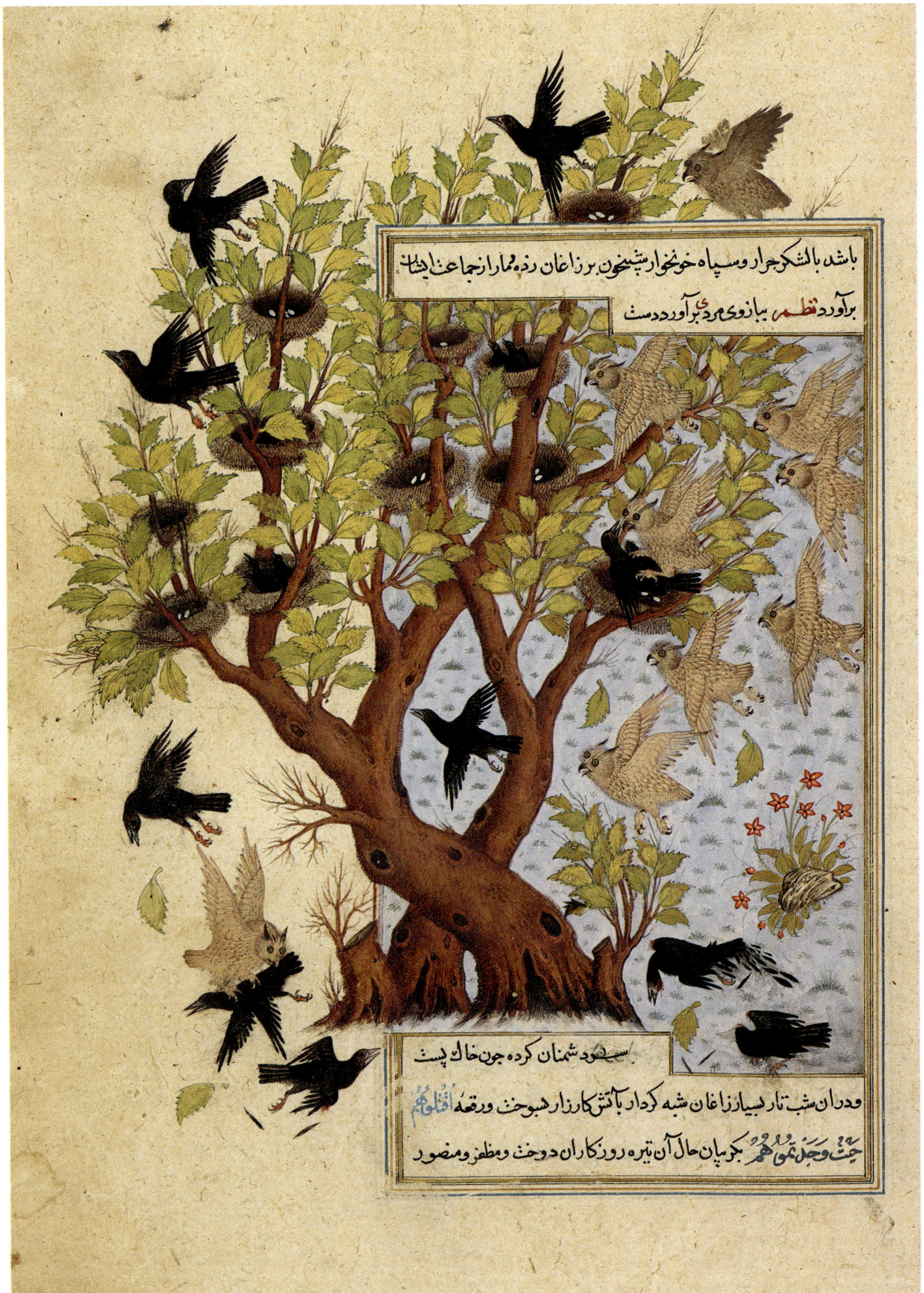

The Battle Between the Owls and Crows is an exquisite example of the illustrated manuscripts of animal fables that traverse cultures and histories with their familiar narratives and unique paintings. The fable collection entitled *Anvar-e Soheyli* (Lights of Canopus) is a twelfth-century translation of an Arabic version known as *Kalila wa Dimna*, itself translated around 750 CE from a Syriac version derived from a Pahlavi edition of the Sanskrit collection of the fables called the *Panchatantra* (Five Principles), which was composed in India in the third century BCE. Created in sixteenth-century Iran, this painting shows the owls' vicious attack on the crows on top of a magnificent tree. The crows later orchestrate a witty revenge against the owls using wisdom rather than force.

The Battle Between the Owls and Crows
Folio 167r of the *Anvar-e Soheyli* (Lights of Canopus)
Rendered into Persian by Kashefi (d. 1504–05)
Attributed to Sadeqi Beg
Qazvin, Iran, 1593
Opaque watercolour, ink, and gold on paper
30.3 × 20.6 cm (11⅞ × 8⅛ in.)
AKM289

An agitated fruit seller is pulled into a fight by one of his customers while an incredulous crowd gathers around them to intervene or just to observe. The scene is set in an open space in front of shops housed beneath a whitewashed arcade near the city gate. The arcade's pointed arches and diamond-shaped spandrels are precisely drawn. The artist creates depth in the painting's composition through a clever placement of individuals and the articulation of buildings. The fruit seller is at the focal point of a perspective formed by the gesticulating onlookers, and further depth is provided by the three-dimensional representation of the arcades. This approach to space and architecture is typical of early Moghul painting and is beautifully represented by the twenty-three full-page paintings of this manuscript in the Museum's collection.

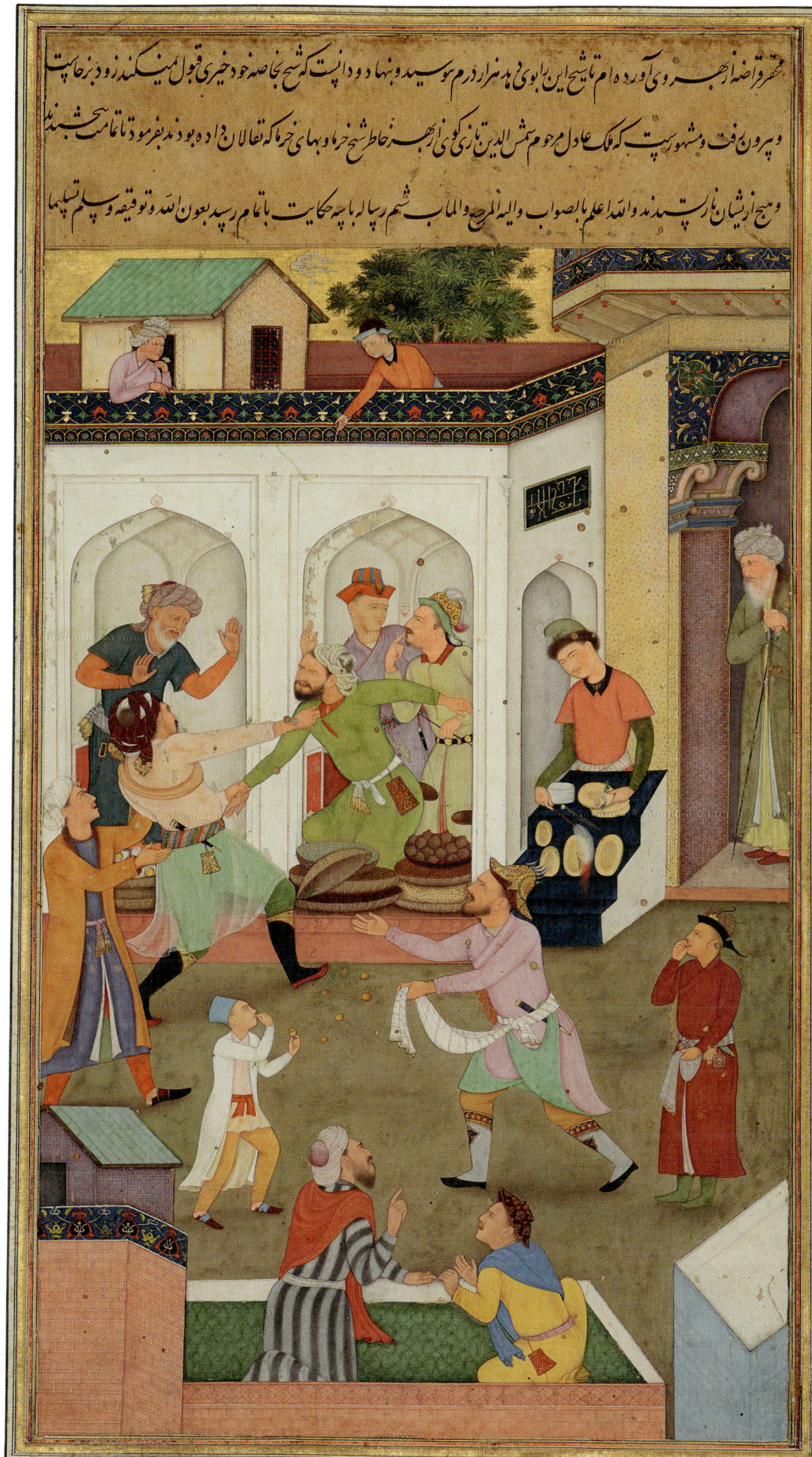

A Fight in the Bazaar (Detail)
Folio 18v from a *Kulliyat* (Assembled Works) of Sa'di (d. 1292)
Agra, India (Historic Hindustan), ca. 1604
Opaque watercolour, ink, and gold on paper
41.8 × 26.2 cm (16½ × 10¼ in.)
AKM284

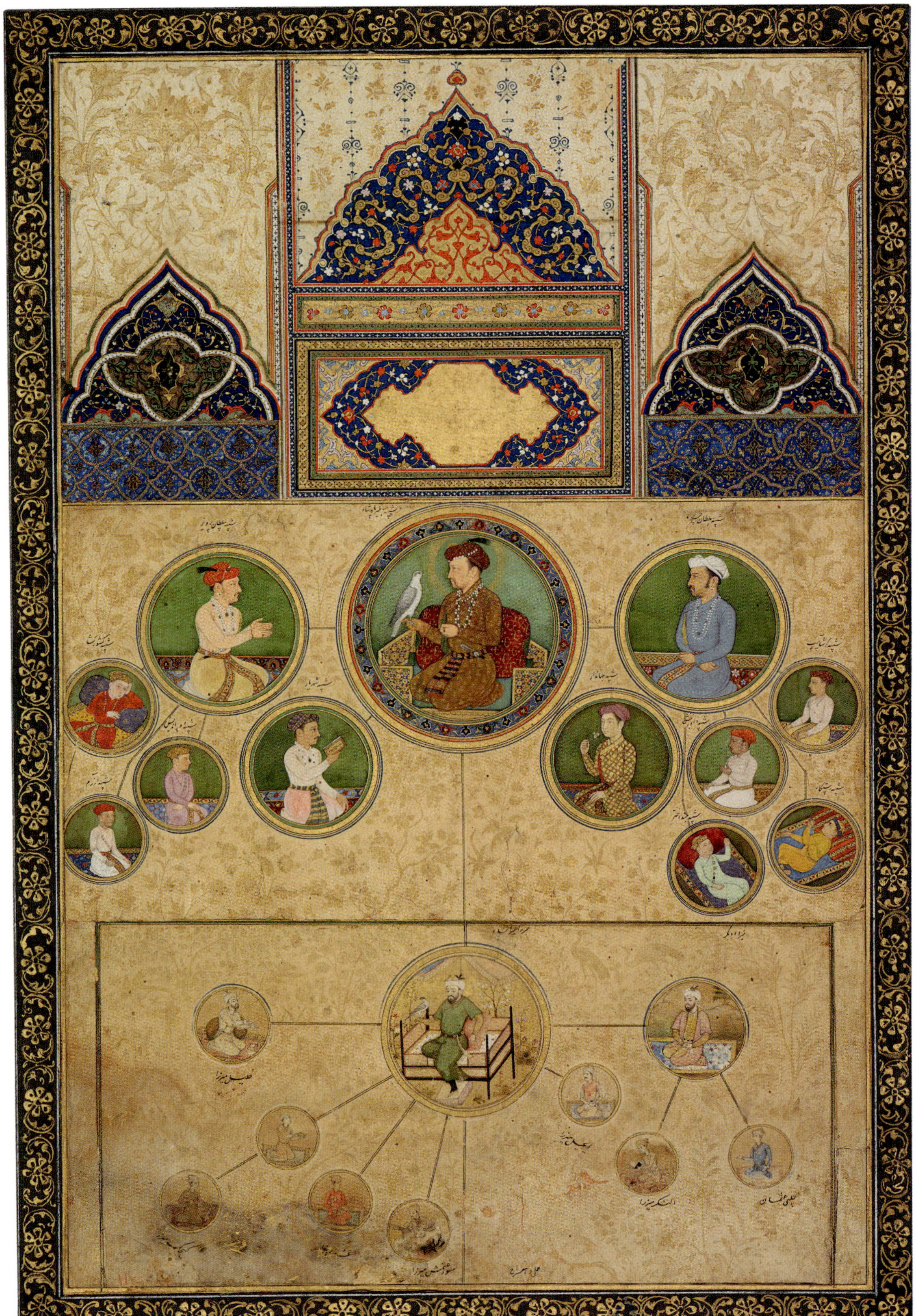

This painting is a composite album page that was skillfully put together most probably before the death of Moghul Emperor Jahangir (reigned 1605–27). The upper portion of the folio has intricately illuminated sections dating to the fifteenth and late sixteenth centuries placed above two genealogical sections from the early seventeenth century. The central medallion with its elaborate border and jewel-like colours features Jahangir at the apex of his immediate family. The emperor is surrounded by portraits of his male progeny, some of whom are still young children. The bottom section of the album page has an earlier genealogy of Jahangir's Timurid ancestors.

Genealogical Chart of Jahangir
Signed by Dhanraj and anonymous artists
Agra, India (Historic Hindustan), 1610–23
Opaque watercolour, ink, and gold on paper
36.2 × 24.2 cm (14¼ × 9½ in.)
AKM151

During the time of Emperor Jahangir, Moghul painting reflected his deep interest in realism, especially in portraiture and in the depiction of natural phenomena such as landscapes. This work, signed by the painter Manohar (active circa 1582–1624), depicts the Moghul emperor sitting on a royal dais with his three sons standing beside him. The figures are portrayed in the typical Moghul portraiture pose with the face in profile and the body in a frontal three-quarter position. The bejewelled and opulently dressed men in this painting, however, are not Jahangir and his sons but rather Jahangir's son, Shah Jahan (reigned 1628–57), and his grandsons. In their quest to legitimize their rule, Moghul emperors saw no harm in taking over pre-existing works of art, as if to place themselves in a more glorious historical past. In this case, new faces with physical features attributed to Shah Jahan, his sons, and his father-in-law, Asaf Khan, replace those of Jahangir, the original patron, and his sons.

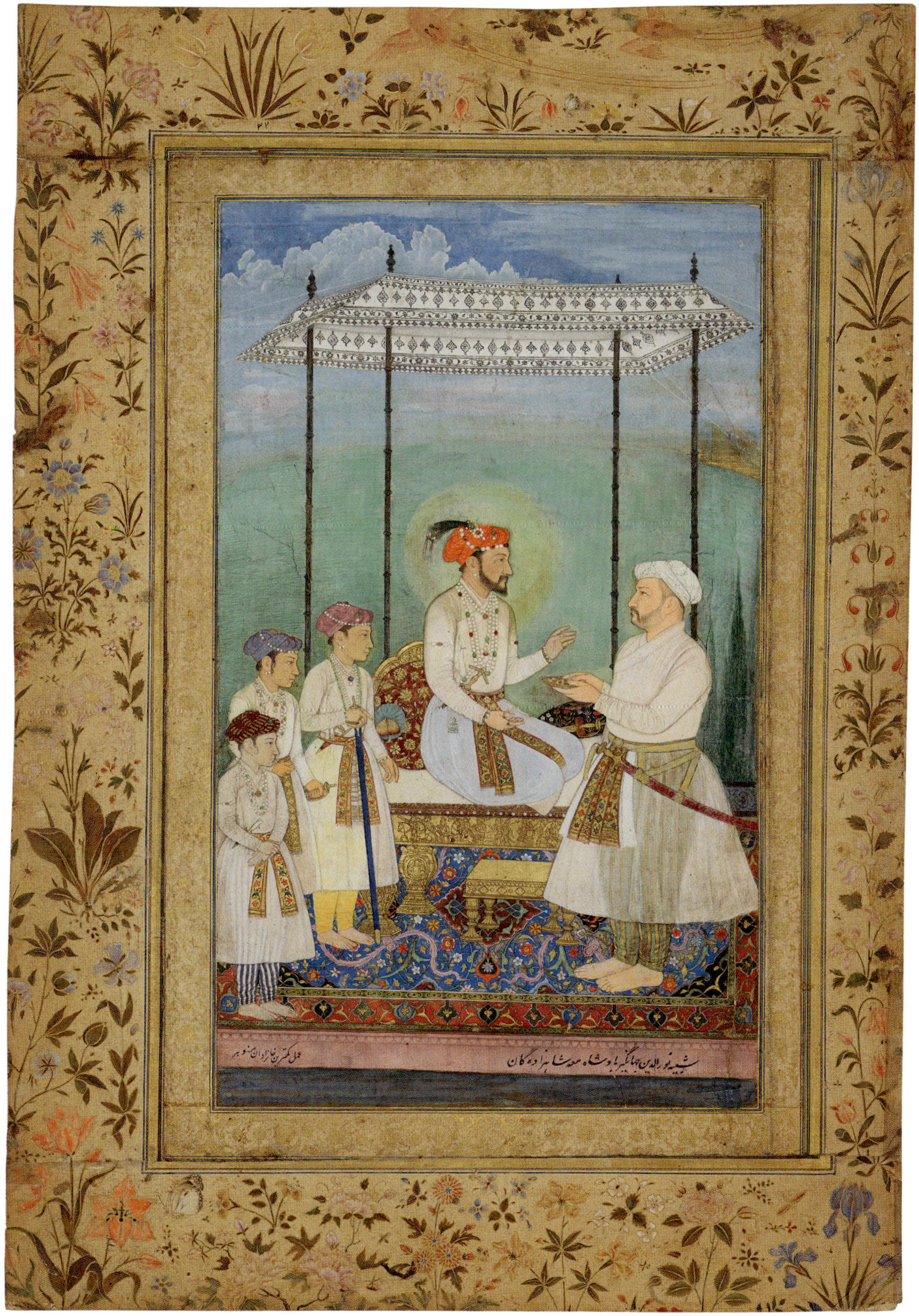

Shah Jahan, His Three Sons, and Asaf Khan

Probably Agra, India (Historic Hindustan), ca. 1628

Opaque watercolour, ink, and gold on paper

35.5 × 24.3 cm (14 × 9⅝ in.)

AKM124

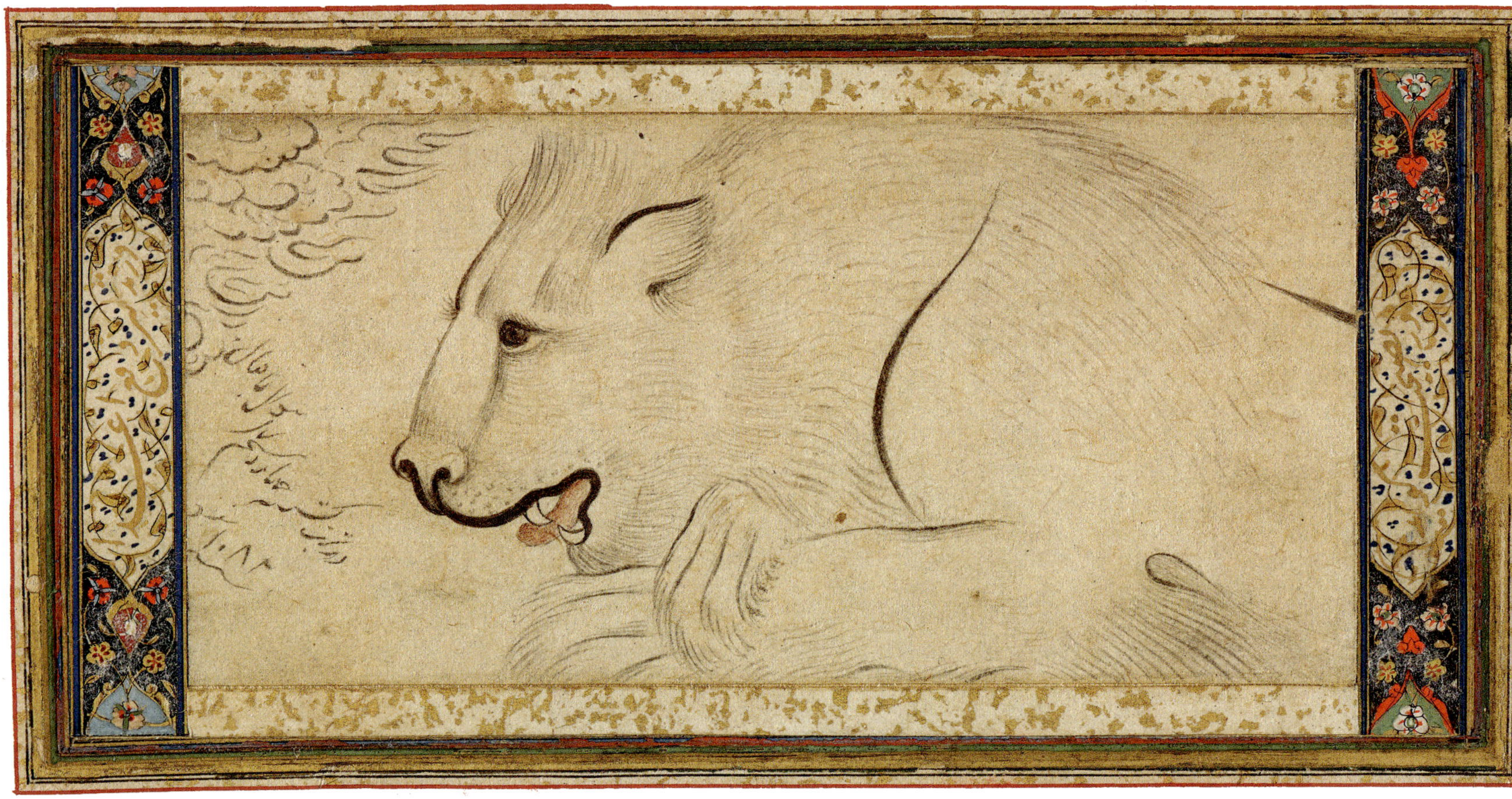

This lion demonstrates a confident style of drawing that evolved in Iran during the sixteenth century and became popular during the seventeenth century. A few fluid lines confidently outline the lion, marking its shoulder, back, mouth, and ear, while the rest of the body is drawn in shorter strokes with finer pens. The drawing is attributed to the Iranian artist Mo'in Mosavvir (active circa 1630–97), who signed two more known line drawings of similar animal topics in 1672 (see also pages 20–21).

A Resting Lion (Detail)
Single-page drawing
Attributed to Mo'in Mosavvir
Isfahan, Iran, 1672
Ink, opaque watercolour, and gold on paper
14.1 × 22.5 cm (5½ × 8⅞ in.)
AKM111

Love and marriage are two central themes in the *Shah-Nameh* that are used as tropes to explore ideas of valour and loyalty. Siyavosh, the son of Iranian King Kay Kavus, is celebrating his marriage to Farangis, the daughter of King Afrasiab, the Turanian enemy of Siyavosh's father. The handsome prince sits with his bride on a raised platform while celebrations take place around a water feature in the palace courtyard. Little does Siyavosh know that the jealousy of other warriors in the court will cause him to send his beloved Farangis to his family in Iran and then have to walk through a raging fire to prove his innocence and loyalty to the king.

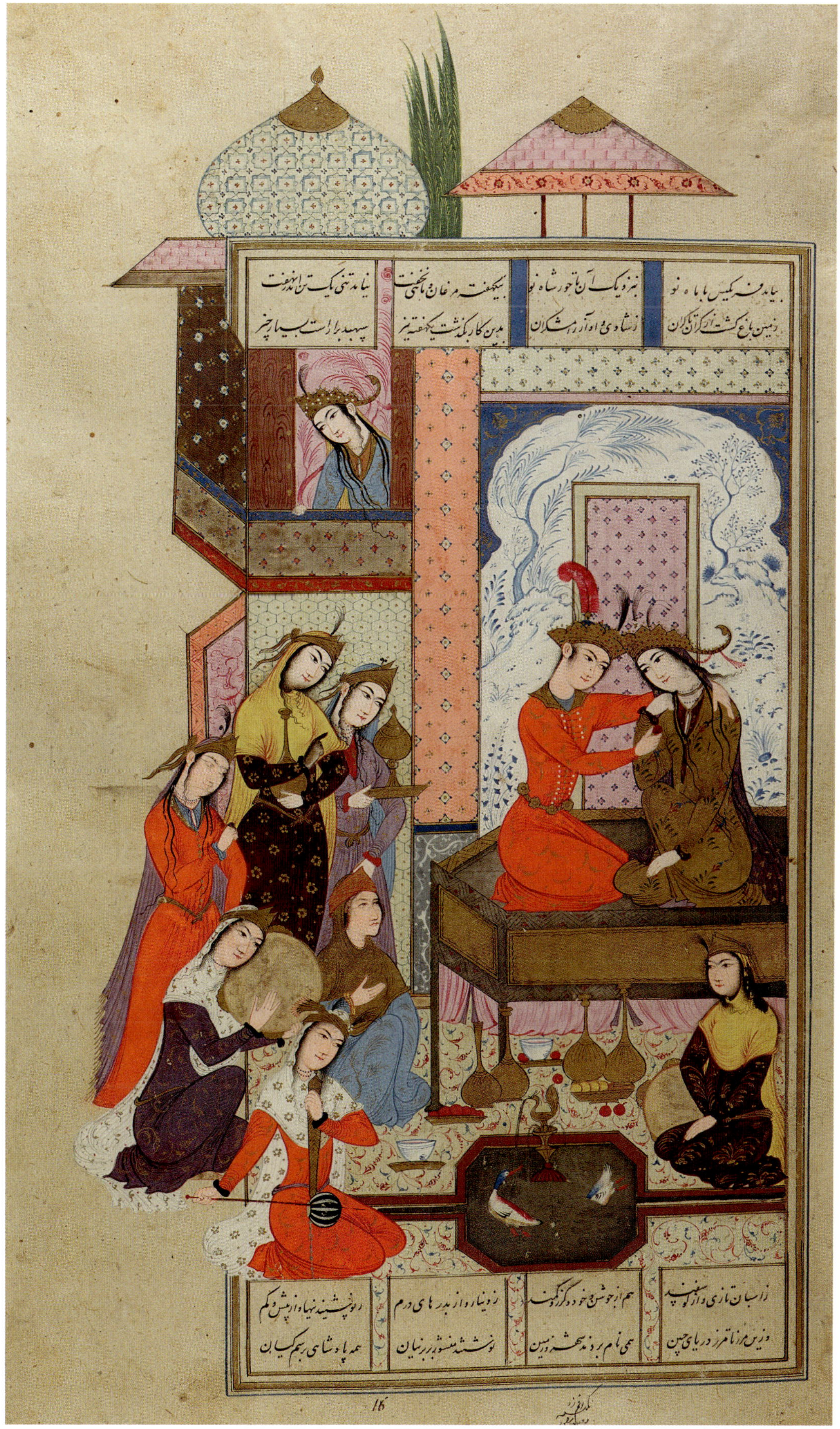

Siyavosh Marries Farangis
Folio 104r from the first volume of a two-volume *Shah-Nameh* (Book of Kings)
Painting by Mo'in Mosavvir
Isfahan, Iran, 1654
Opaque watercolour, ink, and gold on paper
37.9 × 23.5 cm (14⅞ × 9¼ in.)
AKM274

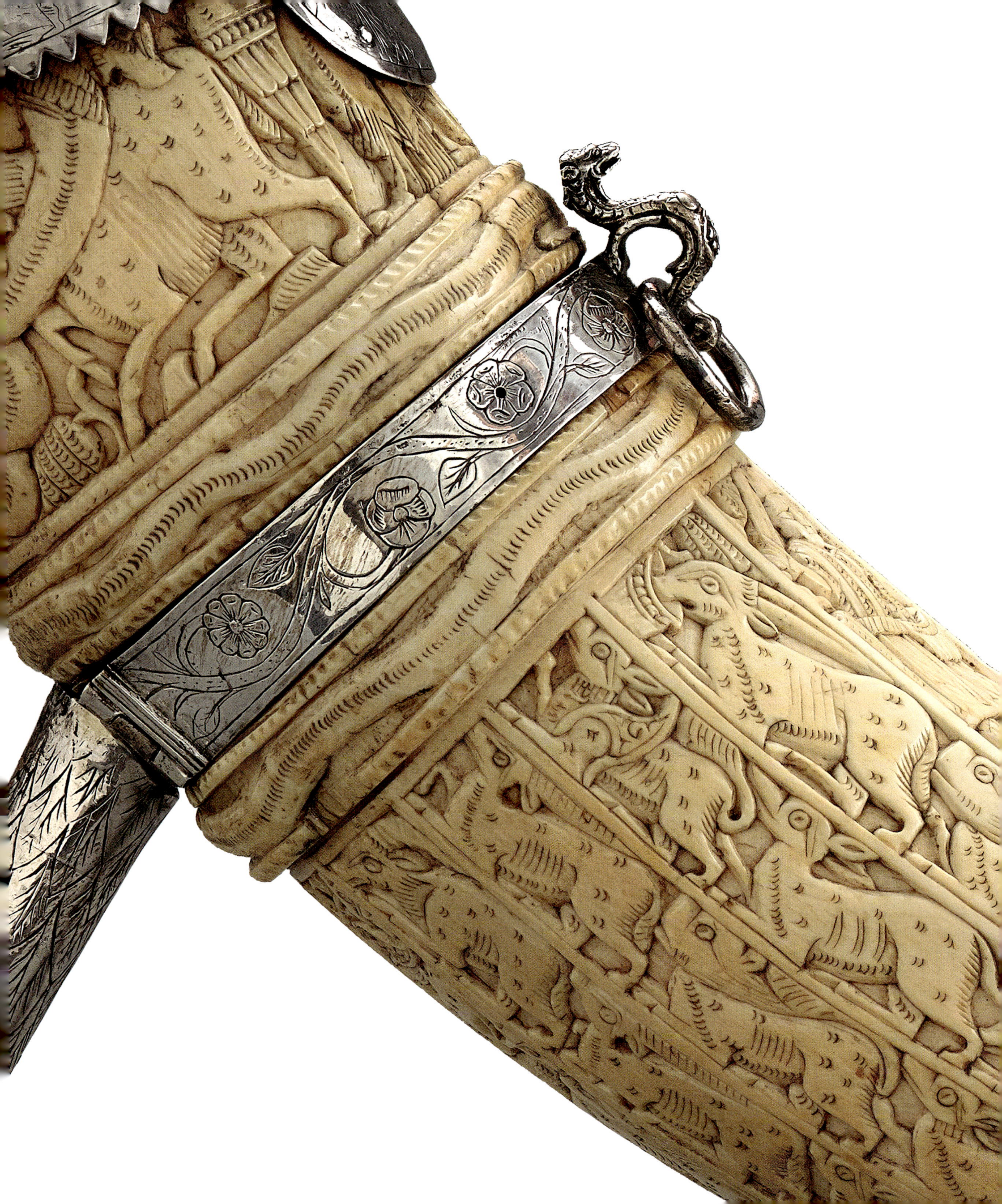

LUXURY OBJECTS

SURROUNDING THEMSELVES WITH THE MOST LEARNED MEN their courts could attract and the most elegant, entertaining, and capable courtiers whose company they could muster, rulers and wealthy patrons also acquired wondrous and luxurious works of art that reinforced an image of status, wealth, and refinement. Artists and men of knowledge followed this insatiable source of patronage at times as part of a court atelier that became a hub of creativity, bringing together artists, aesthetic ideas, and manufacturing techniques from various parts of the world (AKM625 and AKM677).

In addition to commissioning remarkable architectural monuments, luxurious manuscripts (AKM165), and objects in textiles, gold, jade, and ivory, royal patrons were avid collectors of the arts. The Moghul emperor Shah Jahan (reigned 1628–58), for example, collected curiosities, Chinese porcelains (AKM966), manuscripts and calligraphic samples (AKM351), and paintings (AKM124).

High officials and wealthy merchants often copied the passion for luxury and grandeur reflected in the arts produced for court ateliers. The arts of the royal courts of al-Andalus (present-day southern Spain), for instance, are best known from magnificent architectural monuments such as the fourteenth-century Nasrid palace complex of the Alhambra. After the demise of the ruling dynasty, wealthy Christian patrons continued the use of the royal court's style of woodcarving with bone and mother-of-pearl inlay in geometric patterns and abstract plant motifs (AKM634). The beauty and exceptional workmanship of some works of art that have no inscriptions with names of royal patrons (AKM538 and AKM618) bear the hallmark of a discerning benefactor, perhaps not royal, yet eager to own and display a privileged appreciation of the arts.

Detail of Ivory Horn (Oliphant) (see pages 132–33)
Southern Italy, 11th–12th centuries (mount: Great Britain, early 17th century)
Carved ivory with silver mount
Length 64 cm (25¼ in.), height 34 cm (13⅜ in.)
AKM809

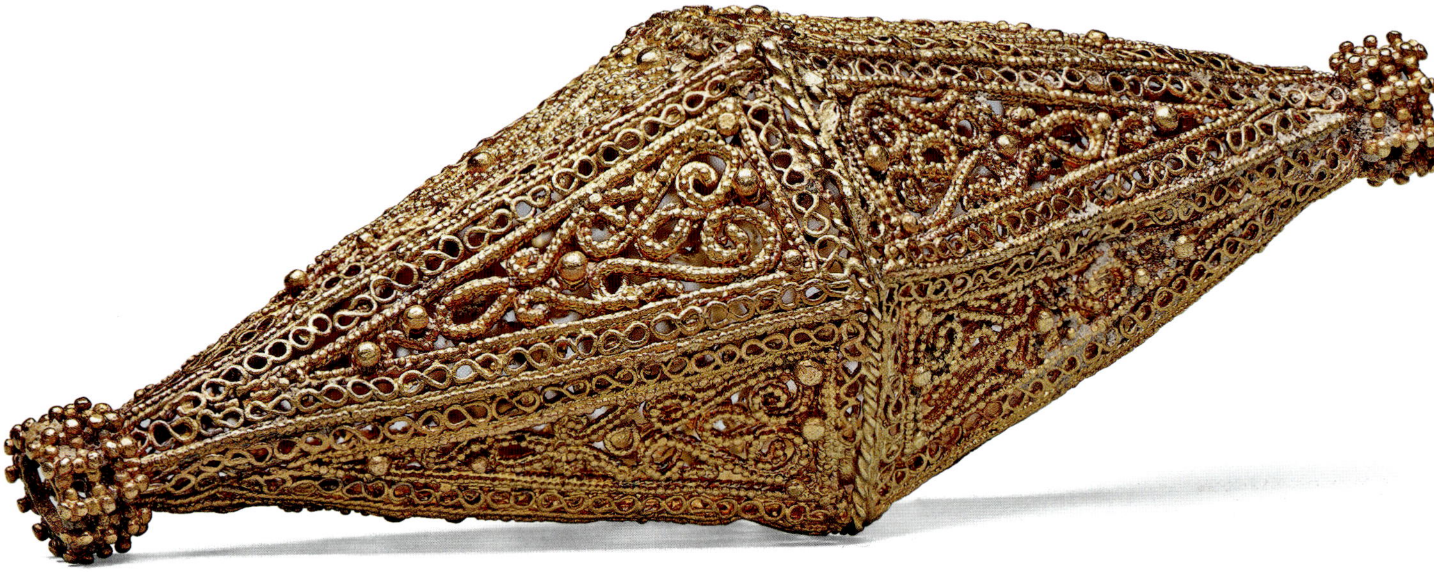

Bead
Egypt or Syria, 11th century
Gold filigree
Length 7.2 cm (2⅞ in.), height 2.9 cm (1⅛ in.)
AKM618

This beautifully made golden bead would have been part of a sumptuous necklace created in the eleventh century during the Fatimid dynasty, which ruled in North Africa, Egypt, and Syria between 909 and 1171. The openwork gold filigree with elaborate granulation is characteristic of the goldsmith technique of the period and is known in historical sources as *mushabbak*. The bead has a box construction in the form of two cones of decorative gold wire strips supporting single or paired S-shaped twisted and granulated wires. The overall impression is one of remarkable skill and lush design befitting the accounts of the Fatimids' great wealth. With their domain straddling the trade routes of Africa, the Mediterranean, and the Indian Ocean, the Fatimids were well-known as avid patrons of art and architecture.

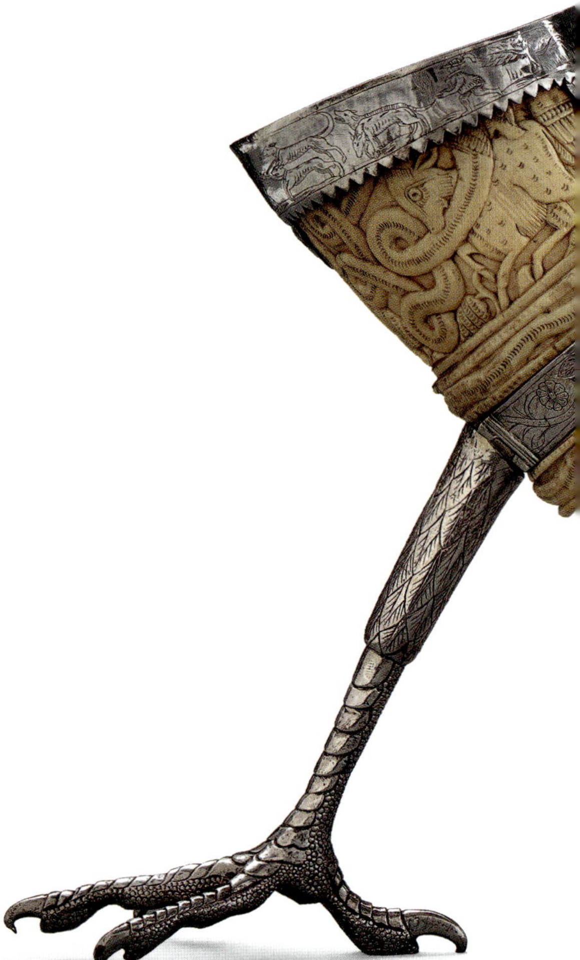

Ivory Horn (Oliphant)

Southern Italy, 11th–12th centuries (mount: Great Britain, early 17th century)
Carved ivory with silver mount
Length 64 cm (25¼ in.), height 34 cm (13⅜ in.)
AKM809

This rare carved-ivory tusk is an exceptional example of the dissemination and exchange of visual culture across the eastern Mediterranean among the Fatimids (909–1171), the Byzantine Empire, and the Italian city-states. It is one of a few examples surviving in major museum collections that were carved in Sicily or southern Italy, with images derived from Fatimid court culture and iconographic style. Known as an oliphant, this tusk is decorated with a hunting scene with real and mythical animals running in file across its length. The first recorded use of the word *oliphant* is in the twelfth-century French epic *La Chanson de Roland* where the hero uses an oliphant as a sounding horn to warn Charlemagne's army against the Muslim attack during the eighth-century Battle of Roncesvalles. Oliphants are also known as hunting horns and indeed hunting and animals are the predominant decorative themes on surviving oliphants. The exquisite carved decoration on this oliphant, and the silver mounts that were added in the seventeenth century, suggest it may have also served a ceremonial role (see also pages 16 and 49).

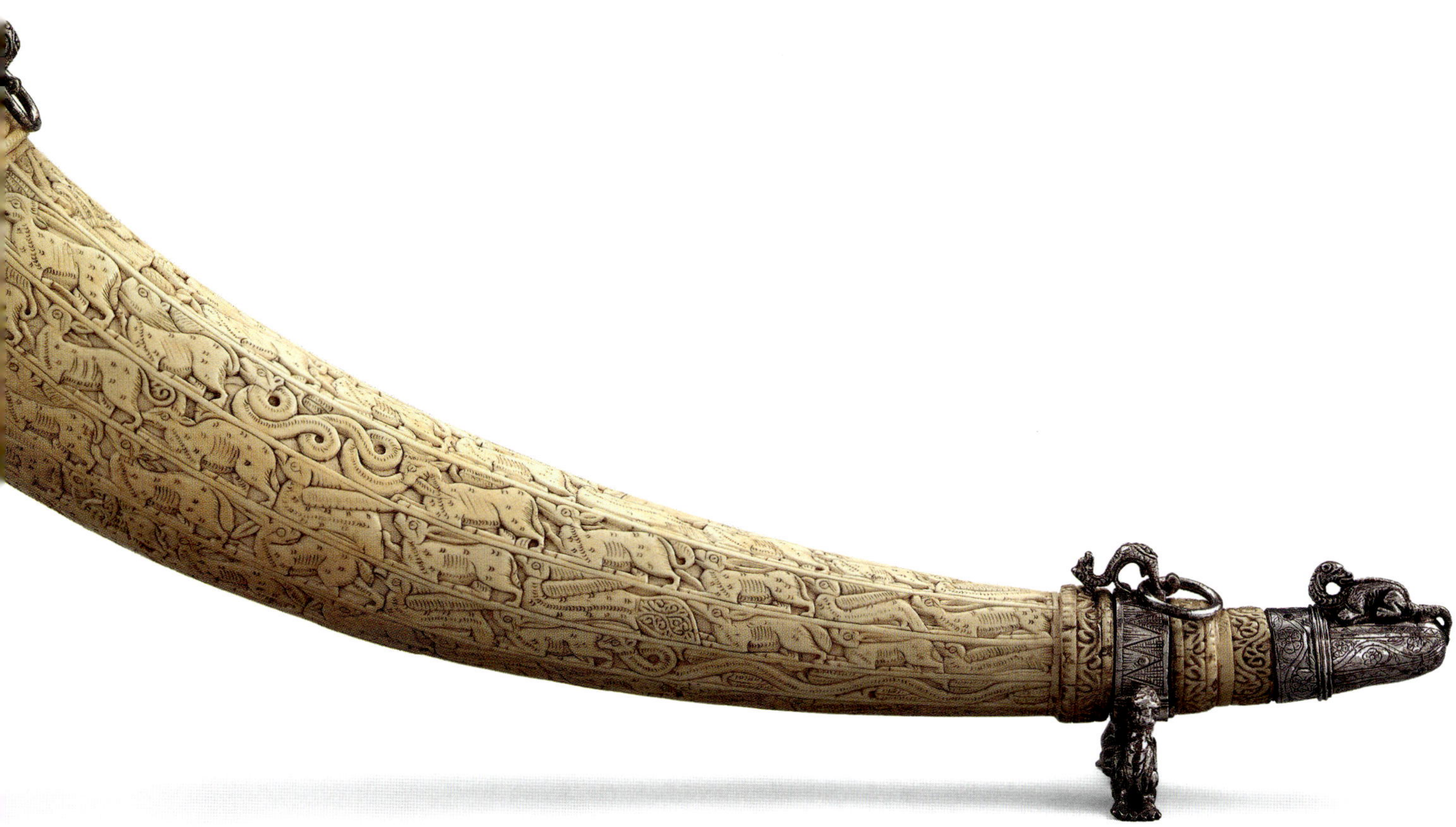

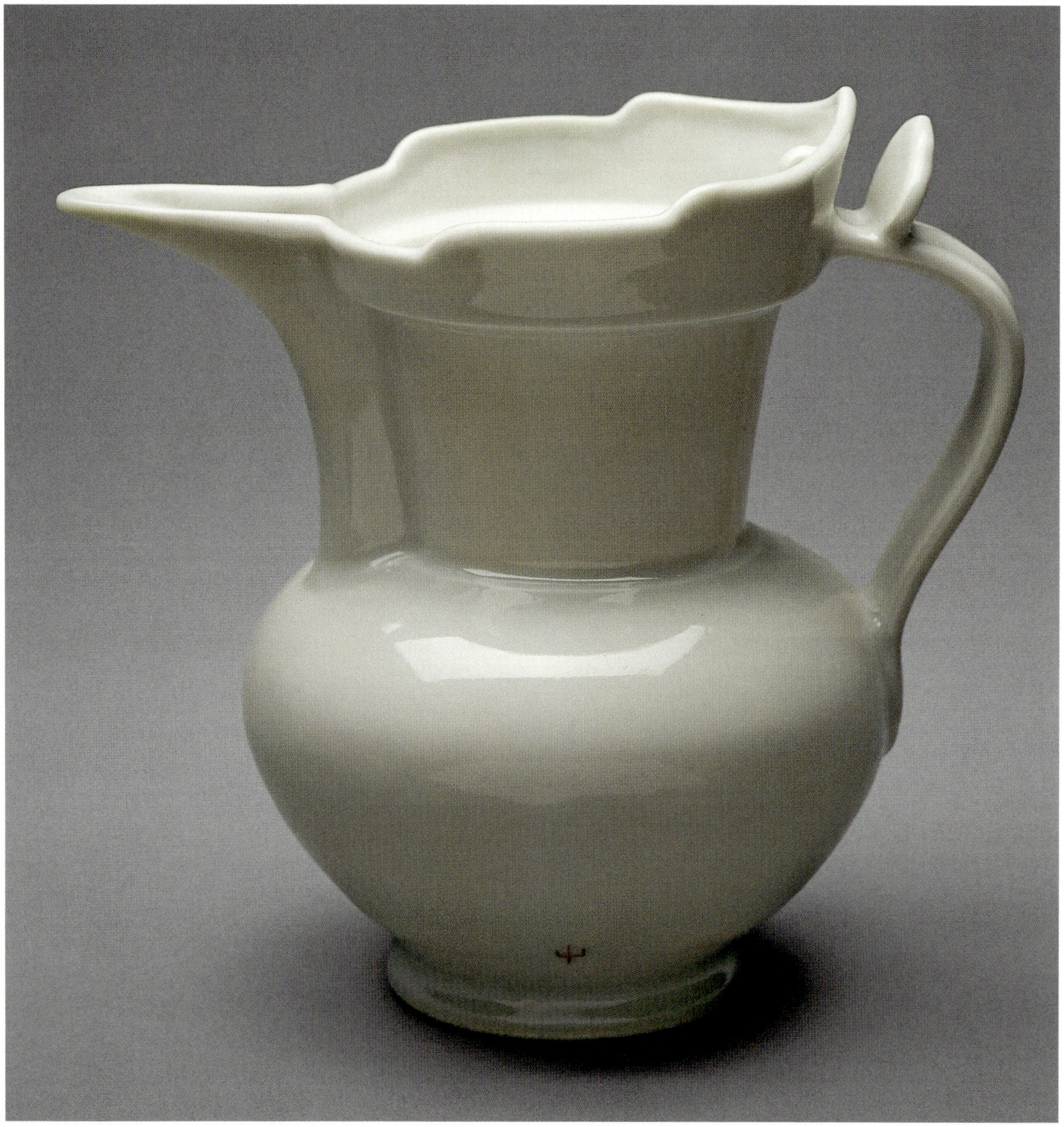

Known to the world as the builder of the white-marble-clad Taj Mahal, Shah Jahan (reigned 1627–58) was an avid collector of the arts. Like Emperors Babur (reigned 1526–30) and Jahangir (reigned 1605–27) before him, he collected curiosities, Chinese porcelains, jade, and objects adorned with precious stones. He also accumulated antiques, especially those made for his Timurid (1370–1507) ancestors, including several jade objects produced for Ulugh Beg (reigned 1411–49), the Timurid ruler of Central Asia. The Aga Khan Museum's rare porcelain ewer, seen here, was made in the imperial kilns at Jingdezhen for the Yongle Emperor of China (reigned 1402–24). By the time it entered the court of Shah Jahan in 1643, it was already an antique created more than a century earlier. One wonders whether Shah Jahan acquired it directly from China or if it was part of the collection of objects he acquired in Central Asia along with the jade objects belonging to Ulugh Beg.

Ewer

China, 1403–24 (with Shah Jahan's dated cartouche, 1643)
Porcelain, glazed
Height 19.3 cm (7⅝ in.)
AKM966

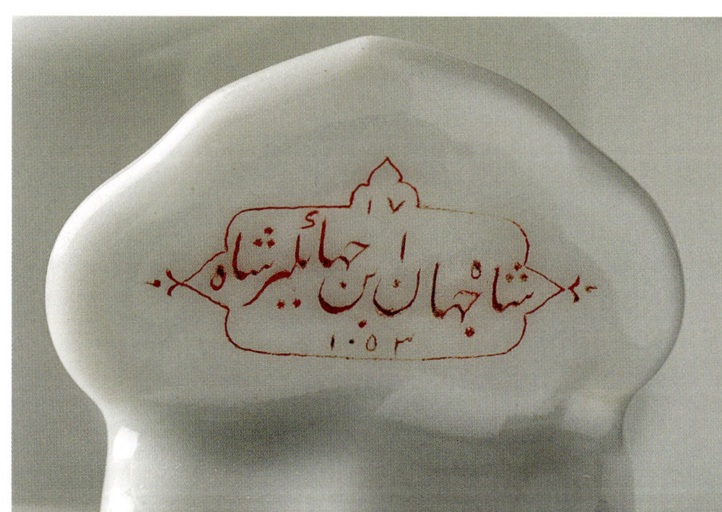

This rare silk robe with a fitted waist, flared skirt, and tiny-button closure is a remarkable example of luxury clothing under the Mongols who governed the area from China to Iran during most of the thirteenth and fourteenth centuries. The vast region under the control of the Mongols established relative peace and safety that facilitated the movement of raw materials, technical knowledge, visual motifs, and able craftsmen, resulting in revolutionary advances in the arts of the Mongol Ilkhans, who ruled Iran between 1256 and 1353 and adopted Islam in 1295. Sumptuous textiles woven from silk cloth wrapped with gold, like this robe, were made in various areas and traded into Europe where they became known as Tartar cloth or *panni tartarici*. The roundels on the Aga Khan Museum robe, however, are decorated with pseudo-writing that suggests it was made in Iran or Central Asia. This robe would have been worn under an open outer coat with short sleeves in order to better display the expensive and beautiful textile underneath. The robe's arms are extraordinarily long and would have been pushed up around the forearm, adding a layer of protection as well as emphasizing the abundance of gold woven silk available to its owner.

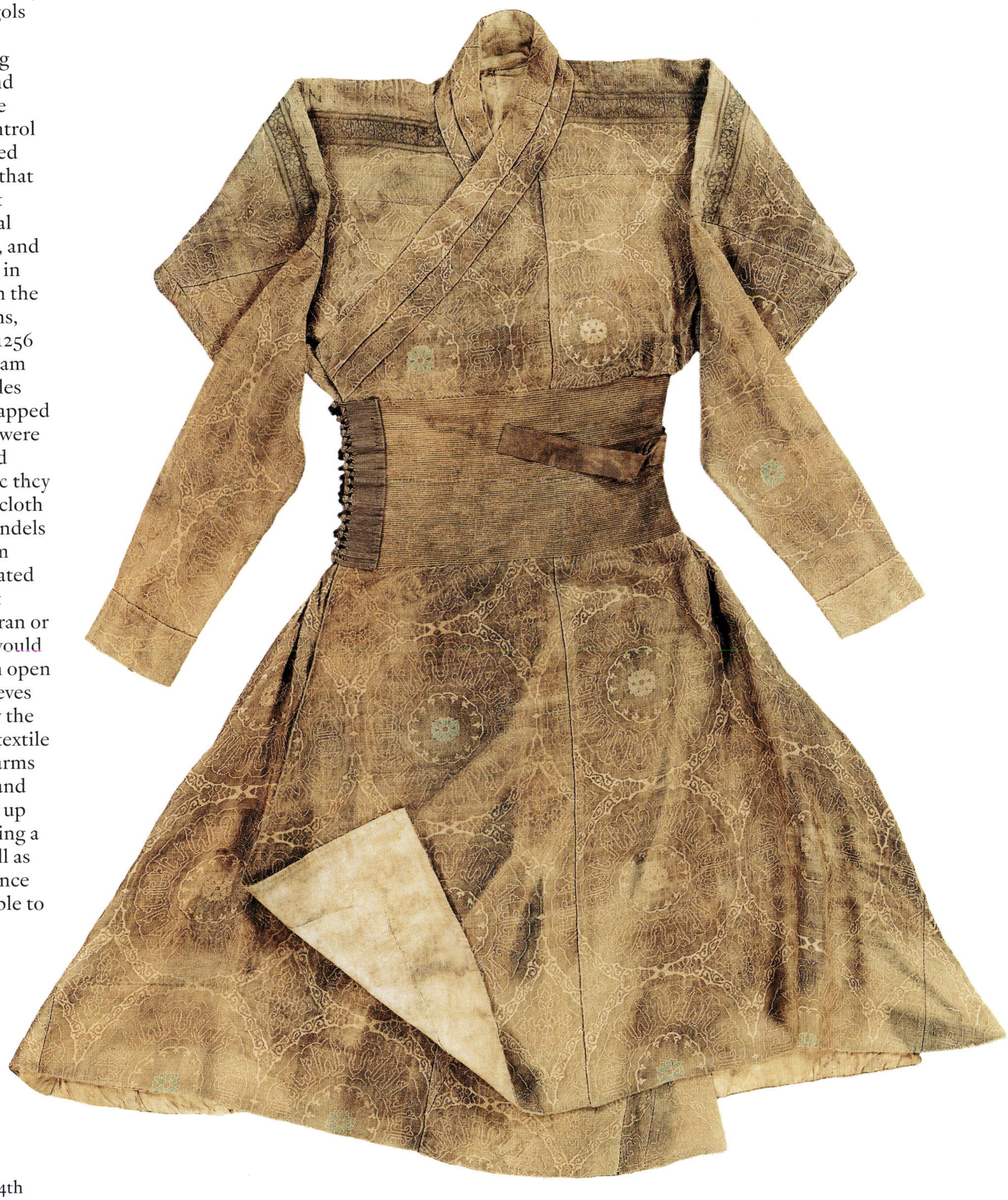

Robe
Iran or Central Asia, 13th–14th centuries
Silk and metal thread
Height 140 cm (55⅛ in.)
AKM677

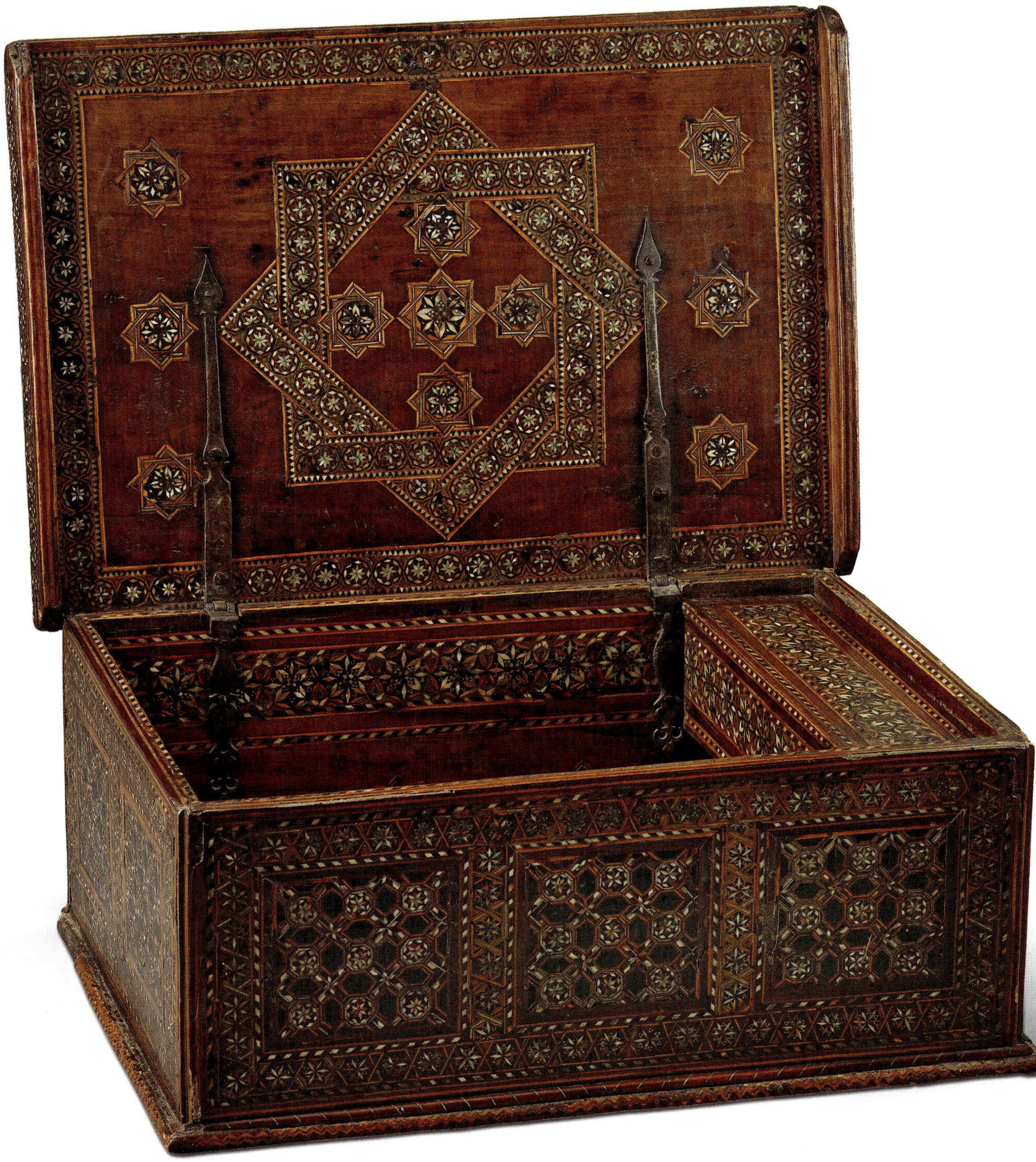

Scribe's Chest

Spain, 15th–16th centuries
Wood inlaid with bone, metal, wood, and mother-of-pearl
22 × 49 × 33 cm (8⅝ × 19¼ × 13 in.)
AKM634

Geometric patterns and plant ornaments continued to be the most prominent decorative features of luxury items made by Muslim craftsmen, known as Mudéjar, who continued to live in Spain after the fall of al-Andalus in 1492. This remarkable walnut box was used to store writing paraphernalia, with an inner, lidded compartment for smaller writing implements. The intricate designs decorating the chest have typical sixteenth-century Mudéjar features, including bone and mother-of-pearl inlay and rosettes in the form of eight-pointed stars with petal-shape arms. The survival of a few examples in major museum collections demonstrates the importance given to luxurious inlaid scribal chests and the continuity of demand for Mudéjar art by the Christian patrons of sixteenth-century Spain.

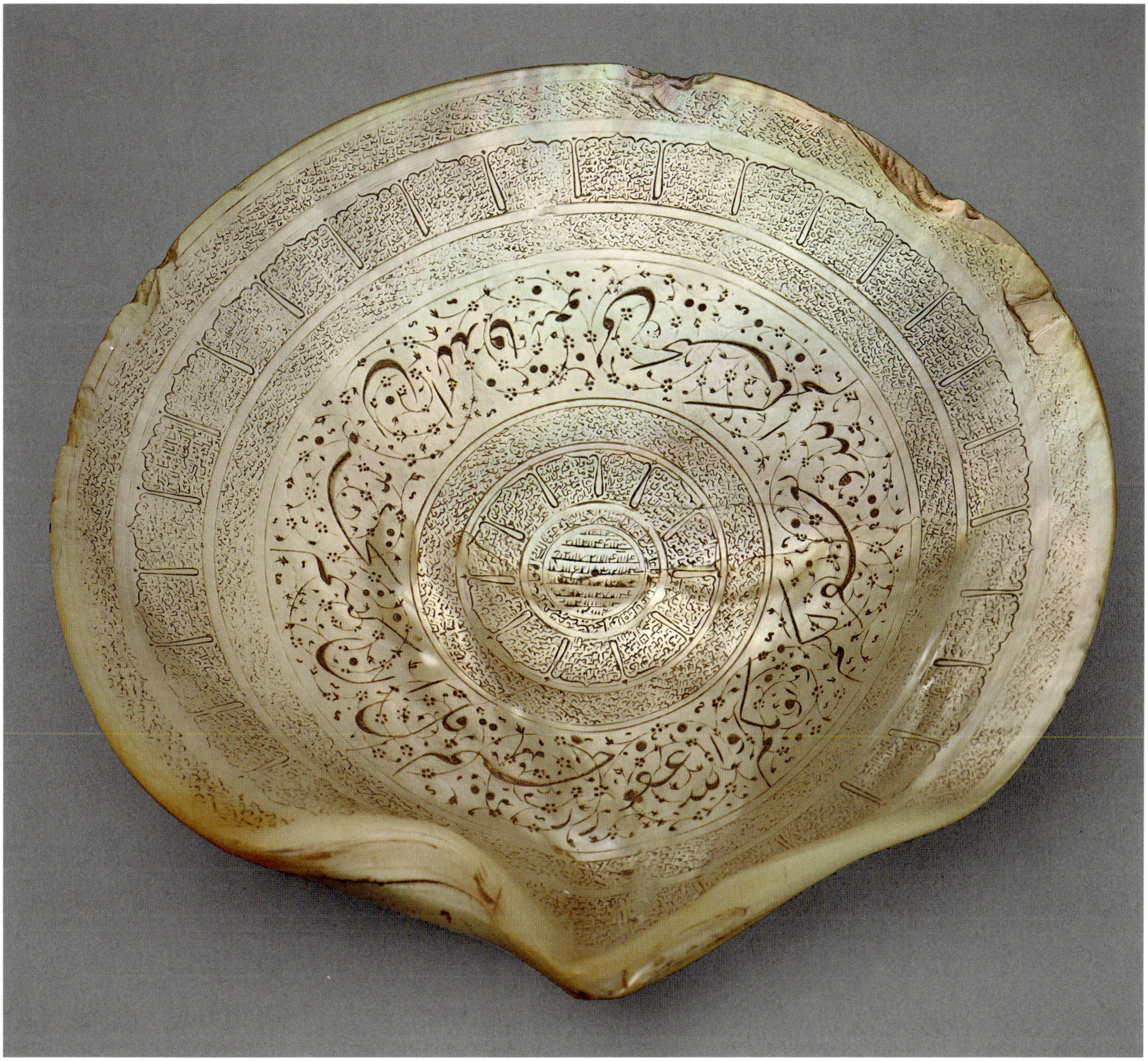

Shell with Inscriptions
India (Historic Hindustan), 18th century
Incised mother-of-pearl
Diameter 14.5 cm (5¾ in.)
AKM665

This palm-size, perfectly shaped mother-of-pearl shell displays an elegant design and an intriguing function. Its luminous surface is engraved with eight concentric rings containing verses from the Qur'an and religious supplications. The variety of the calligraphic styles and their layout make the design both dynamic and quite dignified. Although the intensity of the decorative program on the shell and the attention given to the minutest detail are unique, the shell may have been designed for a specific purpose that demonstrates how Muslims evoked the Qur'an in their everyday lives. The concave shape of the shell and some of its decorative motifs suggest that it may have been used as a drinking vessel. In line with the belief in the protective and therapeutic power of the Qur'an, some Muslims drank water that came into direct contact with Qur'anic verses in order to obtain blessings and protection. Could this have been the role of this singular shell?

Compendium

Iran, 19th century
Enamelled gold
Diameter 9 cm (3½ in.)
AKM625

This astronomical compendium was made in nineteenth-century Iran to reflect the wealth and finesse of its owner. It contains miniature astronomical instruments in a small gold-enamelled box that would have been hung from a chain or held in a pocket. In addition to a universal equinoctial dial and a compass, the compendium holds a depiction of a horseman with a falcon, perhaps that of the owner. The box reflects the Qajar court's (1779–1925) taste for personal luxury objects and interest in scientific knowledge and trade with Europe.

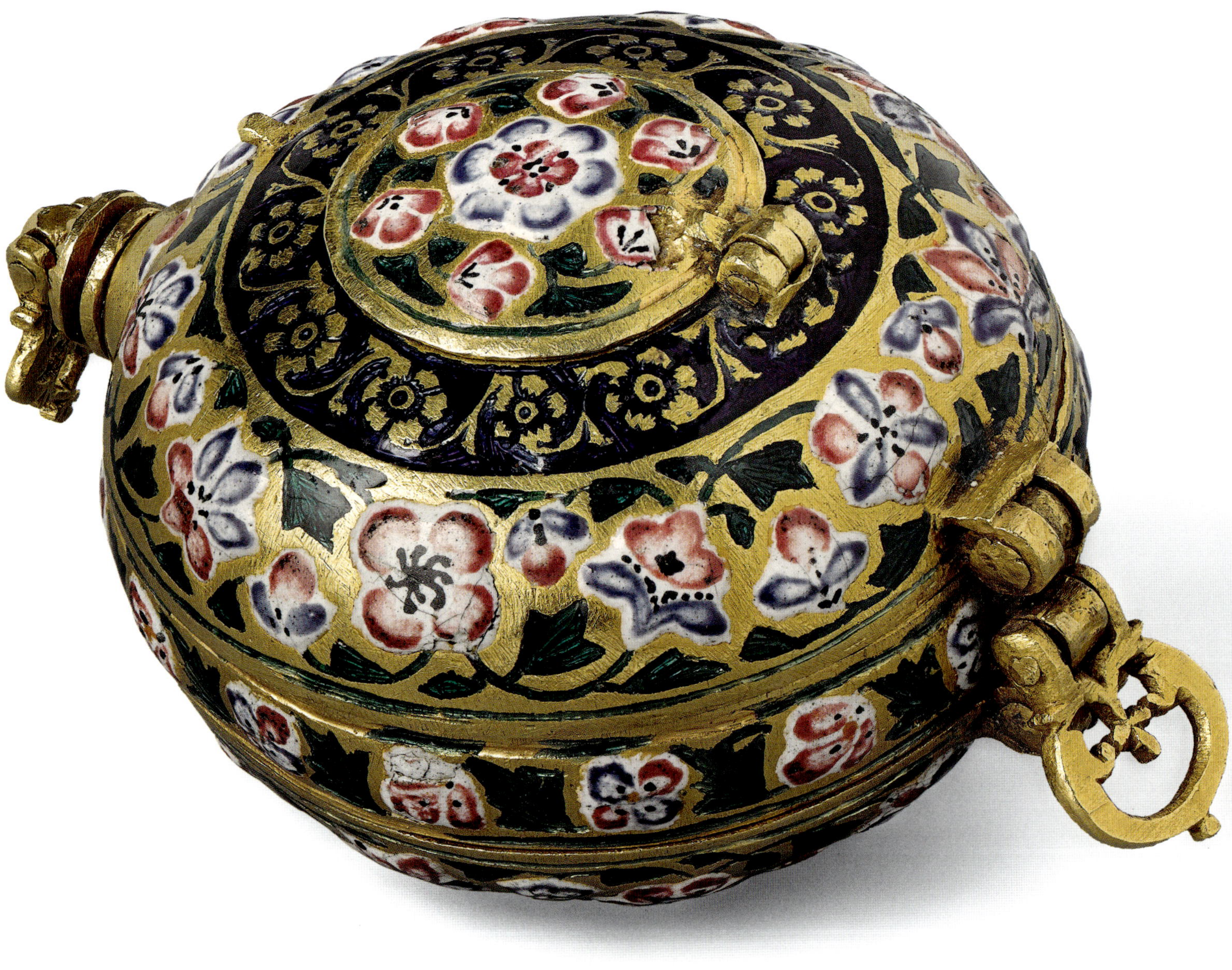

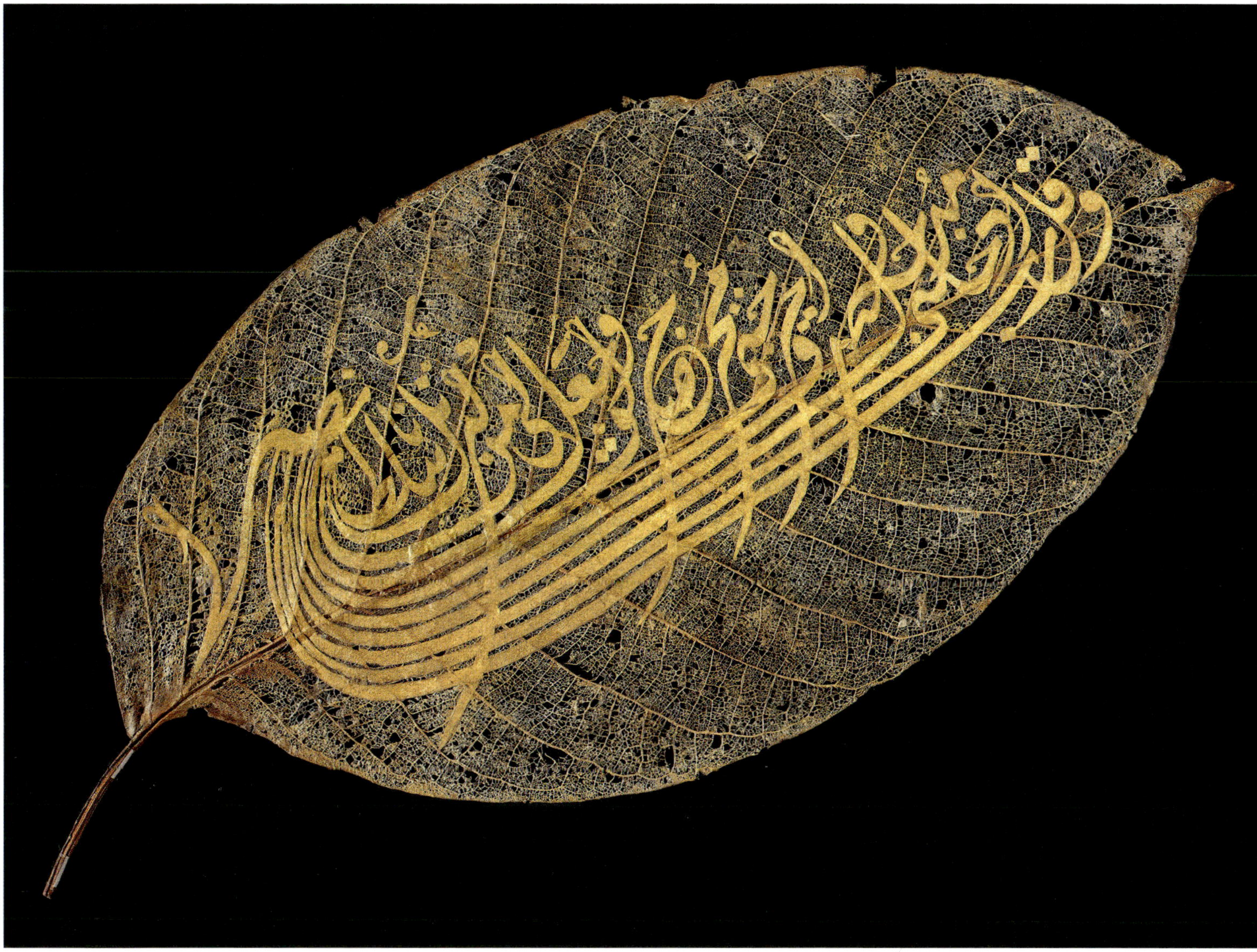

Leaf with Calligraphic Composition

Turkey, 19th century
Gold on chestnut leaf
13.5 × 28 cm (5¼ × 11 in.)
AKM538

The skill and artistic virtuosity required to create this exceptional decorative object reflect the importance given by Muslims to applying Qur'anic verses on a broad variety of objects as a constant reminder of their faith and its centrality to their lives. Here, a sweet chestnut leaf is inscribed with a Qur'anic verse from Surat al-Isra' ("The Night Journey," Q17:80), which reads: "And say, 'Lord grant me a good entrance and a goodly exit, and sustain me with Your power." The calligrapher composed the verse in the form of a boat with the letters forming passengers and oars, perhaps recalling the journey of life. To make this extraordinary leaf, the calligrapher wrote the inscription on the leaf and sealed the writing on both sides with a wax barrier. He then soaked the leaf in an alkaline solution just long enough to dissolve most of the vegetable matter, while leaving the skeleton and the inscription intact. Gold leaf was then applied to the leaf, adding shine, value, and a luxurious effect (see also page 21).

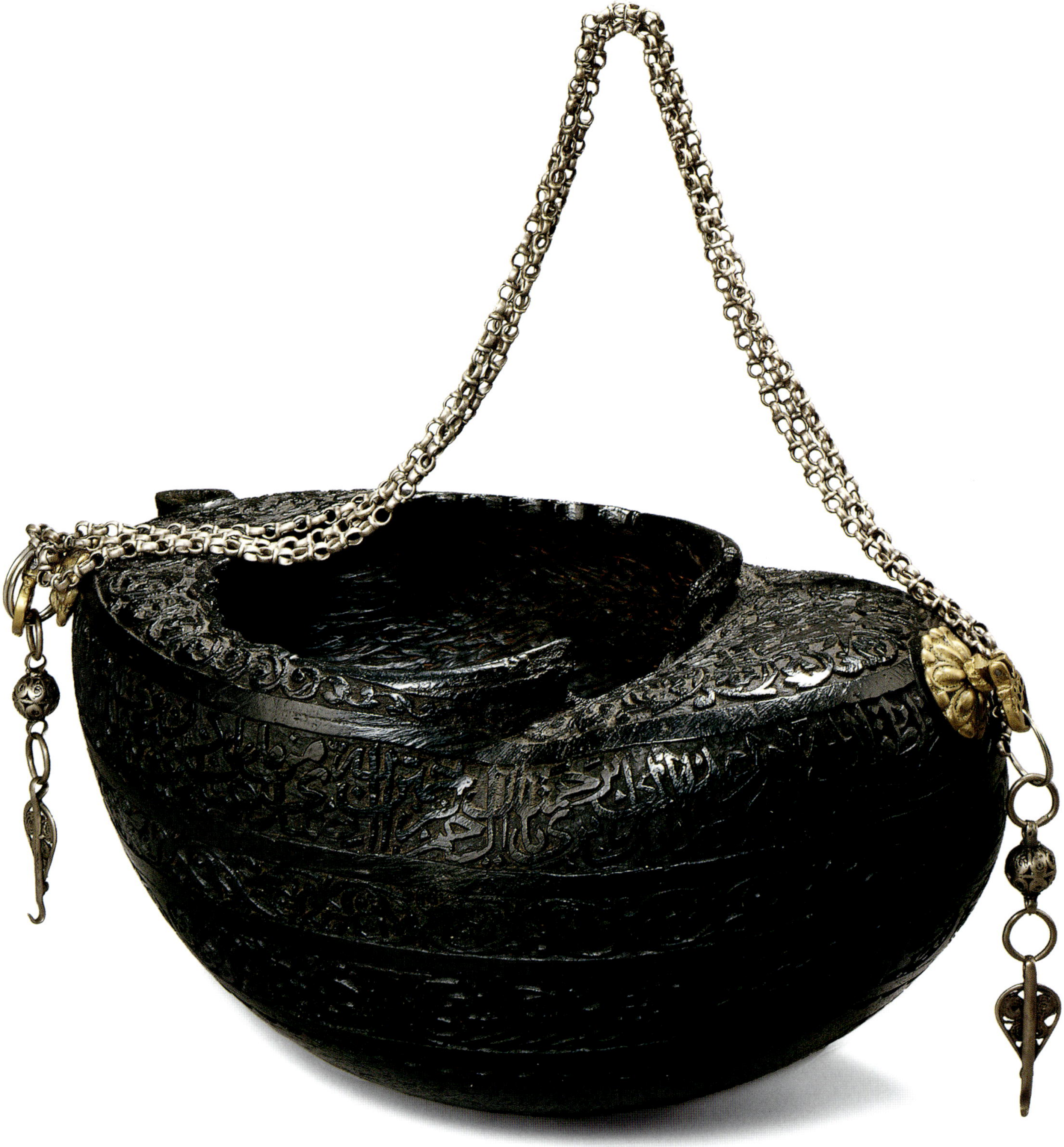

Beggar's Bowl (*Kashkul*)
Iran, 18th century
Carved nutshell
Length 24 cm (9½ in.)
AKM640

Drifting on the ocean from its native habitat on the Seychelles near the coast of southeast Africa all the way to the shores of India and Iran, the coco-de-mer nut (*Lodoicea maldivica*) acquired a mystical significance. Its voyage became symbolic of the journey of the Sufi mystic on the path leading to spiritual knowledge. This mystical connection may have led to the function of this remarkable object as a beggar's bowl (*kashkul*) carried by a Sufi *dervish* as a sign of renouncing all worldly possessions and subsisting on the generosity of humanity. The *kashkul* is fashioned from the shell of half of the nut, with carved inscriptions and supplications in Arabic and Persian. The upper band of inscription contains the Nad-e 'Ali, the devotional prayer to 'Ali. The rest of the prayer reads: "Help me with your hidden kindness, God is higher than the fire of your torture O ... with Your Mercy O You, most Merciful of all those who are merciful, God is my Lord, my aid comes from You O ..."

Pen Box

Iran, 1863–65
Papier mâché, paint, and varnish
Length 26.8 cm (10½ in.)
AKM643

The art of painting on pasteboard or papier mâché under a lacquer varnish (lacquer painting) that decorates this extraordinary pen box was introduced to Iran through the extensive trade and diplomatic contact with China, where the technique originated. Lacquer painting became a prominent technique to embellish the bindings of books and pen boxes under the Safavids (1501–1722) and the Qajars (1779–1925) in Iran. The painter of this box, Muhammad Isma'il, demonstrated his exceptional skill of minutely detailed painting by using an impressive repertoire of subjects. Individual cartouches all over the body of the box are adorned with representations of the Qajar ruler Nasir al-Din Shah (reigned 1848–96), legendary kings from the *Shah-Nameh*, portraits of famous Sufis, and depictions from the poems of Sa'di (died 1291) and Nezami (died 1209). One wonders if this pen box celebrates the art of writing or commemorates instead the painter whose signature and self-portrait decorate its interior.

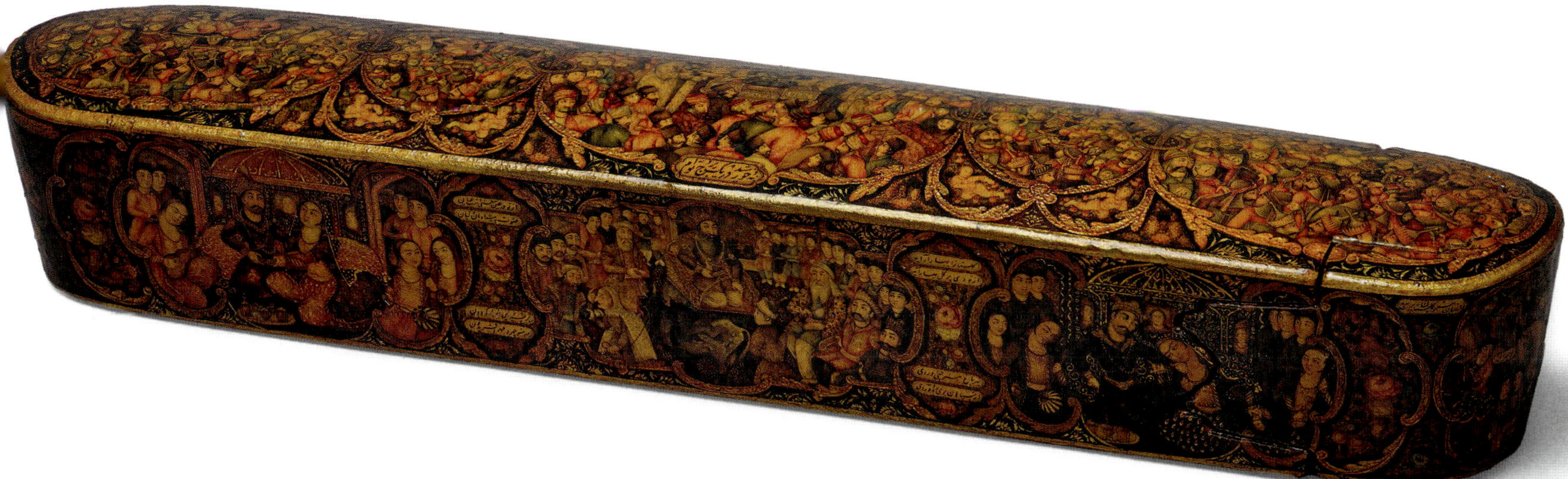

سیاه چشم مشکین خال خامه نخستین جلوه نازکه در ختای بخطای نامه آغاز سپاس خداوند مهربانست و مهربان بخشنده تن و جان سرانرا گردن در بند اوست و دلهارا

و شهریاران آگاه را بر تخت و گاه مایه آرام جهان کرده و جهانیان را شاد و آسوده روان در سایه حمایتشان پرورده بهر فریقی طریقی داده و بهر کیشی دستور

CALLIGRAPHY AND ILLUMINATION

CALLIGRAPHY, THE ART OF BEAUTIFUL WRITING, has a special status in many art traditions, but none more so than in the arts of the Islamic civilizations. Writing is intimately linked with the Qur'an, which Muslims believe to be the Word of God revealed to the Prophet Muhammad in the early seventh century, first orally and then compiled by his followers and written down. The sanctity of the written Word imbued calligraphy more generally with a symbolic status so that calligraphers were highly esteemed, elevating them to the most prominent position among all artists in Muslim cultures. There are more known names and surviving biographies of calligraphers than there are of any other artists.

With the spread of Islam from the Arabian Peninsula to North Africa and Spain in the west, and Iran, Turkey, Central Asia, South Asia, and Southeast Asia in the east, Arabic script came to be used for other languages, including Persian (Farsi), Chaghatai Turkish (AKM227), Ottoman Turkish, Urdu, Malay, and Swahili. While Arabic remained the main language for religious texts, the predominant literary and intellectual tongue was Persian, which was employed by the literary elite of the ruling courts throughout present-day Iran, Central Asia, Turkey, and South Asia.

In the section on Qur'ans in this book (see pages 58–73), calligraphic examples with angular Kufic and cursive scripts were used predominantly for copying the Qur'an. The collection highlights shown here, though, are mostly exceptional single-page literary compositions. Iranian calligraphers developed a new cursive, sloping script during the fourteenth century known as *nasta'liq* that was typically found in literary and poetic compositions. Calligraphy was applied by a variety of reed pens and at times cut from paper (*qat'*) to further demonstrate the virtuosity of the calligrapher (AKM227). The calligrapher's art was highly sought after and collected in albums (*moraqqa'*) with decorative borders in various techniques, including painting (AKM249) and marbling (AKM254).

Detail of Letter from Crown Prince 'Abbas Mirza to Napoleon I (see page 151)
Tehran, Iran, 1808
Opaque watercolour, ink, and gold on paper
120 × 58 cm (47¼ × 22⅞ in.)
AKM251

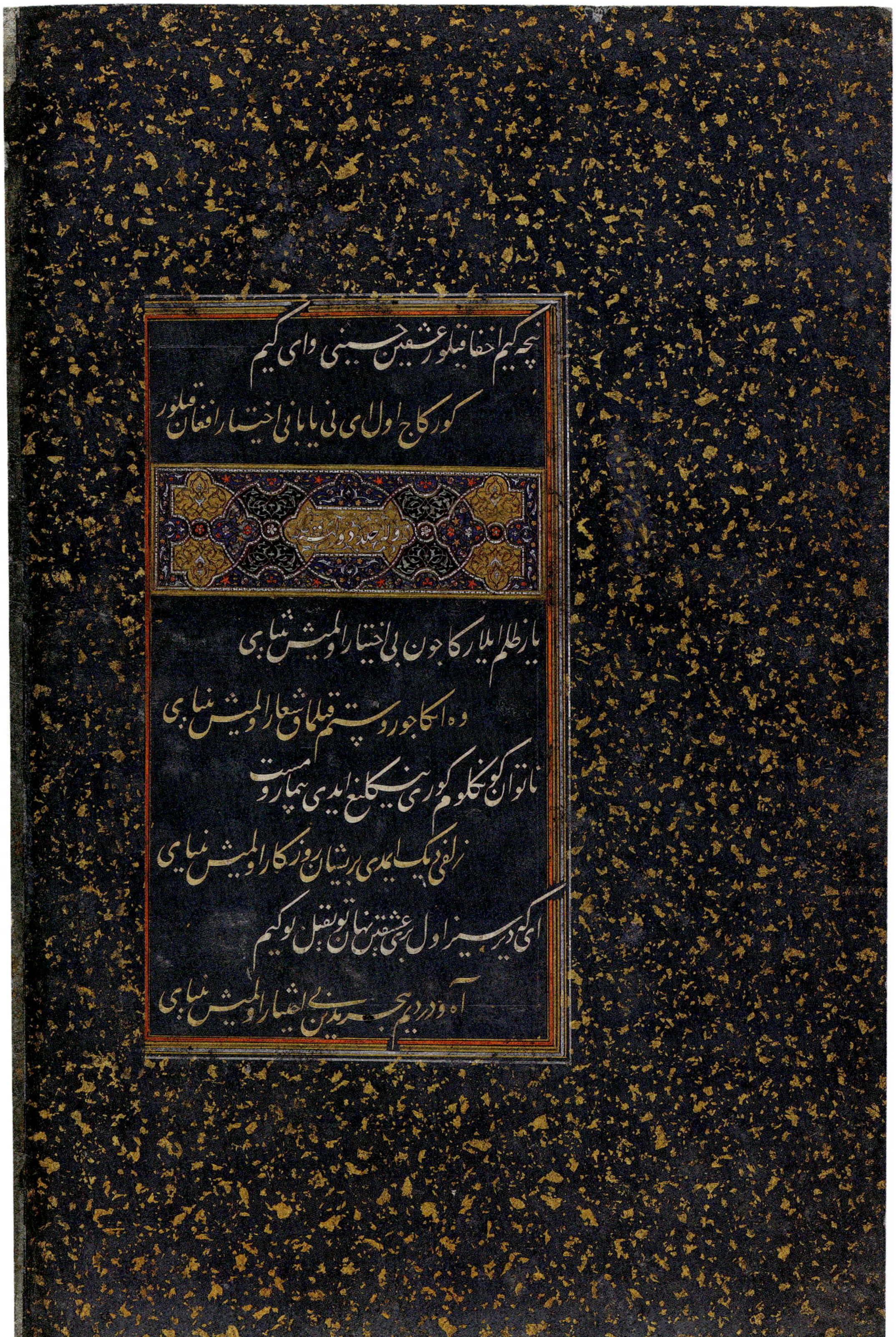

This exceptional composition is from a dispersed collection of poetry (*divan*) composed by the Timurid sultan Hosayn Bayqara, who ruled Herat in present-day Afghanistan from 1469 to 1506. Although Persian was the common literary and administrative language in Central Asia, the Timurids (1370–1507) maintained their native Turkic tongue, Chaghatai, in which these verses are written. Chaghatai became a prestigious literary language in which famous poets, including the founder of the Moghul dynasty, Babur (reigned 1526–30), and the poet-statesman Mir 'Ali Shir Nawa'i (died 1501), left remarkable works. The verses in this example were written in a *nasta'liq* script cut from paper in three different colours, then pasted onto the deep blue background before being set in a gold-speckled paper frame. The most famous practitioner of the cut-calligraphy technique (*qat'*) is Sheykh 'Abdollah of Herat, who signed several other folios from this beautiful manuscript. According to his contemporary Babur, however, the quality of Sultan Hosayn Bayqara's poetry in this *divan* is not good enough. Could this marvellous calligraphic presentation make up for that?

Découpé Calligraphic Example
From a dispersed *Divan* of Sultan Hosayn Bayqara (d. 1506)
Herat, Afghanistan (Historic Iran), ca. 1475
Opaque watercolour, ink, and gold on paper
23.7 × 15.2 cm (9⅜ × 6 in.)
AKM227

Not only did the Moghul ruler Shah Jahan (reigned 1628–58) have a keen interest and discerning approach when acquiring Chinese porcelains (AKM966) and Iranian jades but he was also an avid collector of paintings and calligraphic specimens. A fine example of calligraphy is this Persian quatrain penned by the prolific poet-calligrapher Mir 'Ali al-Soltani (died 1544), who was famous for the diagonal format of his *nasta'liq* poetry. The calligrapher, who is also reported to have designed the lion format of the Nad-e 'Ali (AKM526), was extremely sought after by the Moghul sultans who would have mounted the prized calligraphic specimens in sumptuous albums (*moraqqa'*) and surrounded them with borders of painted floral decoration.

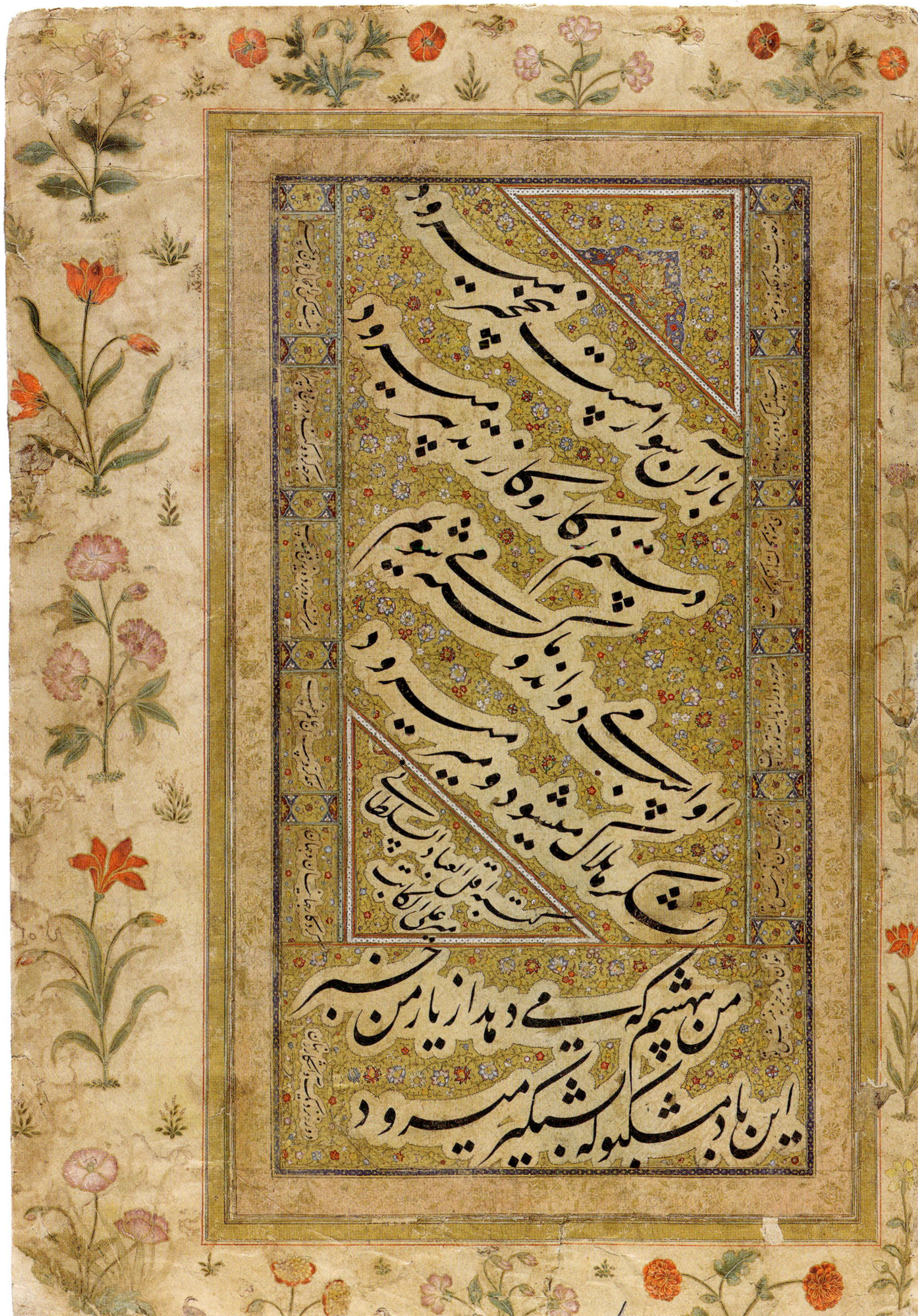

Page of *Nasta'liq* Calligraphy from a Royal Moghul Album
Signed by Mir 'Ali al-Soltani
Calligraphy: Iran, 1520; border: India (Historic Hindustan), ca. 1640
Opaque watercolour, ink, and gold on paper
36.9 × 25.2 cm (14½ × 9⅞ in.)
AKM351

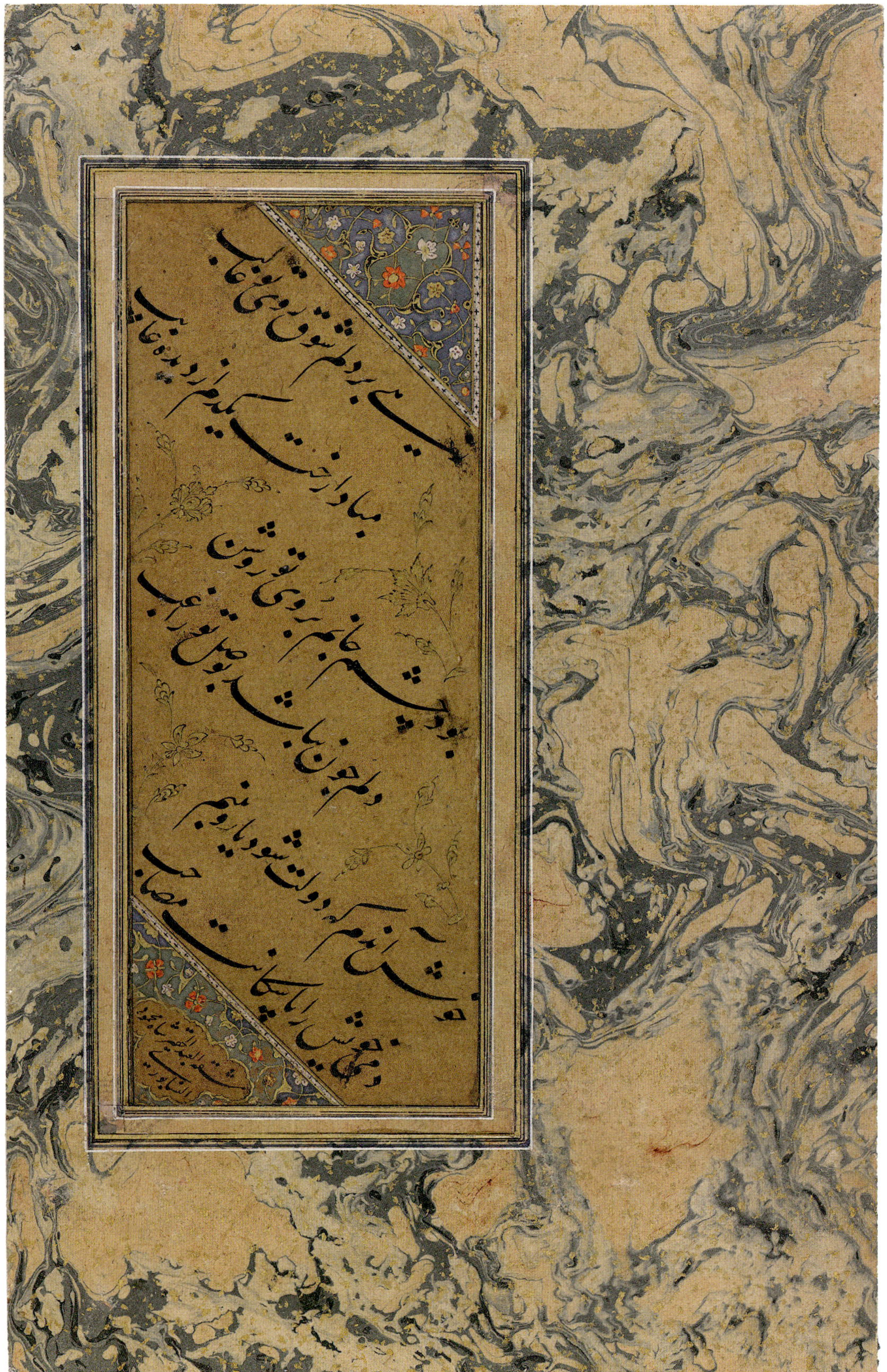

Shah Mahmud Neyshaburi (died circa 1564–65), whose signature is seen in the bottom left triangle of the text panel, was one of the most renowned calligraphers in the court of the Safavid shah Tahmasp I (reigned 1524–76). His masterful works for the shah, including a *Khamseh* of Nezami now in the British Library in London, and a unique *nasta'liq* Qur'an now at the Topkapı Palace Museum Library in Istanbul, earned him the epithets Shahi and Zarin Qalam (Golden Pen). Neyshaburi's calligraphic style is known for its elegant *nasta'liq*, which creates balanced compositions through the rhythmic elongation of horizontal strokes. The border of Neyshaburi's calligraphic panel is decorated with a blue-and-gold marbling effect known as *abri* (*ebru* in Turkish) used in Iran and Central Asia in the fifteenth century. Artists today still use the same method to achieve the elegant swirling effect of marbling by developing the desired pattern and colours in a water bath and then transferring them to paper.

Page of *Nasta'liq* Calligraphy
Signed by Shah Mahmud Neyshaburi
Mashhad, Iran, ca. 1540
Opaque watercolour, ink, and gold on paper
26.7 × 16.7 cm (10½ × 6⅝ in.)
AKM254

The Moghuls (1526–1858) considered calligraphy to be one of the noblest arts that were fit for a prince, and many of the Moghul emperors were fine calligraphers. They also collected elegant calligraphic compositions and writing examples by renowned masters in lavishly decorated albums. This superb page was penned by the Moghul prince Dara Shikoh, Shah Jahan's eldest son, who was killed by his brother, Aurangzeb, in a power struggle in 1659. Dara Shikoh was known for his intellectual pursuits and his patronage of the arts. His personal collection of paintings and calligraphy included an exceptional album that he presented to his wife, Nadira Banu Begum, in the 1630s, now in the British Library. Dara Shikoh's calligraphic sample was later mounted in an eighteenth-century album where it was set in a floral border. This border reflects the Moghuls' avid interest in all natural phenomena and the close observation and depiction of animals and flowers as part of album borders or as intricately painted specimen studies.

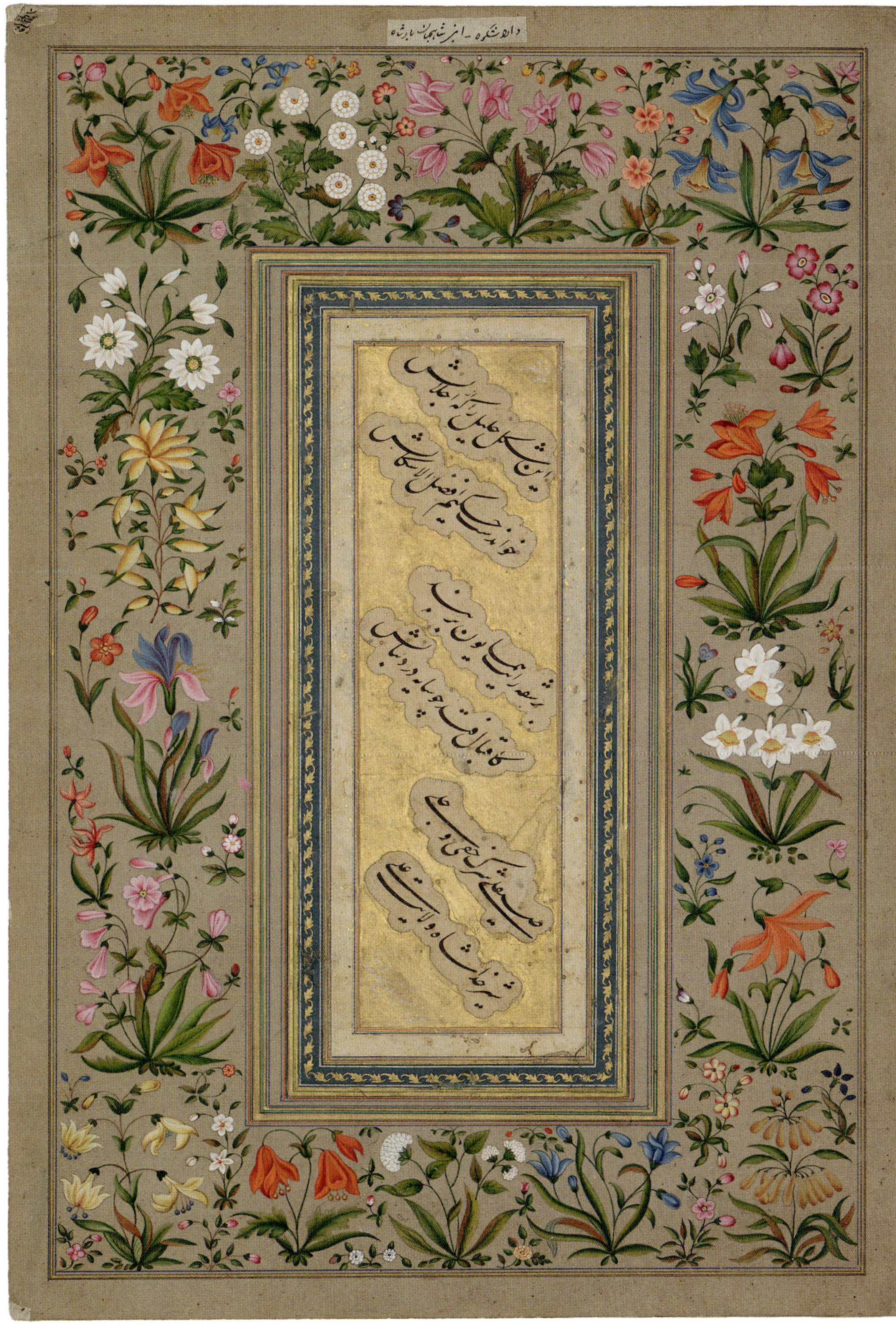

Page of *Nasta'liq* Calligraphy
Signed by Prince Dara Shikoh (d. 1659)
Burhanpur, India (Historic Hindustan), 1631–32 (border 18th century)
Opaque watercolour, ink, and gold on paper
42.3 × 28.8 cm (16⅝ × 11⅜ in.)
AKM249

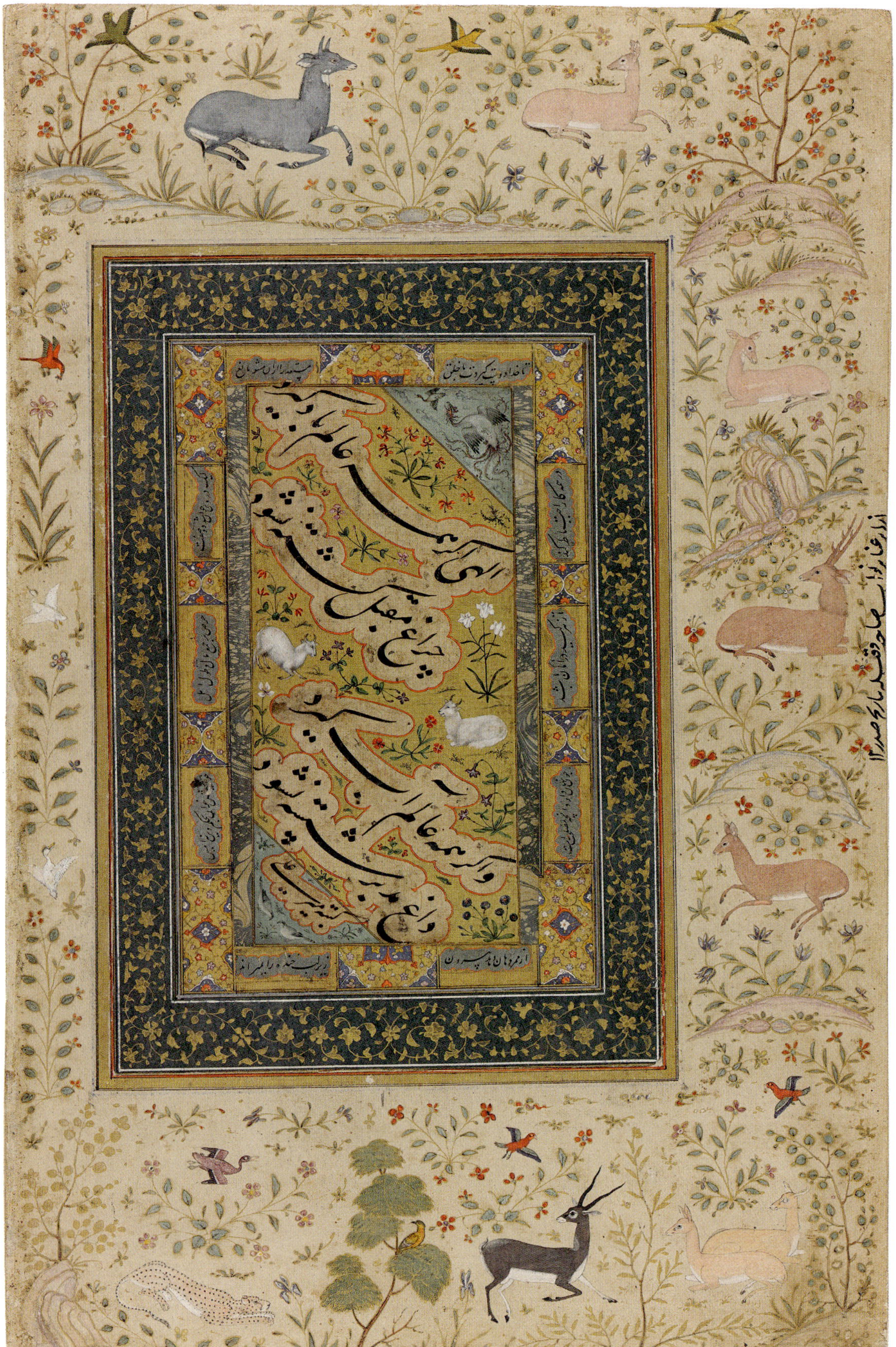

"My God, if the entire universe should be blown by wind

Let not the light of fortune be extinguished

And if the entire universe should become flooded with water

Let not the mark of the unfortunate be washed away!"

The above Persian quatrain, written in a heavy *nasta'liq*, is typical of the hand of the prolific Persian calligrapher Mir 'Ali of Herat (died 1544). Mir 'Ali's work was appreciated by the Moghuls and collected and bound in superb albums (AKM351). Here, this page from an album made for Shah Jahan (reigned 1628–58) uses an elegant collage of different types of papers around the calligraphy, including two narrow bands with marbled paper (AKM254). The paper collage with Mir 'Ali's quatrains at its centre was set in an exceptional border of a natural landscape. The painter of the border, Dawlat Khan, has depicted a finely illustrated group of deer, antelopes, and *nilgai* (blue bull) in a lush landscape with a rich variety of tropical birds, all watched by a crouching cheetah in the bottom left of the border. The precision with which the animals are drawn suggests that the artist drew upon manuals that perhaps came into his possession through Western influences at the Moghul court.

Page of *Nasta'liq* Calligraphy
Signed by Mir 'Ali, ca. 1520
Opaque watercolour, ink, and gold on paper
39.2 × 25.4 cm (15⅜ × 10 in.)
AKM145

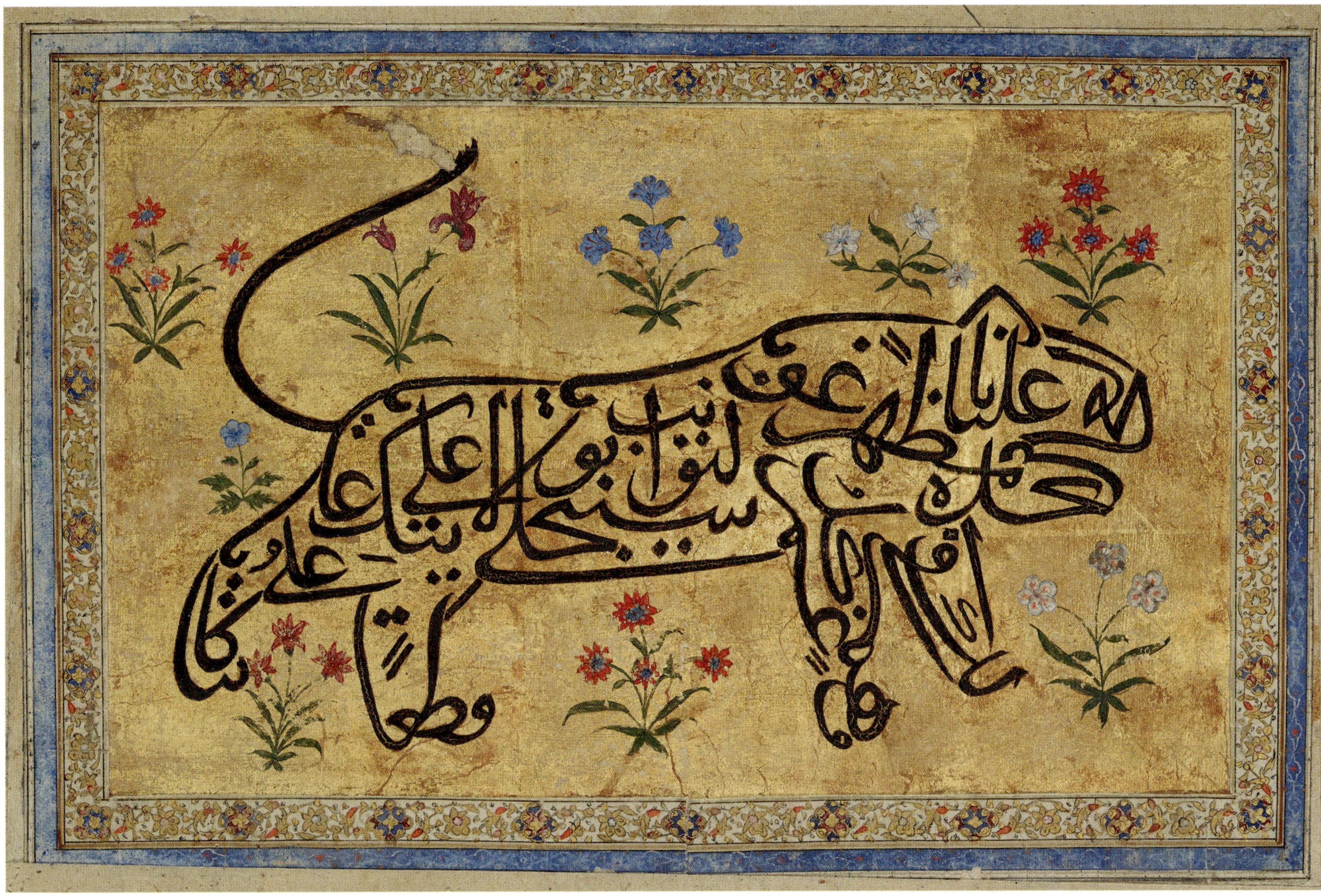

Devotional Calligraphic Composition
India (Historic Hindustan), 17th century
Opaque watercolour, ink, and gold on paper
12 × 19.2 cm (4¾ × 7½ in.)
AKM526

This splendid calligraphic lion is an example of zoomorphic writing where calligraphers blended the arts of writing and drawing by using words to form animal and human shapes. The choice of the lion here is quite pertinent since the Arabic text is a supplication to ʿAli, the Prophet Muhammad's cousin and son-in-law, who was the fourth caliph and first imam. Because of his courage and valour, ʿAli was known to Sunni and Shia Muslims by the epithet "The Lion of God." The prayer, known as Nad-e ʿAli, is typically used by Shia Muslims to seek ʿAli's help and support in times of stress and sorrow. What is interesting here is that the seventeenth-century calligrapher was so faithful in copying from an earlier model that he also replicated the signature of the original sixteenth-century calligrapher, most probably the famous Safavid calligrapher Mir ʿAli Haravi. That signature forms the hind leg of the lion in the original composition.

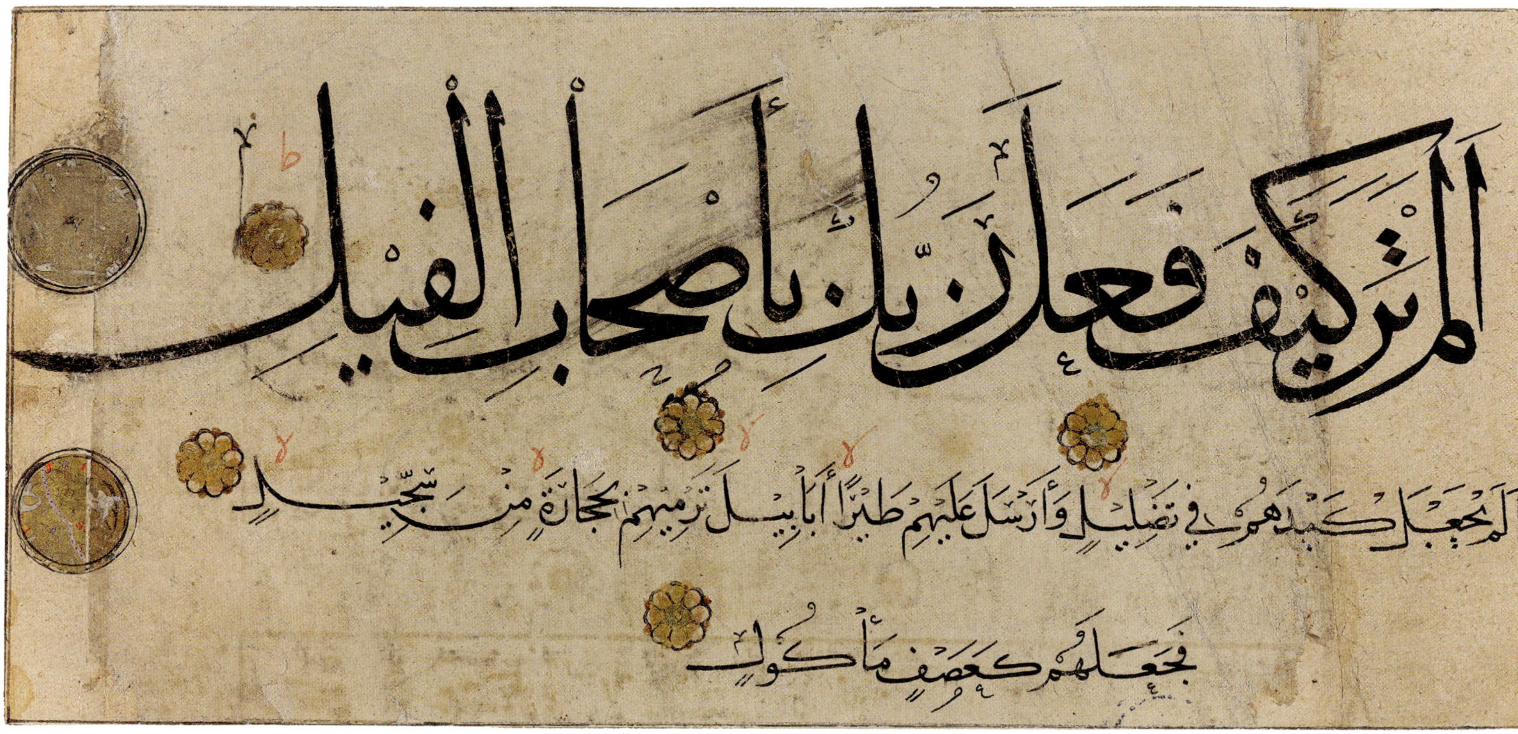

Page of Calligraphic Exercise
Turkey, 17th century
Ink and gold on paper
13.1 × 27.5 cm (5⅛ × 10⅞ in.)
AKM349

Treatises on calligraphy repeatedly warn the student that the only way to attain perfectly proportioned beautiful writing is by continuously copying and repeating a teacher's work. This master-to-pupil training process often produced various copies of a single text at different stages of development, several of which are now in major museum collections. This exceptional composition is an example of a calligraphic exercise, but the pupil here must have been quite advanced in his or her training since the text contains a full chapter of the Qur'an (Surat al-Fil 105:1–5) in two different scripts, as well as all the additional markers that characterize a finished work. While the first line is rendered in a larger-scale angular script with flattened curves known as *muhaqqaq*, the rest is in the simplest and most commonly used cursive script known as *naskh*. Typical of other calligraphic exercises under the Ottomans (1299–1923), this writing specimen would not have been meant for public display but rather it would have been collected in a calligrapher's *moraqqa'* or teaching album.

Although the main purpose of this diplomatic letter was to seek French support against Russia, one-third of its length is filled with a decorative gold-illuminated heading. The magnificent heading was meant to express to its recipient, the French emperor Napoleon Bonaparte (reigned 1804–14), the importance of the sender, the crown prince ʿAbbas Mirza, son of Qajar ruler Fath ʿAli Shah (reigned 1797–1834). The broad, empty margin on the right and the exaggerated distance between the written lines were also intended to convey a sense of prominence. Following a long Persian chancery tradition, the letter is written in a controlled *nastaʿliq*, a cursive, sloping script that evolved in fourteenth-century Iran and was typically used for literary and poetic compositions (AKM227 and AKM145).

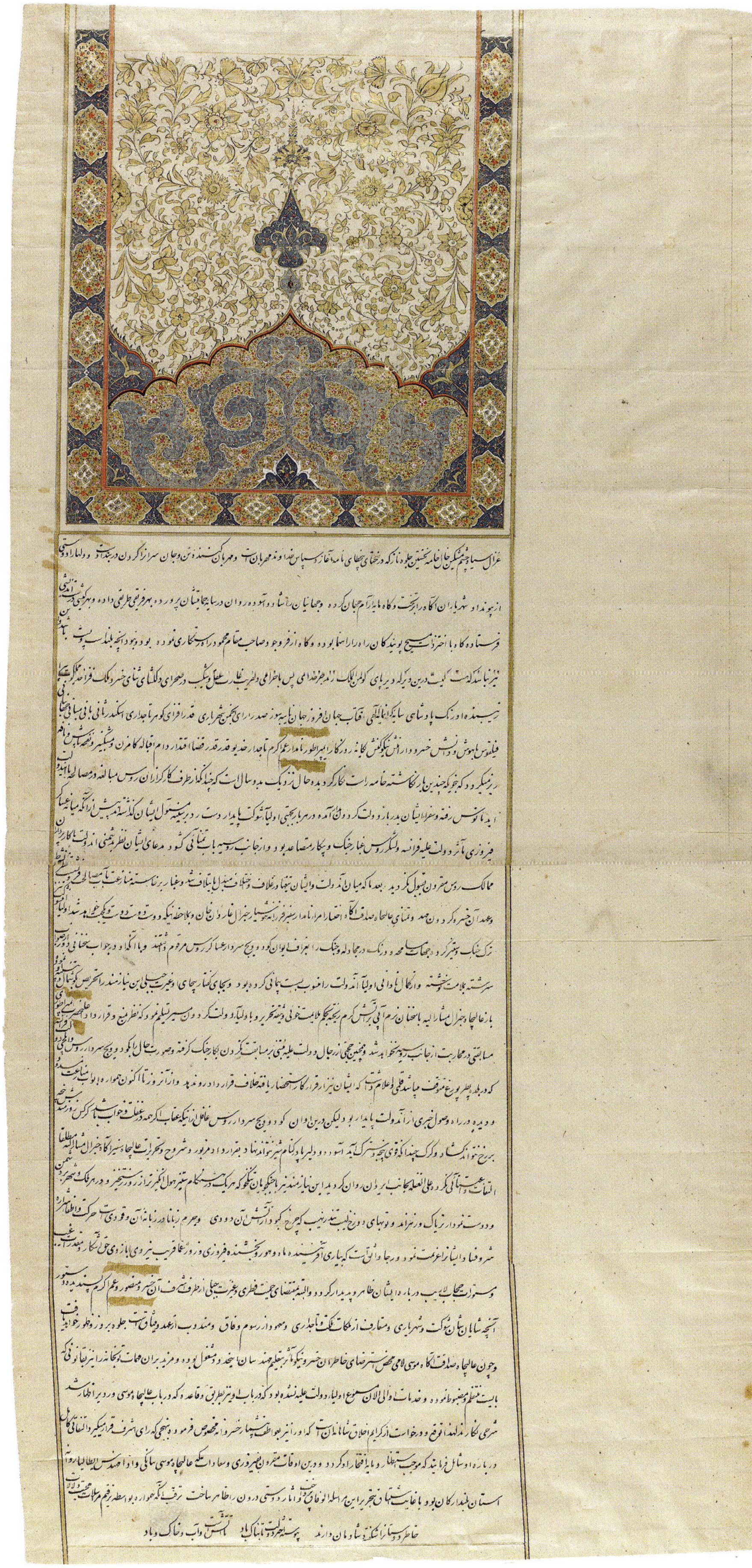

Letter from Crown Prince ʿAbbas Mirza to Napoleon I
Tehran, Iran, 1808
Opaque watercolour, ink, and gold on paper
120 × 58 cm (47¼ × 22⅞ in.)
AKM251

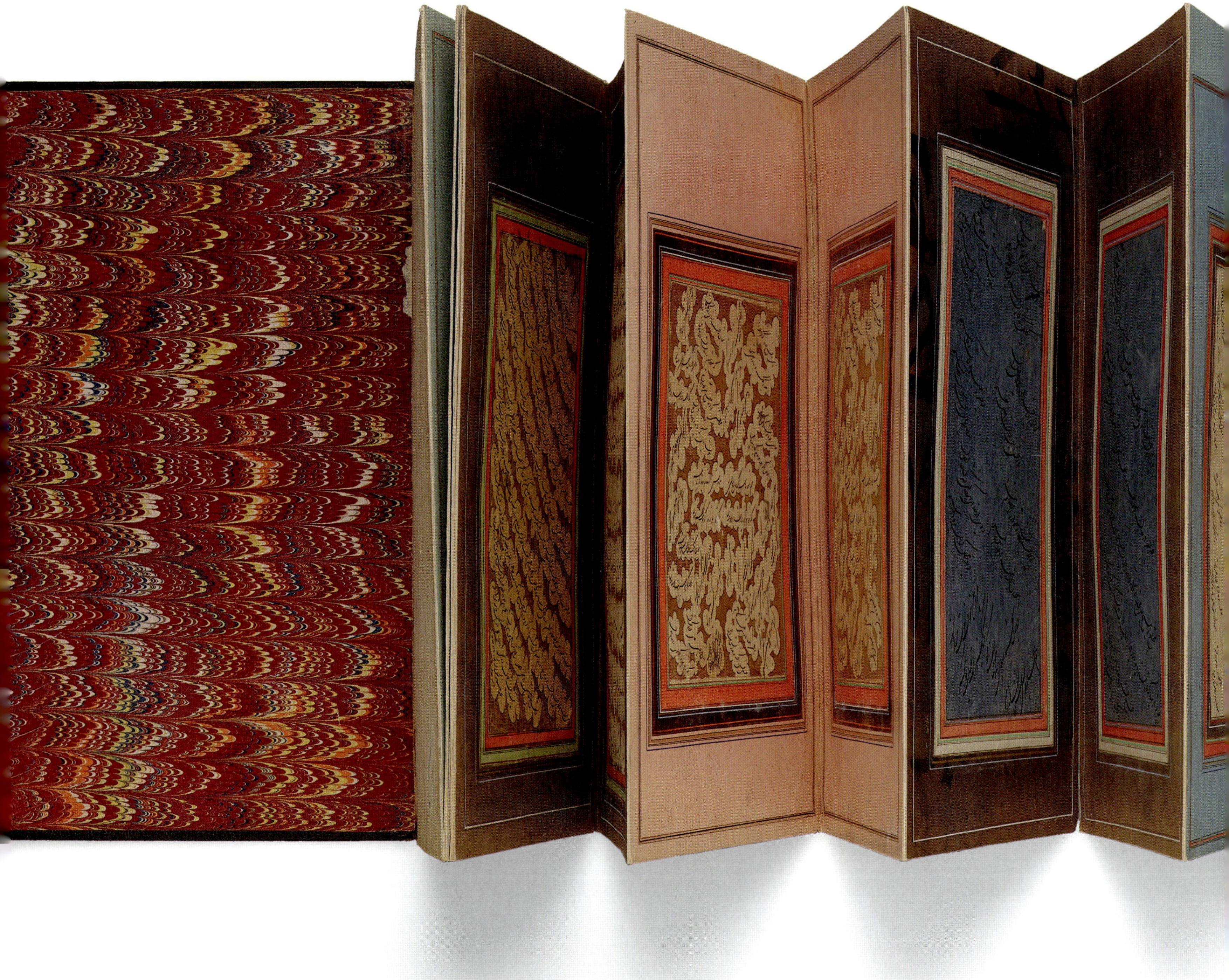

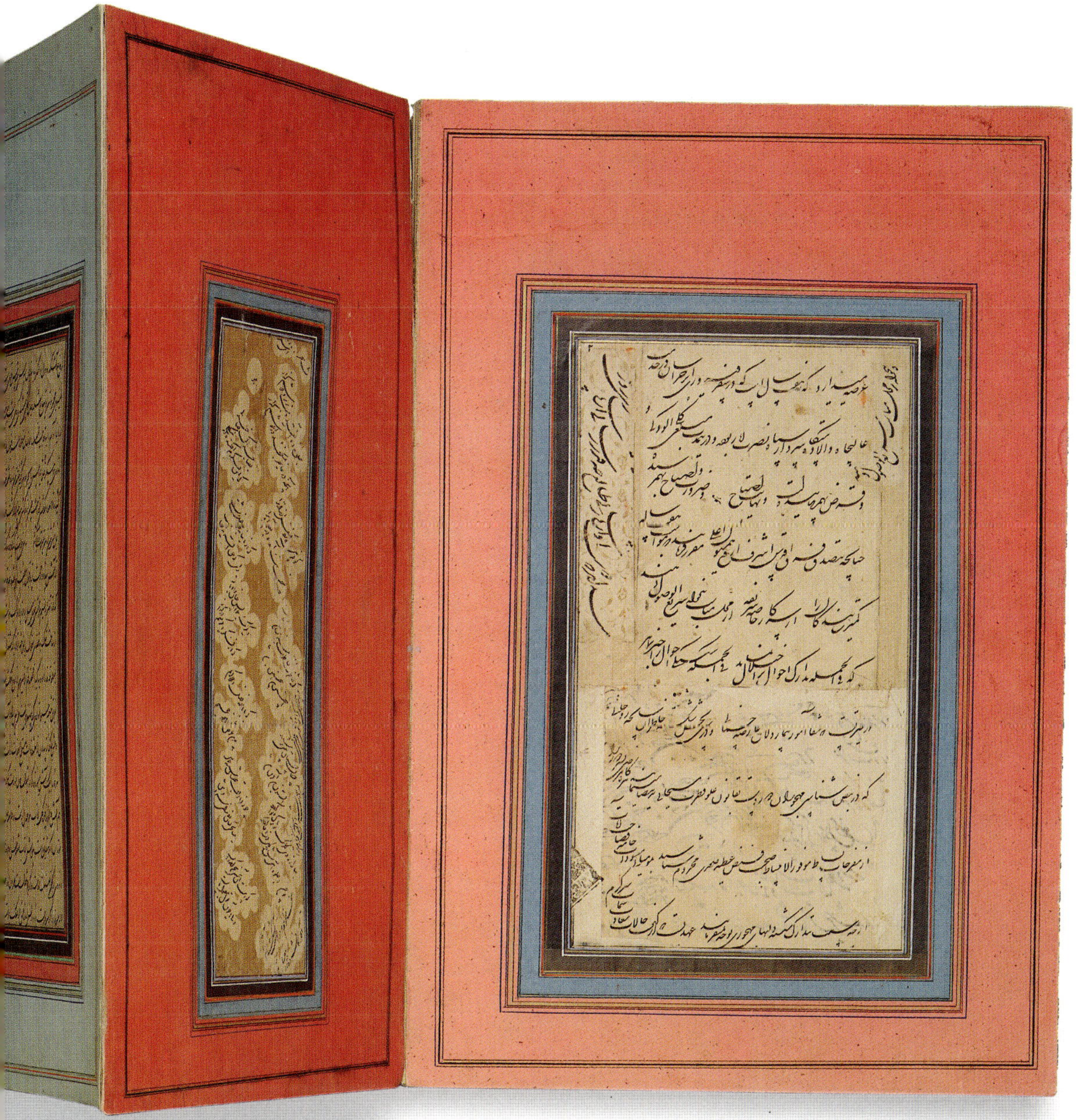

This forty-eight-page album displays different calligraphic examples of the script known as *shikasteh* (also *shikasteh nasta'liq*). Developed predominantly to enable the scribe to write faster by smoothing the articulation of each letter, then linking letters and, at times, entire words, *shikasteh* became the favoured script for official documents and administrative correspondence. Each page in this album is a demonstration of the virtuosity of the calligrapher, showing different compositions and hands. The album is in the form of an accordion (also known as a concertina-type album) that was popular under the Qajars, who ruled a united Iran between 1794 and 1925. Each calligraphic specimen is set within plain-coloured borders on an undecorated coloured background. The folios were then hinge-linked, creating an accordion effect.

Accordion Album of Calligraphic Examples in *Shikasteh Nasta'liq*
Iran, 1800–50
Ink and gold on paper with leather binding
29.2 × 19 cm (11½ × 7½ in.)
AKM360

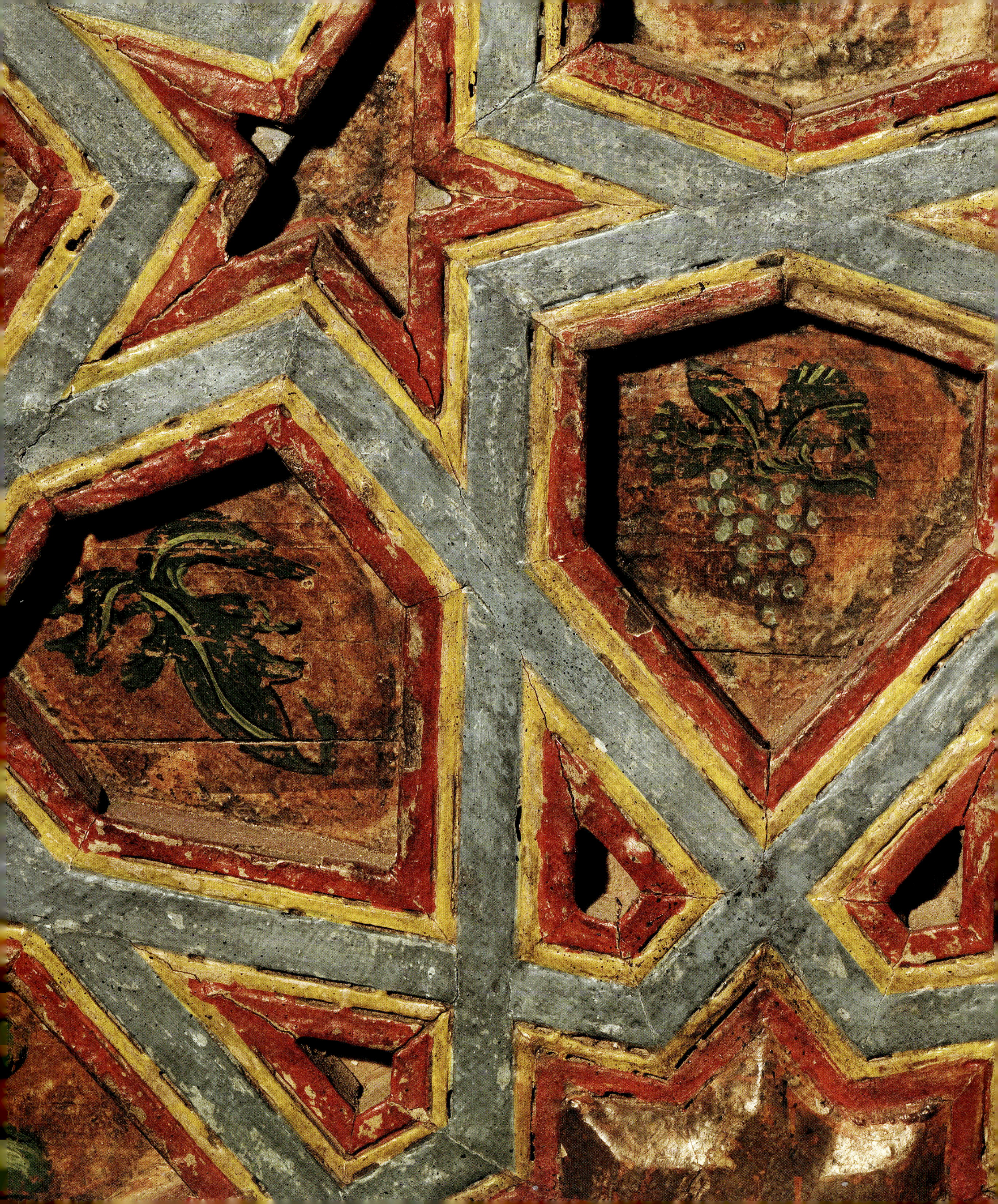

ARCHITECTURAL DECORATION

Muslim civilizations inherited the use of architectural elements decorated with intricate designs of geometric, calligraphic, figural, and floral motifs from the diverse cultures that preceded them. By the eleventh century, the creative combinations of abstract floral patterns (also known as arabesque), geometric interlace (*girih*), and stalactite vaults (*muqarnas*) established a new aesthetic that was both dynamic and distinctive of Islamic civilizations. While the application of these elements was widespread, the technique of decoration and its location on a building reflected the various regional styles and local building traditions of the places where they were built.

Common among the decorative elements in the following examples from the Aga Khan Museum's collection are patterns based on a seemingly infinite repetition of designs and motifs. Division and repetition of abstract forms of vegetation, for example, are extended indefinitely and used in tiles to decorate the interior (AKM584) and exterior (AKM572) of a building. Geometric interlace patterns (*girih*) also follow the same structural principle; these decorative compositions are based on the folding and repetition of circles, triangles, and squares (AKM730). The resulting patterns are mathematical in nature, and their aesthetic value lies in the artist's choices regarding what aspect of the pattern to highlight, which material and technique to use, and which colours to apply.

Calligraphy played an important role in architectural decoration. Whether the content of an inscription is historical, giving the date of a building; a foundation inscription commemorating a patron and listing his or her titles; literary quotations (AKM631); or verses from the Qur'an (AKM628), these inscriptions were placed inside or outside the building where they were clearly seen and appreciated. Inscriptions are found above doors, entrances, windows, and niches; as friezes adorning the upper parts of walls; covering the interior and exterior of domes; and as overall exterior decoration.

Detail of Ceiling Panel
(see page 161)
Spain, 15th–16th centuries
Carved and painted wood
Base 170 cm (66⅞ in.),
sides 171.8 cm (67⅝ in.)
AKM730

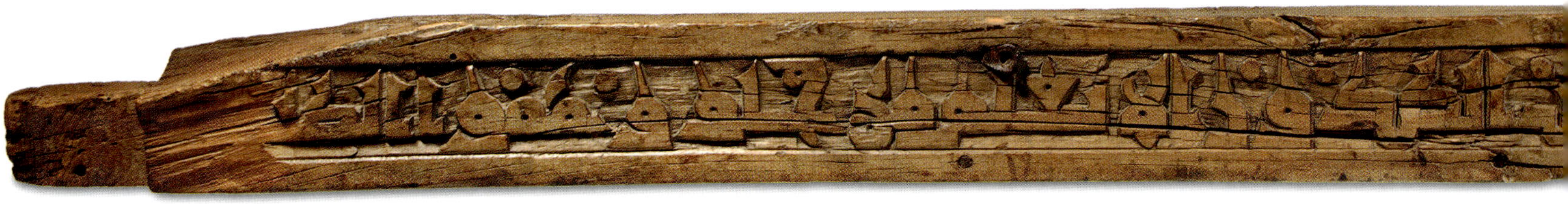

Beam
Egypt, 9th century
Carved wood
Length 120 cm (47¼ in.)
AKM701

This beam is a rare example of decorative carved wood surviving from Egypt before the Fatimids (909–1171). Although we do not know its original function, the beam was initially part of a longer frieze of Qur'anic inscriptions (here containing verses Q67:13–14). The Arabic letters are carved in a heavy, angular Kufic script with decorative pointed finials. The fashion for similar wooden beams with carved Qur'anic inscriptions can still be seen in the Mosque of Ibn Tulun built during the Tulunid dynasty (868–905) that governed Egypt under the Abbasids (750–1258). The austere exterior of the mosque is contrasted by the architectural decoration of its interior, which features carved plaster (stucco) and wooden beams with elaborate decorative patterns and inscriptions.

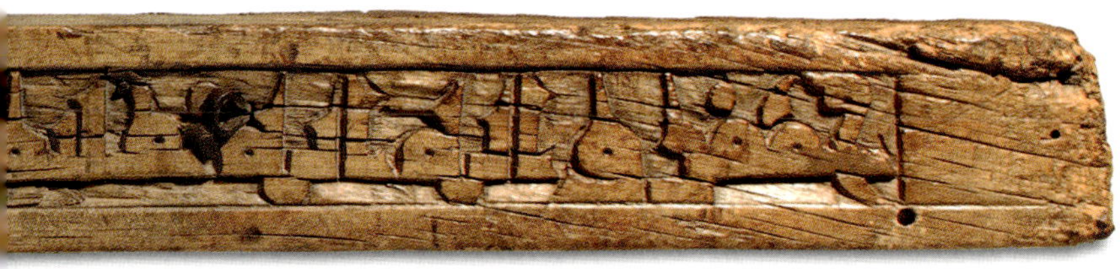

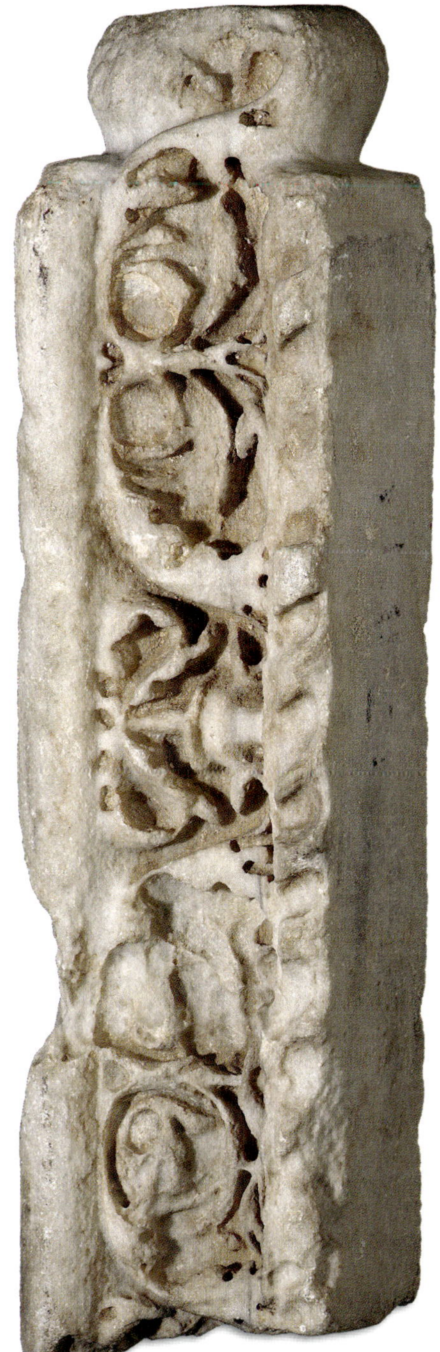

Marble *spolia* from the remains of Pre-Islamic Classical buildings were widely reused throughout history, especially in places where marble was rare or quarries were no longer productive. Here, a Roman panel with a deeply carved acanthus scroll formed the back of a funerary stele dating to December 986. This cultural adaptation of architectural elements was common under Muslims in North Africa. Indeed, the Mosque of ʿAmr, first established in Fustat (present-day Cairo) in 642, has a plethora of repurposed marble columns.

Funerary Stele
Egypt or North Africa, 987
Carved marble
Height 59.7 cm (23½ in.)
AKM662

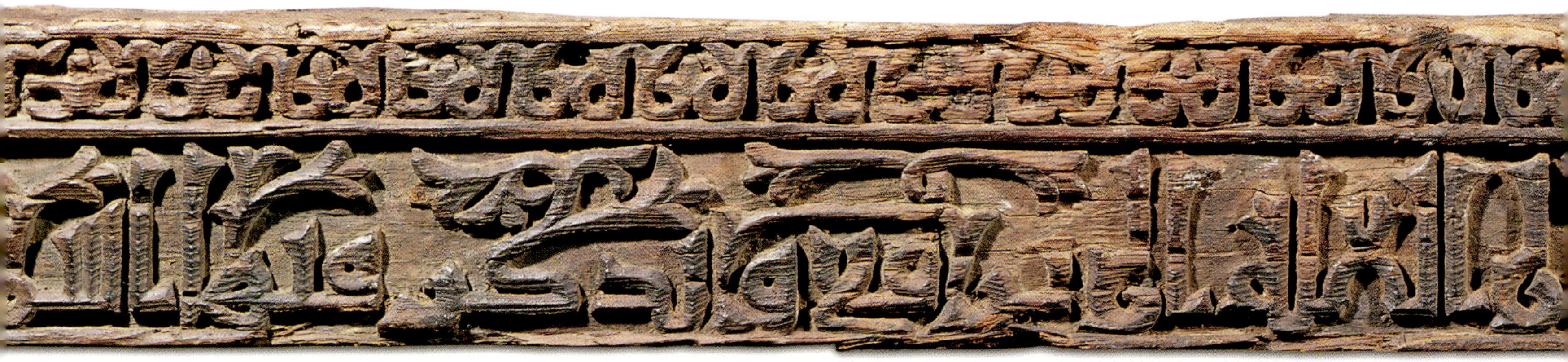

Beam with Surat al-Nur
Spain (Historic al-Andalus), 10th–11th centuries
Carved wood
427 × 16.7 cm (168⅛ × 6⅝ in.)
AKM628

A rare survival from the Umayyad period in Spain (756–1031), this architectural fragment would have been part of the decorative frieze of the interior of a mosque. The inscription bears the Qur'anic verse of light (Surat al-Nur), which is an allegorical reference to Divine Light. The verse was commonly used to adorn mosques, especially their vase-shaped lamps. The inscription is carved in deep relief in a foliated Kufic script surmounted by a repetitive floral element.

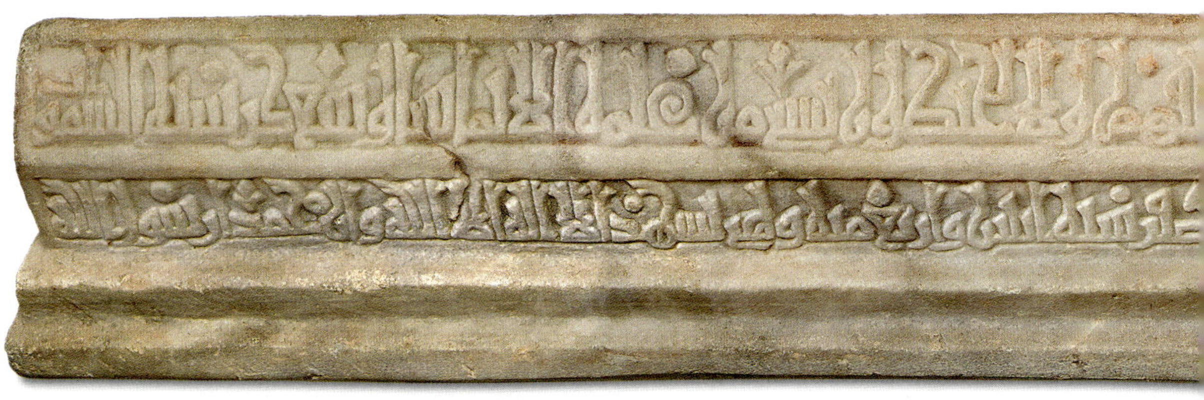

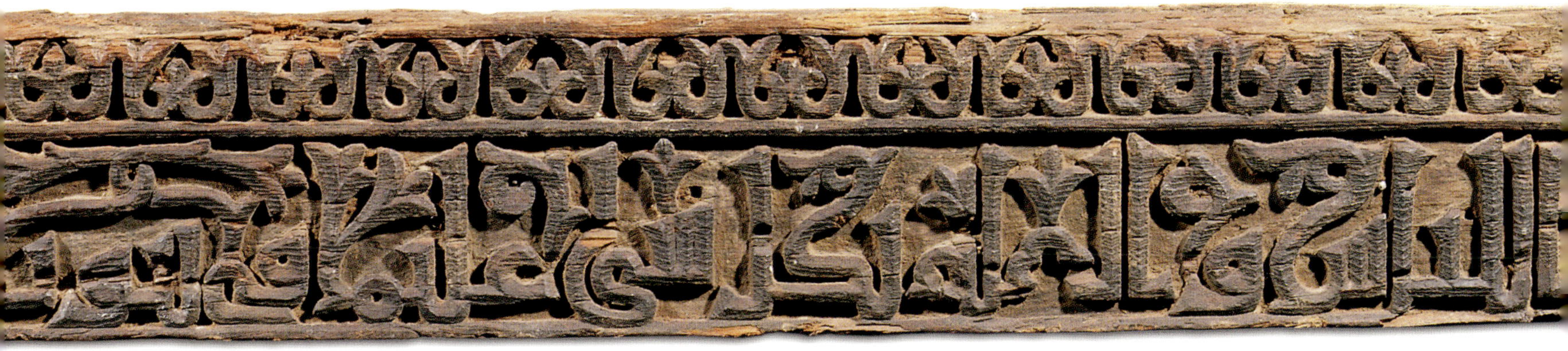

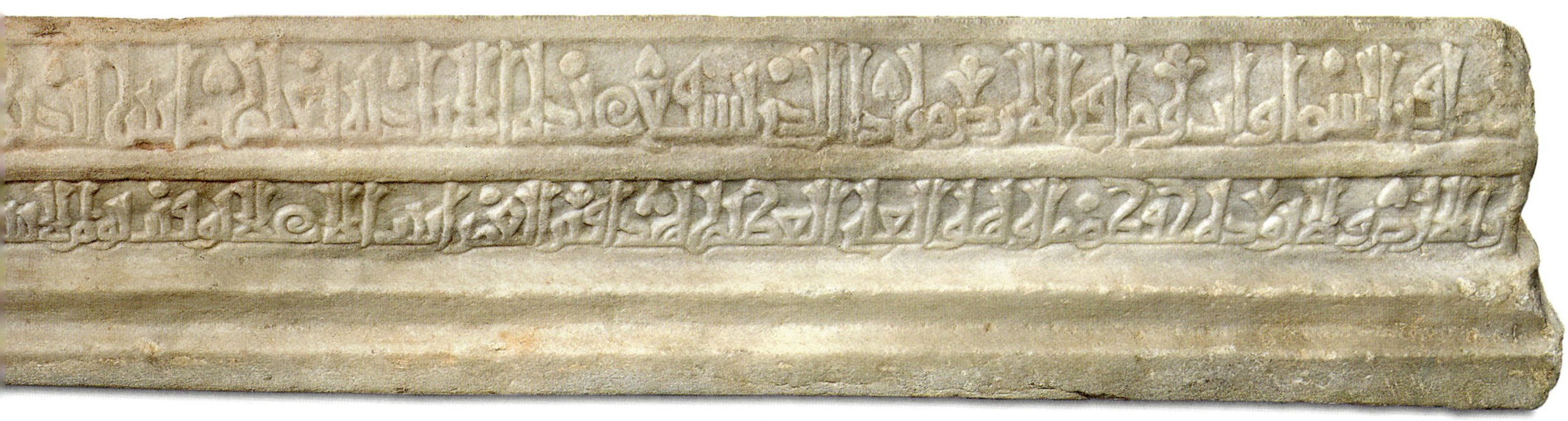

Cenotaph

Egypt or Tunisia, 1011
Carved marble
160 × 22 × 17 cm (63 × 8⅝ × 6¾ in.)
AKM912

This type of cenotaph with its fine carving and elaborate inscription would have been part of the tomb of a notable individual. The inscription carries the name of an anonymous female, "al-Qamar, daughter of al-A'la," who died in September 1011. Qur'anic verses and the Muslim profession of faith (*shahada*) cover the remaining sides of the upper section of the cenotaph. The inscriptions are carved in a foliated Kufic script with curling leaves decorating the uprights of all the letters. The form of the cenotaph, the calligraphic style, and the half-palmette element that decorates the end panels are typical of carved marble cenotaphs from North Africa dating to the Fatimid period (909–1171). This one, however, is the earliest known.

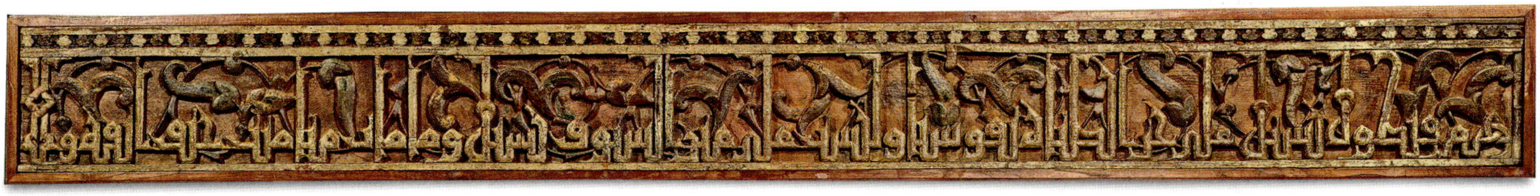

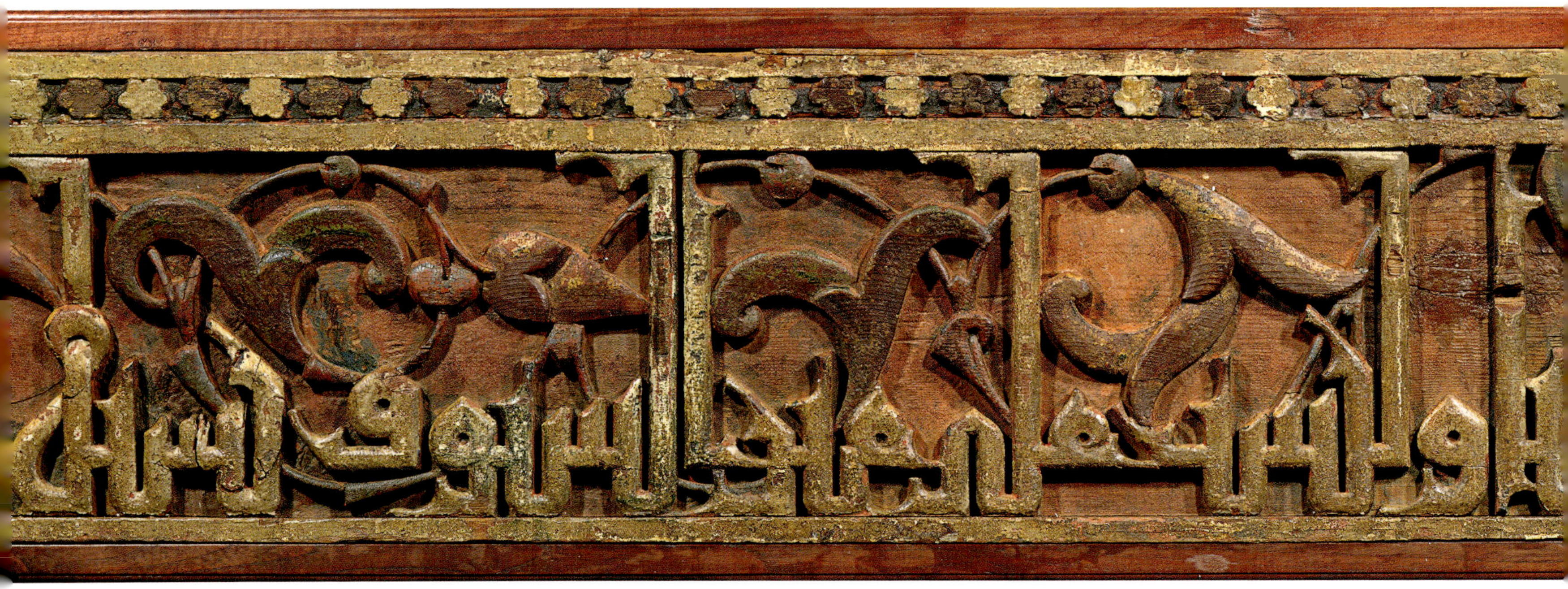

Beam

Morocco or Spain (Historic al-Andalus), 12th–13th centuries
Carved and painted wood
313 × 30.8 cm (130¼ × 12⅛ in.)
AKM631

One of a pair of beams belonging to a carved frieze, this object would have been part of the interior walls of the residence of a learned patron. The angular Kufic script carved in relief on an elegant leafy scroll background is part of a Pre-Islamic Arabic poem that extols valour in the face of danger and boasts of courage in battle. The combination of the nostalgia symbolized by the use of classical Arabic poetry and the focus on courage and warfare are characteristic of the Almohads, a Berber dynasty from North Africa that ruled Morocco and parts of Spain between 1150 and 1269. The Almohads were avid builders of city walls, madrasas, and mosques, including the Great Mosque of Seville and its famous minaret La Giralda. Such structures would have also been decorated with similar wood friezes. Surviving examples in other museum collections demonstrate that the same design and script were also used for Qur'anic inscriptions.

Ceiling Panel

Spain, 15th–16th centuries
Carved and painted wood
Base 170 cm (66⅞ in.),
sides 171.8 cm (67⅝ in.)
AKM730

This triangular panel is part of a carved wood ceiling that embellished a zone of transition linking the walls of a room to its ceiling. Considering the elaborate design and the overall effect, the room would have been quite spectacular. Interlacing star patterns in various materials and techniques were a hallmark of the arts produced in Spain under the Nasrids (1232–1492). The eight-pointed star at the centre of this triangular panel and the wooden strapwork it generates can also be seen in the architectural decoration of the Nasrid fort palace of the Alhambra in Granada as well as in the sumptuous silk textiles typical of the period.

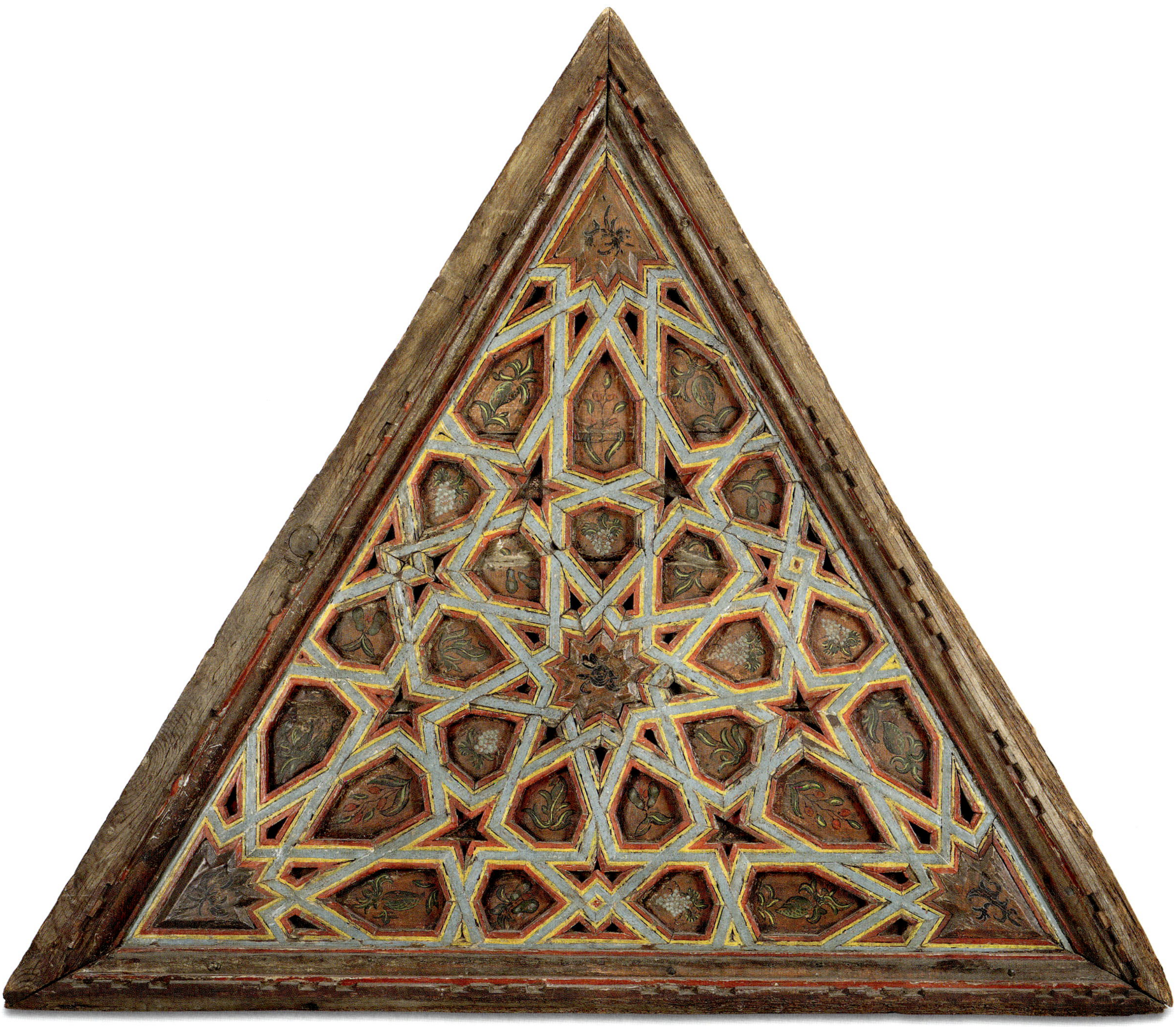

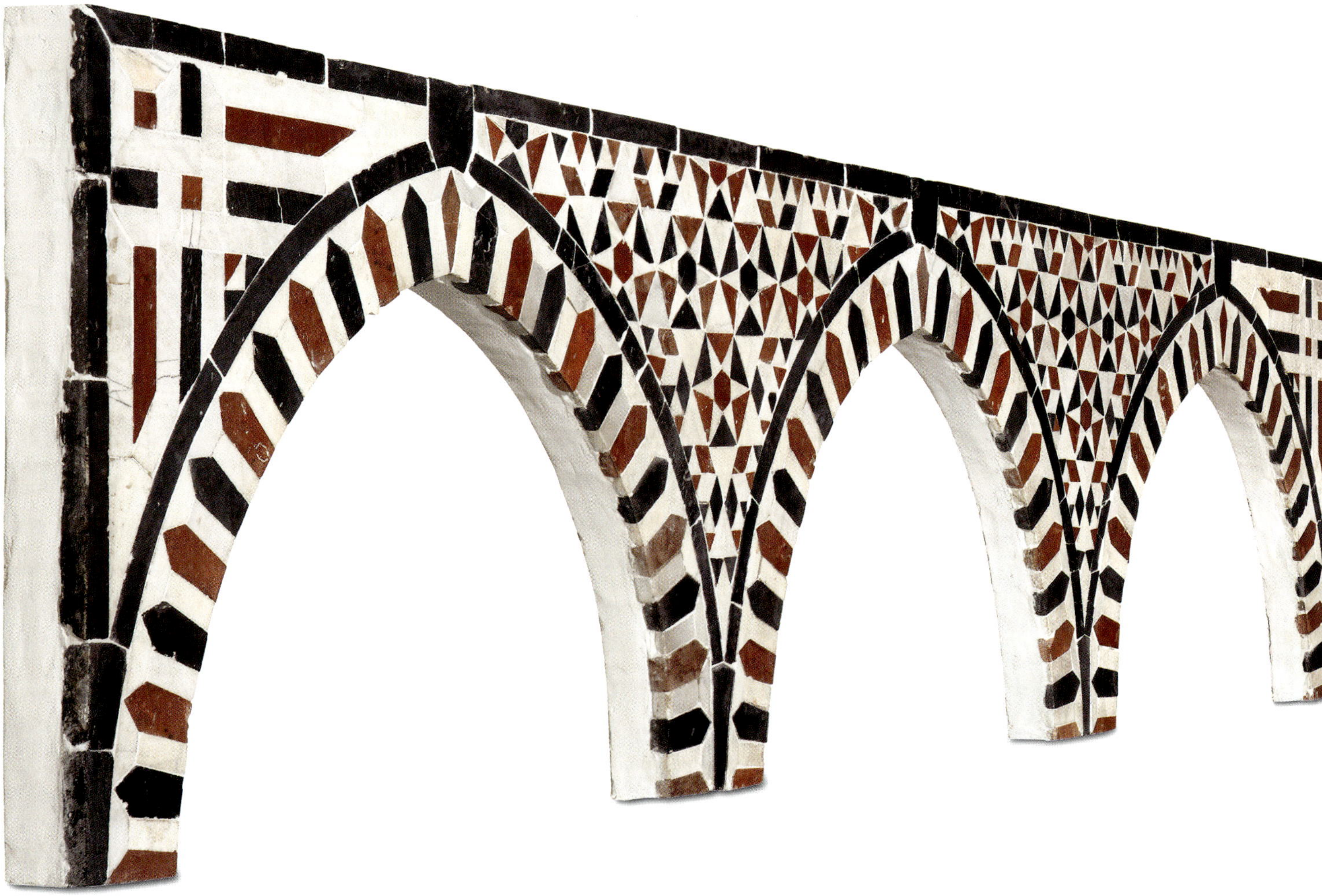

Panel

Egypt, 15th century
Marble and stone mosaic
225 × 49 × 5 cm
(88⅝ × 19¼ × 2 in.)
AKM571

Typical of the decorative approach to stone, this triple-arched wall panel uses the natural variety of stone colours to produce intricate polychrome compositions. Different stones and marble were cut according to the desired design, here forming a star-and-hexagon mosaic with knot-like interlace on the end spandrels. The stone mosaic was then fixed together with a layer of plaster applied to its back, turning it into a single panel easily fitted onto a wall or used as an arcade. This panel would have decorated a reception room in a residential building in Egypt or Syria of the Mamluk period (1250–1517) where arched panels, similar to this one, separated the central hall with its gushing fountain from the two raised reception areas that flanked it.

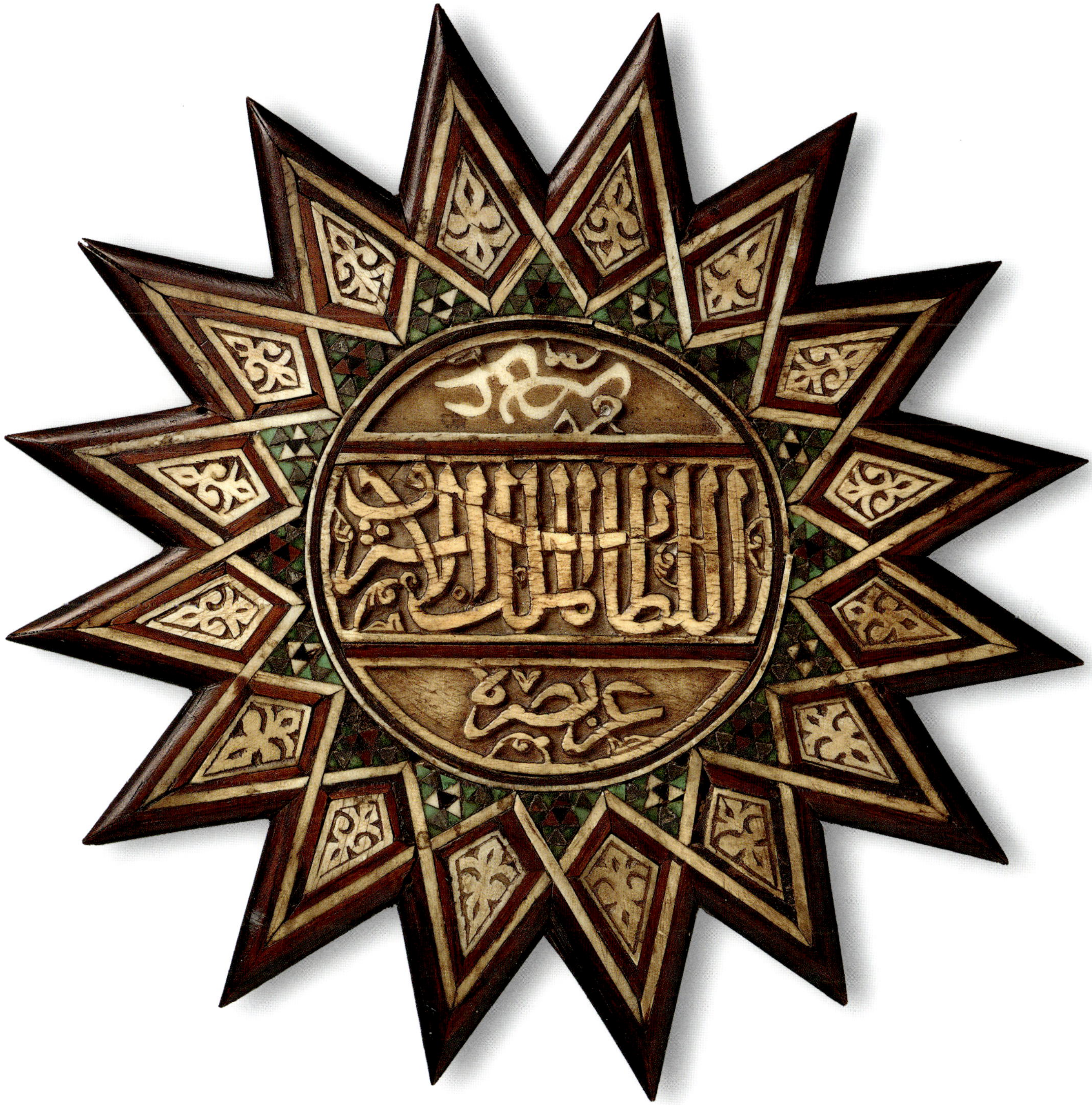

Panel

Egypt, second half of 15th century
Ivory, wood, and metal in a wooden frame
Diameter 22 cm (8⅝ in.)
AKM703

Geometric compositions based on stars and polygons were a common feature of the decorative language of Egypt and Syria under the Mamluks (1250–1517). This sixteen-point star-shaped panel inlaid with finely carved ivory was probably a central piece in a repetitive pattern that adorned the interior of an important building. The inscription in the centre of the panel is the heraldic blazon of the Mamluk Sultan al-Ashraf Qaytbay who ruled between 1468 and 1496. The star-shaped panel was probably meant for one of his architectural projects and bears resemblance to the superb star patterns decorating the wooden pulpit (*minbar*) of Qaytbay's complex, which was built in Cairo's north cemetery in the 1470s. Geometric patterns and heraldic blazons were employed extensively by the Mamluks on a broad variety of objects and in different media.

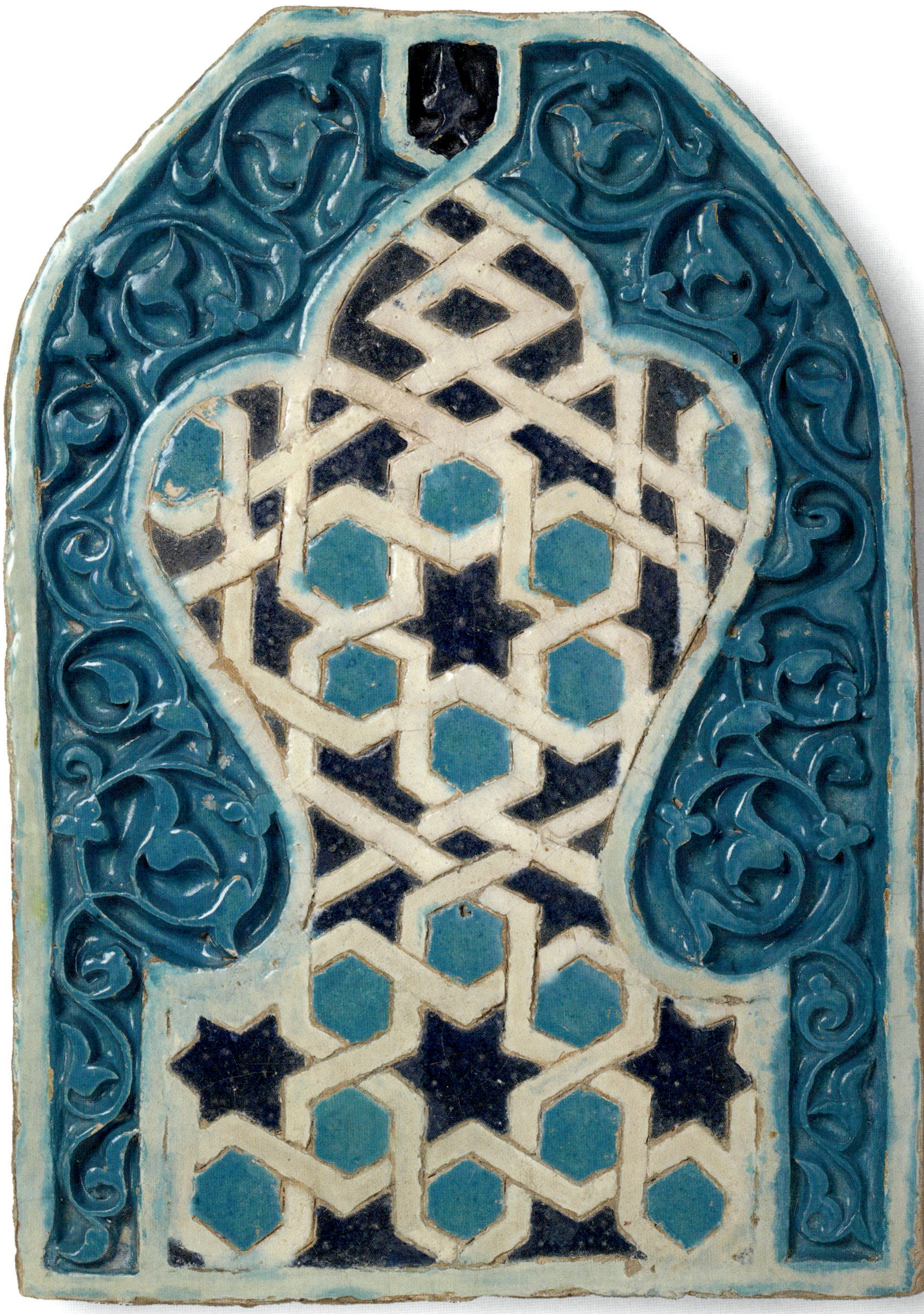

This arch-shaped tile is an example of the opulence of Timurid (1370–1507) architectural decoration in Central Asia that can be seen in Timur's (or Tamerlane's) mausoleum (circa 1400–04) or the royal necropolis of Shah-e Zendeh in Samarqand in present-day Uzbekistan. Here, the artist demonstrates an immense skill by combining two techniques of carving and rendering them in the typical palette of Timurid architectural decoration: turquoise, blue, and white. The turquoise frame has an abstract vegetal motif of a continuously unfolding vine that was deeply hand-carved into the surface of the tile. This frame surrounds a perfectly balanced geometric interlace with a star pattern incised in its central field. The carving was done while the tile was still soft, with the glazing applied in the form of powdered minerals fused into shiny glazes of different colours when baked in the kiln.

Tile Panel

Central Asia, 14th century
Earthenware, carved and glazed
56 × 39 cm (22 × 15⅜ in.)
AKM572

Part of a larger decorative composition, this single tile would have covered the exterior of a building in the second half of the fourteenth century, most probably in present-day Uzbekistan. The shape of the tile indicates that the overall design may have been developed on paper and later transferred to individual tiles. The design consists of two deeply carved elements separated by a flat, incised frame covered in white glaze. The section on the right has an inscription in Arabic stating that "sovereignty belongs to God" where the uprights of the letters are interlaced and knotted to create a complex pattern. The left panel comprises repetitive vertical cartouches of a typical Timurid split-palmette motif alternating with a six-point star. The whole design is carved in relief and glazed in a copper compound fluxed in an alkaline coating to produce the turquoise colour typical in the architectural embellishment of Central Asia.

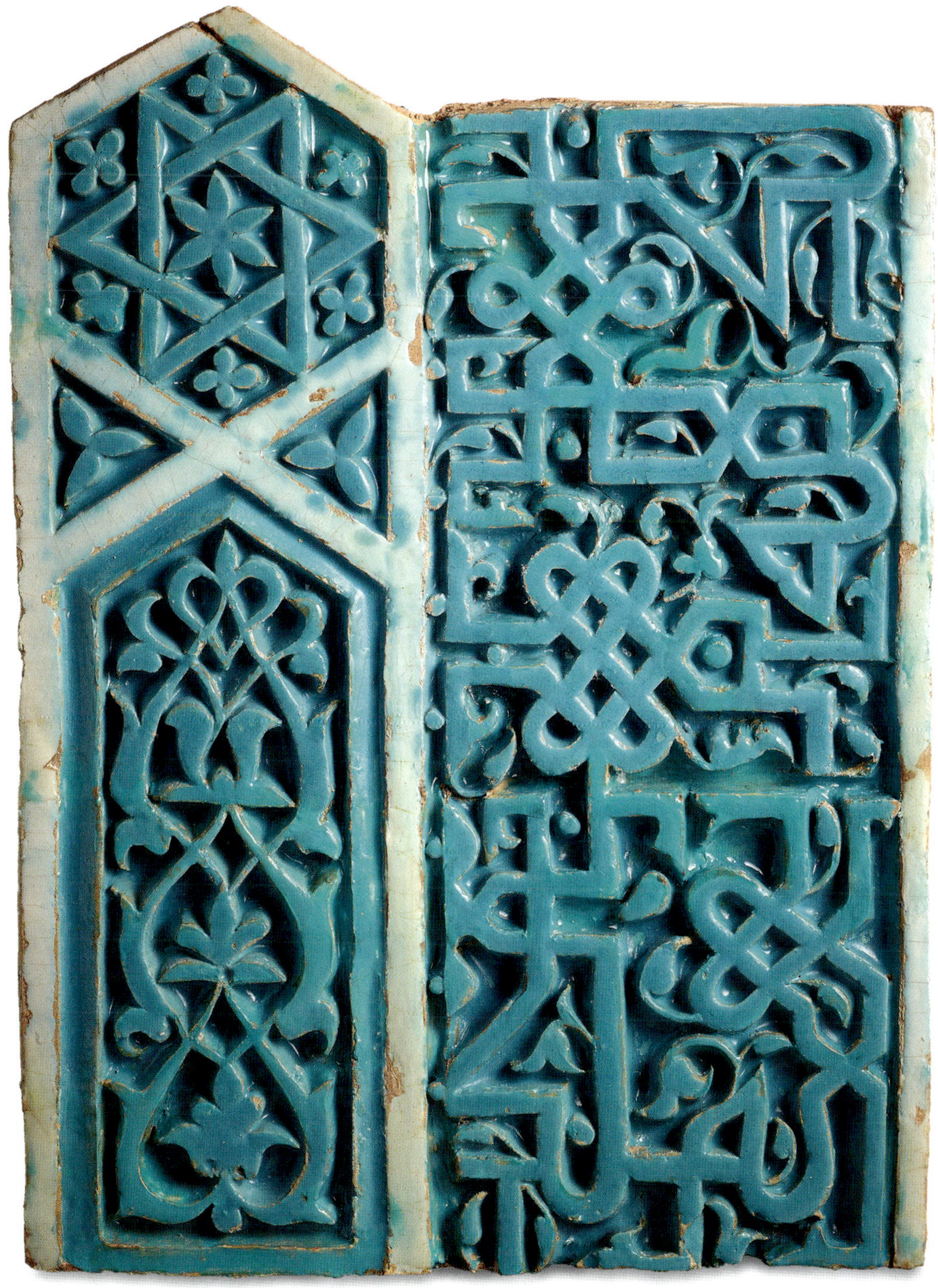

Tile Panel
Central Asia, second half of 14th century
Earthenware, carved and glazed
51.8 × 37.5 × 6.4 cm
(20⅜ × 14¾ × 2½ in.)
AKM827

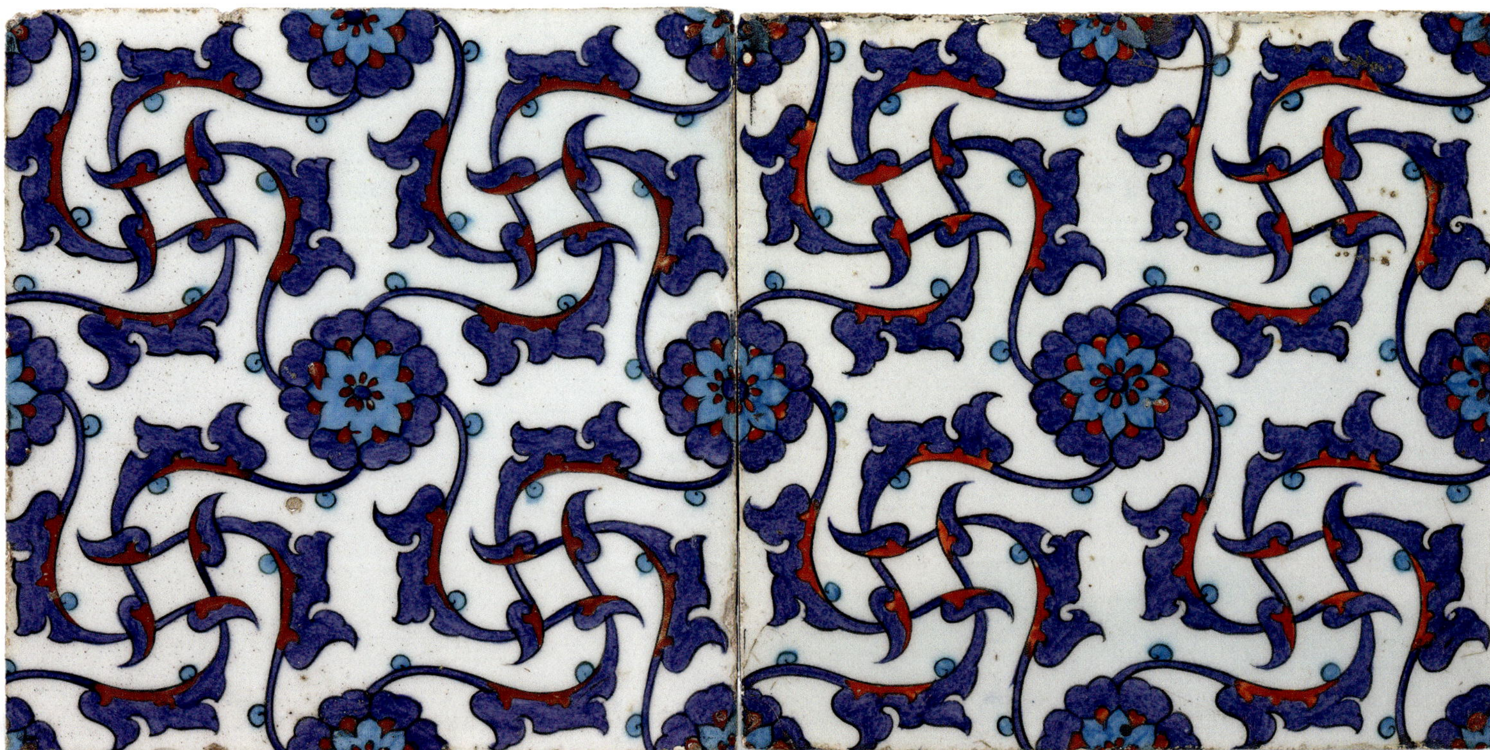

Tiles

Iznik, Turkey, ca. 1560
Fritware, underglaze-painted
Each 25 × 24.5 cm (9⅞ × 9⅝ in.)
AKM583 and AKM584

By the sixteenth century, mosques and palaces built under the Ottomans (1299–1923) had predominantly plain ashlar exteriors with a profusion of colours and patterns on the interior in the form of glazed tiles, carpets and textiles, painted ceilings, and monumental inscriptions. These tiles are part of a repeat-pattern composition, an example of which adorns the walls of the sixteenth-century Rüstem Pasha Mosque in Istanbul. Typical of tiles with repeat patterns, the underglaze-painted design would have been applied to the tile through the use of a stencil. The design itself is highly complex. It is an exquisite example of a floral spray around a central motif demonstrating the folding, rotation, and repetition of patterns that characterize Islamic art. The colours are also representative of the Ottoman taste with combinations of turquoise, cobalt blue, white, and red.

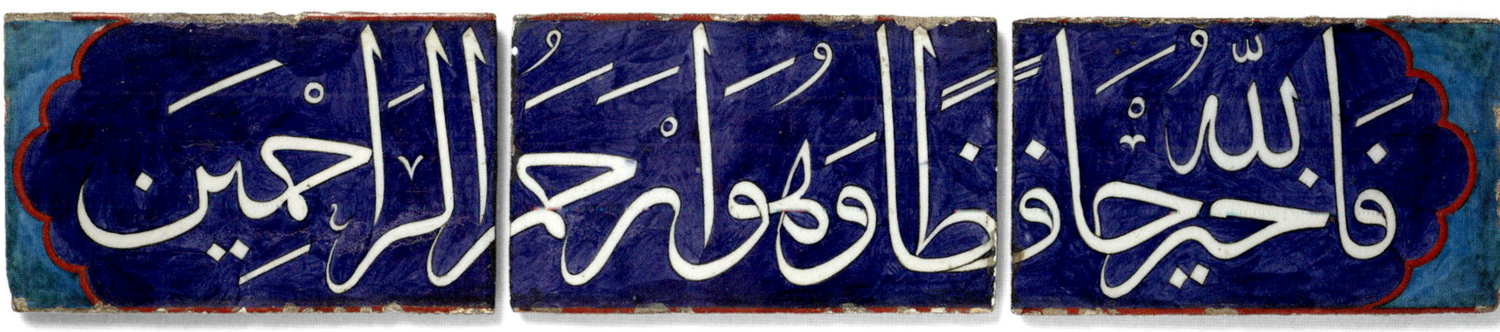

Tile Frieze
Iznik, Turkey, ca. 1570
Fritware, underglaze-painted
15.5 × 75 × 1 cm
(6⅛ × 29½ × ⅜ in.)
AKM698

This tile frieze is inscribed with verse 64 of the twelfth sura of the Qur'an: "Allah is the best guardian, and He is the most merciful of the merciful." It would have formed an integral part of a decorative program in an Ottoman mosque in the second half of the sixteenth century. Cartouches with Qur'anic verses painted under a clear glaze and calligraphic panels with the names of the Prophet, the first four caliphs, and the Prophet's two grandsons, Hassan and Husayn, as well as painted floral motifs, were the predominant decorative elements in Ottoman mosque interiors. The distinctive tomato-red colour used to frame the calligraphic cartouche here indicates a date later than the 1550s when this red was first employed in Ottoman tile production at Iznik in present-day Turkey.

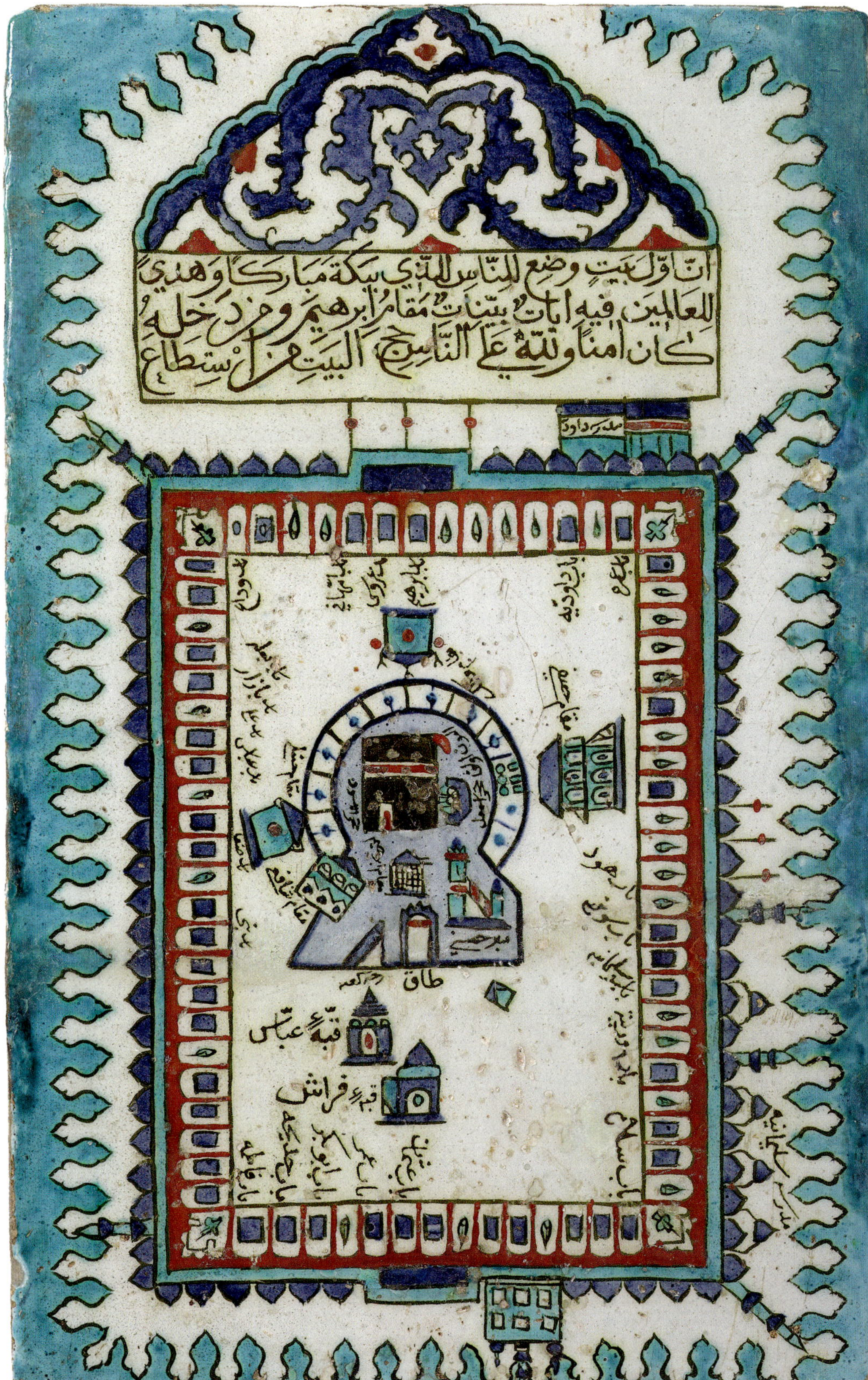

Using bright colours under a clear glaze, this single tile depicts a topographical representation of the Ka'ba and the Masjid al-Haram in Mecca. The Ka'ba, distinguished by its rectangular form and the black cloth with a gold trim cover (known as *kiswa*), is believed by Muslims to be the place that the patriarch Abraham built to worship God. This is reflected in the main inscription beneath the arch that contains a verse from the Qur'an reminding believers of Abraham's faith and the importance of pilgrimage (*hajj*) to Mecca (Sura 3:96–97). Tiles of this type were common under the Ottomans (1299–1923) and were used to decorate the *qibla* wall of mosques and religious buildings, indicating the direction of prayer and commemorating pilgrimage.

Tile

Iznik, Turkey, 17th century
Fritware, underglaze-painted
52 × 32 cm (20½ × 12⅝ in.)
AKM587

These two tiles are exquisite examples of the natural illustration of flowers and plants in architectural decoration common in India and Iran in the seventeenth century. Here, the clump of irises with long, flowering stems and sword-shaped leaves would have been part of a larger composition surrounding an arched opening. Artists used a tilework technique known as *cuerda seca* (dry cord) to create complex designs with clearly defined components. The black outline of the design consists of a waxy material that acts as a resistant or separator to the different-coloured compartments of the design. The colours are then applied in the form of various powder minerals that fuse in the kiln into the desired colours. This technique allowed the artist to present a close depiction of his subject, which in some cases included a variety of birds and animals.

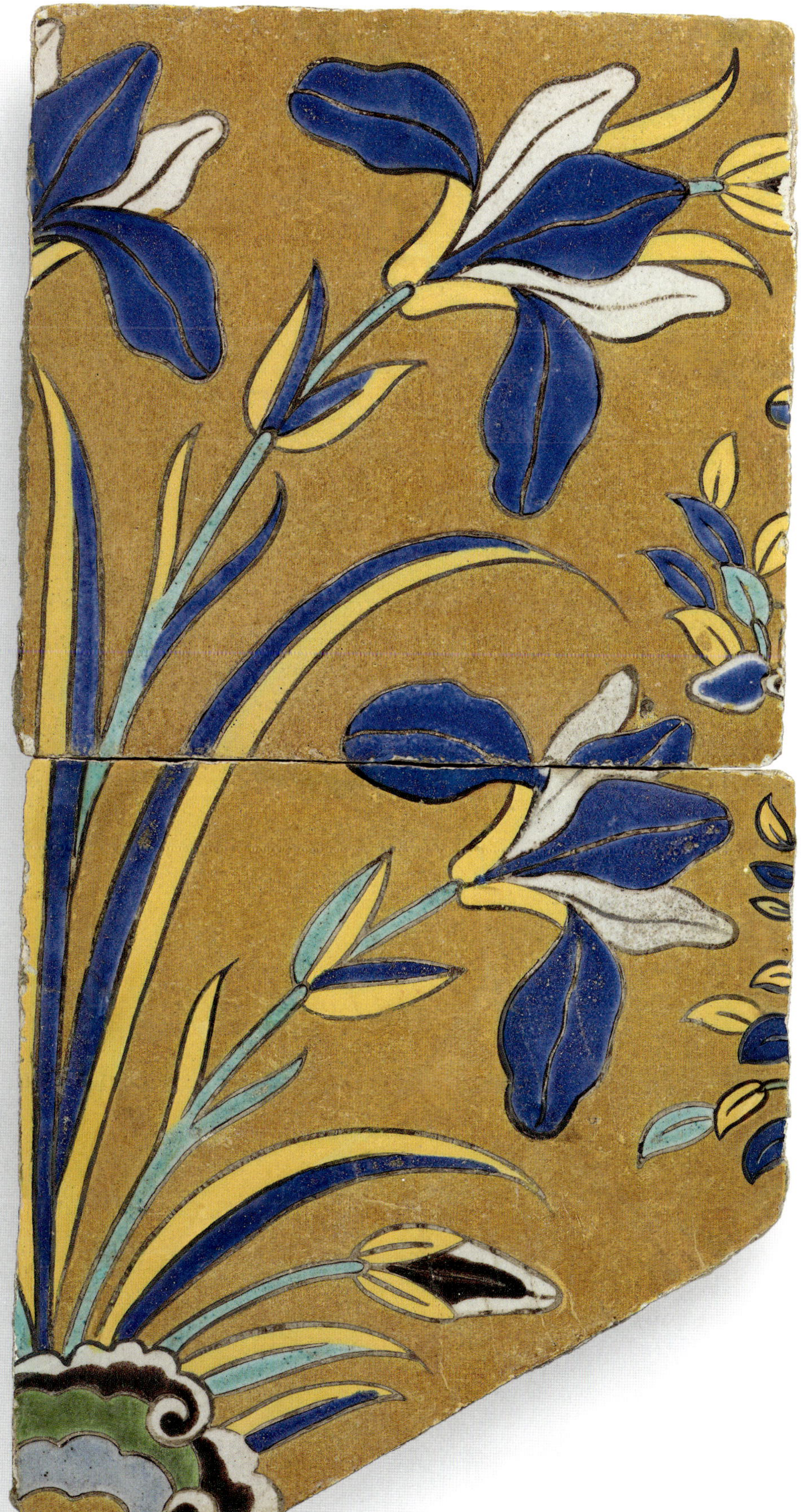

Tile Panel
Iran or India (Historic Hindustan), 17th century
Earthenware, *cuerda seca* and glazed
47.8 × 24 cm (18⅞ × 9½ in.)
AKM590

CONTRIBUTORS' BIOGRAPHIES

Philip Jodidio has written or edited more than a hundred books on architecture and art, including *Discovering Architecture: How the World's Great Buildings Were Designed and Built* (2013), *Under the Eaves of Architecture: The Aga Khan: Builder and Patron* (2007), and the *Architecture Now!* series of books (2001–ongoing). For more than twenty years he was Editor-in-Chief of *Connaissance des Arts* in Paris.

Ruba Kana'an is the Head of Education and Scholarly Programs at the Aga Khan Museum in Toronto, Canada. She is a specialist on the urban histories of Pre-Modern Muslim societies as well as on the interface between art and law in Muslim contexts. Dr. Kana'an has taught extensively at the graduate and undergraduate levels on various aspects of Islamic art and Islamic studies and developed Oxford University's first online course on Islamic art.

Henry S. Kim is the Director and CEO of the Aga Khan Museum in Toronto. An ancient history scholar and classical archaeologist by training, Kim joined the Aga Khan Museum from the University of Oxford where he taught, curated collections, and managed capital projects at the Ashmolean Museum from 1994 to 2012. Educated at Harvard and Oxford, he served as Curator of Greek coins and university lecturer in Greek numismatics at the university. From 2004 to 2011 he was the Project Director for the Ashmolean Redevelopment Project, a redevelopment and transformation of the museum.

Assadullah Souren Melikian-Chirvani is the Curatorial Director of the Aga Khan Trust for Culture and is an internationally renowned cultural historian of the Iranian world and its sphere of influence, including the Persian-speaking courts of Islamic India. A Research Director at the National Centre of Scientific Research in Paris, which he joined in 1970, he retired in 2004. Throughout his career he focused on the connection between the written word and the visual arts. His groundbreaking discoveries include the demonstration of the Buddhist background to the depiction of ideal beauty, the "Moon-Faced Buddha," in literature and art; the role of the *Shah-Nameh* as a behavioural model in the *Shah-Nameh* visual and auditory environment of Iranian courts; and the universal correlation between motif and literary concepts in Iranian culture. He is the author of numerous scholarly articles and five pioneering books, among them *Islamic Metalwork from the Iranian World, 8th to 18th Centuries* and *Le chant du monde: L'art de l'Iran safavide*. From 1969 to 2013 he wrote a weekly column in the *International Herald Tribune* under the name "Souren Melikian" and retired as the Art Editor for that newspaper in October 2013.

Luis Monreal is the General Manager of the Aga Khan Trust for Culture in Geneva, Switzerland. He is a conservation specialist, art historian, and archaeologist, and has held various positions, including Secretary-General of the International Council of Museums at UNESCO, Paris, France (1974–85); Director of the Getty Conservation Institute, Los Angeles (1985–90); and Director General, La Caixa Foundation, Barcelona, Spain (1990–2001). Monreal is the author of several books that have been published in many languages and has also been involved in the creation and establishment of a number of museums.

D. Fairchild Ruggles is Professor of Landscape History at the University of Illinois at Urbana-Champaign and is the author of *Islamic Art and Visual Culture* (2011), *Islamic Gardens and Landscapes* (2008), and *Gardens, Landscape, and Vision in the Palaces of Islamic Spain* (2000).

ILLUSTRATION CREDITS

Copyright © Aga Khan Museum, 2014 (photos by Gérald Friedli): pages 2, 19 (top), 43, 48 (bottom left), 49, 50, 52, 54, 58, 67–73, 78, 95–98, 100–01, 105, 114, 120–22, 135, 140, 154, 156–57, 158–59 (top), 160, 162.

Copyright © Aga Khan Museum, 2014 (photos by Sean Weaver): pages 4, 16–18, 19 (bottom), 20–21, 41, 44, 47, 48 (top), 53, 61–66, 74, 76, 77, 79, 80–88, 90–94, 99, 102, 104, 106–13, 117–19, 123–30, 132–34, 136–39, 141, 142, 144–52, 158–59 (bottom), 161, 163–69.

Copyright © Aga Khan Development Network, 2014: pages 6 (photo by Moez Visram), 11–13, 25 (photo by Gary Otte), 33, 36 (bottom), 37 (top right).

Tom Arban Photography: pages 10, 23, 24, 26, 29, 31.

Copyright © Imara (Wynford Drive) Limited, 2014: pages 27, 32, 35.

Copyright © Studio Adrien Gardère, 2014: page 28.

Copyright © Maki and Associates, 2014: page 30.

Copyright © Vladimir Djurovic Landscape Architecture, 2014: page 36 (top).

Copyright © iStock, 2014: pages 37 (top left), 46.

Copyright © Trustees of the British Museum, 2014: page 40 (photo by Dudley Hubbard).

Copyright © Victoria and Albert Museum, London, 2014: page 48 (bottom right).

INDEX

Page numbers in italics indicate illustrations.

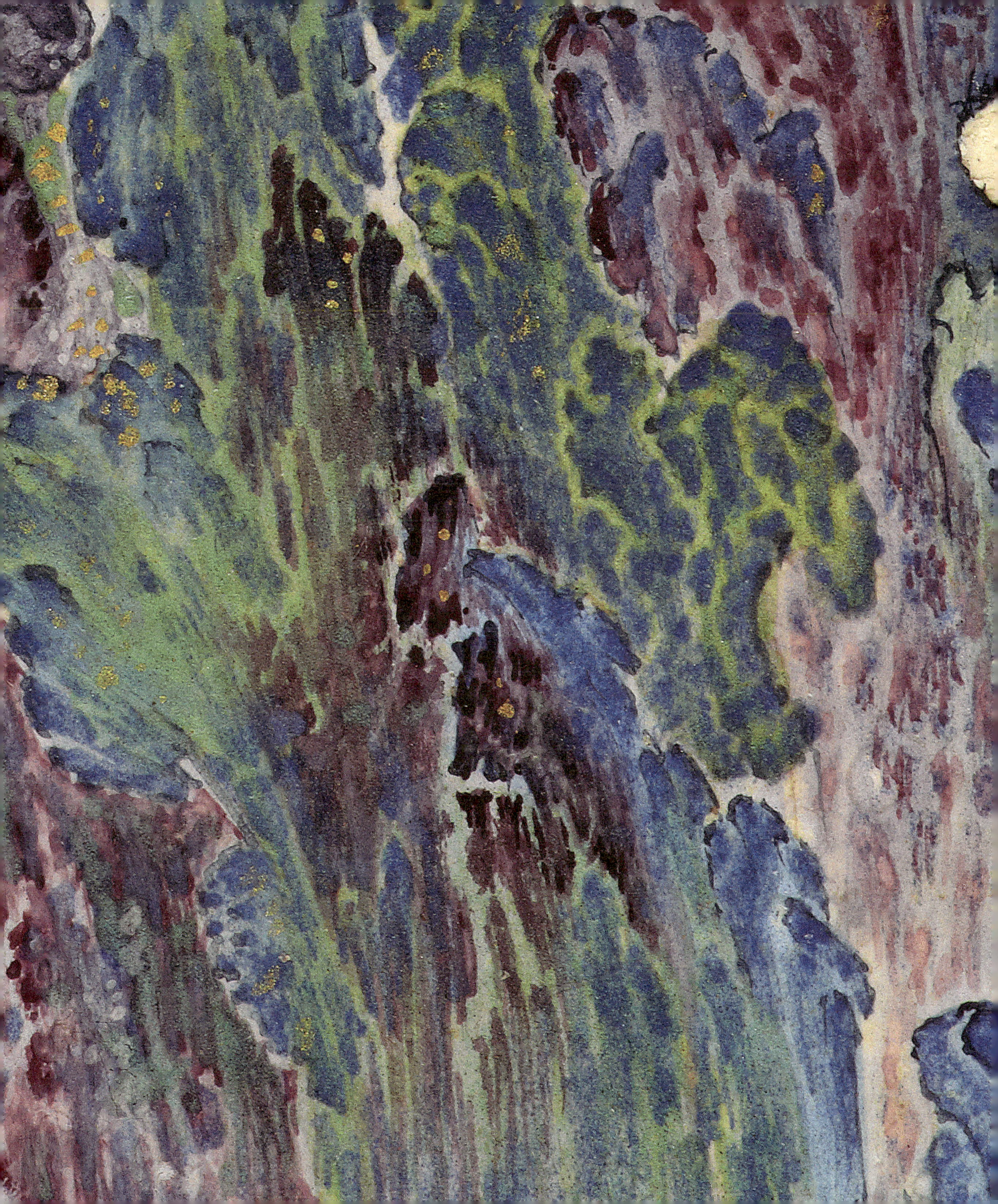

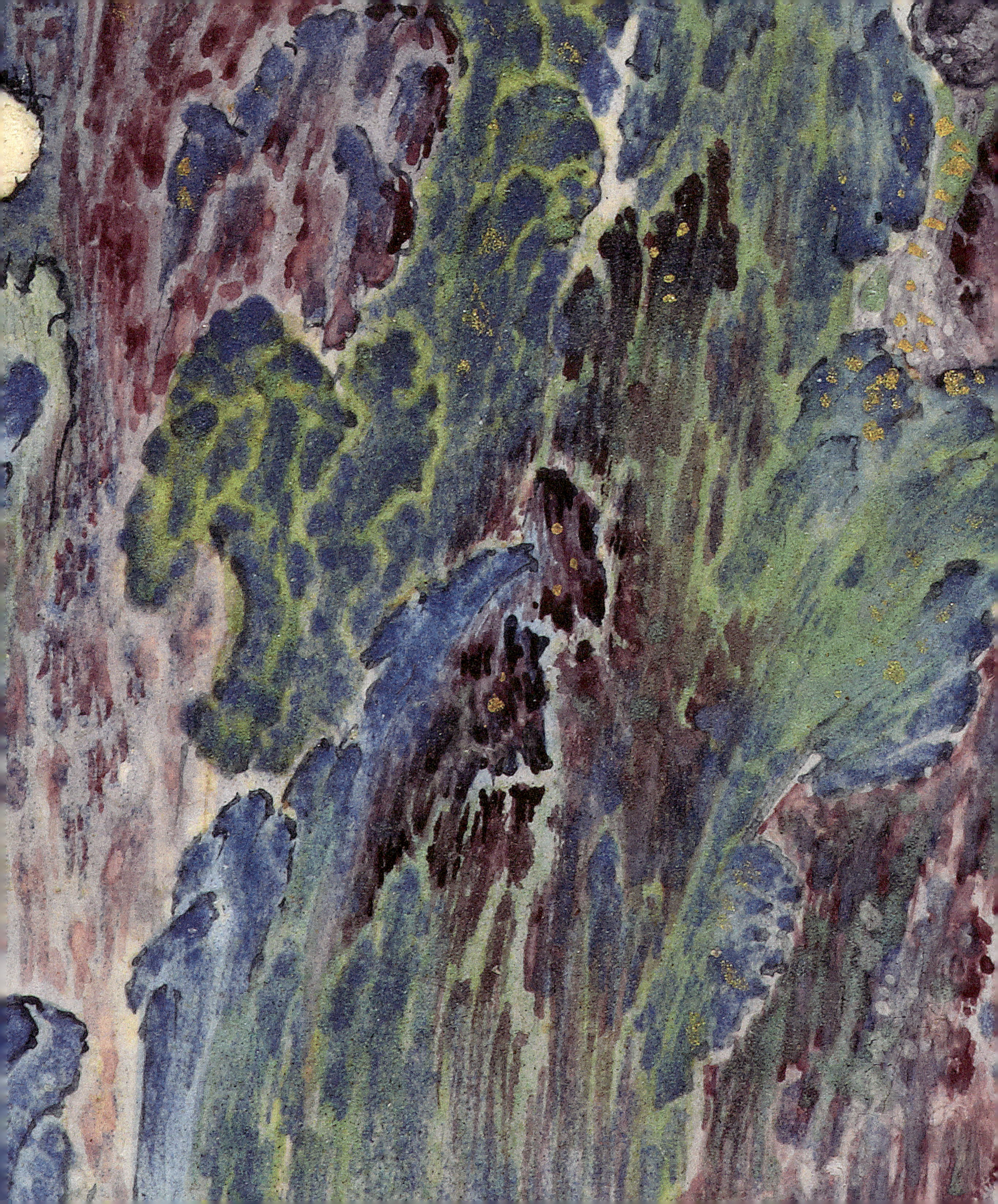